Revolution in Warfare?

Revolution in Warfare?

Air Power in the Persian Gulf

Thomas A. Keaney
and
Eliot A. Cohen

Naval Institute Press
Annapolis, Maryland

Originally published as *Gulf War Air Power Survey Summary Report* in 1993 by the U.S. Government Printing Office. Naval Institute Press edition published in 1995.

Library of Congress Cataloging-in-Publication Data

Keaney, Thomas A.
  Revolution in warfare? : air power in the Persian Gulf / Thomas A. Keaney and Eliot A. Cohen.
      p.   cm.
  Rev. ed. of: Gulf War Air Power Survey. 1993.
  Includes bibliographical references (p.) and index.
  ISBN 1-55750-131-9 (alk. paper)
  1. Persian Gulf War, 1991—Aerial operations, American. 2. United States. Air Force—History—Persian Gulf War, 1991.   I. Cohen, Eliot A.   II. Gulf War Air Power Survey.   III. Title.
DS79.724.U6K43   1995
956.7044'248—dc20   95-32745

Printed in the United States of America on acid-free paper ∞

02 01 00 99 98 97 96 95   9 8 7 6 5 4 3 2

First printing

To the members of the Gulf
War Air Power Survey

Contents

List of Illustrations   viii
List of Tables   x
Preface   xi
Introduction   xiv

One What Happened?   1
Two What Was the Air Campaign Plan?   22
Three What Did the Air Campaign Accomplish?   45
Four What Was the Role of Intelligence?   105
Five Who Ran the Air War?   124
Six What Were the Conditions in the Theater?   138
Seven What Were the Instruments of Air Power?   152
Eight What Supported the Air Power?   173
Nine Was Desert Storm a Revolution in Warfare?   188
Ten What Does Desert Storm Tell Us about the Future of Air Power?   213

Appendixes

One Gulf War Chronology, April 1990 to February 1991   227
Two Statistical Appendix   238
Three The First Twenty-four Hours of the Air War   282
Four Summary Data for F-117 and F-111 Strikes   290
Five Attrition of Armor and Artillery in Iraqi Heavy Divisions   296
Six Gulf War Air Power Survey Principal Staff and Review Committee   297

A Note on Sources   299
Glossary   302
Index   307

Illustrations

1 Map of the Region   3
2 Shift to the West by U.S. XVIII Corps and VII Corps   6
3 Coalition Plan for Ground Attack   8
4 Iraqi Deployment in Kuwaiti Theater of Operations on 17 January 1991   9
5 Coalition Air Strikes by Day against Iraqi Targets   10
6 Coalition Air-to-Air Sorties by Day   11
7 Attacks of the Iraqi III Corps, 29–31 January 1991   17
8 Chokepoints for Retreating Iraqi Troops in the Kuwaiti Theater   20
9 Phases of Desert Storm Campaign Plan   42
10 Iraqi Flight Activity versus Coalition Kills   50
11 Coalition Fixed-Wing Combat Attrition by Cause   52
12 Coalition Strikes by Target Category and Air Power Function (17 January–28 February 1991)   56
13 Precision Strikes against Leadership and Telecommunications/ Command, Control, and Communications   59
14 Strikes against Electricity and Oil   62
15 Estimated Drawdown of Iraqi Electric Power   63
16 Iraqi Nuclear Target System   68
17 Iraqi Nuclear Facilities by Location   68
18 Tuwaitha (C11) Baghdad Nuclear Research Facility   69
19 Coalition Strikes against Nuclear, Biological, and Chemical Targets   70
20 Daily Scud Launches during Desert Storm   74

Illustrations

21 Coalition Strikes against Scuds   75
22 By-Week Launch Totals and Maximum Salvo Size for Iraqi Scuds   77
23 Damaged Bridges in Iraq (DIA)   81
24 Status of Bridges along Routes from Baghdad to Kuwaiti Theater of Operations, 28 February 1991   82
25 Prewar Route Capacities, Baghdad to Kuwaiti Theater of Operations   83
26 Route Capacities (Baghdad to Kuwaiti Theater of Operations), 28 February 1991   84
27 Fixed-Site Iraqi Naval Targets   88
28 Strikes Targeted by Kill Box, 17 January–28 February 1991   91
29 Chokepoints for Retreating Iraqi Troops in the Kuwaiti Theater   100
30 Relative Distances in the Area of Operations   142
31 Formation of a "Package" for Attacks into Iraq   143
32 Map of Iraq and Kuwait   145
33 Map of Region Depicting Major Air Bases Used by Coalition Air Forces during Desert Storm   147
34 Coalition Aircraft Totals in Key Elements of Air Power Support   154
35 Aerial Refueling Tanker Tracks over Saudi Arabia and Nearby Regions   161
36 Coalition Attack Aircraft Sorties by Time on Target, 17 January–28 February 1991   169
37 Deployment of Selected USAF Assets   177

Tables

1 Internal Look 90 Target Lists   26
2 Growth of Targets, August to December 1990   35
3 Listing of Selected Munitions Employed in Desert Storm, 17 January–28 February 1991   90
4 Operational-Strategic Summary   102
5 Total Sorties by U.S. Service/Allied Country by Aircraft Type   156
6 Desert Storm Attack Aircraft   167
7 Missiles Employed in Desert Storm Strikes   168
8 Desert Shield/Desert Storm U.S. Weapons Expenditures   171
9 Precision versus Non-Precision Target Coverage   206

Preface

From 16 January through 28 February 1991, the United States and its allies conducted one of the most operationally successful wars in history, a conflict in which air operations played a preeminent role. On 22 August 1991, Secretary of the Air Force Donald B. Rice created the Gulf War Air Power Survey to review all aspects of air warfare in the Persian Gulf. Although commissioned by the Air Force, the Survey was directed to assess all aspects of air power in the gulf, including air operations by all American and allied armed services. The Survey produced reports on planning, the conduct of operations, the effects of the air campaign, command and control, logistics, air base support, space, weapons and tactics, as well as a chronology and a compendium of statistics on the war. It prepared as well a summary report, shorter papers, and an archive of paper, microfilm, and electronic records now lodged at the Air Force Historical Research Agency at Maxwell Air Force Base, Alabama.

The *Gulf War Air Power Survey Summary Report* was originally published by the U.S. Government Printing Office (GPO) in 1993. Because GPO bookstores are not as widely accessible as commercial outlets, and out of a desire to provide a more useful one-volume work on the air war in the Persian Gulf, the authors proposed to the Naval Institute Press publishing a revised version of the *Summary Report*. Since the original Survey was completed on government time, we have thought it proper to have any royalties generated by this book's sales donated to charity.

The current volume differs from the original *Summary Report* in three important ways. First, chapter 9—"Was Desert Storm a Revolution in Warfare?"—consists of chapters 9 and 10 of the original *Summary Report*, with minor deletions. Second, some new text has been added. In chapter 3 we have included material from an article by Thomas A. Keaney on the difficulties of measuring military effectiveness.[1] The new chapter 10—"What Does Desert Storm Tell Us about

---

1. Thomas A. Keaney, "Surveying Gulf War Airpower," *Joint Force Quarterly* (Autumn 1993): 25–36.

the Future of Air Power?"—consists chiefly of extracts from an article by Eliot A. Cohen that attempted to explain some of the lessons of the Survey for a broader audience.[2] By its nature, this chapter is more speculative in tone than the others in the book. Third, we have added chronological and statistical appendixes drawn from the vast quantities of data in volume five of the complete Survey. Aside from these changes, however, we have made few alterations to the original text, save for correcting an occasional infelicity in expression.

The Survey was not a definitive history: that will await the passage of time and the opening of sources (Iraqi records, for example) that were not available to Survey researchers. Nor was it a summary of lessons learned. Rather, the Survey provided an analytical and evidentiary point of departure for future studies of the air campaign. It concentrated on the operational level of war in the belief that this level of warfare is at once one of the most difficult to characterize and one of the most important to understand.

The Survey, directed by Eliot A. Cohen, was staffed by a mixture of civilian and military analysts, including retired officers (most are combat veterans) from all of the American armed services. Its seven task forces were directed, with one exception, by civilians working temporarily for the Air Force. The Survey was examined by a distinguished review committee, which included scholars and retired general officers from the Army, Navy, and Air Force, as well as former and current senior government officials. The names of the senior staff and review committee of the Survey appear in appendix 6 of this book. The Survey strived to conduct its work in a spirit of impartiality and scholarly rigor. Its members had as their standard the observation of Mr. Franklin D'Olier, chairman of the U.S. Strategic Bombing Survey during and after World War II. "We wanted to burn into everybody's souls the fact that the survey's responsibility . . . was to ascertain facts and to seek truth, eliminating completely any preconceived theories or dogmas."

The Survey's members owed a great debt of gratitude to Secretary Rice, who conceived the original project, provided it with resources, and set for it the highest standards of independence and objectivity. Many organizations and individuals gave generously of their resources and time to support the Survey's researches. Various branches and commands of the Air Force were particularly helpful in providing material for and, in some cases, personnel to conduct the study. The U.S. Navy, Marine Corps, and Army aided this study in different ways, including the sharing of data pertaining to the air war. A number of the United States' Coalition partners also made available individuals and

---

2. Eliot A. Cohen, "The Mystique of U.S. Air Power," *Foreign Affairs* (January/February 1994): 109–24.

Preface

records that were vital to the Survey's work. Many participants in the war, including senior political officials and officers from all of the services, were willing to speak with the Survey and to share their recollections of Desert Shield and Desert Storm. Private students of the Gulf War also volunteered their knowledge of the crisis and conflict. Wherever possible and appropriate, such assistance has been acknowledged in the text.

The authors are grateful to the staff of the Naval Institute Press and, in particular, to Ms. Anne Collier, who saw this project through to completion, and Ms. Linda O'Doughda, who edited the manuscript with a light but firm touch. We also wish to recognize the work of Mr. Barry D. Watts, who wrote portions of chapters 3, 4, and 9, and Dr. Wayne W. Thompson, who wrote portions of chapter 5. Both gentlemen provided extensive comments on early drafts. The *Summary Report*'s first draft also benefited greatly from the comments and contributions of Mr. Lawrence M. Greenberg, Col. Richard J. Blanchfield, Col. Emery M. Kiraly, Col. Mark L. Tarpley, Lt. Col. Daniel T. Kuehl, Capt. Jeffrey A. Hodgdon, and Mr. Steven L. Orton. Some graphics and tables were done by Mr. Alan P. Heffernan, Mr. Barry D. Watts, and Mr. Lawrence M. Greenberg. Finally, a special word of thanks for the work of the primary typists, Ms. Peggy Kramer and Ms. Cecelia A. French; the editors, Mr. Lawrence J. Paszek, Ms. Anne Predzin, and Mr. Chris Pankow; the layout designers, Mr. Michael O. Bowers and Barbara L. Gardien; and Judith Cohen, who revised the index.

The passage of two years since the completion of the Survey has reinforced our appreciation for the enormous labors of its staff, upon which we have relied throughout. Under conditions of great time pressure, and confronting an enormous task, they completed a piece of work that scholars will draw on for years to come. In editing the original *Summary Report* we recalled not only their professional diligence, but also the pleasure we took in their company during two years of hard collective work. We dedicate this book to them, with our gratitude and in friendship.

Introduction

This book, as with the *Summary Report* from which it is derived, captures some of the key findings of the ten reports of the Gulf War Air Power Survey (GWAPS). It does not, however, merely offer an executive summary of each report; rather, it asks a number of questions that cut across each of the reports. In all cases, the main reports of the Survey contain far fuller treatment of any given issue than is possible here. Furthermore, the authors of this study could not treat some issues, particularly in the realm of space and intelligence operations, in an unclassified forum such as this.

Chapter 1, What Happened? gives a brief overview of Desert Shield, the deployment to the Arabian Peninsula following Iraq's invasion of Kuwait in August 1990 and a longer account of the Gulf War. It sets a chronological context for the discussions that follow. Chapter 2, What Was the Air Campaign Plan? describes the evolution of the air campaign plan that Gen. H. Norman Schwarzkopf, commander in chief, Central Command (CINCCENT), authorized for execution on 17 January 1991. Chapter 3, What Did the Air Campaign Accomplish? evaluates the effects and effectiveness of the air campaign. Chapter 4, What Was the Role of Intelligence? examines the many aspects of intelligence as they related to air operations in the Gulf War, including strategic estimates and bomb damage assessment. Chapter 5, Who Ran the Air War? examines the organizations that orchestrated the air campaign and some of the controversies that emerged, including those centering on the role of the Joint Force Air Component Commander (JFACC) and the lengthy Air Tasking Order (ATO) that coordinated the vast majority of sorties. Chapter 6, What Were the Conditions in the Theater? briefly treats the political considerations and physical constraints of distance, terrain, weather, and basing structure that shaped the employment of air power in the gulf. Chapter 7, What Were the Instruments of Air Power? covers the role of different air platforms, with particular attention to the unique contributions of the United States. Chapter 8, What Supported the Air Power? discusses some of the other elements of air power, including munitions and logistical support required for the conduct of operations. Chapter 9, Was

Introduction

Desert Storm a Revolution in Warfare? asks whether the success of air operations in this war augurs a broader transformation of warfare. Chapter 10, What Does Desert Storm Tell Us about the Future of Air Power? explores some of the implications of the war for the American use of air power in the future.

Secretary Rice gave the Survey a mandate to examine the widest possible range of issues relating to air power in the Gulf War. In this endeavor the Survey soon became aware that it suffered from both a glut and an insufficiency of source materials. The glut is easily understood. In the age of the personal computer and copying machine, organizations create vast quantities of paper, including incremental modifications of working documents. The professional historians of the Air Force and other services conducted interviews (subsequently transcribed), collected and microfilmed key papers, and in a few cases directly recorded events as they happened. Subsequently, a host of private and public research organizations conducted studies on virtually every aspect of the war, uncovering further material and producing their own secondary sources. The Survey assembled its own archive of all available material on the Gulf War (see "A Note on Sources" in this book), an archive subsequently shipped to the United States Air Force Historical Research Agency, Maxwell Air Force Base, Alabama.

The insufficiency of information requires some explanation. Much important discussion in this war took place via telephone conversations—rarely did participants, pressed as they were for time, take notes of these conversations. The prevalence of the briefing (rather than the memorandum) as a form of official communication further obscured the historical record. Briefing slides usually consist of "bullets," cryptically phrased assertions or observations that take on meaning only in the context of a discussion—for which notes rarely exist. Such slides usually contain numbers or factual assertions of unknown provenance; very often the Survey began tracking a number down only to find itself caught in a circle of briefings referring to briefings.

Individuals rarely retained electronically recorded information (target databases, for example, or videotapes of bombing runs) in archives; rather, they updated or recorded over computer disks and videotapes. Many of the computer management systems that should have captured adequate information suffered partial or complete breakdowns under the stress of operations on a vast scale and were replaced by ad hoc combinations of computer and paper records that sometimes did not survive the war. Organizations (fighter wings, for example) placed very different emphases on the accurate recording of some of the most important kinds of operational data; the mission reports of many attack sorties, for example, present inadequate information to determine what an aircraft had struck and sometimes even where it had dropped its bombs.

We have attempted to render, in as clear a fashion as time and skill permitted, a comprehensive account of how air power, and above all American air power, shaped the confrontation with Iraq from 2 August 1990 to the end of the Gulf War on 28 February 1991. The GWAPS reduced the uncertainties surrounding the use of air power in the 1991 Iraq war but did not eliminate them. In this book, as in the Survey, we have attempted to frame and answer important questions about the employment of air power in the Gulf War, bearing in mind that the issues raised herein have considerably more than a purely historical interest. To be sure, we hope that this book will help scholars seeking to improve our understanding of the Gulf War. But we also hope that it will help those men and women, civilian and military, who will have to consider and create the instruments of American air power in the future. Should this book and the GWAPS's reports prove of use to them, we will have accomplished our most important purpose.

Revolution in Warfare?

One | What Happened?

Iraq invaded Kuwait before dawn on 2 August 1990. During the subsequent five and a half months, in an operation named Desert Shield, U.S. and Coalition forces poured into the theater to deter further Iraqi aggression and to set the stage for offensive actions. Operation Desert Storm, the combined attack on Iraq, began in the early hours of 17 January 1991 with an independent air campaign and ended on 28 February 1991 after a four-day combined forces ground and air assault. Coalition forces evicted Iraqi forces from Kuwait and destroyed much of Baghdad's military machine. From the outset, U.S. air power was central to the accomplishment of United States's and the United Nations's political and military objectives. It enabled the Coalition to deploy its forces and subsequently cripple Iraqi military capabilities, paving the way for Baghdad's defeat on the battlefield. The following pages briefly describe air operations from August 1990 through February 1991, set in their political and military context.

The August 1990 crisis was preceded by increasingly contentious negotiations between Iraq and Kuwait concerning territorial claims and financial obligations. Neither the Persian Gulf states nor the United States, however, anticipated Iraq's invasion of Kuwait. As late as July 1990, the intelligence community assessed the deployment of eight Iraqi Republican Guard divisions to the Kuwait border as an attempt to pressure Kuwait in the negotiations, not as a prelude to war. Even when the negotiations foundered on 1 August, Kuwait refrained from placing its military forces on full alert. Iraqi forces entered Kuwait City hours after the invasion began on 2 August and reached the Kuwait–Saudi Arabian border the next day. Surprised and overwhelmed, the Kuwaitis offered only sporadic resistance, and the Kuwaiti air force fled to Saudi Arabia after destroying a number of Iraqi helicopters and vehicles with their A-4 and Mirage F-1 aircraft.

Most American military and political leaders had also failed to anticipate the Iraqi invasion, which occurred on the very day that President George Bush gave an important policy address on the future of American national security policy. Yet, although preoccupied with Europe and the end of the Cold War, military planners had taken preliminary steps to reorient their focus from a global war with the Soviets to regional contingencies. Beginning in the fall of 1989, U.S. military planning for Arabian Peninsula security shifted from a potential Soviet threat to a regional threat with Iraq as the focus. By the spring of 1990, U.S. Central Command (CENTCOM) had prepared a draft operations plan (OPLAN 1002-90, Defense of the Arabian Peninsula) to address such a contingency. The plan only slightly resembled the operations that would unfold, however. Defensive in nature, it called for an early deployment of U.S. forces to trade space for time, while reducing the attacking Iraqi forces until sufficient U.S. forces could deploy for a counteroffensive to recapture lost territory.

Two days after the Iraqi invasion, President Bush convened a meeting of the National Security Council to discuss U.S. options. After briefing the president on possible military options—including those in CENTCOM's draft contingency plan—Gen. H. Norman Schwarzkopf, commander CENTCOM, and his staff prepared for a deployment of forces to Southwest Asia.[1] Their deployment plan would take four months to execute (plus an additional two months for the forces added later) and would depend on the use of some twenty-five regional bases, including some not mentioned in existing plans. Ultimately, it would also involve command arrangements with forces from thirty-eight countries. Weeks would be needed to deploy enough troops to defend Saudi Arabia against the Iraqi forces across the border in Kuwait. Schwarzkopf and his planners understood the precariousness of the situation and placed priority on deploying combat units first, at the expense of support and sustainment personnel and equipment.

General Schwarzkopf depended on air power as the essential shield for the buildup of forces necessary to defend the Arabian Peninsula. The only forces he had immediately available in the region were a carrier battle group (USS *Independence*), two KC-135 tankers, a mobile operations center deployed (Operation Ivory Justice) to Abu Dhabi at the request of the United Arab Emirates, and the six Navy ships of CENTCOM's Joint Task Force Middle East. On 6 August, Saudi King Fahd requested military assistance following a meeting in Riyadh with a U.S. delegation that included Secretary of Defense Richard B. Cheney, General Schwarzkopf, and Lt. Gen. Charles A. Horner, commander, Air Force Component, Central Command (CENTAF). Schwarzkopf designated Horner the CENTCOM forward commander, placing him in charge of the reception of forces that began flowing into the theater within days, while Schwarzkopf returned to the United States.

Under an umbrella of Saudi F-15Cs and AWACS on twenty-four-hour

---

1. U.S. Department of Defense, *Conduct of the Persian Gulf War*, Final Report to Congress, April 1992, 32, 334, 350; hereafter *Conduct of the Persian Gulf War*. See chapter 2 of this book for a discussion of planning for the air campaign.

What Happened? 3

Figure 1   Map of the Region
Source: *Conduct of the Persian Gulf War.* Appendix D.

defensive air patrol, the buildup of Coalition forces on the Arabian Peninsula began. The first aircraft in the region included the *Independence* carrier air wing, the First Tactical Fighter Wing (F-15Cs) and E-3 Airborne Warning and Control Aircraft from the United States, and RC-135 (Rivet Joint) reconnaissance aircraft from Europe. Troops from the 82d Airborne Division assumed defensive positions around the airports. By the end of August, the Royal Air Force had two fighter squadrons in place with accompanying tanker and maritime patrol aircraft, and U.S. forces had increased to fourteen tactical fighter squadrons (U.S. Air Force and Marine Corps), three carrier battle groups, a B-52 squadron, four tactical airlift squadrons, seven Army and Marine Corps brigades with attack helicopters, and a Patriot air defense system. By the end of the war, more than thirty-eight hundred U.S. fixed- and rotary-wing aircraft, half a million personnel, and almost three million tons of cargo had arrived in the theater.

Moving such a large force over eight thousand miles to Southwest Asia put a tremendous strain on the military transportation system. Over the months of Desert Shield, sealift brought about 95 percent of the equipment and supplies to the region, and strategic airlift (C-5, C-141, KC-10, and Civil Reserve Air Fleet) brought 99 percent of the personnel. In the early days of deployment all supplies and equipment except for that prepositioned on ships in the region came by air.[2] Moving personnel and equipment from the few points of debarkation in the theater to the many airfields and staging areas required almost seventeen thousand C-130 tactical airlift sorties. On 18 August the president authorized the first-ever activation of the first stage of the Civil Reserve Air Fleet, and on 22 August he signed Executive Order 12727 authorizing the call-up of two hundred thousand reservists for a period of up to 180 days.[3] Without these measures the U.S. airlift, taxed to the limit, could not have sustained the required buildup in the theater.

When General Schwarzkopf returned to the theater in late August, an Iraqi invasion of Saudi Arabia seemed less imminent. In retrospect, it appears unlikely that Iraq had ever intended to invade Saudi Arabia immediately after seizing Kuwait. Once in Kuwait, Iraqi forces quickly assumed a defensive posture, and Saddam Hussein's determination to retain Kuwait was beyond all doubt. Baghdad remained unmoved by the U.N. resolutions of 2 and 6 August, which condemned the invasion, called for the restoration of Kuwait, and authorized a multinational embargo of all trade to Iraq. Saddam Hussein declared Kuwait the nineteenth province of Iraq,[4] took Americans and other foreigners in Kuwait and Iraq hostage, and pronounced in October that if war came, Iraq would launch missile attacks against Saudi Arabia and Israel. Since Iraq was known to possess chemical munitions and was believed to have biological weapons, these threats raised the prospect of grave danger to the gulf states, Israel, and deployed Coalition forces.

As Coalition forces grew, a dual chain of command evolved, with Saudi Lt. Gen. Prince Khalid Bin Sultan al-Saud as the commander, Joint Forces and Theater of Operations, and General Schwarzkopf as the commander of all U.S. forces in the theater. General Horner assumed operational duties as the area air defense coordinator, the airspace control authority, and the joint force air component commander (JFACC) responsible for planning, coordinating, allocating, and as-

---

2. Chapter 8 discusses equipment and supplies brought to the theater. Appendix 1 contains a chronology of activity, April 1990 to 28 February 1991.

3. Chapters 7 and 8 contain further discussion on the airlift forces employed.

4. Radio Baghdad broadcast, 8 August 1990.

signing personnel to theater air operations derived from General Schwarzkopf's apportionment decisions.[5] Horner exercised his authority through the daily air tasking order (ATO), which provided detailed direction—with some exceptions—for all Coalition flight operations during both Desert Shield and Desert Storm.

The daily ATO became a subject of contention. It comprised some two hundred pages in standard message format, or approximately eight hundred pages on the Computer-Assisted Force Management System. It contained times, targets, altitudes, call signs, radio frequencies, and other necessary mission information. CENTAF found its daily construction and dissemination to all units concerned a massive task. Each of the U.S. armed services and Coalition forces accepted the need for a single authority to coordinate an air campaign and to provide safe separation of the two- to three-thousand aircraft sorties flown per day in the theater's limited airspace. They had reservations, however (to varying degrees), about General Horner's authority to select the targets and prescribe the flight operations for the many elements of the Coalition air forces. Eventually, the ATO directed almost all Coalition fixed-wing aircraft sorties, although it did not always impose tight control over these aircraft.[6] Helicopters flying at less than five hundred feet above the ground were exempted from direct JFACC control, as were naval aircraft on overwater flights.

From the first, General Horner had to concern himself with getting forces to their bases and planning for the defense of the Arabian Peninsula. Early on, he appointed U.S. Air Force Brig. Gen. Buster Glosson director of a special planning group—known as the Black Hole—to prepare offensive air operations against Iraq. This effort, in turn, drew on Instant Thunder, a plan developed in early August by the air staff. The Black Hole consisted primarily of Air Force officers but eventually included officers from all the services as well as British and Saudi representatives. Working in great secrecy, the Black Hole had a plan ready for implementation in mid-September, ahead of the arrival of the main ground forces. Their plan sought to dislodge the Iraqi forces from Kuwait by attacking key Iraqi targets such as leadership and command and control systems; key nuclear, biological, chemical, electrical, military, and oil-production facilities; bridges, railroads, and port infrastructures; and air defense, naval, missile, and ground forces, particularly the Republican Guard.

This offensive air campaign supported the CENTCOM plan, which

---

5. Message, USCINCCENT, 101100Z, August 1990, para. 3E26, GWAPS, CHC 12–15. See "A Note on Sources" at the end of this book for an explanation of GWAPS citation formats used in footnotes.

6. Discussion of the JFACC organization and procedures is contained in chapter 5. Sorties from Turkey (Proven Force) did not appear in the ATO.

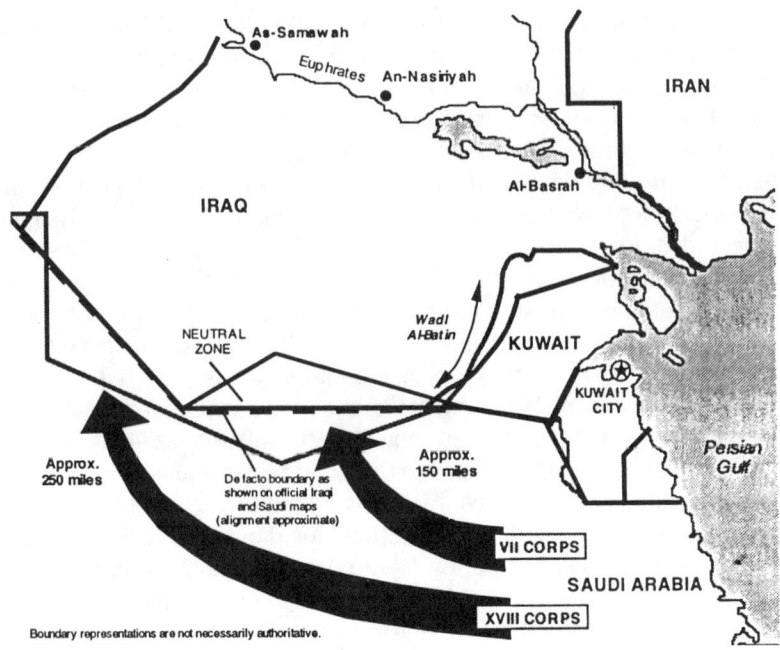

Figure 2　Shift to the West by U.S. XVIII Corps and VII Corps
Source: *Conduct of the Persian Gulf War,* 247.

called for four phases: Phase I, a strategic air campaign against Iraq; Phase II, suppressing enemy air defenses in the Kuwaiti theater of operations; Phase III, preparing the battlefield; and Phase IV, a ground campaign. The Black Hole's air campaign plan was accepted by the president in October. More troublesome was the plan for employing the Coalition ground forces, since the lack of such forces limited the ground-attack options to a frontal assault into Kuwait.

Because a Coalition frontal assault raised the likelihood of heavy Coalition losses, the president authorized the addition of more ground and air forces to enhance Schwarzkopf's options. As a result, a second phase of deployment, begun in late November 1990, increased the forces already in the theater by four hundred Air Force aircraft, three carrier battle groups, and more than four Army and Marine divisions, including the European-based U.S. VII Corps. The new deployments also entailed activation of more reserves. Arab and European Coalition members proportionally increased their forces. Arrival of the additional forces coincided with the deadline set for Iraq to evacuate Kuwait—15 January 1991.[7] By mid-January, the Coalition force in-

---

7. On 29 November 1990 the U.N. Security Council voted to authorize force to expel Iraqi forces from Kuwait if they had not evacuated by 15 January 1991.

cluded nearly eighteen hundred combat aircraft from twelve countries, a large naval force in the Persian Gulf and Red Sea, and approximately 540,000 ground troops from thirty-one countries. The total Coalition force numbered in excess of 660,000.[8] The increased number of Coalition air and ground forces allowed Schwarzkopf to concentrate on his main goal: enveloping the Republican Guard and Iraqi regular army divisions. To do this he would launch Phases I, II, and III of the air campaign, while he repositioned the bulk of his forces to the west in preparation for Phase IV.

During the preceding months the Coalition air forces had honed their skills and learned to operate together through exercises that not only rehearsed planned missions but also desensitized the Iraqi air defenses to Coalition flight patterns. Once the air campaign began, effectively shutting off Iraqi surveillance of the Coalition ground forces, the U.S. XVIII Airborne Corps and VII Corps would deploy to the west (see figure 2) to set the stage for enveloping the Iraqi ground forces. As the Marines (MARCENT) and two Arab corps (JFC-N and JFC-E) attacked to hold Iraqi forces in place, and as the 4th Marine Expeditionary Brigade faked an amphibious assault, the two westward corps would attack the Iraqi force on the flank (see figure 3).[9]

Iraqi ground forces facing the Coalition also grew over the months of the Coalition's buildup. Beginning with the fourteen divisions estimated to be in the theater in September, the Iraqi army increased gradually until November, when Baghdad announced it would send another 250,000 troops to the theater in response to the announced Coalition increase, bringing the number of Iraqi troops to a nominal 680,000.[10] In January 1991 the Defense Intelligence Agency estimated that Iraq had forty-two to forty-three divisions in the theater with 540,000 troops, more than forty-two hundred tanks, twenty-eight hundred armored personnel carriers, and approximately thirty-one hundred artillery pieces. In addition to its ground forces, Baghdad had more than seven hundred combat aircraft and a multilayered air defense system, a navy of missile-firing patrol boats, and Silkworm surface-to-surface missiles for coastal defense.[11]

---

8. *Conduct of the Persian Gulf War*, 85–86. As of 15 January 1991, CENTCOM strength was 454,128: ARCENT, 247,637; CENTAF, 48,679; NAVCENT, 67,851; MARCENT, 85,447; SOCCENT, 3,279; and CENTCOM Headquarters and JCSE, 1,235. By 27 February 1991, CENTCOM strength had grown to 541,376 (GWAPS, *Statistical Compendium*, Table 14, Theater CENTCOM Personnel Strength at Weekly Intervals, 60).

9. This brief summary does not identify all of the ground forces engaged in this attack. For instance, a French division was attached to the XVIII Corps and a British division to the VII Corps. Maps are extracted from *Conduct of the Persian Gulf War*, 244, 247.

10. *New York Times*, 20 November 1990, A-1.

11. *Conduct of the Persian Gulf War*, 11–13, 84–85.

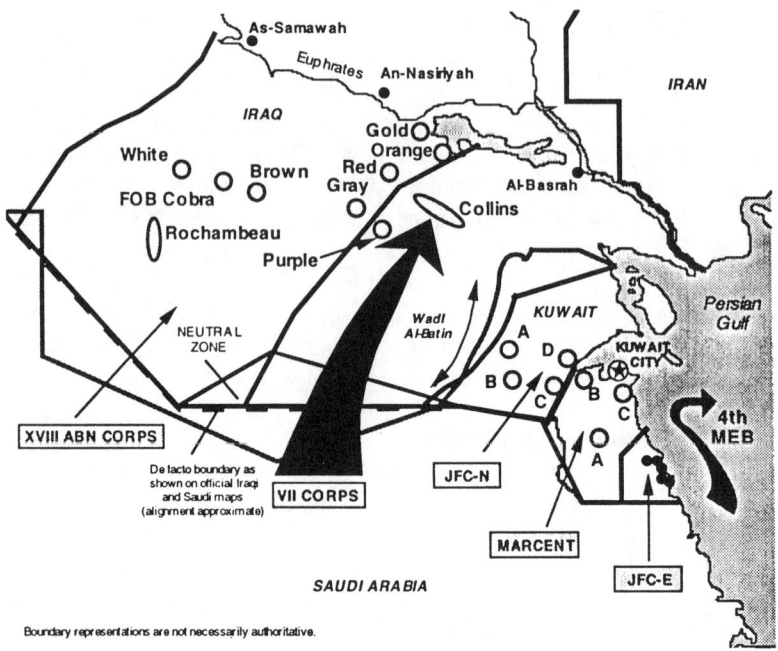

Figure 3   Coalition Plan for Ground Attack
Source: *Conduct of the Persian Gulf War*, 244.

Postwar analysis confirmed this number of Iraqi divisions but concluded that the number of troops, armor, and artillery in these units was overstated. Most divisions deployed understrength, particularly those on the front lines in the western part of the theater (total undermanning, 120,000).[12] Also, Iraqi policy allowed frequent leaves, meaning that a large number of soldiers, absent when the air campaign began, never rejoined their units. The Survey authors judge that 20 percent, or eighty-four thousand troops, were either on leave or had deserted when the air war began.[13] Applying these decrements to the original Defense Intelligence Agency estimate results in a revised

---

12. Such a disposition of divisions would make sense in light of the Iraqi anticipation of a Coalition attack coming up the coast road or from the area of the Wadi al Batin (into either the Iraqi IV or III Corps areas). Note, however, that some units deployed at close to full strength. As a result, any theater-wide assessments based on manning of frontline units should be made with caution.

13. Having such a large portion of the army on leave with an attack pending appears unusual, but numerous prisoner of war reports confirm the practice. The program of frequent leave appears to have been used to keep troop morale up and desertions down. A like system was in place during the Iran-Iraq War. Desertions before 17 January are counted within the 20 percent authorized to be on leave. This decrement could be greater if there was a substantial early-desertion rate in addition to the numbers on leave.

What Happened?

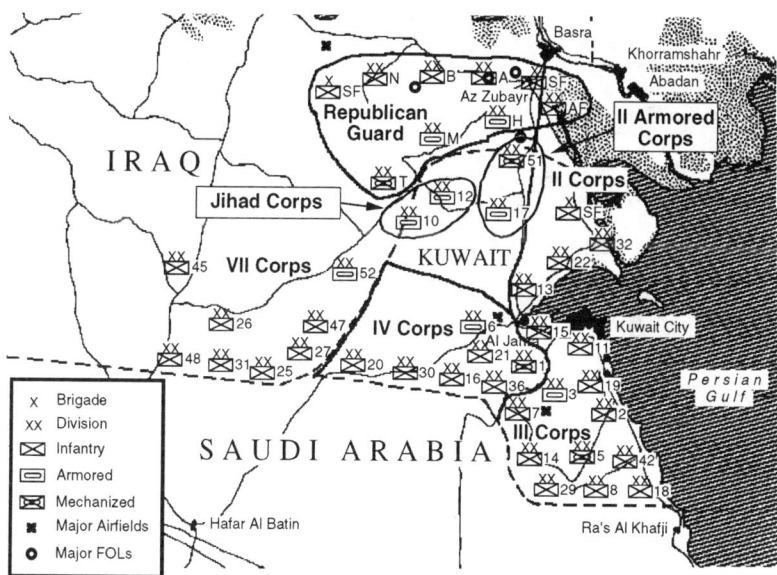

Figure 4   Iraqi Deployment in Kuwaiti Theater of Operations on 17 January 1991

estimate of no more than 336,000 Iraqi troops in the theater on 17 January 1991.

While exact numbers were unknown, U.S. planners had a fairly accurate overall picture of Iraqi deployments in the theater by the beginning of the war (see figure 4). Coalition reconnaissance clearly established the purpose and general location of Iraqi ground forces, which had deployed in three defensive lines or echelons. The frontline forces—closest to the Kuwait-Saudi border—were intended to slow and attrit the initial Coalition attack and allow the Iraqi military leadership to determine its main axis. The frontline forces consisted of infantry divisions from three corps arrayed east to west with Iraqi III Corps facing MARCENT and JFC-E, IV Corps facing JFC-N, and VII Corps west of Wadi al Batin.

The second Iraqi echelon comprised the tactical and operational reserves of armored and mechanized divisions deployed throughout central Kuwait and southern Iraq. Their mission was to reinforce other units and block Coalition penetration of the front lines. (The tactical reserves were the 1st, 3d, 5th, 6th, and 52d Divisions. The operational reserves were the 17th and 51st Divisions, the II Armored Corps, and the 10th and 12th Divisions, the Jihad Corps.)

The Republican Guard formed the third echelon north and west of the Kuwait border. These divisions, including the heavy divisions of the Guard—the Tawakalna, Madinah, and Hammurabi—were the strategic

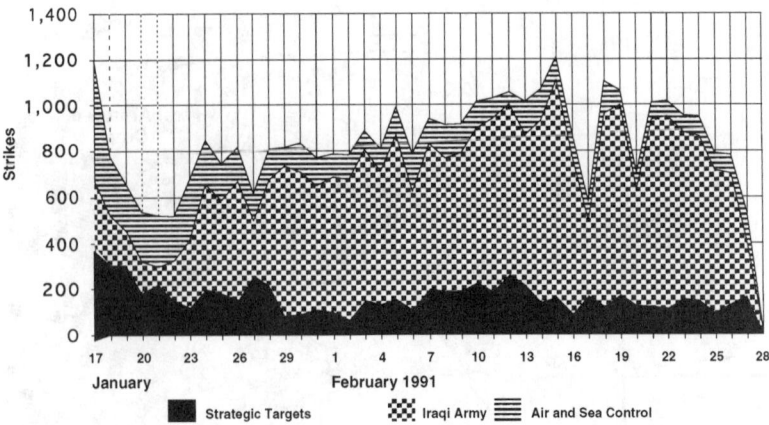

Figure 5   Coalition Air Strikes by Day against Iraqi Targets
Note: Strategic targets are defined in chapters 2 and 3 (see in particular figure 12). Iraqi army strikes include attacks on equipment, troop concentrations, and logistics sites of the Iraqi army in the Kuwaiti theater. Air and sea control includes attacks on airfields, air defense sites, and Iraqi naval and coastal defense targets. (For data on each target set and aircraft, see appendix 2.)
Source: GWAPS Database.

reserve poised to counterattack the main Coalition offensive.[14] Other infantry divisions of Iraq's II Corps deployed north of Kuwait City along the shoreline with general missions of reinforcing the main body, protecting the coast, and defending against possible airborne attacks into central Kuwait. CENTCOM assessed the three lines of defensive formations as twenty-five committed, nine reinforcing, and eight theater reserve divisions.[15]

Early on 17 January, the Coalition launched a concentrated air campaign against strategic military, leadership, and infrastructure targets in Iraq (see appendix 3). Even before the first shots were fired at 0238 local time by helicopters attacking an early-warning radar site in southern Iraq, B-52s from Barksdale Air Force Base in Louisiana were en route with conventional cruise missiles, Navy ships had fired salvos of Tomahawk land-attack missiles (TLAMs), and F-117 stealth aircraft were approaching Baghdad. Waves of aircraft followed, rapidly sweeping into Iraq to attack airfields, nodes of the integrated air defense system, leadership command and control systems, known Scud (the NATO

---

14. *Conduct of the Persian Gulf War*, 110–12. Note: heavy division is a term that describes either an armored or mechanized division. Appendix 2 contains further data on numbers of Coalition aircraft in the region.

15. USCENTCOM Situation Report, 23 February 1991, GWAPS, CHST 68.

What Happened?

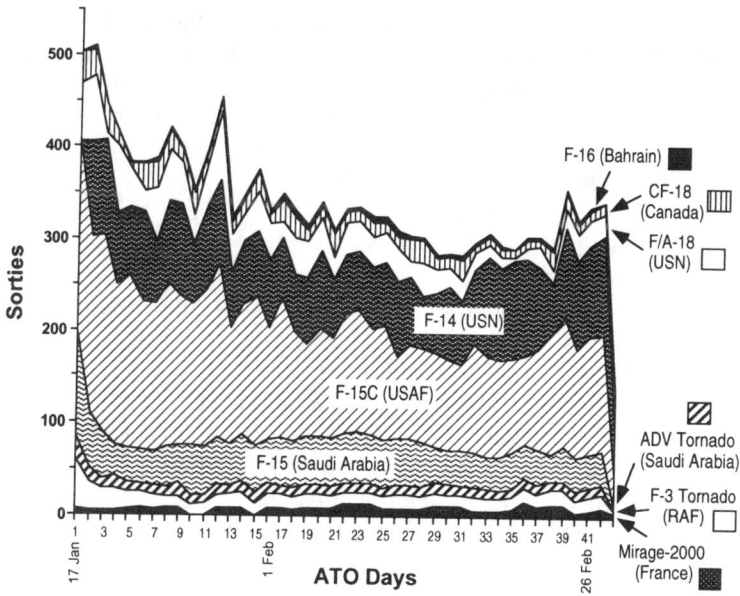

Figure 6 Coalition Air-to-Air Sorties by Day (Defensive Counterair and Combat Air Patrol)
Source: GWAPS Database.

designation for the Soviet-produced SS-1 ballistic missile) sites, nuclear/chemical/biological production sites, and electrical power facilities. By dawn, the attacks spread to include ground forces in the Kuwaiti theater of operation—defined as Kuwait and that part of Iraq south of 31° North and east of 45° East.

The second night and day were characterized by more of the same attacks, with oil production and storage facilities and naval sites coming under assault. The first two days of air operations were the most thoroughly planned and the most complex of the war, as Coalition commanders attempted to dismember Iraqi air defenses and at the same time attack targets across the entire spectrum of strategic target sets. To accomplish this, planners employed their entire arsenal of air weapons, including stealth F-117s, Tornados with JP-233 runway attack munitions, F-15Es, attack helicopters, drones, and conventional air-launched cruise missiles. The Coalition hit virtually every target set on the initial strikes, although the greatest weight of effort was directed against air defenses, airfields, and command elements of the Iraqi regime. Although sortie rates remained at similar levels throughout the war (with 2,759 flown the first day, including 432 refueling sorties), subsequent strikes were never as complex or focused, nor perhaps did they need to be (see figures 5 and 6).

The prime concern of commanders during the first days was to gain and maintain air superiority. To do this they employed an array of specialized aircraft that included dedicated air-to-air fighters (F-15Cs and F-14s); airborne warning, control, and intelligence aircraft (E-3s and RC-135s); electronic jamming support aircraft (EF-111s and EA-6s); and aircraft firing high-speed antiradiation missiles (HARMs) at Iraqi search and tracking radars. Additionally, two types of radar-decoy drones stimulated Iraqi radar activity, thereby deflecting attention from strike aircraft and encouraging surface-to-air missile radars to remain active and therefore vulnerable to HARM missiles. The F-4Gs alone expended 118 HARMs the first night. Almost half of the 1,961 HARMs expended by the services were launched during the first week of the war. After that, just the threat posed by the HARMs kept most Iraqi radars off the air. The decoys were likewise used principally during the first week of the war, most on the first night and only sparingly after that.

Not surprisingly, most Iraqi air combat sorties and air-to-air losses (fourteen) to Coalition fighters occurred during that same first week of the war. Subsequent losses occurred when Iraqi aircraft attempted to flee to Iran, not while trying to defend Iraqi airspace. By 27 January, air supremacy was achieved.

The nature of the strategic targets in Iraq required careful weaponeering (choice of weapons to match particular targets) to achieve the desired effects and accuracy, to avoid excessive collateral damage, and to reduce the risk of delivery aircraft having to conduct repeat attacks. Some target systems succumbed quickly—electrical power, for example. Other target sets consisting of a greater number of individual targets (for example, almost six hundred hardened aircraft shelters) required repeated strikes throughout the war.

Most targets in these categories required precision-guided weapons with a capability to penetrate hardened buildings. The softer area targets such as oil storage facilities could be struck with nonprecision gravity bombs. Virtually all American laser-designating aircraft participated in the strategic air campaign in Iraq. Since the risk of flying aircraft over Baghdad during daylight was high, TLAMs were used to keep the pressure on during daylight. Aircraft capable of employing precision weapons were at a premium, so much so that such aircraft could not be spared to attack bridges until the second week in the war. While most of the laser-guided bombs and surface-to-surface and air-to-surface missiles expended in the course of the forty-three-day air campaign were directed against industrial, government, and communications facilities, a large number were used against air installations and Iraqi ground forces, mainly in the course of direct attacks against armor.

Although strikes in Iraq required the use of precision weapons, the aircraft within the Scud launch areas for more immediate targeting, attacks on communication links thought to be transmitting Scud launch authorization, attacks of suspected sites, and strikes against Scud production and storage facilities. By war's end, nearly every type of strike and reconnaissance aircraft employed in the war participated in the attempt to bring this threat under control, but with scant evidence of success.

A second redirection of targeting involved digging the Iraqi air force out of its shelters. Subject to almost immediate engagement by Coalition aircraft ranging over their bases, the Iraqis elected not to contest control of Iraqi airspace and sought protection in hardened aircraft shelters that they thought immune from Coalition attack. On 23 January, airfield attack operations shifted from attacking runways to destroying aircraft shelters to remove the threat of these aircraft. Attacking the nearly six hundred Iraqi shelters required a substantial shift of resources, mainly F-117s and F-111Fs dropping laser-guided bombs. For two weeks F-111Fs devoted approximately 60 percent of their strikes to these shelters. They were then drawn off for use against tanks and other ground force equipment. Twenty-eight percent of the total British precision-bombing effort was against hardened shelters. Meanwhile, F-117s continued to prosecute shelter attacks until the last week of the war.

The shelter campaign took away the Iraqi air force's last chance of surviving the war reasonably intact. Unable to maintain the force as a strategic reserve (as it had during the Iran-Iraq War), Baghdad attempted to evacuate its combat aircraft to Iran. In the four-day period beginning on 26 January, nearly eighty aircraft fled across the border. By the end of the first week of February, a total of more than a hundred aircraft fled and were interned by the Iranian government. The Coalition established air patrols between the Iraqi air bases and the border in an attempt to stem these escapes and shot down several Iraqi aircraft. Other Iraqi aircraft, in their efforts to escape in low-level dashes, ran out of fuel and crashed.

The Iraqis also dispersed their remaining aircraft around airfields, on roads, in residential neighborhoods, and even near archaeological sites, taking advantage of the Coalition's known desire to avoid collateral damage. Through these measures, some Iraqi aircraft survived the war, but the Iraqi air force ceased to operate as an effective combat force. In fact, Baghdad's only known attempt at an offensive air strike took place on 24 January when two Iraqi F-1s attempted a low-level dash over the Persian Gulf, most likely to attack Coalition ships. A Saudi F-15C pilot downed both aircraft before they could reach their target.

Though air strikes with precision weapons continued throughout Iraq, the weight of effort by nonlaser-designating aircraft shifted to the

Kuwaiti theater beginning in the second week. Air attacks attempted to fix the Iraqi ground forces in place, seal off the area from resupply by attacking traffic within the area, and destroy equipment. Together with the bombing effort, psychological operations increased as Coalition leaflets in the millions, radio broadcasts, and loudspeakers encouraged Iraqi soldiers to lay down their arms.

After a week of air attacks against Iraq and its forces in the Kuwaiti theater, Baghdad began taking desperate measures to precipitate a ground war. While Iraq had anticipated an initial period of air attacks, the actual attacks were longer and more severe than expected, and a Coalition ground attack still appeared no closer to getting under way. Before the war, Saddam Hussein had boasted of the Iraqi advantage in a ground war; he predicted that mounting casualties would split the Coalition and turn the U.S. public against the war. On 22 January, Iraq set fire to two oil refineries and an oil field near the Kuwait-Saudi border. A day later Iraq opened oil manifolds in several offshore terminals, allowing crude oil to pour into the Persian Gulf. Whether Iraq's intent was to provoke a ground war or to make an amphibious assault more difficult is not known, but attacks by two F-111Fs using GBU-15 precision bombs on the oil manifolds at the Al Ahmadi refinery on 27 January stopped the oil flow into the gulf.

On 29 January, the Iraqi army attempted to prompt a ground war by launching attacks into Saudi Arabia from several points in southeastern Kuwait; the most prominent attack was against the Saudi Arabian town of Al Khafji (see figure 7). Saddam Hussein ordered the attack to induce the Coalition into a ground war, heighten the morale of his own forces by taking the offensive, and take prisoners as a source of intelligence in order to determine the Coalition's intentions.[19] The result was a defeat for the Iraqis in several ways. They occupied the abandoned and unguarded town of Al Khafji for a day, but Coalition forces quickly evicted them. Attempts to assemble Iraqi reinforcing columns in Kuwait were detected by a variety of night reconnaissance systems, including the newly arrived JSTARS (Joint Surveillance Target Attack Radar System) E-8 aircraft, and the columns were routed by air attacks. Having failed to precipitate a greater ground war, the Iraqis simply took to their defensive emplacements to await their fate.

While the action at Al Khafji provided the first instances of combined ground action involving the Coalition Arab forces and U.S. forces and the first true instances of close air support in the war, it also proved

---

19. Although Saddam Hussein's precise intentions may never be known, this synopsis follows the widely accepted interpretations of Iraqi action by CENTCOM and Washington intelligence organizations during and after the war. Enemy prisoner of war reports provide positive confirmation of this interpretation of events, and no reports dispute it (Message, Defense Intelligence Agency, dtg 151959Z February 91, subject: NADA INTSUM 207-91, GWAPS, CHST 45-33).

What Happened?

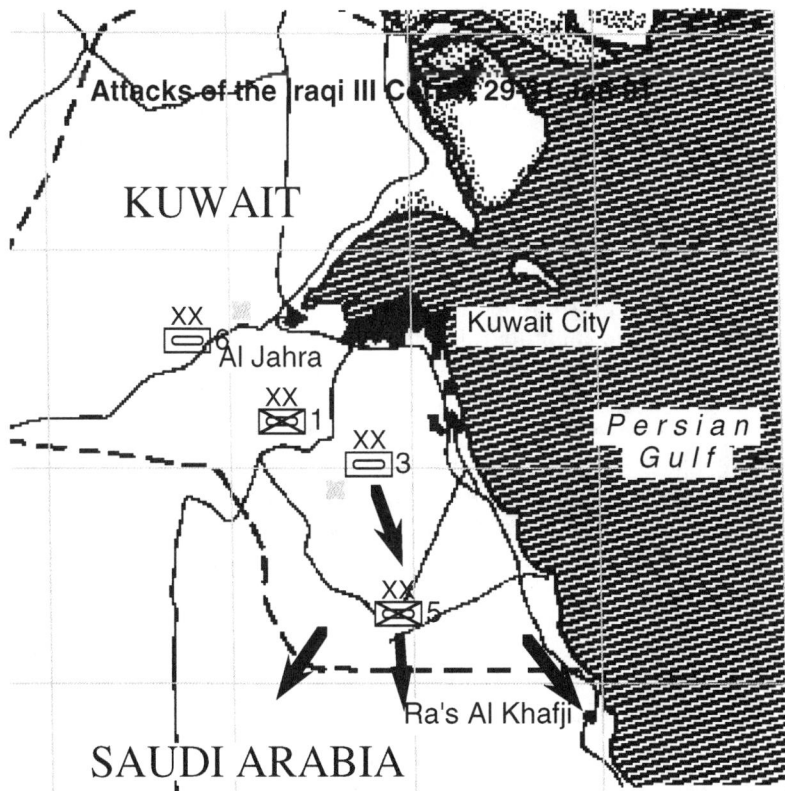

Figure 7 Attacks of the Iraqi III Corps, 29–31 January 1991

costly. The engagement produced several incidents of fratricide: thirteen Marines and four Saudi soldiers were killed in three incidents, two occurring during air-to-ground attacks.[20] It also resulted in the single greatest loss of Air Force personnel when an AC-130 gunship was shot down with its fourteen-man crew.

Before and during the Al Khafji attacks, Coalition aircraft destroyed nearly all Iraqi missile boats. Many of them were destroyed as they apparently attempted to flee to Iran, much as Iraqi aircraft had done several days before. The Iraqi navy was small, but even the presence of small missile-firing boats posed a threat to the Coalition battle groups and amphibious forces. The destruction of the missile boats allowed freer action for the Coalition forces in the northern gulf, although the

20. Office of Assistant Secretary of Defense (Public Affairs), *News Release No. 504-91*, 13 August 1991.

presence of Silkworm missile sites along the coast remained a threat throughout the remainder of the war.[21]

In early February, as CENTCOM's focus shifted to the Kuwaiti theater in preparation for the ground offensive, the effectiveness of the air attacks against the Iraqi army (planning was based on an attrition rate of 50 percent of Iraqi armor, artillery, and armored personnel carriers) came into question. Washington and the theater leaders disagreed over the level of damage actually achieved against Iraqi forces as well as the counting rules used to tally the damage. This disagreement brought several reactions in the theater. In addition to some adjustments to the counting rules, the theater air commanders modified some of the air operations. To increase the lethality of the attacks, the pilots of A-10s—aircraft thought to be the most effective against armor—decreased their attack altitude from above ten thousand feet to between four- and seven-thousand feet.[22]

A second adjustment, one that led to far better results, was the employment of laser-guided bombs against Iraqi armor. F-111F crews conducted night tests during the first week of February using their infrared sensors to detect the hot skin of the tanks (or any other metal equipment) contrasted against the cooler sand that surrounded them. Following these tests, F-111F, F-15E, and A-6 aircraft flew laser-guided bomb attacks against Iraqi armor in a procedure known as "tank plinking." From that point, the number of recorded armor and artillery kills climbed rapidly.[23]

During the later stages of the air attacks to prepare the battlefield for the ground attack, the weight of effort shifted from the Republican Guard and other heavy divisions in the Iraqi theater reserve to more direct attacks on the Iraqi frontline divisions. More B-52 sorties flew against the frontline forces to effect breaching operations. MC-130s dropped BLU-82 (fifteen-thousand-pound) bombs to clear mine fields and support psychological operations. Following the loss of two A-10s sixty nautical miles north of Kuwait City in mid-February, which

21. The missile boats and Silkworm missiles were not the only threat to the naval forces. Aircraft with air-to-surface missiles could launch from Iraqi (and possibly Iranian) bases and pose a longer-range threat to the fleet. Information drawn from two Center for Naval Analyses reports: Peter P. Perla, *Desert Storm Reconstruction Report, Vol. I: Summary*, and Jeffrey Lutz, et al., *Desert Storm Reconstruction Report, Vol. VI: Antisurface Warfare* (Alexandria, VA: 1991).

22. During this same period, the employment of F-16 killer scouts (Pointers) began, and F-16 pilots were directed to release bombs below eight thousand feet (see Colonel Lewis point paper, "Corps Air Support at Desert Storm," 3 July 1991, GWAPS, CHST 22-15); and 23/354 TFW(P) "Battle Staff Directive No. 26," 31 January 1991, GWAPS, Microfilm Roll 26554.

23. See discussion in chapter 3.

prompted General Horner to restrict A-10s to targets along the Saudi-Kuwait border in Kuwait, a greater concentration of A-10s attacked the Iraqi regular army forces in the front lines. Specific objectives included preparing breaching sites in Iraqi defenses, destroying artillery in the breach areas, and bombing the pumps used to fill Iraqi fire trenches.

As air power began to focus on the upcoming ground campaign, the continuing strategic air campaign momentarily drew increased attention with the attack on the Al Firdos bunker on the night of 12–13 February. Coalition planners did not know that the bunker, a legitimate military target, had also served as a civilian shelter when F-117s struck it. The resulting controversy over the deaths of several hundred civilians resulted in tightened control from Washington of attacks into downtown Baghdad.

In preparation for the Coalition ground offensive, air and ground units began rehearsing close air support procedures. As part of these preparations General Horner established new rules of engagement to support the ground campaign. He eliminated minimum-altitude restrictions and instructed crews to press their aerial attacks in every way possible to protect Coalition ground forces while maintaining an appropriate level of caution for aircrews. General Horner summarized his guidance: "The weather considerations that were valid last week are no longer valid. There are people's lives depending on our ability to help them if help is required. So I want a push put on. I want people feeling compulsion to hit a target. I do not want fratricide. So if in doubt don't shoot."[24]

While air power employed during the incursion at Al Khafji was an unrehearsed response to an unexpected action, the air power supporting the ground offensive of 24 to 28 February was well planned. The date for the offensive was known, sorties apportioned, and the procedures practiced. Air operations were coordinated and geared to support the ground offensive with large numbers of aircraft sorties planned for close air support and to interdiction across the Kuwaiti theater.

The bulk of the Coalition aircraft not scheduled for close air support were assigned the task of flying interdiction sorties. Commanders intended these sorties to destroy supplies and prevent Iraqi reserve forces from reinforcing the front lines or to catch retreating troops by striking headquarters, roads, and bridge networks. Attacks by Coalition aircraft extended throughout the theater, with Navy (from the gulf carriers) and Marine sorties concentrating on eastern Kuwait. Many

---

24. Comments from log of 24 February 1991, Headquarters CENTAF Office of History, *Daily Comments of Lt Gen Charles A. Horner, 17 January through 28 February 1991*, GWAPS, CHP 13B.

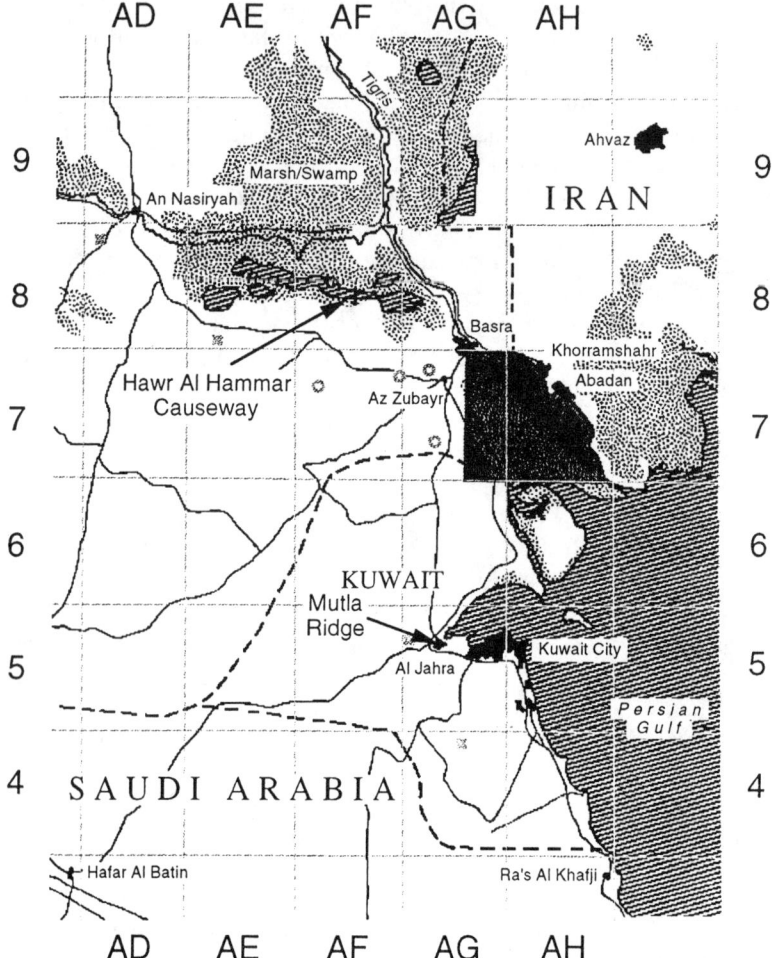

Figure 8   Chokepoints for Retreating Iraqi Troops in the Kuwaiti Theater

Note: Shaded area depicts no-strike areas declared on 27 February.

of the night flyers (F-111s, F-15Es, A-6s, and the LANTIRN-equipped F-16s)[25] focused on targets in the northern part of the theater to damage the heavy divisions further and to disrupt road traffic. B-52s flew around the clock: on the first day, they hit breaching sites and frontline forces; on subsequent days they struck headquarters and staging areas just south of the Euphrates River in Iraq.[26] The plan intended to put

25. Two squadrons of F-16s had navigation pods of the low-altitude navigation and targeting infrared for night (LANTIRN) system.

26. Master Attack Plans, 24 through 27 February 1991, GWAPS, BH 1.

What Happened?

maximum pressure on the Iraqi forces with every type of strike aircraft at the Coalition's disposal.[27]

When the ground offensive began at 0400 local time on 24 February, the system needed all the flexibility it could muster to deal with the rapidly changing conditions. More than three thousand sorties flew that day, mostly in the confined airspace over the battlefield. The generally light opposition to the rapid ground advance generated few targets for close air support aircraft, and a period of poor weather and restricted visibility caused by oil fires limited the ability of many aircraft to perform close air support.

Fortunately, Coalition planners enjoyed a comfortable surplus of available close air support sorties that could engage alternate targets well ahead of the rapidly moving ground advance. Aircraft equipped with radar-aimed release systems used this less accurate tactic, while many of those not so equipped had to return with their bombs. While some sorties of true close air support did fly, most of the effort, and the subsequent destruction, fell on the heavy reserve divisions and the retreating columns of the Iraqi army as it fled Kuwait. The highway proceeding northwest out of Kuwait City and Al Jahra and over Mutla Ridge, the "highway of death," was one such bottleneck of traffic that came under attack during this retreat (see figure 8).[28]

In the later stages of the war the air effort focused on supporting the ground campaign. Air attacks throughout Iraq continued, however, destroying bridges to the theater, military support facilities, and communications within the theater, plus attacking surviving or newly identified Scud, chemical, biological, and nuclear sites. In addition, Baghdad, which generally had been spared since 13 February, came under renewed air attack during the final four days of the war, as U.S. planners made a last attempt to cripple the national leadership. This last effort included an F-111F attack on deep bunkers with GBU-28 deep-penetrator weapons.

The war ended with a Coalition-declared cease-fire at 0800 on 28 February 1991. The Iraqi army had been driven into a corner of southern Iraq, south of the Euphrates River and west of a canal near Basra. Neither waterway was easily passable. Coalition ground forces had reached the banks of the Euphrates River and had approached to within thirty miles of Basra. Arab forces occupied Kuwait City. By any measure, Iraq had suffered a crushing military defeat, and air power had proved central to that outcome.

27. Although the F-117s and Tornados only marginally so: F-117s continued to hit strategic targets in Iraq, and Tornados were employed principally against airfields in Iraq. The Proven Force F-16s and F-111s, which could not reach the Kuwaiti theater, continued to strike targets in northern Iraq.

28. See discussion in chapter 3.

Two | # What Was the Air Campaign Plan?

On 8 August 1990, two days after King Fahd of Saudi Arabia had approved the deployment of American forces to defend his country, and one day after those forces began to deploy, President George Bush outlined U.S. objectives in the region. One, secure the immediate, unconditional, and complete withdrawal of Iraqi forces from Kuwait. Two, restore the legitimate government of Kuwait. Three, assure the security and stability of the Persian Gulf region. And four, protect American lives.[1]

On 25 August 1990, less than three weeks after the U.S. decision to commit troops to defend Saudi Arabia, General Schwarzkopf briefed Gen. Colin L. Powell, chairman of the Joint Chiefs of Staff (JCS), on the outlines of a four-phased plan to eject the Iraqis from Kuwait. Although the ground forces concept of operations remained unclear, the concept of the air campaign had already evolved:

> **USCINCCENT's Intent**
>
> We will initially attack into the Iraqi homeland using air power to decapitate his leadership, command and control, and eliminate his ability to reinforce Iraqi ground forces in Kuwait and Southern Iraq. We will then gain undisputed air superiority over Kuwait so that we can subsequently and selectively attack Iraqi ground forces with air power in order to reduce his combat power and destroy reinforcing units. . . .[2]

In the months that followed, increased forces became available for war, and planners developed specific elements of the air and ground campaign. The four-phase structure of the air campaign remained un-

---

1. Address to the Nation Announcing the Deployment of United States Armed Forces to Saudi Arabia, in *Public Papers of the Presidents of the United States: George Bush, 1990* (Book II) (Office of the Federal Register, National Archives and Record Administration, 1991), 1108. These objectives were a restatement of those put forward by the U.S. State Department on 6 August. U.N. Resolutions 660 and 661 of 2 and 6 August also contained the first two of these objectives.

2. Viewgraph from briefing, "Offensive Campaign: Desert Storm," Headquarters, Central Command, 24 August 1990, GWAPS, NA 208. Notice the use of the term "decapitate."

What Was the Air Campaign Plan?

changed, however: a strategic air campaign into Iraq, air supremacy over the Kuwaiti theater, preparation of the battlefield by attrition of the Iraqi army, and air support for the ground attack. Turning this concept into reality would require a great deal of time and labor.

No single "air campaign plan"—recognizable as such—existed. Rather, the air campaign plan executed by Coalition forces at the outset of the Gulf War consisted of three elements:

- a broad statement of purpose, including the idea of a four-phased war;
- extremely detailed air tasking orders for the first two days of the war, plus additional staff work on the third day of operations; and
- a more diffuse set of expectations about how the air war would unfold and what it would accomplish against any given target set.

The air campaign plan was imbedded in the operations plan for all forces and consisted of an amalgam of thick scheduling documents, an extensive series of briefings (each slightly different from the last), and a set of intentions captured only sporadically on paper. Nonetheless, the result was a unified concept for applying air power against Iraq.

Pre-crisis Planning

The plan for using air power in Desert Storm had surprisingly little to do with planning done before August 1990. The Soviet threat and the nature of the theater had long shaped the expected role of air power in the defense of the oil-producing areas in the gulf region. The distance of the theater from the United States, and the lack of any in-place forces on the ground, made airlift and sealift critical to any defense of the region. American planners expected air forces, land- and sea-based, to serve as the first line of defense in the early stages of a conflict that might last months until large ground forces could arrive. In the early weeks of war in the gulf, planners expected air power to interdict and delay the attacking ground forces, be those forces Soviet, Iranian, or Iraqi. On the basis of those expectations, the planned use of air power was defensive, with little thought given to offensive employment or any other independent use of air power.

Until 1989 Southwest Asia was, in the global context of U.S. planning, a secondary theater; the United States would fight a limited defensive campaign, conserving its resources for a far larger and more important struggle with the Warsaw Pact on Europe's central front. Furthermore, as in Europe, the offensive use of air power in a war involving the Soviet Union seemed to pose unacceptable risks of escalation. In October 1989 General Powell, newly appointed JCS chairman, directed General Schwarzkopf to concentrate planning for a Southwest Asia conflict on a scenario of regional conflict without Soviet involvement, not on operations in the context of a global superpower war.

Furthermore, that planning would reflect a political assessment that Iraq, not Iran, had become the primary threat to regional stability. The demise of the Warsaw Pact would allow CENTCOM to draw on greater resources for planning than would have previously been available. As a result, the forces planned for a Southwest Asia contingency doubled, and in some cases tripled. Staff officers had prepared a draft of the new plan, "Operations Plan 1002-90, Defense of the Arabian Peninsula," by the spring of 1990. In the normal course of events, they would have completed an approved plan by the summer of 1991.[3]

Pre-August 1990 planning for the Persian Gulf, as for most regions, concentrated on the requirements for deploying forces over vast distances. Planners thought more about the means of moving the fighting and logistical units to the theater—a vast task—than about the tasks of the units once they got there. The sketchy operational planning that did exist envisaged three phases. During the first phase, deterrence, American forces would attempt to discourage an aggressor who had already demonstrated hostile intent. Air forces would arrive first on the scene; Air Force tactical fighter squadrons, airlift squadrons, aerial tankers and airborne command and control aircraft, two Navy carrier groups and one battleship battle group, and Marine Corps and brigade-size Army aviation assets would arrive within the first two weeks. A B-52 squadron and a third carrier battle group would follow shortly.

During a second phase, defensive operations, the United States would gain air superiority against an attacking enemy, protect the air and naval bases used for debarking forces, and interdict enemy lines of supply and communication in order to disrupt the attacking force. In addition, air power would provide any necessary close air support.

A third phase, counteroffensive operations, was anticipated after sufficient forces had assembled and the enemy's combat power had declined by an unspecified level of attrition. The specifics of this last phase received almost no treatment in the plan other than a reference to the tasks of defeating enemy forces and regaining control of key facilities.[4]

CENTCOM leaders examined the draft operations plan in a com-

---

3. Notes, Col. Bryan A. Sutherland, USA, CENTCOM J-5, handwritten notes, 3 October 1990, GWAPS and AFHRA 00881768; Fact sheet, "USCINCCENT OPLAN 1002-90—Arabian Peninsula," Col. John L. Buckley, USCENTCOM J-5-P, 1 June 1990, GWAPS and AFHRA 00881768, reel 23630; and USCINCCENT OPLAN 1002-90 Concept of Operations, 16 April 1990, 19–20, GWAPS, CHC 13.

4. USCINCCENT OPLAN 1002-90, second draft, 18 July 1990, Concept of Operations, 20–26.

What Was the Air Campaign Plan?

mand post exercise, Internal Look 90, that took place in July 1990 and ended just days before the Iraqi invasion of Kuwait. CENTCOM designed the exercise to test the draft plan and uncover potential difficulties in its execution. An important addition to the exercise force list were the Air Force's stealth aircraft, the F-117s. F-117s did not figure in the draft plan (their existence had become public only in November 1988), but theater commanders could now begin to tap them for regional operations plans. The exercise revealed several shortfalls: not enough precision-guided munitions, a shortage of aircraft tankers to accommodate the aircraft of the carrier battle groups, and impediments to obtaining timely bomb damage assessment for use in planning further air strikes.[5]

The exercise proceeded through its phases to counteroffensive operations when, on the final two days of game play, the National Command Authority granted players "cross-border authority." As a result, the staff ordered aircraft to strike several leadership and command and control targets in Baghdad.[6] But these attacks differed greatly from those later carried out during Desert Storm. They came as the final element of the campaign rather than as its critical opening phase. Exercise-ending attacks against the enemy homeland reflected the decades of planning for East-West conflict in Europe in which such strikes were closely associated with the escalation to nuclear conflict. Furthermore, CENTCOM classified the Internal Look 90 simulated attacks as "long-range interdiction," a term considerably different in its connotations from the "strategic targets"[7] of Desert Storm. And finally, the concluding strikes of Internal Look 90 in no way matched the weight and intensity of the air campaign that began on 17 January 1991.

Internal Look 90 did serve usefully in some areas, however. The targets selected by staff for the scenario served as a valuable starting point for the eventual Desert Storm target list. Two lists were drawn up in the summer of 1990 for Internal Look: a CENTAF list and a CENTCOM composite list, using nominations from the service components. Both lists are shown in table 1.

Too much can be made of the differences between these early lists, some of which derived from the access of the service components to

---

5. *Whirlwind War*, draft of June 1992. U.S. Army Center of Military History, Washington, D.C., 85, GWAPS, NA 304; and USCINCCENT, *Desert Shield/Desert Storm and Internal Look 90 After Action Reports*, 15 July 1991, GWAPS, NA 9.

6. Fact Sheet, Maj. John Heidrick, 9 AIS, "9 TIS/INT Planning Procedures for Internal Look 90 and Operation Desert Shield," 4 May 1992, 1, GWAPS, NA 267; and USCINCCENT, *Desert Shield/Desert Storm*, Appendix L, GWAPS, NA 9.

7. In the planning of the Desert Storm air campaign, these targets were identified as "strategic" targets; in the mission reports accomplished after each mission, the strikes were identified as "interdiction."

Table 1 Internal Look 90 Target Lists

Target Categories	CENTAF Target List	CENTCOM Joint Target List
Leadership	3	4
Command, Control & Communication	14	21
Air Defense	72	4
Airfields	37	58
Nuclear	1	0
Biological	1	1
Chemical	1	1
Military Production & Support	22	81
Electric	6	0
POL	22	19
Scuds	7	0
Republican Guard	0	0
Ground Forces	0	8
Lines of Communications	25	79
Naval Forces (Ports)	7	17
TOTALS	218	293 *

*Installations listed under more than one category in the Joint Target List have been counted no more than once. For example, Al Basra Naval Base was listed eleven times, but it was counted twice in this table: once as a naval installation and once as a naval headquarters.

Source: Target Study, 9 TIS, "Iraqi Target Study, 15 June 1990, GWAPS, NA-168; and Document, "USCENTCOM Joint Target List," Tab A to Appendix 4 to Annex B to USCINCCENT OPLAN 1002-90, 27 June 1990, GWAPS, NA 41.

specific target intelligence. Nevertheless, two aspects of the lists are noteworthy: first, the emphasis by CENTAF on attacking the air defense system as a prelude to other attacks; second, the negligible attention of both lists to nuclear, biological, chemical, and Scud facilities. Planners lacked information on the location and extent of such facilities, which, in any event, were not central to the war envisioned in Internal

What Was the Air Campaign Plan?

Look 90. In addition, detailed information needed for actual mission planning did not exist for most of the targets nominated on the lists.

Internal Look 90 and the draft plan from which it flowed had a defensive purpose, and the planned air employment reflected this imperative. The list of aircraft missions provided in order of priority by General Horner, the CENTAF commander, carried no reference to attacks on what came to be called the strategic targets of Desert Storm. The priorities did, however, anticipate the defensive planning performed in the early days of Desert Shield.[8]

Desert Shield Planning

Iraq's invasion of Kuwait on 2 August 1990 created a situation quite different from the scenario envisioned in OPLAN 1002-90 (which anticipated thirty days' warning of an invasion of Saudi Arabia). If anything, the change made the use of air power even more crucial. When General Schwarzkopf and General Horner laid out options for President Bush at a National Security Council meeting on 4 August, it was clear that all the early options involved air power. The initial land- and carrier-based air power could arrive within days; twelve fighter squadrons, a bomber squadron, and two carrier battle groups could be in the region when only an airborne division and a Marine brigade would be available. Forces for a ground offensive, if necessary, would not be ready for more than four months, and even deploying sufficient ground forces to establish a defense would take several weeks.[9]

General Horner briefed the meeting on the employment of air power as envisioned by the operations plan: gaining air superiority, interdicting the attacking Iraqi forces, and defending the ports and rear areas. He also briefed a second plan of offensive retaliatory strikes against targets in Iraq, if Iraq used chemical weapons against U.S. or allied forces.[10] As forces began to deploy to the theater, the CENTAF staff developed employment plans for these two options.

The two initial options were captured in the format of ATOs[11]: the

---

8. Letter, Col. Richard B. Bennett, USAF, Director Combat Plans, subject: "Internal Look 90 COMUSCENTAF Air Guidance Letter," 24 July 1990. GWAPS, NA 163.

9. Briefing, "USCENTCOM Preliminary Planning, 2–6 August 1990," GWAPS, NA 117.

10. *Conduct of the Persian Gulf War*, 40; and Letter, Tactical Air Command Historian to 9th Air Force Historian, 12 June 1991, subject: General Horner Questions and Answers, with two attachments, GWAPS, CHP 13A.

11. There was no complete operations plan or operations order in existence that captured the essence of the planning taking place. The air tasking order is the final distilled product of the planning involving objectives, aircraft sortie allocation, and target selection, issued in terms of a daily schedule of aircraft sorties matched with missions, targets, times, and all the coordinating instructions necessary for units to accomplish the

"Punishment ATO" and the "D-Day ATO." The first plan of August 1990, the Punishment ATO, may also be seen as the first of the true offensive plans. An outgrowth of General Horner's briefing to the president on 4 August, this ATO involved a single retaliatory strike in reaction to the use of chemical weapons by Iraq. The targets (seventeen total) were economic (oil production and storage facilities and electric power generation), military (including the known chemical, nuclear, and biological facilities), and one political target—the presidential palace. The Punishment ATO assumed no accompanying ground attack. The objectives were punitive to discourage further Iraqi use of chemicals and were not assumed to be a part of any larger campaign: there was no mention of a next step if the punishment did not work.[12]

This effort soon gave way to the larger offensive air campaign, for which planning began in Washington during this same period. Meanwhile, Riyadh planners working on the D-Day ATO concentrated on the possibility of an Iraqi attack into Saudi Arabia and planned for the sorties envisioned in OPLAN 1002-90: that is, to gain air superiority, to attack the invading Iraqi forces, and to defend key facilities in Al Jubayl, Ad Dammam, and Dhahran, the principal bases through which the deploying Coalition forces had begun to enter the theater.

As it existed in August 1990, the D-Day ATO represented a totally defensive air employment, based as it was on the inadequate number of U.S. ground forces in the region in August. CENTCOM's studies at the time indicated that it could not successfully defend the key facilities along the coast against an Iraqi assault until near the end of August, when the 82d Airborne Division and a Marine expeditionary brigade had arrived to protect these enclaves.[13] As more ground and air forces arrived in the theater, the D-Day ATO expanded from its defense-only stance to include more offensive strikes, just as the draft operations plan had envisioned and the staff had practiced in Internal Look 90. Continually updated throughout the period of Desert Shield, the D-Day ATO also served as a focus of the overt planning for an air campaign. The true offensive plan, however, was not the D-Day ATO but a plan being developed by a special planning group, the Black Hole,

---

specific tasks. Although a single day's ATO does not explain an air campaign, the term ATO is used here as it was often used at the time—as shorthand for the series of daily orders for air operations that executed a specific plan. The ATO itself is a controversial subject of the war, and further discussion of this subject is found in chapter 5.

12. The employment of this ATO seems to have anticipated an Iraqi Scud attack with chemical weapons. Headquarters, CENTCOM J-5 Plans, *After Action Report,* Vol. VI, Tab A, "U.S. Air Campaign Plan," August 1990, GWAPS, NA 259.

13. Headquarters, CENTCOM J-5 Plans, *After Action Report* and Supporting Documents, Vol. VI, Tab X, "Combat Analysis Group After Action Report," 21 March 1991, GWAPS, NA 259.

What Was the Air Campaign Plan?

whose existence and planning were known to just a few on the CENTCOM and CENTAF staffs.[14]

Phase I, "Offensive Air Campaign"

Pre-crisis planning had called attention to deficiencies in basic intelligence information, had acquainted staffs with the region in which they would fight, and—perhaps most important—had familiarized them with one another. But these efforts did not shape the Desert Storm air plan. The strategic purpose of the actual war that occurred—an offensive operation to liberate Kuwait and shatter Iraqi power rather than a defensive operation to protect Persian Gulf allies—was utterly different from that of pre-crisis planning. Furthermore, much of the Desert Storm air plan emerged from the preparations of special and ad hoc organizations whose existence no one had anticipated before the war.

Shortly after the Iraqi invasion of Kuwait, a group of air staff officers in the Pentagon began planning an air campaign designed to eject Iraqi forces from Kuwait. Col. John A. Warden III, the air staff's deputy director of Air Force plans for warfighting, supervised this effort. The group initially numbered six but quickly grew to more than one hundred officers from the Air Force and other services, operating out of offices that were previously the facility of an air staff division called Checkmate. This ad hoc group itself became known as Checkmate. Warden and his Checkmate organization developed military objectives, a concept of operations, and a targeting scheme designed to accomplish the president's objectives using air power alone.

The initiative might have ended there had General Schwarzkopf not called the Air Force vice chief of staff, Gen. John M. Loh, and asked for help in planning an air option to retaliate against Iraq. General Schwarzkopf was not looking for an option to eject Iraq from Kuwait by air power alone, nor was he, as a theater commander, predisposed to ask for assistance from a service staff. But at this time (8 August) he had few forces available in the theater and needed a way to retaliate against some new, hostile act by Iraq such as the seizure of the American Embassy in Kuwait or a chemical weapons attack.[15] The Punish-

---

14. Fact sheet, Maj. John Heidrick, 9th AIS, Shaw AFB. "9 TIS/INT Planning Procedures for Internal Look-90 and Operation Desert Shield," 4 May 1992. GWAPS, NA 267 and in Continuity Book, maintained by Captain Heidrick, 9th TIS containing miscellaneous reports, summaries, and charts located at HRA, Maxwell AFB, AL; and interview, Dr. Alexander Cochran with Brig. Gen. Buster Glosson, 12 December 1991, GWAPS Cochran files.

15. General Schwarzkopf had first spoken with JCS chairman, Gen. Colin Powell, about the need for a retaliation plan. Since the Air Force chief, Gen. Michael Dugan, was out of town at the time, his request to the Air Staff went to General Loh. Interview, Diane T. Putney, Center for Air Force History, with Gen. H. Norman Schwarzkopf (USA, Ret.), 5 May 1992, GWAPS, NA 268.

ment ATO provided one such option, but he apparently saw this attack as an insufficient response and his regular staff as too burdened with managing the deployment to develop an alternative. He found Warden's ideas much more suitable.

The plan developed by Warden and Checkmate, named Instant Thunder, called for an intense six-day air campaign designed to incapacitate Iraqi leadership and destroy its key military capabilities. Warden's campaign was organized around "centers of gravity"—key elements of the enemy state and armed forces, the destruction or disabling of which would compel the enemy to yield to American wishes. Because the most important center of gravity was the ability of Saddam Hussein to lead and control his nation, attacks on telecommunication sites and command centers would therefore isolate him from the Iraqi people and his armed forces. Together with a national-level psychological warfare campaign directed against the Ba'athist regime, these attacks would disable or even fatally weaken the regime.

Instant Thunder targeted Iraq's nuclear, chemical, and biological facilities and its national air defense system and airfields. Other targets included electric power, oil production, railroads, and military production. In all cases, however, the United States would strenuously avoid civilian casualties and, indeed, any long-term damage to the Iraqi economy. The United States would visibly demonstrate its intention to attack Hussein, not the Iraqi people. The plan had eighty-four targets (nineteen in the telecommunications set) to strike over six days. Initially, Warden planned to use strictly Air Force assets, including F-117 aircraft.[16] Warden did not consider Instant Thunder a finished product but rather a good first cut.

The plan (which developed constantly from early August on) progressed through a number of versions during the ten days Warden briefed it to Air Force headquarters and the joint staff before introducing it to the theater. The text of the briefing viewgraphs stopped just short of declaring that Instant Thunder alone would force Iraq to withdraw from Kuwait.[17] The Checkmate planners appear to have believed that the conflict would require attacks on Baghdad and Iraq proper and not solely, or even chiefly, on forces deployed in Kuwait.

---

16. Briefing, "Instant Thunder," "Iraqi Air Campaign," and like names, August 1990, contained in GWAPS, CHSH 5 and 7. Warden was predisposed to focus on the command element as the true center of gravity in any case (John A. Warden III, *The Air Campaign* [Washington: National Defense University Press, 1988], 51–58), but the personality of Saddam Hussein made this focus seem particularly appropriate.

17. Versions of the briefing included the following formulation: "degrade Iraqi will and military capability . . . to conduct defensive operations in Kuwait" (8 August); "Create conditions leading to Iraqi expulsion from Kuwait" (11 August); "Peninsula nations would have combat capability to deal effectively with residual Iraqi forces" (17 August), GWAPS, CHSH 5 and 7.

What Was the Air Campaign Plan?

After Warden briefed the plan to General Schwarzkopf on 10 August, and General Powell on 11 August, the latter directed that planners from the other services and the joint staff join the effort. At this stage too the plan expanded to include the Navy and Marine Corps aircraft deploying to the region and the Navy's TLAMs.

The version of the plan that General Schwarzkopf received on 17 August retained Warden's and Checkmate's concepts but included more than Air Force aircraft and, reflecting the joint staff sponsorship, bore the logo of the Joint Chiefs. Instant Thunder offered the American high command an offensive option with air power it would not have for months in any other way. The plan did not receive universal support, however: General Horner (serving as CENTCOM commander, forward, in General Schwarzkopf's stead) gave it a far more critical reception than it had received in the United States.

General Horner thought the plan was seriously flawed in its operational aspects and disapproved of its relative neglect of the Iraqi forces in Kuwait. To produce a more acceptable plan, Horner selected General Glosson, then on another assignment in the region, to direct a secret planning effort for an offensive air campaign.[18] Horner retained in the theater several of Warden's planners who had accompanied him, thereby also retaining some of Warden's concepts. The plan that emerged from Glosson's efforts contained the same target sets, the same focus on Iraqi leadership, and the same intent of isolating Saddam Hussein from the Iraqi people and his forces. Instead of constituting an entire campaign, however, the revised plan became the first phase of a more general plan to eject Iraqi forces from Kuwait.

On 25 August 1990, General Schwarzkopf briefed General Powell on a four-phase plan, code named Desert Storm, to eject Iraqi forces from Kuwait (a briefing from which the quote found at the beginning of this chapter was taken). The first phase, called the strategic air campaign, was essentially the Instant Thunder plan, with an added aim of preventing reinforcement of Iraqi forces in Kuwait. The second phase would gain air superiority over Kuwait. The third phase consisted of air operations to reduce Iraqi ground forces capability before the ground attack. The fourth phase, which still required much work, was a ground attack into Kuwait. This four-phase planning concept was identical to the one executed the following January and February. Schwarzkopf estimated that he could execute the first three phases by early October but could not conduct the ground phase until December.[19]

---

18. Transcript, General Horner's taped responses to written questions by CMSgt. John Burton, CENTAF Historian, March 1991, GWAPS, CHP 13A.

19. Briefing Viewgraphs, "Offensive Campaign: Desert Storm," Headquarters, Central Command, 24 August 1990, GWAPS, NA 208.

The development of the strategic air campaign, now Phase I in a larger plan, was a highly classified process. The Black Hole, directed by General Glosson, operated in secrecy. In addition to normal security concerns, the high classification of the development project stemmed from American and Saudi sensitivity to the concerns of friendly Arab governments that threats of an offensive military action might impede a negotiated settlement. The Black Hole included Army, Navy, and Marine Corps representatives, but Air Force officers predominated. Most of the latter came from outside the CENTAF staff.

Throughout the fall of 1990 the planning effort continued. By mid-September, representatives from Great Britain's Royal Air Force and later from the Royal Saudi Air Force had joined the effort. By 2 September, the Black Hole had prepared, and General Horner had approved, a CENTAF operations order for Phase I. General Schwarzkopf then heard the briefing (3 September), as did General Powell (13 September), Secretary of Defense Dick Cheney, the JCS, President Bush, and members of the National Security Council (10 and 11 October). At these meetings, less developed plans for Phases II and III were briefed; Glosson and the Black Hole continued to concentrate on Phase I.

The CENTAF staff, which prepared the daily ATOs and had custody of the D-Day ATO, worked on plans for the close-in battle in Kuwait, plans that would form the basis for Phase III and the air portion of Phase IV. As noted, this CENTAF planning staff operated in isolation from the Black Hole, with little knowledge of its plans.

The strategic air campaign of Instant Thunder envisioned approximately 150 attack aircraft; the plan briefed to the president in October called for more than 400 attack aircraft, with another 300 (half of them helicopters) reserved for defense against an Iraqi attack and to initiate the third phase.[20] Nonetheless, the concepts of the first phase remained remarkably constant.

According to the operations order for Desert Storm, there were six military objectives, and Phase I was to focus on three "centers of gravity."[21]

Theater Military Objectives

- Attack Iraqi political/military leadership and command and control;
- Gain and maintain air superiority;

---

20. Operations Order, COMUSCENTAF Operations Order "Offensive Campaign—Phase I," 2 September 1990, GWAPS, BH 8-133; and briefing slides in "General Glosson's Brief," GWAPS Box 3, Folder 60.

21. USCINCCENT OPORD 91-001 for Operation Desert Storm, 16 January 1991, paras. 1D, 3B, and 3C, GWAPS, NA 357.

What Was the Air Campaign Plan?

- Sever Iraqi supply lines;
- Destroy chemical, biological, and nuclear capability;
- Destroy Republican Guard forces; and
- Liberate Kuwait City.

Centers of Gravity

- Iraqi National Command Authority;
- Iraq's chemical, biological, and nuclear capability; and
- The Republican Guard Forces Command.

Phase I Targeting

Phase I, the strategic air campaign, called for attacks against twelve interrelated target sets[22] in order to "result in disruption of Iraqi command and control, loss of confidence in the government, and significant degradation of Iraqi military capabilities."[23] First, command of the air was to be gained by attacks on the Iraqi strategic air defense system and airfields. The most important centers of gravity were leadership and command, control, and communications facilities. To eliminate long-term Iraqi offensive capabilities, the nuclear, biological, and chemical weapons research, production, and storage facilities, together with the Scud missiles, launchers, and production and storage facilities, were targeted. The key elements of the Iraqi armed forces and their supporting industries made up the remainder of the target sets: the Republican Guard forces, military storage and production sites, naval forces and ports, railroads and bridges, electricity production, and oil-refining and distribution facilities.

To simplify its task, the Black Hole assigned each target category an alphabetic identifier (e.g., L for leadership, SAD for strategic air defense) and a number for each target in that category (for example, L15, SAD01, etc.). This identification system would cause some confusion during the air campaign, when targeting and intelligence communities outside the Black Hole used a more complicated but standard identification system. Moreover, the simple Black Hole system developed an ambiguous categorization of targets: naval targets, for instance, included at least one air defense site and one petroleum terminal.

The original Instant Thunder plan had begun in August 1990 with a

22. The term strategic air campaign means simply those activities planned as part of Phase I. The term was a controversial one at the time, and discussions continue within the U.S. military concerning the appropriateness of the terms "strategic targets" and "air campaign."

23. OPORD 91-001, para. 3C.

total of eighty-four targets to be struck over a six-day period, and although the target sets remained essentially the same, the total number of targets grew during the fall of 1990. The growth in numbers is shown in table 2. The August date corresponds to the final plan of Warden and Checkmate as it was presented to General Horner; the December date indicates the Phase I plan as it was in its final stages before execution.

The growth in numbers reflected sharply increased knowledge of the Iraqi military forces and leadership structure gained after the United States focused its reconnaissance capabilities on Iraq in the summer and fall of 1990. The growth also came about as an indirect consequence of the increased number of strike aircraft available and the resulting ability to target a larger portion of the Iraqi air defense and military support structure. Throughout the war, in fact, the target list would continue to lengthen. The intensity of the planned campaign also grew, because although its duration remained constant (six days), the number of aircraft available for its prosecution continuously increased.[24]

The air planners' first priority was to gain command of the air. This goal was a basic tenet of air operations, and its achievement would generate at least three specific advantages in the war. First, the incapacitation of airfields and the air defense system would allow sustained prosecution of attacks against the other target sets. Second, command of the air would prevent Iraqi offensive strikes against Coalition forces: in particular, strikes delivering chemical weapons. Third, the Coalition would prevent Iraqi reconnaissance flights that might uncover the shift of ground forces to the west, the surprise to be sprung at the start of the ground offensive.[25] Therefore, the planners directed their most intense and immediate attention to destroying the Iraqi defense system through the use of F-117s, other aircraft employing antiradiation missiles to attack radar systems, and a vast array of electronic countermeasures.

The attacks against the nuclear, chemical, and biological weapons and Scud facilities served short-term and long-term objectives alike. In the short term, their destruction would prevent the employment of such weapons in the Gulf War. Planners believed that the Iraqi nuclear weapons program had not gone beyond research, but they believed Iraq fully capable of using both chemical weapons and Scuds.[26] In the long term, the objective of security and stability in the Persian Gulf required

---

24. The operations order stated six to nine days. OPORD 91-001, para. 3A, 16 January 1991.

25. MR, Lt. Col. David A. Deptula, USAF, subject: Observations on the Air Campaign Against Iraq, August 1990–March 1991, 29 March 1991, 3, GWAPS, Safe #12, D-01.

26. Briefing, Maj. Gen. Robert Johnston, CENTCOM Chief of Staff, to Joint Staff and National Command Authority, "CENTCOM Offensive Campaign," 10 and 11 October 1990, in report CENTCOM J-5 Plans, Augmentation Cell, *After Action Report* [Vol. IX SAMS], Tab C, 28 February 1991, GWAPS, NA 259.

What Was the Air Campaign Plan?

Table 2   Growth of Targets, August to December 1990

Target Sets (symbols used by the Special Planning Group and their explanations)	21 August	20 December
SAD (strategic air defense)	10	27
C (chemical, nuclear, and biological facilities)	8	20
L (leadership)	5	27
CCC (command, control and communication sites)	19	30
E (electric power)	10	16
O (oil facilities)	6	8
RR (railroads and bridges)	3	21
A (airfields)	7	25
N (naval ports and facilities)	1	4
MS (military support facilities)	15	46
SC (Scud facilities)	N/A	13
RG (Republican Guards)	N/A	0
Totals	84	237

Note: Highway bridges were added to the category that was originally railroads alone; Scud facilities were counted as part of the chemical, nuclear, and biological category in August; the Republican Guard was a new target set; specific targets were added at a later date.
Source: Briefing, Joint Chiefs of Staff, "Iraqi Air Campaign, Instant Thunder," GWAPS CHSH 5-3; and Briefing, CENTAF/CC to SECDEF in "General Glosson's Brief."

eliminating Iraqi weapons of mass destruction along with the Scuds that could serve as their delivery means.

Planners knew that the Iraqi ballistic missile force had mobile launchers, some number of which would escape destruction and fire their missiles. Although the Black Hole had planned since August 1990 to attack the fixed Scud sites, neither that group nor anyone else had devised, before the war, a search-and-destroy scheme for dealing with them. The planners in the Black Hole, like CENTCOM's leaders, regarded Iraqi ballistic missiles (even with chemical warheads) chiefly as nuisance weapons that might cause political difficulties for the alliance (particularly if Israel were to retaliate against the Iraqis). They viewed the missiles as posing little tactical or operational threat to the Coalition and intended to reduce the offensive threat they represented by attacking fixed launch sites, support bases, production facilities, potential sites of concealment, and support facilities for mobile launchers, but not the launchers themselves.[27]

Military support facilities and naval ports and facilities were natural target sets. Several other target sets (railroads and bridges, electric power production, and oil facilities), while undeniably forming part of a country's military power, also serve a country's nonmilitary economic power and its civilian populace.[28] Hence, planners attempted to affect the military support provided by these entities while limiting the damage in other respects. The Black Hole did not, however, attempt to avoid inconveniencing the Iraqi population. Rather, they wished to inflict disruption and a feeling of helplessness on the Iraqi public without bringing about severe suffering—all in the hope of weakening Hussein's grip.

As a result, planning for attacks on the industrial power of the country had a dual nature. On the one hand, the objectives were to "cripple production" and "complicate movement of goods and services."[29] On the other hand, planners harbored an "intent to convince the Iraqi populace that a bright economic and political future will result from the replacement of the Saddam Hussein regime" and that "execution planning will emphasize limiting collateral damage and civilian casualties and preserving the Iraqi and Kuwaiti capability to quickly reconstitute their economies."[30]

To comply with this guidance, target selectors tried to distinguish between short-term and long-term damage to electric power generation and oil facilities. Regarding oil targets, this meant that Coalition aircraft would hit oil-refining and storage facilities but not oil-production facilities. Within the refinery target subset, aircraft would hit distribution points, not cracking towers. Regarding electric power targets, they would strike transformers, which were thought to take months to repair, instead of the generator halls, which were thought to take years to repair.[31]

27. Target list (with objectives for each target category, including Scuds), GWAPS, BH, Other Documents, Folder 8.

28. Many of the telecommunications targets would also fall into this category.

29. Briefing, Joint Chiefs of Staff, "Iraqi Air Campaign Instant Thunder," 17 August 1990, GWAPS, CHSH 5-3; and Operations Order, COMUSCENTAF Operations Order Offensive Campaign—Phase I, 2 September 1990, 4.

30. COMUSCENTAF Operations Order, Offensive Campaign—Phase I, 2 September 1990, 3–4.

31. There were no prewar limitations on striking bridges and railroads, though some

What Was the Air Campaign Plan?   37

Attacks against leadership and command and control had political and military dimensions. Separating the national leadership in Baghdad from the military forces in the field would delay the coordination of military operations and show the Iraqi forces the powerlessness of their leaders. Planners also hoped for a more direct political effect. If Saddam Hussein could not communicate with the Iraqi people, he could neither propagandize against the United States and its allies, mobilize the country for war, nor court world opinion. Consequently, the air campaign targeted radio and television transmitters, relay stations, telephone and telegraph facilities, and military command posts.

In addition to facilities that might house Saddam Hussein, the buildings of the Ministry of Defense, Ba'ath Party headquarters, and similar sites came under attack. Planners counted most on these strikes, thus ending the war by air power alone. The strikes, in coordination with others, would not just neutralize the government but would change it by inducing a coup or revolt that would result in a government more amenable to Coalition demands. The final CENTCOM operations plan did not stress these intentions, however, which appeared most forcibly in the CENTAF operations order of September 1990. "When taken in total, the result of Phase I will be the progressive and systematic collapse of Saddam Hussein's entire war machine and regime."[32]

Planners hoped that the air campaign would end in the removal of Saddam Hussein but did not make his death or capture a specific objective. In fact, Generals Powell and Schwarzkopf made statements at the beginning of the air campaign disclaiming such a goal.[33] Before the war, military leaders worried that targeting Saddam Hussein might contravene Executive Order 12333, which prohibits U.S. government involvement in "assassination."[34]

Likewise, U.N. resolutions around which the Coalition had coalesced said nothing about eliminating Saddam. Explicitly setting goals that

---

limits were instituted during the war. This chapter will not go into the effectiveness of this guidance, but later chapters will. For instance, weapons and aircraft accuracy limitations sometimes did not allow such discrimination, and when Iraq began to dump oil into the gulf and employ oil-fired trenches as part of its defenses, some of the pumping stations in southern Iraq and Kuwait were attacked. (Glosson interview, 12 December 1991, GWAPS Cochran files; and Deptula interview, 8 January 1992.)

32. COMUSCENTAF Operations Order, 2 September 1990, 4.

33. General Powell, News Briefing, 16 January 1991 (transcript released by the Office of the Assistant Secretary of Defense for Public Affairs), 5; and General Schwarzkopf, CENTCOM Briefing, 18 January 1991 (transcript released by the Office of the Secretary for Public Affairs), 4.

34. Executive Order 12333—United States Intelligence Activities, 4 December 1981, in Office of the Federal Register, National Archives and Records Administration, *Codification of Presidential Proclamations and Executive Orders* (Washington, 1989), 647.

went beyond those of the United Nations would have necessitated complex and possibly counterproductive negotiations with the allies.[35]

Finally, and perhaps most important, there was no certainty that strikes aimed at killing Saddam Hussein would have their intended effect. Officials remembered the complications involved in tracking down Manuel Noriega during Operation Just Cause the previous year and consequently hesitated to specify an outcome that aerial bombing simply could not ensure.[36]

The political effects of the attacks on Iraq remained of concern throughout the planning effort. The operations plan included rules prohibiting attacks on cultural and historic sites, hospitals, mosques, civilian population centers, and other nonmilitary structures, in accordance with any military operation.[37] "Anything which could be considered as terror attacks or attacks on the Iraqi people will be avoided."[38] A joint no-fire target list dated September 1990 was updated just before the war and then revised several times during the war. The State Department and the intelligence agencies contributed to the list, which included archeological sites, sites of special significance to the Islamic religion, foreign embassies in Baghdad, and camps thought to be holding Kuwaiti prisoners of war.[39]

Just two days before the beginning of the air campaign, Secretary of State James Baker and Under Secretary of State for Political Affairs Robert Kimmitt went to the Pentagon to make a final examination of the target list with Cheney and Powell, and, according to Kimmitt, "It was very clear to both Secretary Baker and me . . . that those political considerations that had been expressed, both at the Cabinet level and [in the NSC Deputies Committee], had been well taken into account,

---

35. President Bush, "Remarks on the Nomination of Edward R. Madigan as Secretary of Agriculture and a Question-and-Answer Session with Reporters," 25 January 1991, in *Weekly Compilation of Presidential Documents*, 28 January 1991, 80; Vice President Quayle, cited in "Quayle on Hussein: 'He is totally irrational,'" *U.S. News & World Report*, 18 February 1991, 27; and Robert Kimmitt, transcript, American Enterprise Institute, "The Gulf War Coerence," 7 December 1991, 293.

36. Robert Gates in "The Gulf Crisis: The Road to War," Program Three, 19; Gen. Colin L. Powell, transcript of News Briefing, 17 January 1991, 6; and Gen. H. Norman Schwarzkopf, in Hearings before the Committee on Appropriations, House of Representatives, *Department of Defense Appropriations for 1992*, Part 2, 102d Congress, 1st session (Washington, 1991), 277.

37. Operations Plan, Headquarters, U.S. Central Command, Combined Operation Desert Storm, 17 January 1991, Appendix 4 to Annex C, "Rules of Engagement," GWAPS, CHC 18-1.

38. COMUSCENTAF Operations Order, 2 September 1990, 3.

39. Messages, USCINCCENT, subject: USCINCCENT Joint No-Fire Target List for Desert Shield, 14 September 1990, GWAPS, CHSH 100-26; and USCENTAF, subject: Joint No-Fire Target List, 16 February 1991, GWAPS, BH 2, Section 4.

What Was the Air Campaign Plan? 39

and we both left the meeting very comfortable from a political perspective."[40]

The Republican Guard received particular attention in CENTCOM planning, enough to have it specified as one of the target sets in the Phase I plan. Planners identified the Republican Guard as a center of gravity of the campaign and a priority target of the air campaign. Not only did the guard serve as the strategic reserve of the Iraqi forces in Kuwait, it also provided essential support to Saddam Hussein's regime. Schwarzkopf's planners intended to rout the Republican Guard so that they could not help Saddam Hussein retain order in the country. The operations order directed that the roads and rail lines south of Basra should be blocked in order to prevent the withdrawal of the Republican Guard forces.[41] While they were seen as a target that had to be dealt with in Phase I of the air campaign, that issue became moot when, because of the number of Coalition aircraft available, the first three phases of the air campaign began at essentially the same time.

Planning for Phases II, III, and IV

The planning for the second, third, and fourth phases of the air campaign dealt with the Iraqi forces in the Kuwaiti theater. Initially deemed unnecessary by Warden and the Instant Thunder plan, attacks on these forces came to play a much larger role once the plan got to the theater. Besides being a part of the offensive campaign that became the Desert Storm plan, attacks on Iraqi forces in the Kuwaiti theater received attention during the fall of 1990 in the planning for a contingency in which Iraq attacked Saudi Arabia. On 14 August, CENTCOM and Saudi officials formed the U.S.–Saudi Joint Directorate of Planning (JDOP) at the Saudi Ministry of Defense headquarters in Riyadh to develop combined operations plans.

The JDOP's first product, "Combined Operations Order 003," published on 20 August, assigned CENTCOM forces missions in concert with Saudi and Coalition regional forces to defend Saudi Arabia as far forward as possible. The concept of operations had Saudi forces establish a picket line close to the northern border while U.S. forces shielded Al Jubayl and Ad Dammam/Dhahran to protect deploying U.S. forces at those major airports and seaports of debarkation.

The JDOP continued its planning efforts throughout Desert Shield and Desert Storm, publishing the final plan for the defense of Saudi Arabia on 29 November 1990, but the locus of planning lay elsewhere.

40. Transcript, American Enterprise Institute, "The Gulf War Conference," 7 December 1991, 236.

41. Operations Order 91-001, para. 3.E.2.b.2; and Glosson interview, 12 December 1991, GWAPS Cochran files.

While the JDOP produced three other combined operations plans dealing with the occupation and defense of Kuwait, it served chiefly as a forum to identify and resolve Coalition problems and, perhaps more important, it provided a conduit for rapid access to Saudi policymakers.[42] Offensive planning took place within CENTCOM: the Black Hole was developing Phase I, and CENTAF and CENTCOM staffs were developing plans for preparing the battlefield and supporting the ground attack. A CENTAF reorganization in December 1990 formally merged the Black Hole with the other elements of the CENTAF planning staff. At this time, all phases of the air campaign came together in the "Desert Storm Operations Plan."[43]

Planners made Phase II, "Air Superiority in the Kuwait Theater," a separate phase only at General Schwarzkopf's suggestion (most of the air planners viewed the Iraqi air defense system as a whole, including the Kuwaiti theater), and this phase received little special elaboration. Phase III, "Battlefield Preparation," however, called on air power to destroy ground forces to a degree not heretofore planned for any air force.

From early August 1990 on, CENTCOM leaders assumed that Iraqi forces would outnumber those of the Coalition and that a successful attack into the Kuwaiti theater would require an extensive preliminary air attack. In the words of one of the earliest briefings on this subject, "[we] therefore must have heavy air attrition prior to ability to wage successful offense."[44]

As early as 14 August, General Schwarzkopf's combat analysis group concluded that for a Coalition offensive to be successful with a single corps, the air campaign would first have to achieve 50 percent attrition of enemy ground forces.[45] General Glosson first discussed the 50-percent goal in September with Col. Joe Purvis, chief of a special group of Army planners that Schwarzkopf had recruited from graduates of the Army's School of Advanced Military Studies at Fort Leavenworth.[46] No one really knew what would constitute a measurable 50

---

42. Operations Plan, Headquarters, U.S. Central Command and Joint Forces and Theater of Operations, Combined OPLAN for Defense of Saudi Arabia, 29 November 1990, GWAPS, CHC 18-4; and USCENTCOM J-5 Plans, *After Action Report*, 5–6, GWAPS, NA 259.

43. The planning organizations were brought together, but the existence and specifics of Phase I remained a closely held secret until just prior to the air campaign's initiation. Horner interview, 4 March 1991.

44. USCENTCOM Briefing, "Preliminary Planning," 2–6 August 1990, GWAPS, NA 117.

45. Report, Combat Analysis Group, 21 March 1991, in Vol. VI of CENTCOM J-5 Plans, *After Action Report*. The Bush administration's November decision to double the forces for a two-corps ground offensive did not change the calculations because intelligence reported that Iraq had also deployed more forces to the Kuwaiti theater.

46. The best description of Army planning for the offensive is Richard M. Swain, *"Lucky War": Third Army in Desert Storm* (Ft. Leavenworth, KS: U.S. Army Command and General Staff College Press, 1994).

What Was the Air Campaign Plan?

percent attrition of combat effectiveness, however. Initial planning called for attrition of troops and all major pieces of equipment, but CENTCOM planners later narrowed these indicators to tanks, armored personnel carriers, and artillery. Moreover, the attrition was left as a theater-wide goal, not attached to specific divisions or areas of the theater.

CENTAF planners divided the air attacks on the Iraqi ground forces into two parts: those directed against the Republican Guard and those aimed at the remainder of the army in Kuwait. The planners earmarked higher performance aircraft (F-16s, F/A-18s, F-15Es, F-111Fs) for attacks against the Republican Guards, reserving the A-10s, AV-8Bs, and attack helicopters for the divisions in Kuwait. Attrition calculations assumed six hundred sorties a day against each of the two parts of the Iraqi army, relying primarily on precision munitions (but not laser-guided bombs—that innovation occurred during the air campaign) and various cluster munitions to achieve the attrition.

On the basis of these criteria, General Glosson briefed General Schwarzkopf in December 1990 that air power could achieve the desired 50 percent attrition in five days against the Republican Guards and in approximately twelve days against the remainder of the forces in Kuwait.[47] Schwarzkopf not only accepted these attrition estimates, he also reduced the time available, issuing an operations plan two weeks later that specified eight days for Phase III (see figure 9).

Some flexibility returned in the operations order for the campaign issued on 16 January. In it, the duration of Phase III was "to be determined."[48] The requirement for 50 percent attrition made the ground campaign depend on unprecedented air power success in destroying an army. Air power had an enormous task in Phase III alone: to destroy approximately five thousand pieces of dug-in and defended Iraqi equipment.

These were not the only targets planned for attack in the Kuwaiti theater. The U.S. Army, Marine Corps, and other Coalition ground force components could all nominate targets such as Iraqi army command posts, supply and ammunition depots, communications sites, and troop concentrations, to name just some of the more prominent ones. In other words, while the attrition calculations seem to have anticipated that the air planners would have a free hand in focusing the air attacks on Iraqi equipment, such a notion was counter to the CENTCOM target

---

47. Briefing to the CINC, Phases II and III, 1 December 1990, in "General Glosson's Brief." Subsequent to this briefing, the Iraqi army in the Kuwaiti theater continued to increase in amount of equipment, but so too did the Coalition air forces. Coalition air did not attain a level of six hundred strikes a day in the Kuwaiti theater on a sustained basis until three weeks into the air campaign. For the first two weeks, air strikes against Iraqi ground forces averaged just over three hundred a day.

48. USCENTCOM OPLAN Desert Storm, 16 December 1990, 13, AFHRA 269602; and USCINCCENT OPORD 91-001, 17 January 1991, 6.

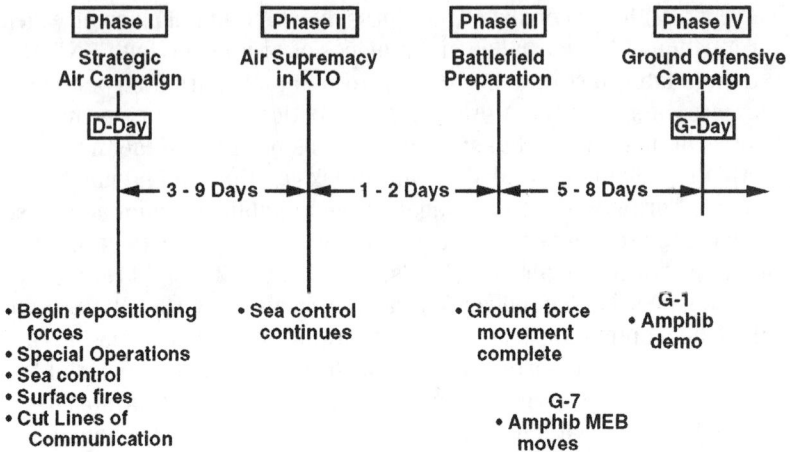

Figure 9 Phases of Desert Storm Campaign Plan
Source: USCINCCENT, U.S. OPLAN Desert Storm, 16 December 1990, np GWAPS, CHC, 18-2.

nomination system. Coalition ground units sought equipment attrition, of course, but they sought that attrition along with the destruction of other elements of the Iraqi army—all before a ground attack.

If all went as envisioned, planners estimated that the final phase, "Ground Offensive Operations," would commence several weeks after the launching of Desert Storm. The objectives for this phase were to liberate Kuwait, cut critical lines of communication into southeast Iraq, and destroy the Republican Guard in the Kuwaiti theater. The ground attack would be "combined with continuous B-52 strikes, TACAIR (tactical air) attacks, and attack helicopter operations." In anticipation of the main attack, "The bridges, roads and rail lines . . . will be cut to block withdrawal of RGFC and to form a kill zone north of Kuwait."[49]

Planners intended to provide close air support for ground forces by using a "Push CAS" system. Flights of aircraft would arrive at locations within the anticipated target areas continuously, sometimes as frequently as every seven minutes. Without waiting for a ground commander to request support, the aircraft sorties were "pushed" to his location. If the commander had no need for the aircraft, they would orbit for a short time, then proceed to attack a planned backup interdiction target, and another flight of aircraft would arrive to fly in orbit at the commander's location. Aircraft were to strike ground targets under the control of the Tactical Air Control Party, naval gunfire liaison team, or an airborne forward air controller.[50]

49. Coalition Combined OPLAN, 6–7; and USCINCCENT OPLAN Desert Storm, 13–14.

50. Coalition Combined OPLAN, 17 January 1991, C-6-2.

What Was the Air Campaign Plan? 43

Targeting in the Kuwaiti theater during the prosecution of both Phases III and IV employed "kill boxes" to orient the attacking aircraft. The theater was divided on the map into squares (the so-called kill boxes), thirty nautical miles on a side, reflecting an already existing Saudi map overlay system. The squares (subdivided further into four fifteen-by-fifteen-mile squares) became the operating areas for attacking aircraft. Sometimes the aircraft flight had a designated target within the kill box; at other times the aircrews were left to find the most appropriate target within the area.

The Final Plan

A final element of the air campaign came together before the campaign's initiation. Aircraft from U.S. European Command had been positioned at Incirlik Air Base in Turkey in hopes that the Turkish government would permit air operations from its territory. While not critical to the success of the campaign, attacks from Turkey would divert Iraqi attention to the north and perhaps prevent the movement of more forces into the Kuwaiti theater. Turkey gave its approval to the U.S. request just hours before the beginning of the air campaign, and the aircraft based at Incirlik, known as Joint Task Force Proven Force, added almost one hundred additional combat aircraft to the air campaign. These aircraft supplemented the Phase I strikes, hitting air defense, chemical weapons, military supply, and industrial targets.[51] Black Hole planners did not count on the Turkish-based force until the war broke out.

In December 1990, the planning efforts of the strategic air campaign came together with the planning for subsequent phases, and a combined Coalition air force operations design emerged. The specific nature of Phase I of the plan, and when it would begin, remained closely held secrets until just before its initiation, so much so that most non–U.S. Coalition air forces could not be included in the opening attacks. The size of the Coalition air forces allowed considerable flexibility in the air assets assigned to the various segments of the air campaign, and the numbers also permitted the first three phases to begin almost simultaneously. By 15 January, the Coalition air forces comprised more than one thousand fixed-wing attack aircraft and another eight hundred air defense fighters and electronic combat aircraft to prosecute the air campaign.[52]

When the air campaign began on 17 January 1991, air planners and commanders were confident. At a relatively low cost—one hundred or

---

51. Schroeder and Raab, *History of Joint Task Force Proven Force*, 50–54.

52. Viewgraph, General Horner Briefing to the Secretary of Defense, 20 December 1990, in "General Glosson's Brief."

so losses, maximum—they thought that the ambitious objectives set in the operations plan could be met. Although they were concerned about the possibility of a preemptive Iraqi attack, they nevertheless thought that merely a few enemy aircraft would penetrate Coalition defenses. Chemical warfare posed a threat, but less to air than to ground forces. Planners had little doubt that within a month the Iraqi army would flee Kuwait or, more likely, lie shattered in place; that Iraqi military industry and the Iraqi air force would be destroyed; and that Saddam Hussein's grip on Iraq would be, if not removed, weakened beyond repair.

Three | **What Did the Air Campaign Accomplish?**

Judging the success of the air campaign must begin with looking carefully at the objectives set by the Coalition and the effects and effectiveness of air operations against the target base in meeting those objectives. The objectives and Iraqi target base identified in the previous chapter form the basis for this assessment. That target base included the fixed targets that CENTAF's Black Hole divided into twelve target categories,[1] as well as Iraqi aircraft, ships, mobile missiles, and ground forces deployed in the Kuwaiti theater. As a way of dealing explicitly with the various objectives and target sets, this chapter considers the air campaign in three major components: control of the air, strategic attacks, and air attacks on surface forces. Although considered separately, these three components obviously reinforced one another in a variety of ways.

In assessing the effectiveness of air power against the various "target sets" devised by air campaign planners, it should be noted that many sets overlapped. Attacks against command and control, for example, affected the ability of the Iraqi leadership to function; attacks against electrical power facilities forced air defense system components to resort to backup generators, which are less reliable and more prone to voltage fluctuations than are normal power supplies. Furthermore, most target categories used by Black Hole planners to structure the air campaign did not constitute homogenous sets. For example, they put the Al Kharhk telephone switching facility in Baghdad—one of the most important telecommunications facilities in Iraq—in the command, control, and communications category. Another important telephone exchange, however, the so-called AT&T building in downtown Baghdad, ended up in the strategic air defense category.[2]

---

1. See chapter 2 (table 2) for a list of these target categories, hereafter referred to as the Black Hole categories.

2. Master Target Folder, GWAPS, BH 2-23; and CHECKMATE Intelligence Target Files, "Baghdad AUTO MPUR-RADREL TERMINAL," GWAPS, CIT 684.

Defining Effectiveness

This chapter focuses on the effectiveness of air power at the operational and strategic levels in the Gulf War, less on the performance of specific weapons systems than on overall results measured against actual military and political objectives. The Gulf War Air Power Survey had no direct access to sites in Iraq nor Iraqi records other than those captured in the Kuwaiti theater during the war. Visitors to Iraq (particularly U.N. inspection teams) provided useful information, but much remains uncertain.

As a result, many of the conclusions here are preliminary and depend heavily on the interpretations of intelligence imagery, the recollections of Coalition participants, and the statements of Iraqi defectors and prisoners of war. The quantum improvement in intelligence-gathering means since World War II, and such Iraqi sources as were available, however, provided enough information to arrive at some conclusions that even site surveys of bombed facilities would probably not affect.

Both direct and indirect, or second-order, effects require consideration. An example of a direct effect would be the destruction of a hardened aircraft shelter with a two-thousand-pound laser-guided bomb that penetrated the structure and detonated inside. An example of an indirect effect would be the Iraqis' subsequent efforts to preserve a portion of their air force in the face of shelter "busting" by dispersing some aircraft in the open and sending others to sanctuary in Iran. Indirect effects can also have more distant second-order consequences. The use of laser-guided bombs to "plink" Iraqi armor in the Kuwaiti theater not only destroyed equipment (the direct effect) but also quickly persuaded Iraqi tank crews to spend less and less time with their vehicles (the indirect effect). By the time the ground war began, the indirect effect appears to have left many Iraqi armor units unable to respond effectively to engagement by Coalition ground forces (the second-order consequence). Naturally, the methodological problems involved in assessing such intangible, but very real, indirect and second-order effects are substantial.

Moreover, determining the effectiveness of these combat operations required several steps: understanding what happened as the result of bomb or missile attacks; determining the proper measurement of the result; and then relating cause and effect—how actions or results achieved objectives of the air attacks. It may be useful to begin with some concrete examples of the complexity of such assessments.

First, consider the evidence available in a photo of a destroyed tank or aircraft. If the tank's turret has been blown off the hull, or the aircraft has been reduced to twisted metal, then the assessment of results is easy: the equipment is unusable. Next, consider the evidence of

What Did the Air Campaign Accomplish?

a photo of a command bunker or aircraft shelter with a hole in the roof of the kind commonly made by a precision-guided bomb with a hard-target-penetrating warhead. Although the bomb obviously hit the target, did it penetrate into and detonate in the interior? And if so, was the structure occupied at the time? The problematic answers to these questions make assessing what happened far more troublesome than in the initial case. Finally, consider a situation where no photo is available, only a pilot report claiming that an Iraqi tank or hardened aircraft shelter was hit with a precision-guided bomb. Uncertainty surrounding such results is even greater than in the second case.

While somewhat idealized, all these cases suggest experiences during and after the Gulf War that confronted analysts attempting to answer the most basic question: What happened? In many instances, more authoritative data that corrected earlier impressions became available only after war's end.

Taking the next step, determining what to measure, requires a knowledge of the objectives sought by the attacks. Not only do the numbers or pictures fail to speak for themselves, they also might not be the correct numbers or pictures. Consider, for example, a comparison of Iraqi and Coalition aircraft shot down as a measure of the effectiveness of the air forces involved, a common indicator used in past wars to determine the performance of opposing air forces. The scorecard would read thirty-three Iraqi aircraft to thirty-eight Coalition, which—in isolation—suggests a slight advantage in favor of the Iraqis.

On the other hand, the Coalition scored thirty-three to one in air-to-air combat, and fixed-wing aircraft flew some sixty-nine thousand "shooter"[3] sorties to an estimate of fewer than five hundred for Iraq—only *two* of which actually penetrated Coalition airspace. Notwithstanding a Coalition/Iraqi combat-loss ratio of thirty-three to thirty-eight, these latter figures indicate that Coalition air forces dominated by overwhelming ratios in air-to-air combat and shooter sorties. This illustrates an extreme case, but it also demonstrates the importance of selecting proper measures as well as the ease with which legitimate evidence can be used to support widely differing interpretations of what happened. In the end, measurement means little until a sensible and reasonably broad set of measures has been selected.

The third step, determining what the data mean, is related closely to the second in that the requirement is to show how results relate to attaining objectives. In this step, one must deal with a hierarchy of objectives: from the tactical (destruction of a tank) to higher levels (preventing an armored attack or degrading the combat capability of a

---

3. This category includes any aircraft whose primary purpose is dropping bombs or firing missiles; omitted, however, are combat sorties flown by electronic countermeasures aircraft.

division or corps). Also note that tactical measures of effects are usually more easily tabulated and understood than operational-level measures. One can count tanks, but how is divisional degradation quantified? As a result, operational-level objectives are quite often presumed to be a direct function of tactical damage assessments. That match is not always improper but, as illustrated by the case of aggregate combat losses due to enemy air defenses for measuring air supremacy, it can be extremely misleading.

Control of the Air

To wage the air campaign, the Coalition had to control the air space over Iraq. When war came, Coalition air forces soon bottled up the Iraqi air force on its airfields and largely prevented effective employment of Iraq's integrated air defense system and radar-guided surface-to-air missiles (SAMs). Save for low-altitude antiaircraft artillery (AAA) and infrared SAMs in highly defended areas like Baghdad and the portions of the Kuwaiti theater occupied by Republican Guard divisions, the Coalition air forces quickly gained relatively unimpeded freedom of action. Air superiority (that is, the ability of one side's aircraft to operate in selected airspace at a given time without prohibitive interference from the other side) was achieved by the end of 17 January 1991; by 27 January, General Schwarzkopf could declare air supremacy, meaning that the Iraqi air force no longer existed as a combat-effective force.[4]

To a considerable extent, the Iraqis conceded control of the air to the Coalition even before the war began. The Iraqi air force on 17 January apparently intended to ride out the initial Coalition bombing raids inside supposedly bombproof shelters while attempting some defensive counter-air action under close control from Iraq's integrated air defense system.[5] The Iraqis may have hoped to disrupt the Coalition air campaign somewhat, inflicting occasional losses on Coalition air forces by attacking stragglers and egressing strike aircraft low on fuel. This limited use of its air force mirrored Iraq's policy in the Iran-Iraq War, when neither side attempted to establish real air superiority. The Iraqi leadership believed that the army, not the air force, determined victory in modern war and that an air force had value primarily as a "force-in-being"—a protected deterrent against regional rivals.[6]

4. *Conduct of the Persian Gulf War*, 124, 127, 129. See the depictions of these operations in appendix 3.

5. Norman Cigar, "Iraq's Strategic Mindset and the Gulf War: Blueprint for Defeat," *The Journal of Strategic Studies*, March 1992, 19.

6. Ronald E. Berquist, *The Role of Airpower in the Iran-Iraq War* (Maxwell AFB, AL: Air University Press, 1988), 51, 55, 74. In November 1980, in a speech to the Iraqi National

What Did the Air Campaign Accomplish?

In the weeks preceding Desert Storm, Saddam Hussein confidently predicted that after the initial air strikes, the Iraqi army would still be "safe and sound and ready for battle" when Coalition ground forces appeared.[7] As in the Iran-Iraq War, ground-based air defenses, rather than Iraqi fighters, would be relied upon to blunt any Coalition air strikes that might occur.[8] In such circumstances, Coalition air-control operations were less a contest between opposing air forces than a concerted effort by the Coalition to minimize its losses while destroying the Iraqi air force on the ground, thereby denying Iraqi's goal of holding its air force in reserve either for a last stand or for postwar use.

Freedom of Action

The opening hours of the war saw Coalition air forces bomb key command and control elements of Iraq's strategic air defense system such as sector and intercept operations centers. Coalition fighters mounted offensive fighter sweeps over the main Iraqi fighter bases with the intent of shooting down any Iraqi fighters that became airborne. British Tornados attacked takeoff surfaces at key airfields with JP-233 (an airfield-attack system containing specialized cratering and mining submunition) in order to limit the numbers of launched Iraqi fighters to quantities the Coalition fighters could readily handle. And sophisticated attacks involving drones and HARMs (high-speed antiradiation missiles) were launched against Baghdad and other areas where Iraq's radar-guided SAMs were concentrated. These efforts were designed to bottle up the Iraqi air force on the ground and eliminate the threat of radar-guided SAMs at medium and higher altitudes, thereby permitting Coalition aircraft to operate there with little risk of significant attrition.

The air-to-air portion of this effort, which averaged some 340 sorties daily over the course of Desert Storm, quickly persuaded the Iraqi air force to stand down. By the ninth day of the war (25 January), Coalition fighters had downed sixteen Iraqi MiG-29s, MiG-25s, and F-1s, and Iraqi flight activity had largely ceased. By the end of Desert Storm, Coalition air forces had shot down thirty-three Iraqi fixed-wing aircraft (five MiG-29s, eight Mirage F-1s, two MiG-25s, eight MiG-23s,

---

Assembly, Saddam Hussein stressed his opinion on the proper utilization of his air force: "We will not use our air force. We will keep it. Two years hence our air force will still be in a position to pound Bani-Sadr and his collaborators" (ibid., 46).

7. Saddam Hussein, speech to the People's International Conference, 11 January 1991, *Sawt-Al-Sha'b* (Amman), 12 January 1991, 15, cited in Cigar, "Iraq's Strategic Mindset," 18.

8. Cigar, "Iraq's Strategic Mindset," 19.

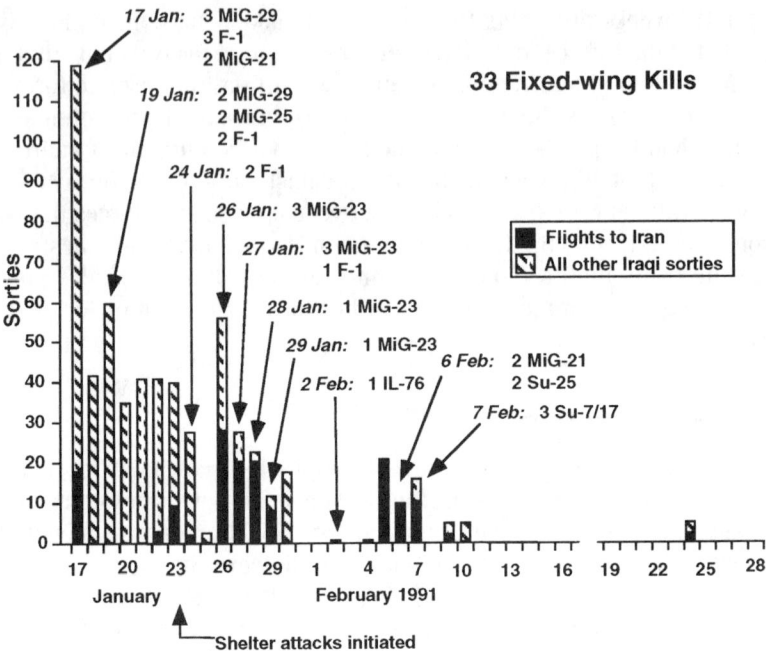

Figure 10   Iraqi Flight Activity versus Coalition Kills

two Su-25s, four MiG-21s, three Su-7/17s,[9] and one IL-76) and five helicopters[10] (see figure 10) while suffering, at most, one air-to-air loss on the opening night of the war.[11]

Although the thirty-three-to-one box score provides some insight into the degree to which Coalition forces dominated in air-to-air com-

---

9. Although these three kills were officially credited as Su-7/17s, they were more likely Su-20 or Su-22 variants (John M. Deur, *Wall of Eagles: Aerial Engagements and Victories in Operation Desert Storm*, GWAPS, NA 399, 41).

10. *Conduct of the Persian Gulf War*, 160; Deur, *Wall of Eagles*, 40–41. Deur's summary also includes the Mi-24 destroyed in the air by a GBU-10 laser-guided bomb from an F-15E on 14 February 1991, for which no "kill credit" was awarded (ibid., 14, 41); and "Tim Bennett's War," *Air Force Magazine*, January 1993, 38.

11. Interview, GWAPS with Comdr. Mark Fitzgerald, 15 May 1992. It was thought, immediately after the war, that no Coalition aircraft had been shot down by Iraqi aircraft. Postwar reexamination of Coalition losses eventually suggested, however, that the lone aircraft lost on the first night of the air campaign, an F/A-18 from the USS *Saratoga*, may have been downed by an Iraqi MiG-25. Detailed reconstruction of the circumstances surrounding the fate of this aircraft produced no positive evidence that it had been lost to an Iraqi radar-guided surface-to-air missile (as was initially believed), and the known presence of an Iraqi MiG-25 in the immediate vicinity when the F/A-18 went down left the Iraqi interceptor as the most likely cause of the loss.

What Did the Air Campaign Accomplish?

bat, it is by no means the entire story. More than 40 percent of the Coalition's kills from 17 January through 28 February involved beyond-visual-range (BVR) shots. The Gulf War was the first conflict in history in which a large percentage of the air-to-air engagements that produced confirmed kills involved BVR shots: namely, the sixteen out of thirty-three victories against fixed-wing Iraqi aircraft credited to Coalition fighters during Desert Storm. These BVR shots were possible because Coalition fighters, operating in conjunction with platforms such as the E-3 AWACS (Airborne Warning and Control System) could shoot BVR with little risk of accidentally hitting friendly aircraft.[12]

Coalition planning against Iraq's ground-based air defenses had two objectives. The first was to destroy the French-built KARI (the French for Iraq, spelled backwards) command and control system—the nervous system of Iraq's air defenses—by directly attacking the system's sector and interceptor operations centers (SOCs and IOCs) and the numerous reporting and listening posts that provided early-warning information. Second, planners intended to suppress Iraq's radar-guided SAMs with drones and large numbers of antiradiation missiles from "Wild Weasel" F-4Gs, F/A-18s, and other aircraft. This Coalition endeavor produced some of the most complex attacks of the air campaign.

The most conclusive evidence of Coalition success in rendering KARI and its associated "strategic" SAMs impotent can be seen in Coalition attrition data (figure 11). From an operational standpoint, the relevant measure of effectiveness against Iraq's ground-based air-defense system was not SOCs, IOCs, or missile-firing batteries physically destroyed but the numbers of Coalition aircraft that were *not* down or damaged while carrying out their missions over Iraq and the Kuwaiti theater of operations. During the first six days of Desert Storm, radar SAMs downed or damaged eight Coalition fixed-wing aircraft; for the rest of the campaign, this segment of Iraq's air defenses damaged or downed another five Coalition airplanes. Given the large numbers of combat sorties flown daily by Coalition air forces—on average, more than 1,600 shooter sorties daily, plus another 540 combat-support sorties—the relatively light losses suffered by Coalition air forces strongly support the conclusion that this portion of the air campaign was highly effective.

The role *not* played in this war by the large numbers of AAA pieces and infrared SAMs deployed around most Iraqi cities and targets and

---

12. GWAPS *Statistical Compendium*, Table 206, "Coalition Air-to-Air Kills Matrix"; Thomas P. Christie, Gary C. Comfort, and Richard E. Guild, *Desert Shield/Desert Storm Air-to-Air Performance Study*, IDA document D-1090 (Alexandria, VA: Institute for Defense Analyses, 1992), 30–31; also Deur, *Wall of Eagles*, 5, 8, 11, 14–15, 18–20, 25–26, 28, 31, 33. In most cases, the rules of engagement for F-15 BVR shots were satisfied by E-3A AWACS aircraft, which were able to confirm "hostile target, no friendlier" (Christie, Comfort, and Guild, C-5).

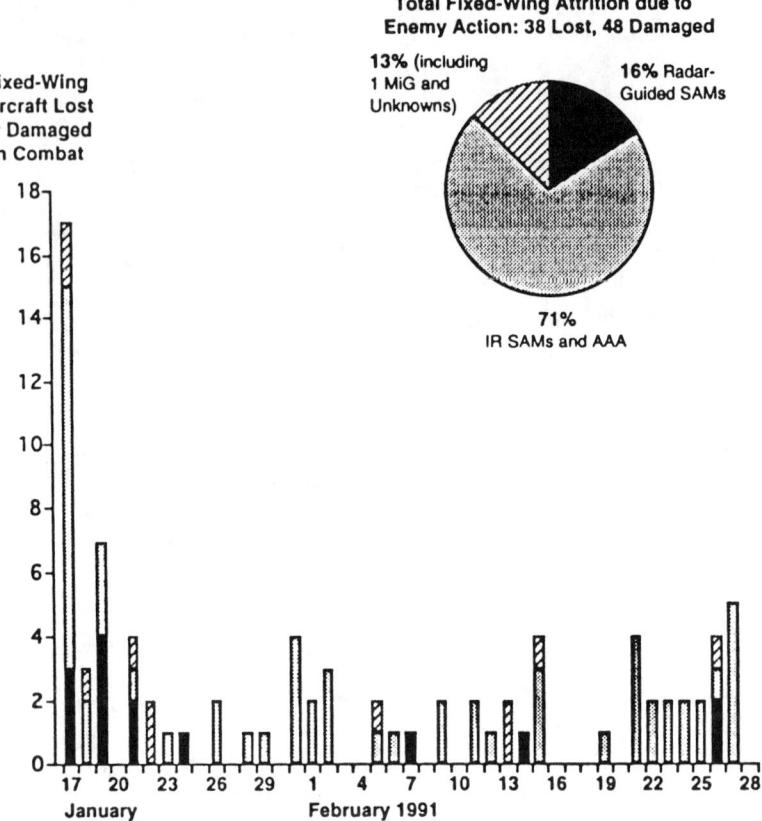

Figure 11 Coalition Fixed-Wing Combat Attrition by Cause

integral to Iraqi ground forces reinforces this conclusion. Such weapons had accounted for the vast majority (85 percent) of U.S. Air Force aircraft losses during the Vietnam War, including the 637 aircraft lost over North Vietnam.[13] The Iraqis probably hoped that their ground-based air defenses could be at least as successful as North Vietnam's had been. By the time Desert Storm ended, however, the Coalition's loss rate was only about one fixed-wing aircraft per eighteen hundred combat sorties. This loss rate was 4.7 times lower than that experienced by the United States over North Vietnam from January to December 1967 and some 14 times lower than the one Ameri-

13. Directorate of Management Analysis, *USAF Management Summary: Southeast Asia Review*, as of 30 June 1973, 28, 30.

What Did the Air Campaign Accomplish? 53

can air forces sustained during Linebacker II.[14] Low losses stemmed from the combination of successful suppression of Iraqi air defense and the decision to bomb from medium altitudes.

How were losses kept so low in Desert Storm? Although some crews initially tried NATO-style low-level ingress tactics during the first few nights of Desert Storm, the sheer volume and ubiquity of barrage AAA, combined with the ability of Stinger-class infrared SAMs to be effective up to twelve- to fifteen-thousand feet, quickly persuaded most everyone on the Coalition side to abandon low altitude, especially for weapon release. Coincident with aircrew reactions to the dangers of low-altitude operations, General Glosson quickly directed the air force units under his command to shift to medium altitude for ingress, weapons release, and egress.[15]

This decision had a price. For aircraft such as the F-16 and F/A-18, which principally employed unguided (or "dumb") munitions during Desert Storm, it entailed a definite sacrifice in bombing accuracy. General Horner stressed in early February 1991 that American support at home for the war depended in large measure on the ability to operate "with less than anticipated" losses of human lives among Coalition airmen, soldiers, sailors, and Marines.[16] Coalition planners thought it imperative not to lose any more aircraft than absolutely necessary.

The final component of the Coalition's efforts to gain and maintain air superiority consisted of attacks on Iraqi airfields. Over the first five days, strikes against runway surfaces—particularly those strikes by Royal Air Force Tornados delivering from low altitude the runway-cratering bomblets and area-denial mines carried by the JP-233 system—were used to limit Iraqi flight activity. Toward the end of the first week of Desert Storm, the Coalition effort against Iraq's main operating bases shifted from runway surfaces to hardened aircraft bunkers and shelters. By then it was clear that Coalition fighters could shoot down virtually any air-to-air opposition that the Iraqis might choose to put into the air. At the same time, Iraqi flight activity had trailed off, which meant that the value of attacks on takeoff surfaces was also de-

14. DOD, OASD/Comptroller, Directorate of Information Operations, Table 311 (22 June 1972) and Table 321 (19 April 1972); and Headquarters Pacific Air Forces (PACAF), Directorate of Operations Analysis, *Summary: Air Operations Southeast Asia*, January 1973, 4-B-1 and 4-B-2.

15. Interview, Maj. Gen. Buster C. Glosson with GWAPS personnel, 14 April 1992. As would be expected, the exact flight and weapon-release "floors" for many aircraft fluctuated during the course of the war in response to tactical conditions and mission requirements.

16. "Daily Comments of Lt Gen Charles A. Horner, Commander USCENTAF, during Operation Desert Storm, 17 January–28 February 1991," entry for 7 February 1991/1700, GWAPS, CHC.

clining. As air planners in both Riyadh and Washington quickly realized, it made little sense to mount JP-233 sorties against runways that the Iraqis were not using.[17]

The campaign to attack aircraft shelters on Iraqi airfields with precision-guided munitions began on the night of 22–23 January, with attacks by F-111Fs delivering laser-guided bombs on about half of the aircraft shelters at Al Asad air base.[18] The Iraqis then began flying combat aircraft to sanctuary in Iran.[19]

Iraq had nearly six hundred hardened aircraft shelters, many of which were only vulnerable to bombs with special penetrating warheads (specifically the GBU-27 and the GBU 24A/B with the I-2000 or BLU-109 warheads). Only two Coalition aircraft, the F-117 and the F-111F, carried these weapons. As a result, the effort against Iraqi aircraft shelters became a relatively slow campaign of incremental attrition. Inevitably, this approach gave the Iraqis an opportunity to play shell games both on and off the airfields with their surviving combat aircraft. By dispersing aircraft into the open on the airfields, they could preclude Coalition aircraft from getting both a shelter and a combat aircraft with a single laser-guided bomb. By moving aircraft in the open regularly—every day or so—they could make it difficult for Coalition planners to target individual aircraft. By dispersing aircraft off the airfields, they could increase the area to be searched. And, last but not least, the Iraqis exploited the Coalition's reluctance to risk damage to cultural monuments such as Islamic mosques by parking combat aircraft near them.

In the end, the Coalition destroyed some 375 aircraft shelters across a total of forty-four major airfields, including three in Kuwait.[20] As for the Iraqi air force, it lost as many as four hundred of the more than seven hundred combat aircraft it had possessed on 17 January, either through destruction or as a result of being retained by Iran. By war's end, the Iraqis still possessed an estimated 300–375 combat aircraft, and the level of destruction of the Iraqi air force was not as complete as the air planners and commanders in Riyadh would have preferred.

---

17. There was much speculation during and after the war that the four GR-1 Tornados the RAF lost before the last JP-233 attacks on 21 January 1991 could be attributed to the low-level ingress and delivery tactics demanded by the JP-233 system. But, in fact, two of these losses were due to radar SAMs, and only one of the four occurred on a JP-233 sortie (Alfred Price, "Tornado in the Desert," *Air Force Magazine*, December 1992, 44).

18. GWAPS Missions Database, entries for the 48th TFW, mission numbers 2601A, 2602A, 2606A, 2607A, 2611A, 2613A, 2614A, 2623A, and 2627A on ATO Day 6.

19. "Fact Paper: IZAF Aircraft to Iran," 11 February 1991, GWAPS, CHC-10, 1.

20. DIA/DX-5B, "Battle Damage Assessment: Iraqi and Kuwaiti Airfields, Summary Report," 10 May 1991.

What Did the Air Campaign Accomplish?

The Coalition's emphasis on aircraft shelters did permit some Iraqi aircraft to survive the war out in the open, while the short flight times (a mere ten to fifteen minutes) to Iranian airspace from fields in central Iraq made it nearly impossible for Coalition aircraft to seal off the Iranian border to fleeing Iraqi aircraft.

Strategic Attacks

In the minds of the Desert Storm air planners, the "strategic core" of the air campaign consisted of the following eight out of twelve target categories: (1) command, control, and communications; (2) leadership facilities; (3) nuclear, chemical, and biological warfare capabilities and weapons programs; (4) military support facilities (for example, ammunition storage, logistics and repair sites); (5) ballistic missile launchers and their supporting infrastructure; (6) electric power; (7) oil refineries; and (8) key bridges and railway facilities. The Black Hole's target list for these eight categories contained 295 targets on 15 January and 535 on 26 February, a growth that reflects a continuing influx of intelligence throughout the forty-three-day war.

Using strikes (meaning occasions on which individual aircraft released ordnance against distinct targets or aimpoints), the eight strategic-target categories absorbed about 15 percent of the Coalition's air-to-ground efforts during Desert Storm.[21] By comparison, attacks against Iraqi surface forces absorbed at least 56 percent of the strikes, and efforts aimed at air control another 14 percent.[22]

The percentage of strikes against the eight strategic-target categories shown in figure 12 may appear relatively small, given the degree of attention devoted to this aspect of the air war by planners and, subsequently, by the public. This attention reflected the importance that a number of the air planners ascribed to attacking the core of Iraqi power and the hopes that some harbored for bringing down the Iraqi regime through the use of air power alone.

An estimated 30 percent of the precision-guided bombs delivered during Desert Storm were targeted against the eight core strategic-

---

21. The traditional input measure for level of effort by air forces has been sorties. Early research, however, revealed that aircraft like the F-117 and F-111F often used precision-guided bombs to hit two or more targets on a single sortie. Strike counts were devised to capture this aspect of Coalition air power in the Gulf War.

22. The total of these percentages falls well short of 100 percent because of the portion of reported strikes that GWAPS was unable to categorize by target category due to incomplete data. The majority of these strikes, though, almost certainly went against Iraqi ground forces. Note too that the more than 340 air-to-air sorties a day that the Coalition averaged during Desert Storm are over and above the roughly 42,000 strikes in the GWAPS Missions Database.

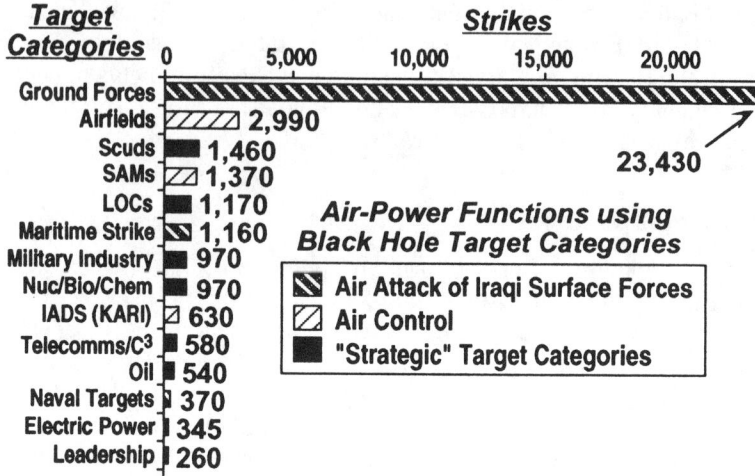

Figure 12 Coalition Strikes by Target Category and Air Power Function (17 January–28 February 1991)

target categories, roughly double the percentage of the total strikes they received.[23] Consequently, these target categories absorbed a disproportionate share of the precision strikes.

The purposes for which the eight core target categories were chosen suggest some natural groupings. These groupings, which will be the subjects of the next three sections, are:

- Leadership and Telecommunications/Command, Control, and Communications (L&CCC),[24]
- Electricity and Oil (E&O), and
- Nuclear/Biological/Chemical Targets and Scuds (C&SC).

Two core strategic categories are ignored by these groupings; namely, railroads and bridges (RR) and military research, production, and support (MS). Bridges and railroad facilities, although defined as a core target category, were, for the most part, attacked to affect the

---

23. GWAPS Missions Database, 2 March 1993. Precision-guided munitions counts were unreliable in the case of certain aircraft, so the percentages given are only approximate. The 30-percent figure for the portion of the precision-guided bombs that were directed against the eight core strategic target categories ignores antiradiation missiles like HARM as well as Mavericks delivered by A-10s.

24. Target-category designators such as "L" for leadership and "E" for electricity were introduced by Colonel Deptula to ease the daily task of reviewing each day's Master Attack Plan. These Black Hole categories were never entirely reconciled with those in DIA's Automated Installations Intelligence File by GWAPS researchers through the end of 1992.

What Did the Air Campaign Accomplish?

supply and support of forces in the Kuwaiti theater; therefore, effects against this target category fall in the discussion of air interdiction operations, treated later in this chapter. Second, the parts of both the MS and RR categories not associated with interdiction mostly fall under the other six core target categories. Examples would include Scud-related targets in MS and bridges in RR that were located in downtown Baghdad or thought to conceal fiber-optic cables linking the Iraqi leadership to Scud units.

Leadership and Telecommunications/Command, Control, and Communications

By attacking the two "leadership" target categories—L&CCC, Black Hole's category designators—campaign planners hoped to disrupt the "central nervous system" of Saddam Hussein's Ba'athist regime. They targeted the various governmental facilities—official residences, government ministries, and command and control bunkers—used by Saddam and his close associates to rule the country, to maintain control over the people, and to direct military operations (the L targets).

The various means by which the Ba'athist leaders communicated with one another, the Iraqi people, the Iraqi military, and the outside world—redundant coaxial and fiber-optic land lines for voice and data, TV and radio stations,[25] microwave radio relays, associated switching facilities (many of them computerized), and satellite communications stations—were identified as a second leadership target category (the CCC targets). Attacking these targets would directly threaten those most responsible for the occupation and pillaging of Kuwait. At the same time, Coalition air planners reasoned that if they could erode the ability of Saddam Hussein and his close associates to exercise tight control of Iraq's military forces, the Iraqi regime would not be able to react effectively to Coalition initiatives or to conduct coordinated military operations.

The strikes that inflicted the bulk of the physical damage to the L&CCC target categories involved precision munitions, carried out principally by F-117s. Given the robust construction, small size, and location in urban areas of many of the targets involved, primary reliance on the F-117/GBU-27 combination made considerable sense, both for certainty of destruction and limitation of collateral damage. Fiber-optic relay stations offer a case in point: only a precision-guided weapon or a lucky hit against the below-ground junction box really effected a cut in the fiber-optic line. Even if strikes against these relay stations with unguided bombs succeeded, incompletely destroying the above-ground

---

25. Radio stations could not only be used to rally the Iraqi populace but were also correctly assessed by Coalition intelligence to be a conduit for triggering Iraqi agents abroad to initiate terrorist attacks.

structures, the fiber-optic line often remained intact unless cut with precision munitions.

The peak levels of precision strikes against Iraqi leadership and its means of communication occurred on the first two nights, and relatively significant numbers of strikes continued for much of the first week. Over the second and third weeks, L targets received less emphasis. CCC, by contrast, got a smaller but fairly steady number of precision sorties over the first three weeks. The level of precision effort against CCC picked up during the fourth week, only to be followed by a more sporadic pattern for the rest of the conflict (see figure 13).

The climax of effort against these leadership targets came toward the end of Desert Storm's fourth week. Master Attack Plans for 9 through 13 February reflected renewed interest in this target category by those in the Black Hole. The F-117 strikes against the Al Firdos district bunker in downtown Baghdad, which were carried out in the early morning hours (Riyadh time) of 13 February, however, precipitated a tightening of higher-level control over strikes on Baghdad in general and on leadership targets in particular.[26] The Al Firdos bunker was one of ten leadership bunkers located in the suburban areas of Baghdad. None of them was hit during the opening weeks of the war because intelligence believed that the Iraqis were not using them.[27] Not until the first week in February did intelligence sources indicate that the Al Firdos bunker had been activated.[28]

Subsequently, various delays, including weather, prevented an attack until the early hours of 13 February.[29] Unknown to Coalition air planners, the upper level of the bunker was, according to the Iraqis, being used at night by families. Hits on the facility by two GBU-27s, both aimed at the same point on the bunker's roof by two different F-117s, were reported that morning by CNN (Cable News Network) as having caused hundreds of civilian casualties.[30] Iraqi sources claimed

26. Harold P. Myers and Vincent C. Breslin, *Nighthawks over Iraq: Chronology of F-117A Stealth Fighter Operations, Desert Shield and Desert Storm* (Office of History, 37th Fighter Wing), 26.

27. As late as 31 January 1991, Checkmate analysts characterized the ten bunkers as "secondary leadership targets" ("Additional Leadership Targets List," Message from Checkmate to the Black Hole, 311730Z, January 1991; and BH, Box 2, Folder 24, Intel/Tgt Info #1).

28. DIA, *Desert Storm Intelligence Bulletin*, "Possible C3 Bunker Activated (63-91)," as of 080530Z, February 1991 (BH, Box 2, Folder 24, Intel/Tgt Info #1). The judgment that the bunker had been activated appears to have been based on the fusion of separate pieces of intelligence.

29. Interview, GWAPS with Lt. Col. David Deptula, 20 and 21 December 1991.

30. Message from Checkmate to the Black Hole, "Additional Leadership Targets List," 311730Z, January 1991 (BH, Box 2, Folder 24, Intel/Tgt Info #1, 3); and GWAPS Mis-

What Did the Air Campaign Accomplish?

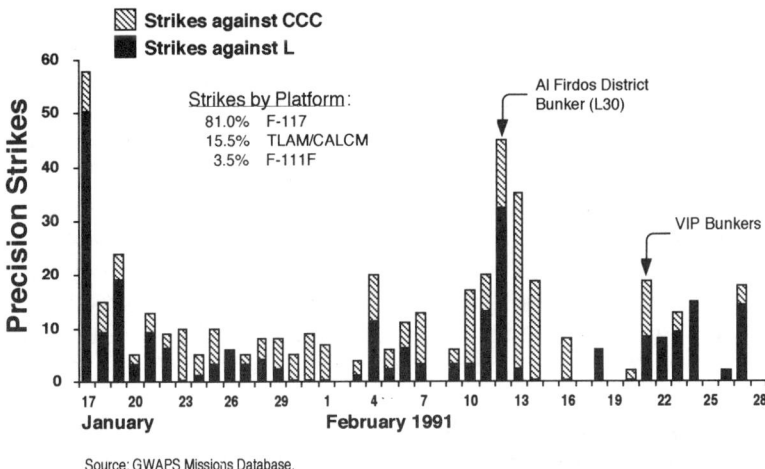

Figure 13 Precision Strikes against Leadership and Telecommunications/Command, Control, and Communications

that two- to three-hundred civilians, including more than one hundred children, died in the bunker,[31] and they quickly exploited the tragedy. In the wake of dramatic television coverage, a sharp reduction in Coalition air strikes against L targets ensued. Among other changes, General Schwarzkopf thereafter personally reviewed any targets selected for air attack in downtown Baghdad.[32]

Consequently, air planners in Riyadh did not resume their efforts until the sixth and final week of the war to "finish off" the L targets.

By the end of the second week of the war, Coalition air planners and intelligence analysts became increasingly convinced that Iraq's national-level telecommunications system had not collapsed as a result of attacks on central switching and microwave relays, despite the

---

sions Database for ATO Day 27. The records on L targets in the Intelligence/Target Information folders used by Colonel Deptula during the war, as well as comments recorded at the time in the Tactical Air Control Center and General Horner's daily briefings all confirm this account of how and why the Al Firdos district bunker came to be struck. It was a legitimate military target, and Coalition planners had no indications before seeing poststrike television coverage over CNN that it had been occupied by civilians.

31. Middle East Watch, *Needless Deaths in the Gulf War* (Washington: Middle East Watch, 1991), 128–29.

32. Lt. Col. David Deptula, GWAPS interviews, 20 and 21 December 1991. Deptula's personal notes from the war confirm that on 13 February 1991 General Glosson was instructed by General Schwarzkopf to begin showing him all targets selected for attack in downtown Baghdad before they were struck.

lethality and precision of the attacks.³³ The system turned out to be more redundant and more able to reconstitute itself than first thought. Fiber-optic networks and computerized switching systems proved particularly tough to put out of action.

How effective were the Coalition attacks on Iraqi leadership and telecommunications/command, control, and communications? Using the Black Hole's target categories, a total of some 260 precision and nonprecision strikes were carried out against the L targets by the war's end; another 580 precision and nonprecision strikes were mounted against the CCC category. Yet, at the war's end, Saddam Hussein was still alive and his Ba'athist regime still in power. Moreover, the Iraqi government had been able to continue launching Scuds during the final days of the campaign.³⁴

Although the capacity of the communications links between Baghdad and its field army in the Kuwaiti theater of operations had been greatly reduced, sufficient "connectivity" persisted for Baghdad to order a withdrawal from the theater that included some redeployments aimed at screening the retreat. Thus, the results of these attacks clearly fell short of fulfilling the ambitious hope, entertained by at least some airmen, that bombing the L&CCC target categories might put enough pressure on the regime to bring about its overthrow and completely sever communications between the leaders in Baghdad and their military forces.

Coalition attacks on the L&CCC target categories need not be judged, however, against this ambitious goal. In retrospect, it may be fairer to ask, how *much* disruption and dislocation did these attacks impose on the functioning of the Iraqi government and its telecommunications? Common sense would argue that strikes against these two target categories must have imposed *some*, if not *considerable*, disruption and dislocation on the Iraqis involved. F-117s carried out the bulk of the 480-plus precision strikes against L&CCC targets. Hits from two-thousand-pound bombs within a few feet of the desired aimpoints on government ministries, national command and control facilities, headquarters, and telecommunications centers forced many elements of Saddam Hussein's government to relocate (in some cases several times) and to shift to backup communications.

Such strikes likewise disrupted normal telephone communications and undoubtedly caused a number of government officials to fear for their lives. Even Saddam Hussein's control of the Iraqi people seems to

---

33. Lt. Gen. Thomas W. Kelly, Director of Operations, JCS, Memo to USCENT COM/J-3, "Iraqi Backbone Telecommunications Vulnerabilities"; also, handwritten note from Checkmate to the Black Hole, 28 January 1991 (GWAPS, BH, Box 2, Folder 24, Intel/Tgt Info #1).

34. The last Scud launches occurred on 26 February 1991.

have been shaken; immediately after the war, rebellions against his rule occurred among the Kurds in the north and Shiite Muslims in the south. Western reporters observed that, for the first time in years, ordinary Iraqi citizens were willing to criticize Saddam Hussein openly.[35]

Yet, the question remains: Given these generalized effects and related symptoms, did the bombing of L&CCC targets come within a hair of shattering Saddam Hussein's Ba'athist regime, or did it fall well short? On the evidence available to the survey, no firm answer can be given. Without access to high-level Iraqi officials and records, the *degree* of disruption and dislocation inflicted by strikes in the L&CCC target categories cannot be quantified, not even roughly. While the Iraqi regime showed signs of being shaken and its telecommunications disrupted, the hoped-for collapse did not occur, and judging how close the Coalition came does not appear possible on the available evidence.

Electricity and Oil

Planners wished to minimize long-term damage to Iraq's economic infrastructure, even as they provided for attacks against both electricity and oil targets. This constraint led air planners and targeting specialists to try to restrict attacks on Iraqi electric power to strikes on transformer/switching yards and control buildings rather than on generator halls, boilers, and turbines in order to minimize recuperation time after the conflict ended.[36] Similarly, attacks on oil production were supposed to concentrate on refined-product storage; distillation and other refining areas were to be aimpoints only if they produced military fuels.[37]

In the case of electric power, however, pilots did not generally refrain from hitting generator halls or their contents, especially during the first week or so of the war.[38] Part of the reason was that the planners elected to go after the majority of Iraq's twenty-five major power stations, and the generator halls offered the most obvious aimpoints. In addition, some of the flying units were not aware that operational planners in Riyadh were attempting to limit long-term damage. Much the same thing occurred with oil targets; in a number of instances, air-

---

35. Chris Hedges, "After the War: Iraq in Growing Disarray, Iraqis Fight Iraqis," *The New York Times*, 10 March 1991, 1, 14.

36. Memo, Brig. Gen. Buster C. Glosson, "Target Guidance."

37. Ibid.

38. That boilers and generator halls were damaged has been well documented by both Coalition wartime reconnaissance and postwar site inspections by members of the international study team that surveyed many bombed facilities from 23 August to 5 September 1991 (Walid Doleh, Warren Piper, Abdel Qamhieh, and Kamel al Tallaq, "Electric Facilities Survey," October 1991, Appendix A; and DIA, *Desert Storm BDA Imagery Review*, DDX-2900-489-91, Vol. 3, 48–53).

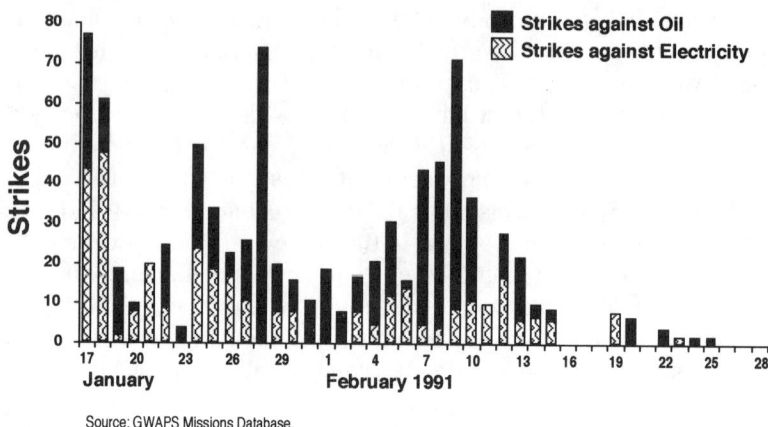

Figure 14 Strikes against Electricity and Oil

craft attacked crude-oil distillation towers despite the intended policy of minimizing prolonged damage.[39] Both discrepancies illustrate the gap that can exist between specifying a target such as a petroleum refinery and picking the particular aimpoints to be hit there.

The twenty-five major generating plants of the Iraqi electrical power system consisted of collocated transformer and switching yards and more than 140 transformer stations (not collocated) linked together on a national grid. The system had a prewar installed capacity of ninety-five hundred megawatts.[40] It generally operated at approximately five thousand megawatts, though—less than 55 percent of installed capacity—prior to the war.[41] Overall, the Iraqi electric power system was relatively modern, redundant, and flexible. It served the needs of Iraq with few of the service interruptions and brownouts typical of many other third-world countries.[42] Similar excess capacity existed in the Iraqi oil industry. Before Operation Desert Storm, Iraq could refine more than 580,000 barrels of oil per day—twice the amount needed to service its own domestic and military needs.

The Coalition mounted some 890 strikes against electric power and oil. The bulk of effort against electricity came early in the campaign, with almost 60 percent of the strikes, including more than sixty by

---

39. DIA, *Desert Storm BDA Imagery Review*, Vol. 3, 12–13, 27–29.

40. Doleh, Piper, Qamhieh, and Tallaq, "Electrical Facilities Survey," 1, in International Study Team, *Health and Welfare in Iraq After the Gulf Crisis: An In-Depth Assessment*, October 1991.

41. Doleh, Piper, Qamhieh, and Tallaq, "Electrical Facilities Survey," 1.

42. Ibid., Appendix A—Reports of Sites Visited, 1–15.

What Did the Air Campaign Accomplish?

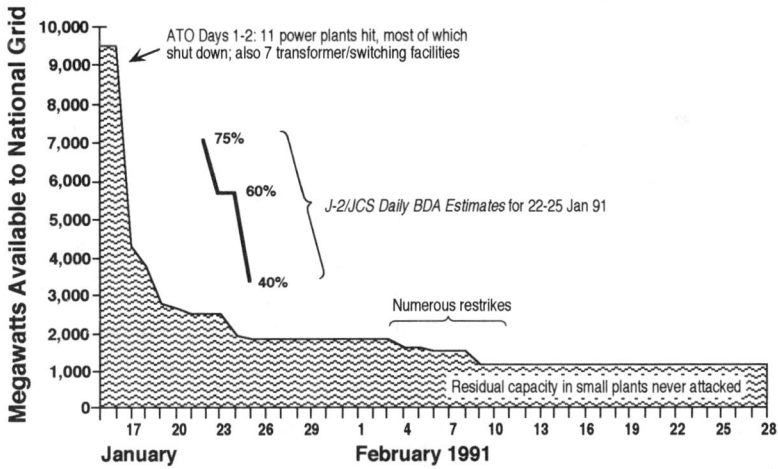

Figure 15 Estimated Drawdown of Iraqi Electric Power

TLAMs, occurring within the first eleven days of Desert Storm. The peak effort against oil, by comparison, came more toward the middle of the campaign (see figure 14).

How effective were Coalition air efforts against the E&O target categories? In the case of electricity, the attacks rapidly shut down the generation and distribution of commercial electric power throughout most of Iraq, forcing the Iraqi leadership and military on to backup power. Ultimately, almost 88 percent of Iraq's installed generation capacity was sufficiently damaged or destroyed by direct attack, or it was isolated from the national grid through strikes on associated transformers and switching facilities, to render it unavailable. The remaining 12 percent, mainly resident in numerous smaller plants that were not attacked, was probably only available locally because of damage inflicted on transformers and switching yards (see figure 15).

In northern Iraq, Coalition aircraft did not have precision munitions; hence, the drawdown of commercial electric power there took place more gradually than in the central and southern portions of the country. U.S. pilots flying missions from Turkey into northern Iraq occasionally reported seeing illuminated towns through the end of January, and Proven Force F-111Es continued to attack northern power plants during the first week of February.[43] Nevertheless, the electric power in central and southern Iraq went down during the initial days of the war, just as the planners had hoped.

How much damage did air attacks ultimately do to Iraq's electric

---

43. GWAPS Missions Database.

power system? Despite the continuation of U.N. sanctions, the Iraqis restored commercial power considerably faster than had been anticipated. For example, planners initially thought that two years would be required to repair the main power plant in Baghdad. But by mid-1992 this plant was reportedly working at 90 percent of its prewar capacity, and, despite a blazing hot summer, not one power blackout occurred in Saddam Hussein's capital even though almost everyone in Baghdad with an air conditioner was running it full blast.[44]

The speed with which the Iraqis restored capacity without external assistance provides evidence that Coalition air inflicted little long-term damage on the Iraqi power system. Even those who charged that the bombing of target systems like electric power had been "unnecessary" readily conceded, on the basis of extensive postwar site inspections, that the strategic air campaign had resulted in remarkably few Iraqi civilian casualties.[45]

Some critics argued, nevertheless, that the bombing of electric power had "contributed to" seventy- to ninety-thousand *postwar* civilian deaths above normal mortality rates over the period April–December 1991, principally because of the lack of electricity in Iraq for water purification and sewage treatment following the cease-fire.[46] These

---

44. Marie Colvin, "Saddam Erases the Scars of War," *London Sunday Times*, 4 October 1992, 16.

45. Greenpeace's estimates of countrywide Iraqi civilian casualties caused by Coalition bombing totaled 2,278 dead and 5,976 injured (William Arkin, briefing viewgraph titled, "Civilian Casualties and Damage," presentation given to GWAPS personnel, 31 October 1991). Arkin, for example, has stated that the air war was "clean on a strategic level," and that he could find no evidence of indiscriminate attacks on cities or civilians, intentional damage for postwar leverage on the government of Saddam Hussein, or extensive collateral damage of civilian structures near targets" ("Tactical Bombing of Iraqi Forces Outstripped Value of Strategic Hits, Analyst Contends," *Aviation Week & Space Technology*, 27 January 1992, 62, 63). After the war, Arkin was able to inspect "13 of the targeted leadership and command bunkers; 49 of the 170 command, control and communications sites; 16 of the 20 oil refineries and distribution facilities, and all of the 75 railroad and auto bridges" hit during the war (ibid., 62).

46. "Tactical Bombing of Iraqi Forces Outstripped Value of Strategic Hits, Analyst Contends," 63. By May 1991, the Harvard Study Team reported sharply increased levels of gastroenteritis, cholera, typhoid, and malnutrition in Iraqi children due to the delayed effects of the Gulf War (*Harvard Study Team Report: Public Health in Iraq after the Gulf War*, May 1991, 12–13). One of the most vocal advocates of this view has been William M. Arkin, director of the nuclear information unit of Greenpeace International. The estimate of seventy- to ninety-thousand additional deaths was derived from a survey conducted in 1991 of some ninety thousand Iraqi households. Based on this data, the additional deaths above the January 1991 "norm" were calculated for April–December 1991 (Arkin, GWAPS interview, 19 October 1992). The final death total as a result of the "indirect detrimental health effects" of the war cited by Arkin was 111,000 (Beth Osborne Daponte, "Iraqi Casualties from the Persian Gulf War and Its Aftermath," 2).

calculations were made without anticipation of the unexpectedly rapid resumption of electric power in Iraq, however.

Coalition planners believed from the outset that if Saddam Hussein's forces were decisively defeated, the Iraqi leader would not long survive the war in power. They further believed that once an accommodation had been reached with the new government in Baghdad, members of the Coalition could provide the parts and anything else necessary to restore electric power speedily throughout Iraq after the war. The political outcome turned out to be something that no one foresaw. Saddam Hussein both retained power and continued to defy the United Nations, thereby causing the continuation of economic sanctions that prevented Coalition assistance in reconstruction or humanitarian relief. To attribute responsibility for Iraq's increased mortality rate in the aftermath of a major military defeat solely, or even primarily, to the damage inflicted on Iraq's electric power system ignores the Iraqi government's responsibility for its own prewar and postwar decisions.

Turning to Coalition efforts against Iraqi oil, strikes against refining capacity appear to have been considerably more effective than those directed against stores of refined products that could be put to military use. Iraq's refining capacity resided in the three large facilities at Baji, Basra, and Baghdad. The CIA eventually concluded that Coalition air strikes had rendered more than 90 percent of Iraq's petroleum-refining capacity inoperative.[47] This judgment was based primarily on damage to distillation towers, inflicted chiefly by a very small number of precision strikes. For the most part, aircraft delivering nonprecision munitions attacked oil storage tanks with more visible but less damaging results. Given the minimum level of effort expended to disable more than 90 percent of Iraq's refinery capacity, this aspect of the air campaign appears to have been both highly leveraged and effective.

How enduring was the damage inflicted on the Iraqi oil industry as a whole? As of October 1992, Iraqi officials claimed that crude-oil production had returned to 800,000 barrels a day and could be increased to 2 million barrels a day (about two-thirds of Iraq's prewar capacity). In addition, restored refineries were supplying more than enough gasoline and heating oil for Iraq's domestic needs and exports to Jordan. Thus, no evidence exists to substantiate that the air campaign inflicted lasting infrastructure damage to Iraq's oil industry.

Finally, how close did the bombing of this target category come to achieving the goal of limiting the fuel and lubricants available to Iraqi forces for military operations? For the most part, the Iraqi air force chose to stay in its shelters and sit out the war; hence, it required little fuel. Iraqi ground forces in the Kuwaiti theater had access to

---

47. CIA, "Imagery Update: #35," 19 March 1991, 1.

Kuwaiti oil facilities and continued to operate the Kuwaiti refining facilities and to use Kuwaiti stocks. Eventually, Coalition air forces began bombing selected Kuwaiti oil facilities to limit use of the stocks. Even so, the amount of diesel fuel available for ground operations at the outset of what turned out to be a one-hundred-hour ground campaign would probably have sufficed for weeks, if not months, of combat.[48]

Before that time, most Iraqi forces in the theater were dug into static positions and had minimal POL (petroleum, oil, lubricants) requirements. Individual units faced local shortages because of distribution problems, most notably caused by Coalition air power striking targets such as trucks and bridges. The limited difficulties caused by local shortages were not the result of Coalition attacks on Iraqi refineries and major petroleum depots, however.

Was the strategic effort against Iraqi oil wasted or unnecessary? Again, one must recall the uncertainties under which the air planners and commanders labored at the time. On the evening of 16 January, no one knew how long the war would last or how well the fourth largest army in the world would resist Coalition efforts to liberate occupied Kuwait. If the ground campaign had become protracted, the efforts against oil might have eventually paid military dividends on the ground. There were sound military reasons for limiting the availability of refined fuels and lubricants as a hedge against the possibility that the war would not proceed as favorably for the Coalition as it did. The effectiveness of these efforts lay, therefore, mainly in limiting the Iraqis' ability to wage a protracted ground campaign. It was prudent to have done so, but attacking oil refineries and storage in Iraq bore no significant military results due to the swift collapse of the Iraqi army.

Nuclear/Biological/Chemical Targets and Scuds

Coalition planners had the explicit military objective of destroying Iraq's chemical, biological, and nuclear capabilities. In the short term, that goal supported the Coalition's generic military objective of destroying Iraq's capability to wage war. In the long term, destroying Iraq's nuclear program and its modified Scud ballistic missile capability would support the political objective of promoting the peace and stability of the Persian Gulf region.

---

48. Desert Storm Studies Group, U.S. Army Intelligence and Threat Analysis Center, "Status of the Iraqi Logistics Systems in the KTO," Annotated Briefing, 2 February 1991, GWAPS, CHST 50-3 & CBDA, Folder 19; also Iraq Regional Task Force, "Iraq: Sustainment Capabilities for the KTO," Desert Storm Defense Special Assessment, DSA 171-91, 20 February 1991, 2). It is not surprising that intelligence estimates varied considerably concerning how many Iraqi combat days might be sustained by on-hand stocks (such as diesel fuel) in the Kuwaiti theater. While these sorts of estimates are always asked for and made, they have inevitably been based on rather speculative methodologies.

What Did the Air Campaign Accomplish?

The U.S. intelligence community agreed during the final months of 1990 that Iraq had extensive nuclear, chemical, and biological warfare capabilities housed in a number of facilities, but the true extent of these programs was unknown. By 1990, Iraq was estimated to be producing as much as one thousand tons of chemical agents annually, including mustard-type blister agents and the nerve agents sarin and tabun, at the Samarra and Habbaniya facilities.[49] Iraq had also used chemical agents against Iranian forces during the Iran-Iraq War, so there was little doubt about the existence of Iraqi chemical-warfare capabilities. What proved harder to predict with certainty was whether, and under what circumstances, Iraq would employ its chemical weapons against the Coalition.

Iraq's biological weapons program dated from the late 1970s, but estimates prior to Desert Storm as to its exact nature and status were much less certain than those on chemical weapons. The United States believed that Iraq had developed anthrax spores and botulinum toxin as agents and that Iraqis were pursuing other toxins and live agents. Enough research, production, and storage facilities suspected of being involved with biological weapons had been identified at various locations (Salman Pak, Taji, and two facilities at Abu Ghurayb) to suggest that the Iraqis had produced such agents in militarily significant quantities.[50]

The Iraqi nuclear program was massive,[51] for most practical purposes fiscally unconstrained, closer to fielding a nuclear weapon, and less vulnerable to destruction by precision bombing than Coalition air commanders and planners or U.S. intelligence specialists realized before Desert Storm. The target list on 16 January contained two nuclear targets, but after the war, inspectors assigned to the United Nations's special commission eventually uncovered more than twenty sites involved in the Iraqi nuclear weapon program; sixteen of the sites were described as "main facilities"[52] (see figures 16, 17, and 18).

Militarily, there were at least two critical areas of uncertainty concerning Iraq's ballistic missile capabilities in the months preceding Desert Storm. One concerned the number of mobile launchers and op-

---

49. Michael J. Eisenstadt, "The Sword of the Arabs": Iraq's Strategic Weapons, Washington Institute for Near East Policy, Policy Paper Number 21, 1990, 5; and Defense Intelligence Agency, "Special Analysis: Degradation of the Iraqi Chemical Warfare Capability," DDB-1620-28-91, 20 February 1991.

50. Eisenstadt, "The Sword," 7–8.

51. After the war, it was determined that the Iraqi nuclear program had employed more than twenty thousand people (David Kay, "Arms Inspections in Iraq: Lessons for Arms Control," 2, GWAPS, NA 375).

52. Security Council, Report S/23215, 7th IAEA on-site inspection (11–22 October 1991), 14 November 1991, 8, 63.

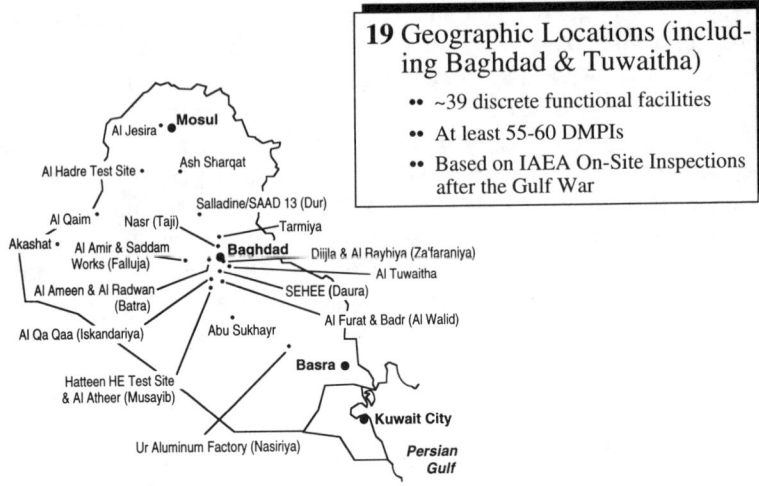

Figure 16 Iraqi Nuclear Target System

erational missiles the Iraqis possessed. The other had to do with how the Iraqis might choose to employ these weapons against Coalition forces.

When Desert Storm began, Coalition planners appear to have assumed that the Iraqis would launch their ballistic missiles initially from fixed or known launch sites, giving Coalition air power a reasonable chance of eliminating the Scud threat—or most of it—in the opening

1. Baghdad:
    Iraqi Atomic Energy Commission
    PC3 Project Headquarters (weaponization oversight)
    Rashdiya Engineering Design Center (centrifuge work)
    National Computer Center (weaponization support)
    Geological & Survey Institute (uranium mining/extraction)
2. Tuwaitha:
    EMIS R&D (Bldgs 80, 85)
    Centrifuge R&D (Bldgs 63, 65)
    Chemical Enrichment (Bldg 90)
    Implosion Work (IRT-5000, Bldgs 9, 10, 15)
    Tammuz II
    Gaseous Diffusion (Bldg 23 until 1987)
3. Tarmiya: EMIS Production
4. Ash Sharqat: EMIS Production
5. Al Jesira (near Mosul):
    EMIS Production
    Centrifuge Production (planned)
6. Batra:
    Al Radwan (EMIS component manufacturing)
    Al Ameen (EMIS component manufacturing)
7. Falluja:
    Al Amir (EMIS component manufacturing)
    Saddam Works (centrifuge component manufacturing)
8. Dur: Salladine (SAAD-13, EMIS component manufacturing)
9. Daura (SEHEE)
    EMIS component manufacturing
    Centrifuge component manufacturing
10. Al Walid:
    Al Furat (centrifuge R&D)
    Al Furat (centrifuge production)
    Badr (centrifuge component manufacturing)
11. Taji: Nasr Works (centrifuge component manufacturing)
12. Nasiriya: Ur Aluminum Factory (centrifuge components)
13. Za'faraniya:
    Al Raybiya (EMIS: calutron components)
    Diijla Electronics (calutron components)
14. Al Qaim: Yellow Cake Production
15. Abu Sukhayr: Uranium Extraction from Carbonate Ores
16. Akashat: Uranium Extraction from Phosphate Ores
    Al Amir (EMIS component manufacturing)
    Saddam Works (centrifuge component manufacturing)
17. Iskandariya: Al Qa Qaa (high explosives)
18. Near Musayib:
    Al Atheer (high explosives work)
    Al Atheer (implosion device work)
    Hatteen Explosive Test Range
19. Al Hatra: Al Hadre (high explosives)

Figure 17 Iraqi Nuclear Facilities by Location

What Did the Air Campaign Accomplish?

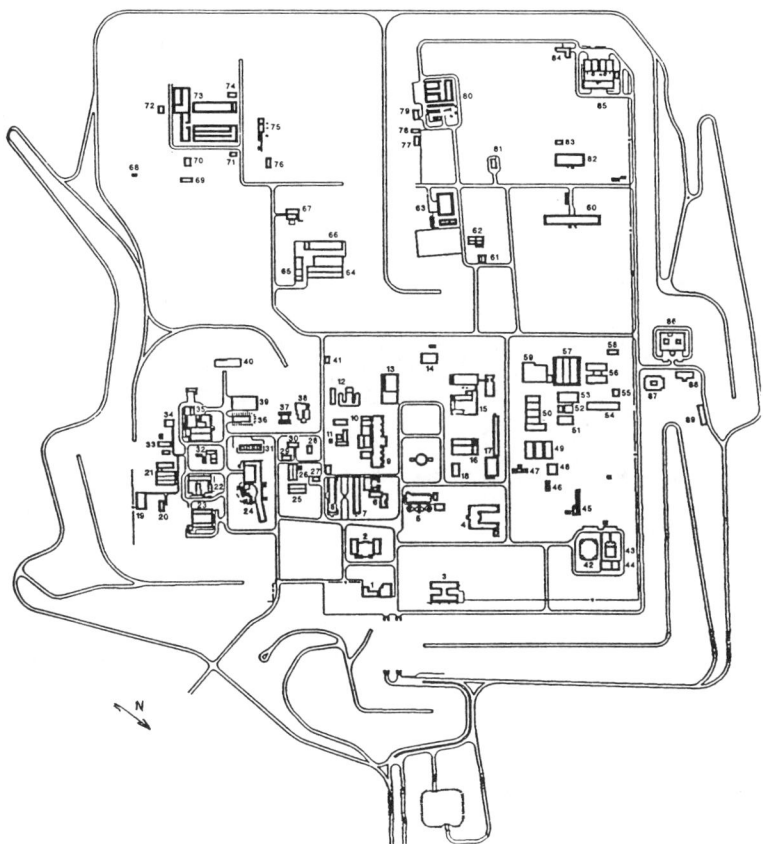

Figure 18 Tuwaitha (C11) Baghdad Nuclear Research Facility

hours of the war.[53] If the Iraqis did shift to mobile operations under attack, Coalition planners assumed that their set-up and launch procedures would resemble those utilized by Soviet Scud units in central Europe. More specifically, the mobile launchers would not only require several hours to launch a missile but also, in the process, would provide distinctive signatures that Coalition forces could exploit to locate and attack them. Planners also assumed that decoys or other "background noise" would not greatly complicate the problem of dealing with Iraqi Scud units. None of these assumptions proved accurate during the war.

53. Interview, GWAPS with General Glosson, 9 April 1992. The GWAPS Missions Database confirms that several hundred sorties were sent against Scud targets during the first four days of the air campaign.

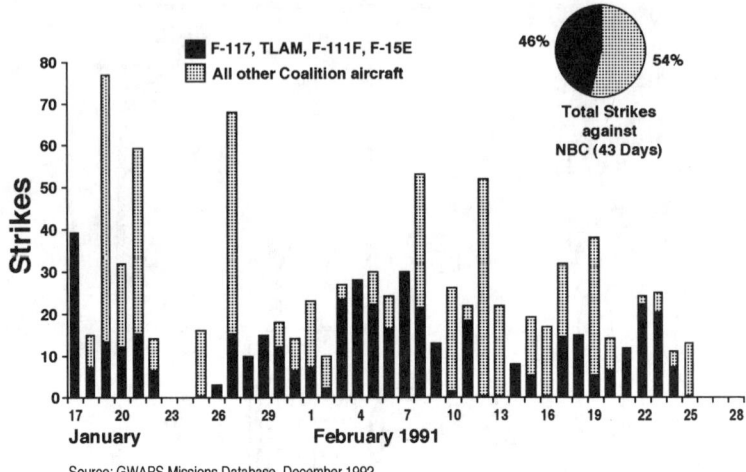

Figure 19 Coalition Strikes against Nuclear, Biological, and Chemical Targets

Overall, the United States did not fully understand the target arrays comprising Iraqi nuclear, biological, chemical, and ballistic missile capabilities before the Gulf War. The Iraqis had, in fact, made these target systems as elusive and resistant to accurate air attack as possible, with some success.

Figure 19 shows the flow of Coalition air strikes against the Iraqi nuclear, biological, and chemical (NBC) targets that made up the Black Hole's "C" target category. In all, the Coalition mounted some 970 strikes against this category. More than 40 percent of the strikes were made with precision weapons, and about 80 percent of those strikes with precision weapons were carried out by F-117s. Aircraft making strikes with nonprecision weapons against NBC targets included B-52s, F-16s, F/A-18s, GR-1s, F-111Es, and A-6s. In addition, F-111Fs and F-15Es conducted a few nonprecision-weapon strikes on these targets.

The bulk of the strikes directed against the C, or NBC, target category focused on Iraqi chemical-warfare capabilities. Target facilities included the three chemical precursor production facilities near Al Fallujah, research centers such as Salman Pak (which Coalition intelligence also associated with Iraqi work on biological toxins), and chemical-munitions production facilities such as Samarra. Suspected storage bunkers for chemical weapons were scattered throughout Iraq, and some of these, notably the "S-shaped" bunkers seen primarily at airfields, had unique signatures. By the time the war began, Coalition intelligence indicated that chemical-warfare units might be operating from Kuwaiti airfields, which transformed virtually all the hardened

What Did the Air Campaign Accomplish?

shelters on those bases into potential storage facilities for chemical munitions. All in all, Iraqi chemical-warfare capabilities offered a large number of potential aimpoints.

Despite Coalition attacks on the chemical-weapons targets, postwar inspections by U.N. special commission teams eventually uncovered some 150,000 chemical munitions.[54] Why, with such a stockpile, did Iraq not use chemical weapons during Desert Storm? One likely answer is that Iraq feared the Coalition's potential for retaliation more than it did the Coalition's destruction of its chemical-warfare capabilities.[55] The portion of the effort aimed at destroying research, development, and production facilities for chemical munitions, though, initiated the process of eliminating Iraq's ability to threaten its regional neighbors with weapons of mass destruction.

Furthermore, the attrition of artillery in demoralized Iraqi frontline units eventually rendered any coordinated, systematic use of chemical munitions nearly impossible to execute against the initial penetration of Iraqi defenses. Even though air attacks against Iraq's chemical-warfare capabilities fell well short of destroying them completely, it by no means follows that those attacks were militarily futile or served no purpose.

How effective was Coalition bombing of Iraq's biological-warfare program? Two basic types of biological-warfare targets were attacked during the air campaign: (1) infrastructure targets such as the Salman Pak and Taji research facilities and Iraq's suspected production plants for biological weapons (one at Al Latifiyah and two near Abu Ghurayb), and (2) the specially designed, refrigerated bunkers scattered throughout Iraq suspected of containing biological or other special weapons.[56]

---

54. Iraq's initial postwar declaration to the United Nations on 18 April 1991 acknowledged nearly ten thousand nerve-gas warheads, some fifteen hundred chemical-weapon bombs and shells, and one thousand tons of nerve and mustard gas (Kay, "Arms Inspections in Iraq: Lessons for Arms Control," 1). By the end of 1992, Iraq had admitted to 150,000 chemical munitions, and the head of the CIA believed that the Iraqis still possessed additional munitions that U.N. inspectors had not found (Robert Gates, "Proposed Remarks to the Comstock Club," 15 December 1992, 12).

55. Asked during a 27 February 1991 press conference why the Iraqis had not used chemical weapons, General Schwarzkopf speculated that air attack—particularly of the artillery in frontline Iraqi units—had probably limited their capability to employ such weapons; he also proffered Iraqi fears of nuclear retaliation as a possible explanation ("Excerpts from Schwarzkopf News Conference on Gulf War," *The New York Times*, 28 February 1991, A-8).

General Schwarzkopf's bottom line, however, was that, while he might never know the answer, he was thankful that chemical weapons had not been used. Much the same view was reiterated in the Defense Department's final report on the Gulf War (*Conduct of the Persian Gulf War*, 155).

56. Some eighteen bunkers were known before the war, and others were discovered during the course of the campaign. Not all of those eventually identified were hit before the cease-fire.

Although the facilities were destroyed, U.N. inspectors could not confirm after the war that the Iraqis had actually produced any biological weapons before 17 January 1991. As in the case of attacks on chemical weapons, however, attacks against known or suspected research and development facilities for biological weapons served the long-term goal of reducing Iraq's postwar threat to its neighbors.

The relationship of weapons delivered on aimpoints to achievement of operational and strategic effectiveness was particularly strained in the case of the Iraqi nuclear program. We now know that the Iraqis' program to amass enough enriched uranium to begin producing atomic bombs was more extensive, more redundant, further along, and considerably less vulnerable to air attack than was realized at the outset of Desert Storm.

Moreover, once the war began, Iraqi willingness to take such unorthodox measures as dispersing nuclear fuel or critical machinery from known nuclear installations like Al Tuwaitha quickly made Iraq's nuclear program even less vulnerable to bombing, no matter how accurate, than it had been during Desert Shield. In this sense, elements of the Iraqi nuclear program were transformed into targets that could be, and were, mobile. Bombing known locations, therefore, failed to achieve the objective of *eliminating* the existing Iraqi nuclear weapons program. The Iraqi nuclear program's redundancy, advanced status on the eve of the war, and elusiveness, in conjunction with the extraordinary measures the Iraqis took immediately after Desert Storm to conceal its extent by destroying certain facilities, led the United Nations to conclude that the air campaign no more than "inconvenienced" Iraqi plans to field atomic weapons.[57]

Efforts by Coalition air forces to suppress Iraqi launches of Scud missiles against Israel, Saudi Arabia, and other Persian Gulf nations during Desert Storm ran into many of the same problems evident in the case of the Iraqis' nuclear weapons program. Key portions of the target set—notably the pre-surveyed launch sites and hiding places used by the mobile launchers—were not identified before 17 January, and, even in the face of intense efforts to find and destroy them, the mobile launchers proved remarkably elusive and survivable.

Although Iraq's average weekly launch rate of modified Scuds during Desert Storm (14.7 launches per week) was lower than it had been during the 1988 "war of the cities," and while launch rates generally declined over the course of the Gulf War (see figure 20), the actual destruction of any Iraqi mobile launchers by fixed-wing Coalition aircraft remains impossible to confirm. Coalition aircrews reported destroying

---

57. The judgment that the bombing at most "inconvenienced" the Iraqi nuclear program was offered by an American who participated in some of the IAEA inspection teams that went into Iraq under U.N. Resolution 687 in 1991.

What Did the Air Campaign Accomplish? 73

around eighty mobile launchers[58]; another score or so were claimed by special operations forces.[59]

Most of these reports undoubtedly stemmed from attacks that did destroy objects found in the Scud launch areas. But most, if not all, of the objects involved now appear to have been decoys, vehicles such as tanker trucks that had infrared and radar signatures impossible to distinguish from those of mobile launchers and their associated support vehicles, and other objects unfortunate enough to provide "Scud-like" signatures.

Over the forty-three days of Desert Storm, roughly fifteen hundred strikes were carried out against targets associated with Iraqi ballistic missile capabilities. This total includes missions reported as having bombed mobile launchers (TELs and MELs), suspected hiding places for the mobile launchers (highway culverts, overpasses, etc.), fixed launch sites (such as those at the H-2 airfield in western Iraq), and Scud-related production and support facilities.[60] Nearly half of the approximately fifteen hundred "Scud" strikes delivered ordnance against either fixed sites or structures such as culverts and highway overpasses suspected of being potential hiding places for mobile launchers; some 30 percent struck ballistic missile production and infrastructure; only 15 percent—just over 215 strikes—were reported to have involved attacks on mobile launchers (see figure 21).[61]

That last percentage (particularly when placed alongside the roughly one thousand "Scud patrol" sorties that dropped on targets other than Scud launchers) begins to give a quantitative sense of how elusive Iraq's mobile launchers proved to be. The numbers also confirm, how-

---

58. Immediately after the war, the A-10s alone claimed to have destroyed fifty-one Scud launchers ("Operation Desert Storm: A-10 Combat Recap: 23/354 TFW[P], 17 January 1991 to 28 February 1991," slide entitled "A-10 Mission Results: Targets Destroyed-Confirmed," GWAPS, NA 292). F-15Es were reported by General Schwarzkopf to have destroyed six to ten mobile launchers on the night of 29 January 1991 (DOD, "Special Central Command Briefing," Riyadh, Saudi Arabia, 30 January 1991, transcript #672561). Hence, an estimated total of some eighty mobile launchers claimed to have been destroyed by Coalition aircrews is consistent with wartime claims, as well as information presented during a GWAPS visit to Nellis AFB, Nevada, in February 1992.

59. GWAPS members visited the U.S. Special Operations Command in March 1992.

60. The "AIF" total for Scud strikes/sorties in the GWAPS Missions Database is substantially lower than the roughly twenty-five hundred Scud sorties widely reported after the Gulf War (see, for example, Richard P. Hallion, *Storm Over Iraq: Air Power and the Gulf War* [Washington: Smithsonian Institution Press, 1992], 181). The principal reason for this difference stems from "Scud patrol" missions that were *launched* to hunt mobile Scuds but, when unable to locate any, "dropped on" other targets of opportunity.

This example also illustrates the kinds of problems that affected many of the figures concerning the Desert Storm air campaign that were circulated in the immediate aftermath of the war.

61. GWAPS Missions Database, 14 December 1992.

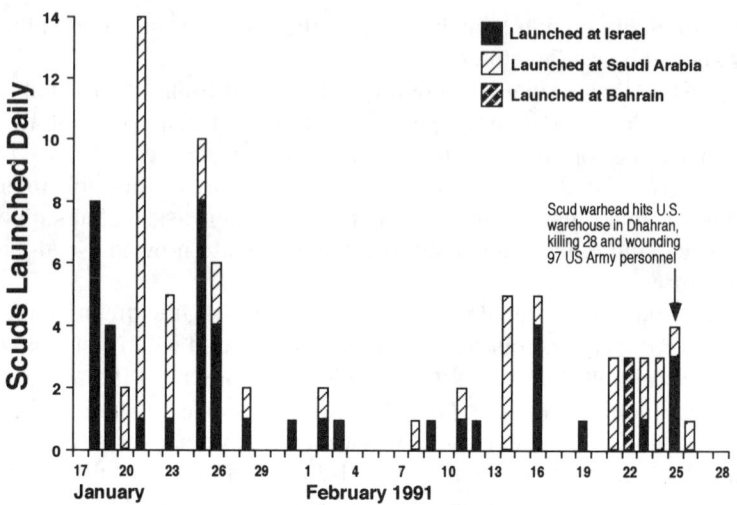

Figure 20 Daily Scud Launches during Desert Storm (Riyadh time)
Data Source: Thomas P. Christie, William J. Barlow, et al., "Desert Storm Scud Campaign," IDA paper P-2661, April 1992.

ever, that the diversion of air assets to the "great Scud chase" was not large relative to more than forty-two thousand strikes recorded during the war by Coalition fixed-wing aircraft.

While Coalition efforts against ballistic missile production and infrastructure served the postwar goal of eliminating Iraq's offensive threat to its regional neighbors, efforts directed against the fixed launchers do not appear to have been totally effective in suppressing Scud launches *during* the war. However prudent and necessary it may have been to strike the fixed sites in order to preclude their later use, the Iraqis, contrary to expectations, opted to rely exclusively on mobile launchers. In hindsight, it now appears that a good portion of the mobile Scud force—perhaps the bulk of it—dispersed from central bases by the end of August 1990, although some dispersal actions may have still been going on toward the end of Desert Shield.[62]

As a result, the initial hope of the air planners in Riyadh that heavy attacks on the fixed Scud sites during the opening hours of the air cam-

---

62. GWAPS discussions with DIA analysts 30 September 1992; also, DIA, "Mobile Short-Range Ballistic Missile Targeting in Operation Desert Storm," OGA-1040-23-91, December 1991, 1. DIA analysts who followed Iraqi ballistic missile capabilities during Desert Shield indicated that many signs of dispersal were observed in the sense of seeing vehicles and activity incrementally disappear from central support bases and other known locations. But the inability to find the places to which vehicles and activities had been moved resulted in caveated reporting whose broader operational import was not readily understood by air planners in Riyadh as pointing to widespread dispersal.

What Did the Air Campaign Accomplish?   75

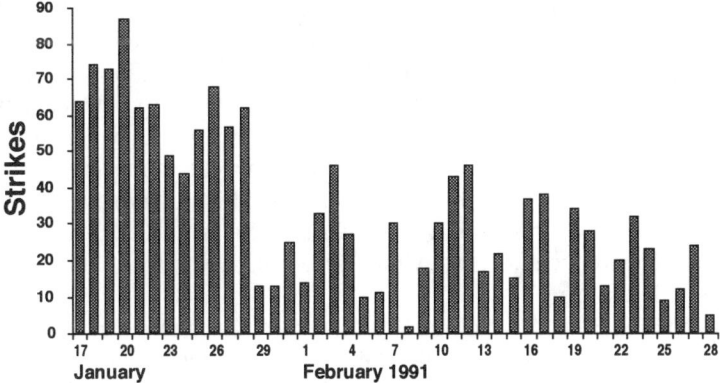

Figure 21 Coalition Strikes against Scuds

paign would largely eliminate Iraq's capability to launch ballistic missiles against Israel or regional members of the U.S.–led Coalition proved to be illusory.[63] The fixed Scud launchers in western Iraq functioned, on the night of 16–17 January, as decoys that diverted attention away from the mobile launchers that had already deployed to their wartime "hide" sites, and the first of Iraq's extended-range Scuds were fired at Israel the following night.[64]

Once Scuds started falling, first on Israel and on Saudi Arabia two days later, the next best military option would have been to locate and attack mobile launchers before they had time to fire. Soviet exercise patterns in central Europe with Scud-Bs and Iraqi practice during the Iran-Iraq War indicated that if the Iraqis followed prior practices, there might be enough prelaunch signatures and time to give patrolling aircraft some chance of attacking mobile launchers before they fired. During the Gulf War, however, the Iraqis dramatically cut their prelaunch set-up times, avoided any prelaunch electromagnetic emissions that might give away their locations before launch, and seeded the launch areas with decoys (some of which were extremely high fidelity[65]) and other vehicles.

63. Getting F-15Es and other strike aircraft cleanly through Iraq's air defense during the opening moments of the air campaign so that they could strike the fixed Scud launchers in western Iraq was a central feature of the Master Attack Plan for ATO Day 1.

64. The first launches against Israel occurred around 0300 on the morning of 18 January 1991, Riyadh local time.

65. U.N. observers, who eventually oversaw the destruction of both mobile launchers and decoys, reported that the high-fidelity decoys were impossible to distinguish visually from the real thing outside of twenty-five yards—even on the ground. The Iraqis also made use of relatively low-fidelity decoys.

The next tactical option was to mount airborne Scud patrols in the hope that, once launches were detected, the strike aircraft would be able to identify the firing locations quickly enough to locate the launchers with onboard sensors and destroy them before they could leave the scene. The weakest link in this chain was the ability of the sensors on strike aircraft to identify and acquire vehicles whose radar and infrared signatures were easily masked and terribly difficult to distinguish on any reliable basis from background clutter, trucks and other vehicles, or countless objects located within the Scud launch areas in western and southeast Iraq.

More than 80 percent of the Scud launches during Desert Storm occurred at night. Even an F-15E orbiting near a fleeting target the size of a MAZ-543 mobile launcher had little chance of identifying and acquiring the vehicle before it reached a hide site. The clearest evidence of this can be drawn from the forty-two occasions on which Scud launches were visually observed by orbiting strike aircraft. In only eight of these cases were aircrews of strike aircraft able to visually acquire the target sufficiently to deliver ordnance.[66] Even allowing for the long distances at which a Scud launch could be seen at night, aircraft such as the F-15E and the FLIR-equipped F-16L experienced fundamental sensor limitations that rendered the probability of finding Iraqi mobile launchers extremely low—even when the launch point could be localized into a relatively small area in near real time by either aircrew visual sightings or offboard sensors providing coordinates.

Some eighty-eight extended-range Scud variants were launched at Israel, Saudi Arabia, and Bahrain during Desert Storm. Thirty-three of those occurred within the first seven days of Desert Storm. Hence, the number of launches over the remaining thirty-six days of the war—a total of fifty-five firings—reflects more than a threefold lower average level of activity (1.5 launches per day versus an average of 4.7 launches per day during the first week). It is reasonable to attribute this reduction in the average number of daily launches to the Scud-hunting efforts of Coalition aircraft.

Nevertheless, the maximum number of Scud launches on any single day—fourteen—does not exceed the total number of mobile launchers known to have survived the war.[67] So the observed launch data are consistent with the possibility that the Iraqis started the war with a total mobile-launcher inventory in the high twenties to mid-thirties. Furthermore, the period of lowest activity spans the third and fourth weeks of the war, and Iraq's Scud units seemed to have recovered

---

66. Defense Science Board (DSB), Office of Director of Research and Engineering, "Lessons Learned during Desert Shield and Desert Storm"—"For Comment Draft," May 1992, 72.

67. The total number of mobile launchers known to have survived the war is nineteen.

What Did the Air Campaign Accomplish?

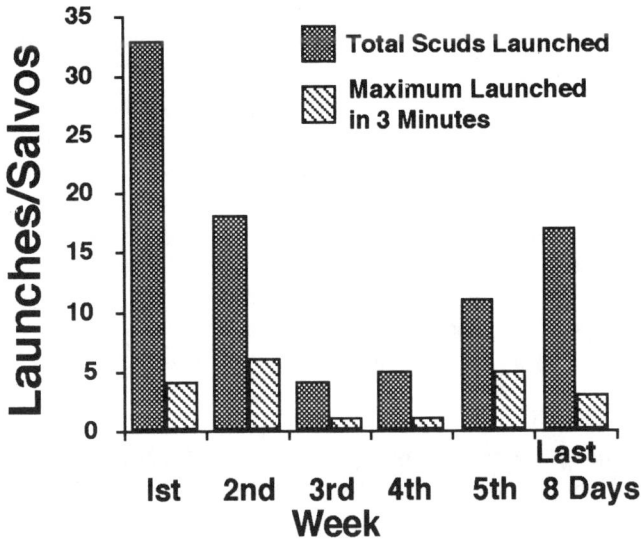

Figure 22 By-Week Launch Totals and Maximum Salvo Size for Iraqi Scuds

Data Source: Thomas P. Christie, William J. Barlow, et al., "Desert Storm Scud Campaign," IDA paper P-2661, April 1992.

somewhat during the final two weeks of the campaign. This pattern can be seen more easily in the week-by-week launch totals depicted as solid bars in figure 22. Relative to the first week, the weekly launch totals reflect a substantial reduction of Scud launches through the fourth week. But the solid bars in figure 22 indicate that some degree of recovery occurred in the fifth week, and the launches during the last eight days of the war are comparable with the total numbers of Scuds launched during the second week.

A somewhat similar story emerges from considering the maximum salvo size in each week. The striped bars in figure 22 depict the maximum salvo size, which has been somewhat arbitrarily defined as the maximum number of missiles fired within a three-minute period during a given week. This measure attempts to represent the Iraqis' potential to overwhelm Patriot defenses by launching many missiles against targets in Saudi Arabia or Israel within ninety seconds. The by-week data suggest that after the low launch rates of the third and fourth weeks, the Iraqi Scud units recovered enough in the fifth week to launch a salvo size comparable to that of the second week. For the final eight days, the salvo size decreased—again presumably because of the pressure put on Scud units by Coalition forces—but it was still greater than that achieved during the third and fourth weeks.

The Desert Storm air planners did reach fairly accurate assessments of how the Iraqis might plan against or respond to air attack. The reactions of Iraqi surface-to-air missile defenses in Baghdad to decoys and HARMs on the opening night, and the possibility that the Iraqi air force would not seriously contest air superiority in the opening days of the air campaign, constitute instances in which the Coalition assessed Iraqi behavior with reasonable accuracy before 17 January. In the case of the Iraqi Scud units, however, the evidence suggests that a series of incorrect assumptions was made by intelligence analysts, air planners, and commanders alike. (See chapter 4 for a further discussion of the estimates of Scud launch operations.) In such circumstances, it should not be surprising that a full picture of the history and extent of the Iraqis' Scud-decoy program was not developed until some months after the war ended.

In retrospect, nothing in the launch or other data bearing on the anti-Scud effort is incompatible with an Iraqi Scud force that had, at most, thirty or so mobile launchers at the start of the war. Certainly, Scud-hunting operations by Coalition aircraft and special forces harassed the launch operations of these units. More important, in conjunction with the perceived effectiveness during the war of Patriots in defending against incoming Scuds, the Iraqi Scud campaign failed in its strategic purpose of fracturing the U.S.–led Coalition. Nevertheless, the fundamental sensor limitations of Coalition aircraft, coupled with the effectiveness of Iraqi employment tactics (including the use of decoys), suggest that few mobile Scud launchers were actually destroyed by Coalition aircraft or special forces during the war. Given the level of effort mounted against mobile launchers, a few may have been destroyed, but nowhere near the numbers reported during the war. Once again, there is no indisputable proof that Scud mobile launchers—as opposed to high-fidelity decoys, trucks, or other objects with Scud-like signatures—were destroyed by fixed-wing aircraft.[68]

The Strategic "Core" in Retrospect

Regardless of the private hopes airmen may have had during the Gulf War that air power might achieve the Coalition's military objectives

---

68. For example, on 30 January 1991 the videotape from an F-15E "Scud hunt" mission was shown at a U.S. Central Command press conference as proof of Coalition success. While it was confidently asserted on this occasion that at least three—and possibly seven—of the vehicles in question were mobile launchers, it appears far more likely that the objects were, in fact, commercial fuel trucks (DOD, "Special Central Command Briefing," Riyadh, Saudi Arabia, 30 January 1991, transcript #672561; also, discussions with DIA analysts and Air Force officers who were involved in bomb damage assessment during the war and saw the tape when it was broadcast over CNN).

What Did the Air Campaign Accomplish?

without a ground campaign,[69] the modest fraction of the air-to-surface attacks focused against the strategic core concentrated primarily on the more pragmatic objectives laid out in this and the previous chapter. Planners wished to exert pressure from the outset directly against the heart of Iraqi power, an idea consistent with other strategic bombing campaigns.[70] Strategic air attacks were, in some cases, less effective than air planners had hoped for or believed, as in the case of the Iraqi nuclear weapons program. By mid-1992, for example, U.N. Security Council inspection teams had identified and destroyed more of Iraq's nuclear missile programs than had the air campaign.[71] In other cases, such as that of Iraq's electrical power system, the Coalition met its immediate military objectives. In yet other cases, such as the L&CCC target categories, effectiveness cannot be precisely estimated.

Air Attacks on the Iraqi Surface Forces

The vast weight of the Coalition air effort in the war flew either directly against Iraqi ground forces in the Kuwaiti theater or against the supply lines to those forces. These ground forces absorbed the preponderance of the attack sorties of the war and an even larger proportion of the bomb tonnage. This portion of the air war was characterized by the gradual attrition of Iraqi forces rather than by a sudden change in Iraqi capabilities such as had characterized the attacks on the Iraqi air force, air defense system, and electrical power grid. Bomb damage assessment focused more on measuring the cumulative effort of many sorties over time than on scoring the successes of individual sorties.

The planners of air attacks against the Iraqi army recognized the important status of the Republican Guard units, but those forces proved a formidable target. They were singled out as a center of gravity for the part they played as the strategic reserve in the Iraqi ground scheme of maneuver and for their political role as defender of Saddam Hussein's regime. CENTCOM planning, in fact, addressed the possibility of staging an earlier-than-planned ground attack if it discovered that Republican Guard forces were about to retreat into the interior of Iraq before the planned ground offensive got under way. Fearing an early

---

69. Asked if he had hoped that the Iraqis might quit before the ground offensive, General Horner replied, "Of course. I'm an airman" (GWAPS interview, Shaw AFB, NC, 10 March 1992).

70. Noble Frankland argued in 1963 that the core idea behind the strategic air offensive against Nazi Germany during World War II—namely, to put pressure directly on the heart of the enemy nation—was, especially for Great Britain, a logical successor to a naval blockage (Noble Frankland, *The Bomber Offensive against Germany: Outlines and Perspectives* [London: Faber & Faber, 1965], 21, 25).

71. Kay, "Arms Inspections in Iraq: Lessons for Arms Control," 5.

withdrawal, General Schwarzkopf directed that bridges be struck early in the air campaign (in Phase I), not simply to stop the flow of supplies into the theater but also to block the retreat of the Guards.[72] Still, the position of those forces, which were the farthest back in the theater, made them the most difficult units to observe and to attack and allowed several of the Republican Guard divisions to be among the least damaged Iraqi units by the end of the war.

The bombing altitudes employed by the Coalition aircraft limited both the prosecution and effectiveness of the air campaign in the Kuwaiti theater. Crews bombed from much higher altitudes than those at which they had trained in order to remain above the effective altitude of the AAA and infrared SAMs. As a result, aircraft delivering unguided munitions lost accuracy because of the greater slant ranges to the targets and the resulting magnification of aiming errors. Some of the munitions operated best when released at lower altitudes (particularly the cluster mines or bomblets) and were thus less effective because of their excessive dispersion pattern when released from higher altitudes. In addition, aircrews had a much greater problem in identifying targets and assessing damage.[73] Precision weapons did not suffer as much from changes in release altitudes.

Attacks on the surface forces consisted of several components: (1) air interdiction of supplies and transport to and within the Kuwaiti theater; (2) attacks on the Iraqi navy; and (3) the main component, attacks on the Iraqi army while it remained in place during the air war, during engagements at Al Khafji, and during the ground war.

Air Interdiction

Air interdiction operations aimed to cut the flow of supplies to the Kuwaiti theater and to stop the movement of forces. Given that most Iraqi ground forces were in the Kuwaiti theater by the start of the air campaign, the need to block reinforcements was limited. Of greater concern was the need to prevent Iraqi forces from departing the theater intact. Because the principal lines of communication between Baghdad and the theater generally followed and frequently crossed

---

72. Headquarters, U.S. Central Command, Combined Operation Desert Storm, 17 January 1991, para. 3.f.(1)(b)3, GWAPS, CHP 18-1.

73. This subject is treated in depth in the Survey's Weapons, Tactics and Training Report. See also USAF Fighter Weapons Center, "Tactical Analysis Bulletin, Vol. 91-2," July 1991, GWAPS, NA 216; Headquarters, Strategic Air Command, "B-52 Desert Storm Bombing Survey," 15 December 1991, 33; Frank Schwamb, et al., *Desert Storm Reconstruction Report, Vol. II: Strike Warfare* (Alexandria, VA: Center for Naval Analyses, 1991), 5-24 through 5-29; and U.S. Marine Corps Research Center, "Aviation Operations in Southwest Asia," Research Paper #92-0003, U.S. Marine Corps, Quantico, Virginia, June 1992.

What Did the Air Campaign Accomplish?

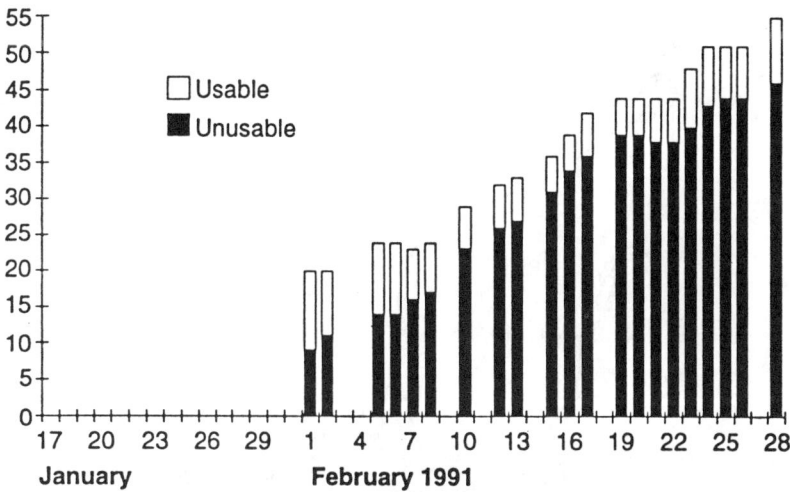

Figure 23   Damaged Bridges in Iraq (DIA)

rivers, bridges became the key targets. Nine railroad bridges and 126 highway bridges lay south of Baghdad, and by the end of the war, roughly half were included in the Black Hole's RR target category. In addition to the bridges, seven rail yards in Iraq were targeted as transportation chokepoints, but the damage to them was not a major factor in eliminating rail traffic between Baghdad and the theater. The destruction of rail bridges was of much greater consequence.

Figure 23 presents the first-order effect of the anti-bridge strikes, a steady increase in the number of damaged bridges in Iraq.[74] In most cases, the damage left the bridge unusable. By the time of the ceasefire, thirty-seven highway bridges and nine railroad bridges were devastated. Another nine highway bridges were severely damaged, though serviceable.[75] As shown in figure 24, roughly two-thirds of these bridges lay on the lines of communication from Baghdad to the theater. Basra, As Samawah, and An Nasiriyah suffered the largest number of damaged bridges.[76]

---

74. Figure 23 reflects data derived from various Defense Intelligence Agency assessments produced during the Gulf War. Dates correspond to the dates of the DIA documents in which damage to bridges was reported.

75. Defense Intelligence Agency, *Final BDA Status Report*, 90–91, GWAPS, NA 519.

76. Figure 24 is based on information derived from *Final BDA Status Report*, 90–98; paper, DIA/DB-8B, list of damaged Iraqi bridges, railway yards, and ferry facilities, 24 February 1991, DB-8B Desert Shield/Desert Storm Translog; large map with overlay, 28 February 1991, DIA/DB-8B; and background paper on Iraq's Logistics.

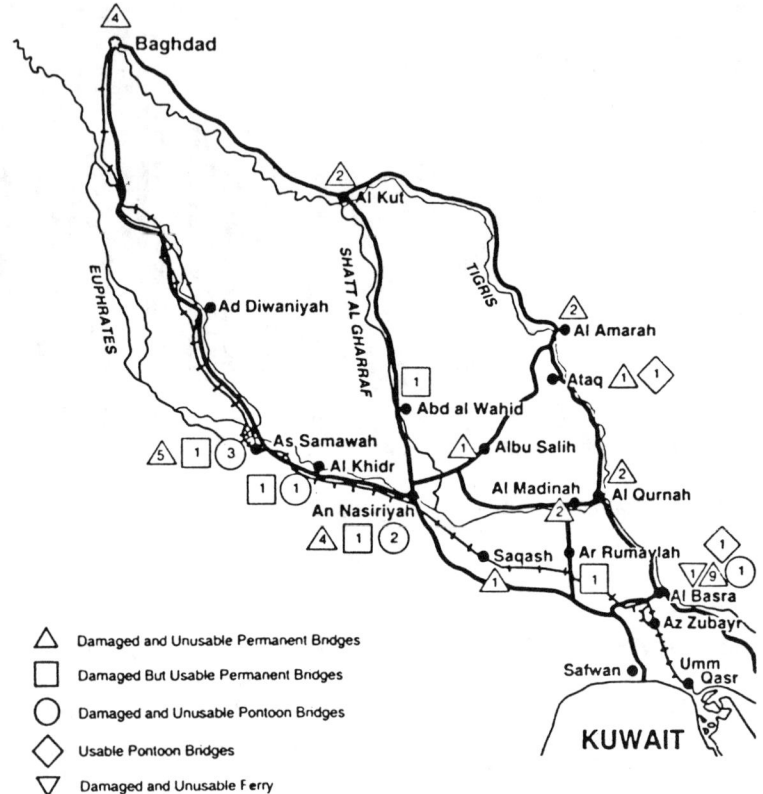

Figure 24   Status of Bridges along Routes from Baghdad to Kuwaiti Theater of Operations, 28 February 1991

Throughout the war Iraq attempted to offset the destruction of its permanent bridges by rerouting traffic, constructing temporary bridges, using amphibious ferry vehicles, and building earthen causeways. The Iraqis did not attempt to repair major structural damage to bridges, perhaps because of the brevity of the conflict and the threat of further strikes. Resupply traffic moving south used secondary routes to bypass damaged bridges, but rerouting became more laborious as bridge damage spread. The skill the Iraqis exhibited in coping with the destruction of their permanent bridges led General Horner after the war to caution: "Anybody that does a campaign against transportation systems [had] better beware! It looks deceivingly easy. It is a tough nut to crack. [The Iraqis] were very ingenious and industrious in repairing them or bypassing them. . . . I have never seen so many pontoon

What Did the Air Campaign Accomplish?

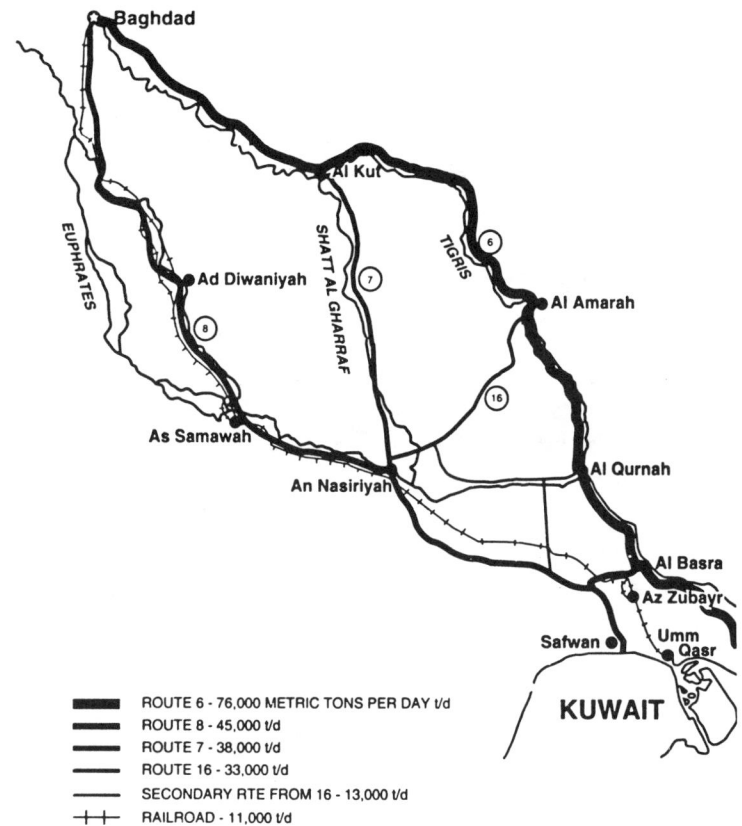

Figure 25   Prewar Route Capacities, Baghdad to Kuwaiti Theater of Operations

bridges. [When] the canals near Basra [were bombed], they just filled them in with dirt and drove across the dirt."[77]

Decreases in the capacities of individual routes to the Kuwaiti theater can be seen in figures 25 and 26.[78] Note that the thickness of each highway line (as well as the line for the railroad) is proportional to its relative capacity. By the end of the war, all but Routes 6 and 8 effectively were closed, and even those two retained only fractions of their prewar capacities.

77. Interview, Perry Jamison, Richard Davis, and Barry Barlow, Air Force History Program, with Lt. Gen. Charles A. Horner, 4 March 1992, GWAPS, NA 303, 49–50.

78. Data for the figures were derived from *Final BDA Status Report*, 93–97; and background paper on Iraq's Logistics.

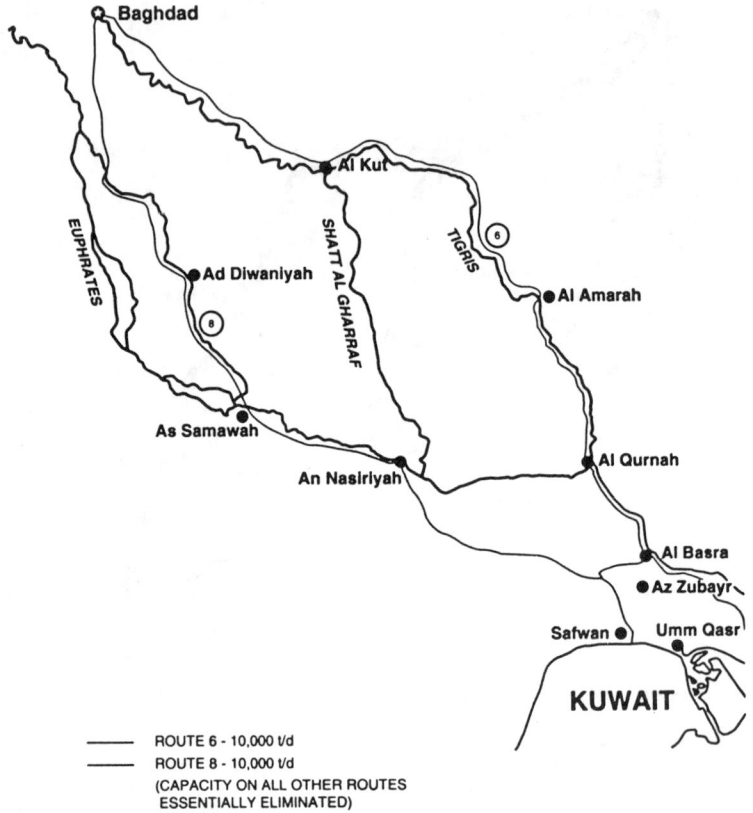

Figure 26 Route Capacities (Baghdad to Kuwaiti Theater of Operations), 28 February 1991

The capacity of the Baghdad-to-Basra rail line was entirely eliminated by the bridge damage described previously. The loss of the rail line was potentially more significant than these numbers alone would suggest, for before the air war, it was the principal means for transporting armor and self-propelled artillery from central Iraq to the Kuwaiti theater. After the line was closed, these vehicles could have used the highways, but only with great difficulty.[79]

During February, various strike aircraft (notably F-16s) flew armed reconnaissance missions along sections of the main highways leading into the Kuwaiti theater. Besides destroying trucks and their cargo, "road recce" forced the enemy to take steps that hampered resupply.

---

79. Report, Intelligence and Threat Analysis Center, U.S. Army Intelligence Agency, *Iraqi Resupply and Sustainability*, ATC-WP-1150-032-91, November 1990, 3, GWAPS, CIM Folder 46; and memo, Dimon to Distribution, 7 February 1991.

What Did the Air Campaign Accomplish?

Iraqi countermeasures to deal with the air threat led to the diminution of the supply flow. By the third week in February, resupply movements were largely restricted to the night hours, as Iraqi vehicles sought refuge in the darkness.[80] The capability of Coalition aircraft to operate at night, however, undercut the effectiveness of this standard response to air interdiction. In addition, Iraq shifted from multi-vehicle convoys to single trucks to make its supply transports less detectable and lucrative targets for Allied aircraft.[81] Yet, this change also reduced the supply tonnage reaching the theater each day.

Attacks on Iraqi stockpiles and transportation *within* the Kuwaiti theater completed the effort to cut off that theater from Iraq. Kuwait afforded few bridges or chokepoints; instead, the attacks fell on the trucks deployed with units and those making supply runs. Information from EPW (enemy prisoner of war) reports suggests that air attacks eliminated more than half the trucks in the theater. The reports indicated that most of the trucks were out of service. They had broken down for want of spare parts, were destroyed by air attacks, or lacked drivers willing to travel the roads in the theater.

The effects on the Iraqi army units, as in other cases, were mixed. Prisoner of war reports from frontline forces showed a general pattern of units low on food and water and lacking in resupply capability. At the same time, there were reports of other units having plentiful supplies of water and hot meals. Prisoners captured at Al Khafji were described as being in wretched health and malnourished but wearing new uniforms and boots; in the Republican Guard areas, on the other extreme, U.S. VII Corps soldiers found trailers of quality foods such as canned mackerel and crackers.[82]

The pattern that emerges from the evidence is not of an army facing starvation, but of an organization in which the distribution system had ceased to function: distributions appeared illogical, and goods were generally absent, hoarded, or lying unused. Air power had dismembered the Iraqi army's transportation system within the theater, and communication between army units, which might have remedied some of the supply problems, was itself under attack.

While the Coalition undertook to isolate the Iraqi army from communications with Baghdad, in-theater efforts were aimed at prevent-

---

80. Briefing, J-2 Daily BDA Assessment for Operation Desert Storm, 19/20–23/24 February 1991, GWAPS, NA 353.

81. Report, Defense Intelligence Agency, *Persian Gulf War: Trends and Outlook (19–24 February 1991)*, Defense Intelligence Memo 61-91, February 1991, 3, GWAPS, CBDA Folder 37.

82. Battlefield Reconstruction Center, Asst. Chief of Staff, G2, Headquarters, VII (U.S.) Corps, "Battlefield Reconstruction from Enemy Perspective (24–28 February 1991)," 47.

ing divisions and corps from communicating with one another, thereby preventing the theater and strategic reserves from reacting promptly to the Coalition ground attack. The communications targets proved tough to attack successfully, however. Even when they were hit, the extent of damage was difficult to assess because of successful—but costly—Iraqi countermeasures.

Prisoner of war reports describe Iraqi measures to preserve their equipment. Those measures included using messengers, prohibiting the use of radios after the start of the air attacks, and even pronouncing death sentences for those who used two-way radios or telephones. Also, the Iraqis laid extensive wire, buried throughout the theater to preserve emergency communications. Wire was strung between units, which were sometimes as far apart as fifty kilometers. Bombing cut the wire at times, but Iraqis often repaired the lines within a day.

Effective communication required more than the ability to warn another unit of attack, though; if the warned unit could not undertake some sort of coordinated action in response, the warning was of little value. Here, the system collapsed. Reports show that once the units tried to move, wire strung between units no longer sufficed, and the lack of communications became debilitating: units either tried to talk, unsuccessfully, on radios susceptible to jamming or simply did not attempt to communicate with one another.[83] Reports after the battle at Al Khafji provided examples of Iraqi units lost in the desert or unable to coordinate actions because the Coalition jammed their communications tronically.

Given the above evidence of the effects of Coalition air attacks against Iraqi supply lines both to and within the theater, what conclusions can be drawn regarding the operational effectiveness of air interdiction in Desert Storm? Strikes against key bridges on the main lines of communication between Baghdad and Basra, as well as armed reconnaissance flights along those routes, succeeded in reducing the flow of supplies to the Iraqi army, even if the air attacks did not completely sever those lines and totally isolate the theater. Because of the limited requirements of an essentially inert army, the overall capacity of the supporting transportation net, and the use of countermeasures (temporary bridges and alternate routes), Iraq was able to move sufficient supplies to the Kuwaiti theater in the weeks before the ground war, despite the air campaign—that is, enough to sustain an inert army.

Whether several more days or weeks of air interdiction operations alone would have eliminated all resupply of the theater is a matter of speculation. What is certain is that the outbreak of large-scale ground combat increased the demand for supplies (especially ammunition and

---

83. U.S. signals intelligence personnel depicted the Iraqi army as having committed "Emcon (electronic emissions control) Suicide."

What Did the Air Campaign Accomplish?

POL) to the point where the residual route capacity and daily supply flow would not have been sufficient to sustain the Iraqi army in a prolonged conflict.

Attacking the Iraqi Naval and Coastal Defense Forces

Coalition aircraft attacked Iraqi naval targets to secure freedom of action in the northern Persian Gulf. The Iraqi navy was small, but the presence of even small missile-firing boats posed a threat to Coalition battle groups and amphibious forces. Carriers and battleships carried firepower to support the ground attack, and the amphibious forces had to be in position to carry out the strategic deception plan and be ready for landings, if necessary. The targets included Iraqi ports and facilities at Basra, Az Zubayr, and Um Qasr; numerous operating locations in Kuwait and on islands; oil terminals; Silkworm missile sites along the coast (see figure 27); and a fleet of patrol boats, missile-firing boats, and minelayers. Of the total of 178 vessels in this navy, the 13 Iraqi missile boats posed the greatest threat.[84]

U.S. Navy aircraft prosecuted the attacks against the Iraqi navy, assisted by Great Britain's Royal Navy attack helicopters; other Coalition aircraft attacked the naval facilities. The aircraft carriers involved were the *Midway, Theodore Roosevelt,* and *Ranger,* with the *America* joining on 15 February. Just as in the case of targets on land, the lack of adequate bomb damage information prevented timely assessment of the damage to the Iraqi boats. Later analysis showed that all of Iraq's missile boats had been damaged or destroyed as of 2 February, except for one that escaped to Iran, but the U.S. Navy's antisurface warfare commander could not declare the threat defeated until 17 February.[85]

Even after the threat was eliminated, however, numerous maritime strikes took place on the many patrol boats that remained on Faylakah Island, Bubiyan Island, and coastal artillery positions and Silkworm missile sites. As a result of all engagements, 143 Iraqi boats were damaged or destroyed, including 12 of the 13 missile boats. On the eve of the ground attack, however, just two of the seven known Silkworm sites (five of them in Kuwait) were believed destroyed.[86]

The attacks against the Silkworm sites contained many of the same frustrations as in the attacks on Scud sites. Although intelligence identified seven Silkworm sites before the war, repeated strikes on those

---

84. Peter P. Perla, *Desert Storm Reconstruction Report, Vol. I: Summary,* and Jeffrey Lutz, et al., *Desert Storm Reconstruction Report, Vol. VI: Antisurface Warfare* (Alexandria, VA: 1991).

85. Perla, *Reconstruction Report,* 78.

86. Lutz, *Reconstruction Report,* 4-1; and viewgraph, "BDA, Tactical Systems, Naval Forces," J-2 Briefing to the President and JCS, GWAPS, NA 353.

Figure 27 Fixed-Site Iraqi Naval Targets

sites did not remove the threat. There were forty-five strikes in all, beginning at the end of January, and half of those were during the ground offensive. The fixed sites were suspected of being decoys: an increasing number of strikes were not made against the identified sites but against suspected sites in adjacent areas.[87] Only two launches of Silk-

---

87. Lutz, *Reconstruction Report*, 5-6 to 5-8.

What Did the Air Campaign Accomplish?

worm missiles were recorded during the war, from a site south of Kuwait City on 25 February; the missiles were fired probably just before the site's capture: one of the missiles apparently crashed into the sea immediately, and the other was shot down by a missile fired from HMS *Gloucester*.[88]

Just as for anti-Scud operations, one cannot judge to what extent the attacks suppressed launches. The Iraqis may have retained the missiles for use solely in the event of an amphibious landing, or they may simply have lacked sufficient targeting data to attack Coalition ships.

Attrition of Iraqi Ground Forces

Air campaign planners aimed to decrease the combat effectiveness of the Iraqi army by 50 percent. The quantitative measure of that attrition was destruction of Iraqi armor and artillery to that level throughout the theater. But a variety of factors came into play. The factors included a more extensive target set to attack than simply armor and artillery, fewer sorties than planned, poorer bombing accuracy from aircraft operating from higher release altitudes, and worse-than-planned weather. Perhaps the greatest change from the plan entailed the munitions employed. Prewar planning computed attrition by relying heavily on the use of air-to-surface missiles—Mavericks—by several types of aircraft (F-16s, A-10s, and AV-8Bs) and a variety of special munitions.[89] As table 3 shows, a significant number of Mavericks were fired, but almost exclusively by A-10s (5,013 of the 5,296 employed by the Air Force). Pilots also used some antiarmor munitions (CBU-89 and GATOR), but not nearly as many as general-purpose bombs.

Air strikes targeted against Iraqi ground forces started on the first day of the air campaign and continued with increasing intensity throughout the war, apart from daily variations based on weather in the region. Air strikes against Republican Guard divisions and other Iraqi heavy divisions in central Kuwait reached their highest daily totals in the first two weeks of February. Daily totals for air strikes against Iraqi frontline divisions peaked just prior to the ground attack on 24 February. Figure 28 displays wartime totals for air strikes against each of the principal kill boxes. Note that the highest totals are for those kill boxes containing the heavy divisions of the Republican Guard and other nearby heavy divisions in central Kuwait (AF7, AE6, and AF6).

Several adjustments in tactics and munitions took place before Iraqi

88. Robert W. Ward, et al., *Desert Storm Reconstruction Report, Vol. VIII: C3/Space and Electronic Warfare* (Alexandria, VA: Center for Naval Analyses, 1992), 4-6 to 4-10.

89. In addition to Mavericks, CBU-89 (Gator) and 30-mm cannons were planned for use against armor; and CBU-52 (fragmentation bomb) and MK-20 (Rockeye) were planned against artillery. Viewgraph, CENTAF/CC Briefing to the SECDEF, 20 December 1990, in "General Glosson's Brief," GWAPS, Box 3-60.

Table 3 Listing of Selected Munitions Employed in Desert Storm,*
17 January–28 February 1991

Munitions	Expended			Total
	Air Force	Navy	Marine Corps	
General-Purpose Bombs				
Mk-82 (500 lb)	59,884	10,941	6,828	77,653
Mk-83 (1,000 lb)		10,125	8,893	19,081
Mk-84 (2,000 lb)	10,467	971	751	12,289
Mk-117 (B-52)	43,435			43,435
CBU-52 (fragmentation bomb)	17,831			17,831
CBU-87 (combined effects munition)	10,035			10,035
CBU-89/78 (Gator)	1,105	148	61	1,314
Mk-20 (Rockeye)	5,345	6,814	15,828	27,987
Laser-Guided Bombs				
GBU-12 (laser/Mk-82)	4,086	205	202	4,493
Air-to-Surface Missiles				
**AGM-114 Hellfire (AH-64 and AH-1W)	Army = 2,876	30	159	3,065
AGM-65 All Models (Maverick)	5,255		41	5,296

*The selected munitions were those most often employed in the Kuwaiti theater. Other types of laser-guided bombs and air-to-surface missiles were used in the war, but not, principally, in the Kuwaiti theater. Totals given are those employed on all targets, however, not just those in the Kuwaiti theater. See cited tables for a listing and totals of all weapons expended during the war.

**The Navy and Marine Corps also fired a total of 283 BGM-71 TOW munitions from helicopters.

Source: Table derived from GWAPS *Statistical Compendium*, Tables 188, 189, 190, and 191 (these tables also appear in appendix 2); also Briefing, HQ DA, ODCOPS, "Aviation Division, Apache in Desert Storm," nd, enclosed in a folder, Army Aviation in Desert Shield/Storm (U.S. Army Aviation Center, FTR, AL: 1992), GWAPS, NA 337.

equipment attrition began to rise at a satisfactory rate. Those adjustments included an increased number of sorties to the Kuwaiti theater,[90] CENTAF's direction that the F-16s and A-10s lower attack and release altitudes, and increased proficiency of the crews as they gained experience. A sharp increase in the destruction of Iraqi equipment also occurred at the end of January during the battle of Al Khafji, when the

---

90. Text of CENTCOM briefing, 26 January 1991, GWAPS, CHST 28; and General Horner Comments, 26 January 1991, GWAPS, CHP 13-B.

What Did the Air Campaign Accomplish?

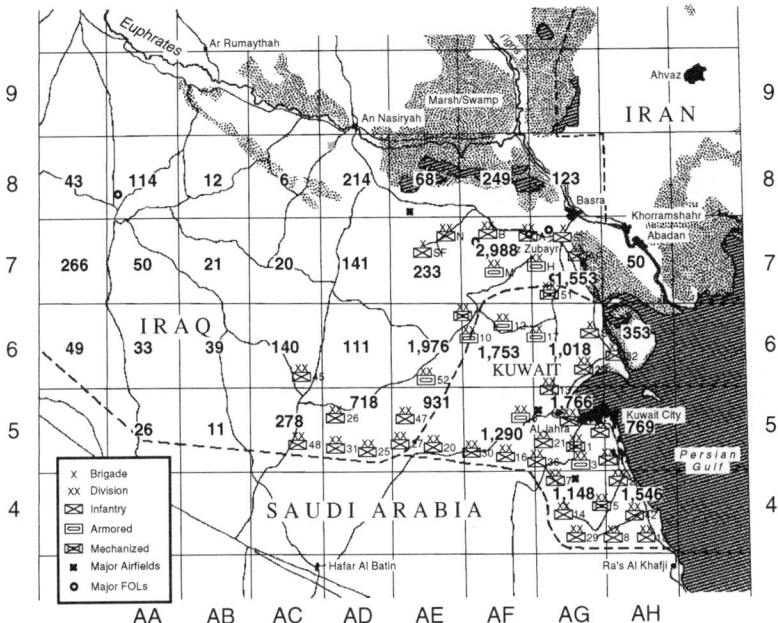

Figure 28 Strikes Targeted by Kill Box, 17 January–28 February 1991

Iraqi armored vehicles left their revetments and moved on roads.[91] By far, though, the greatest impact on Iraqi equipment attrition was rendered by employing laser-guided bombs on Iraqi armor, beginning on 6 February and continuing for the duration of the war. These changes increased the rate of Iraqi armor and artillery attrition, but the 50 percent goal for the Kuwaiti theater was not attained in the theater as a whole before the ground war began.

The amount of equipment attrition suffered by the Iraqi army before the ground war was a highly contentious issue at the time, and postwar reconstructions can only partially update these wartime estimates. On the eve of the ground war, Central Command estimated that there had been 39 percent attrition of Iraqi tanks, 32 percent of armored personnel carriers, and 47 percent of artillery.[92]

At the same time, the Central Intelligence and Defense Intelligence Agencies held to far lower estimates, differences that caused controversy between the theater and Washington.[93] By that time, however, General Schwarzkopf and his staff had rethought the practice of tying

---

91. This battle is discussed later in the chapter.

92. USCINCCENT Situation Report, dated 23 February 1991, GWAPS, CSS 29.

93. See chapter 4 for a discussion of these differences.

Iraqi unit effectiveness directly to equipment attrition. General Schwarzkopf refused to allow briefings that focused on specific percentages of equipment attrition, opting instead for a more subjective assessment of Iraqi unit capability, with equipment attrition as only one of the variables. According to this system, on the eve of the ground war CENTCOM estimated the frontline Iraqi divisions to be below 50 percent effectiveness and the rear divisions, in general, at approximately 75 percent effectiveness.[94]

Since the war, several sources of additional information have become available: photography of the *entire* theater at the beginning and the end of the campaign (15 January and 1 March 1991); photography of *portions* of the theater during the air war; *partial* battlefield studies of Iraqi equipment; and reports on individual divisions from Iraqi prisoners of war.[95] These sources permit the following general assessments:

- The Iraqi army had approximately eight hundred fewer tanks and six hundred fewer artillery pieces at the beginning of the air war than originally thought (that is, approximately 20 percent fewer).

- Prior to the ground war, the Republican Guard heavy divisions[96] had suffered an approximate 24 percent armor attrition, at a time when CENTCOM estimated a 34 percent attrition.

- Enemy prisoner-of-war reports indicate great variations in unit armor attrition during the air war, from 10 percent for an armored division in the middle of the theater (12th Armored) to nearly 100 percent for divisions close to the front lines (52d Armored, 25th, 30th, and 48th Infantry Divisions). Prisoners citing less attrition usually attributed the differences to protective berms, since those same units suffered substantially higher attrition of trucks that were not so protected.

- By the end of the war the Iraqi army had suffered an approximate 76 percent attrition in tanks, 55 percent in armored per-

---

94. *Conduct of the Persian Gulf War*, 256.

95. Directorate of Intelligence, Central Intelligence Agency, "Operation Desert Storm: A Snapshot of the Battlefield," Report IA 93-10022, September 1993. See tabular data from this report in appendix 5. Memo, Lt. Col. Allan W. Howey, USAF, subject: Tank Kills in the KTO, 26 February 1992, GWAPS, NA 167; memo and viewgraphs, Foreign Science and Technology Center, "Joint Intelligence Survey Team Report," 14 January 1992, GWAPS, NA 167; and U.S. Marine Corps Research Center, "Armor/Antiarmor Operations in Southwest Asia," Research Paper #92-0002, USMC, Quantico, Virginia, July 1991.

96. A heavy division being an armored or mechanized division. The Republican Guard had a total of three in the theater: the Tawakalna (mechanized), Madinah, and Hammurabi (both armored).

What Did the Air Campaign Accomplish?

sonnel carriers, and 90 percent in artillery. The Republican Guard heavy divisions had suffered an attrition rate of about 50 percent in these same categories.

- Battlefield study groups have had access to only a total of 163 tanks (6 percent of the 2,633 that had been destroyed or abandoned). Of this sample, between 10 and 20 percent had been hit by air-delivered munitions and about half (78 of 163) were not hit by munitions at all.

The data support several conclusions. First, CENTCOM's initial counts of equipment destroyed were inflated, but so too was the target base, and the errors offset one another. In other words, CENTCOM's *percentages* of equipment destroyed by the beginning of the ground war were in line with later observations, though the *numbers* of pieces destroyed were inflated. Second, equipment attrition did not occur evenly throughout the theater but varied from high attrition to lower attrition by division, moving south to north and from west to east in the theater. Highest attrition took place in the western frontline divisions; lowest in the divisions in the northeast corner of the theater.[97]

A related issue to Iraqi attrition of equipment is the Iraqis' loss of personnel during the air war. CENTCOM produced no estimates of Iraqi personnel losses during or after the war, nor did the 1991 Department of Defense *Conduct of the Persian Gulf War.* Iraq itself has given estimates on number of Iraqi noncombatants killed but has not addressed its military losses. Prisoner reports that addressed the number of soldiers in each unit that were killed, wounded, or had deserted during the air war enable some estimates of the size of the Iraqi army in the theater at the beginning of the ground war. Starting from a figure of 336,000, the estimated personnel manning the Iraqi army at the beginning of the air war as described in chapter 1, the Iraqi army saw desertions of 25–30 percent. In addition, that army suffered a smaller number of casualties to the air attacks—probably less than 10 percent of the force. As a result, the remaining strength of the Iraqi army by 24 February numbered approximately 200,000 to 222,000.

The air interdiction, the damage to the communications and supply systems, along with the equipment attrition during the air war, clearly affected the Iraqi soldiers beyond the inflicting of casualties during that period. The Iraqi soldier, by and large, lost his determination to fight. The Iraqis did not defect or surrender in droves during the air and ground war because their armor and artillery were being destroyed (in fact, statements by Iraqi prisoners of war indicate they appreciated the discrimination of the air forces in aiming at the equipment and not

---

97. Lower equipment attrition in the east would coincide with the far lower rate of employment of precision munitions by the Marine Corps and Navy aircraft used in that area.

them) but because many were short of food and water. The true effects of these attacks, in other words, came not from specific targets destroyed but from the combination of targets attacked and the intensity with which those attacks took place.

The pervasive impression left by the interrogation reports of prisoners was the sense of futility felt by the Iraqis after weeks of extensive bombing.[98] When the bombing started, their ground transportation began to crumble. Many, particularly the frontline forces, ran short of water, food, fuel, and all spare parts. Some units had their supply stocks destroyed. Training in the units ceased. Soldiers moved apart from their equipment because they well understood what the targets were. Many captured Iraqis stated that they thought the air campaign would last several days to a week at most. When it did not end, the sense of futility and inevitability of the outcome became more apparent. Some frontline soldiers decided not to fight, others deserted, and still others remained in place; but the effect on the capability of the Iraqi units was the same. The deserters from the frontline divisions told their interrogators that most of those remaining in their units would surrender at the first opportunity without any resistance. That is exactly what happened.

The ground offensive ended quickly, but units qualified to fight and willing to resist may well have remained. Few of those units were in the front lines, however. When the soldiers and officers in these frontline units decided not to resist, any opportunity for an organized defense in the theater collapsed. The Iraqi strategy called for the operational and strategic reserves to move to resist the points of the Coalition ground attack, but these reserve forces were fooled not only by the direction of the attack but also by how fast it was upon them. The utter collapse of the Iraqi front lines made any planned movements by the reserves irrelevant. The reserve forces were themselves under attack before they had a chance to maneuver or present an organized defense.

Air Power with Engaged Ground Forces

The effectiveness of air power in supporting engaged ground forces during Desert Storm is particularly challenging to assess because the support took place only during the one-hundred-hour ground war and briefly during the Iraqi incursion into the Saudi town of Al Khafji. The brief time involved and the conditions under which the engagements took place—against thoroughly demoralized Iraqi troops, many in full flight or surrendering even before being engaged—make any generalizations based on these circumstances questionable. Moreover, the

---

98. The following paragraphs draw on multiple prisoner-of-war reports.

What Did the Air Campaign Accomplish?

speed of the ground action added to the complexity of making a precise accounting of specific actions that took place. After the war, no theater-wide survey was undertaken, although various organizations attempted reconstructions of some of the battlefield engagements.

Even the limited data make clear, nevertheless, that Iraqi forces were significantly more vulnerable on the move, day or night, than they were dug in and surrounded by air defenses. The JSTARS aircraft, a test aircraft brought to the theater just before the air war, proved enormously capable of identifying the path of attacking or retreating columns of Iraqi equipment and provided both battlefield intelligence and targeting information. Moreover, vehicles out of revetments and on the move were vulnerable to more weapons, such as aircraft cannon fire and air-delivered mines. It is not surprising, then, that the success of attacks on moving columns of armor was substantially greater than those attacks on similar forces protected by berms, camouflage, and other defensive and deceptive measures.

From 29 through 31 January—the time of the Al Khafji battle—Iraqi ground movements were a subject of much conjecture. While Iraqi forces were detected moving south in eastern Kuwait, CENTCOM suspected that the move was a feint for a larger maneuver farther to the west, at the tri-border area, by perhaps the Republican Guard divisions.[99] This suspicion was helped along by pilot reports indicating that the Tawakalna Division had moved from its previous position (and was unlocated) and that the Madinah Division was observed moving south.[100] In this situation, the JSTARS capabilities took on tremendous value, to both evaluate the amount and nature of movement throughout the theater and track the specific movements of Iraqi forces in southeast Kuwait.

All indications are that the air attacks on the Iraqi army during the Al Khafji incursion had a devastating effect. Iraqi equipment attrition as recorded by CENTCOM increased fourfold for the period 29 January to 3 February over what it had been for the entire air campaign up to that point. Even allowing for overcounting of the losses, the impact on the Iraqis was tremendous. While a number of prisoner-of-war reports mention the effects, the most telling one was the comment by a veteran of the Iran-Iraq War, who remarked that his brigade underwent more damage in thirty minutes than it had in eight years in the previous war.

---

99. TACC Log, intelligence briefing on 28 and 29 January 1991, and a notation of a telephone call from the CENTCOM J-3, Major General Moore, warning that the Al Khafji attack may have been a feint. GWAPS, microfilm roll 10263.

100. CENTAF Historian Notes of TACC Operations, 29–31 January 1991, GWAPS, NA 200.

Subsequent to the experience at Al Khafji, the Iraqi army attempted no other attacks. They constructed more berms, dug deeper, dispersed supplies, changed to the use of smaller convoys in the Kuwaiti theater, moved headquarters locations frequently, and increased the use of decoys in many areas.[101] Perhaps the greatest theater-wide impact of Al Khafji was its effect on the Iraqi army commanders. Their forces dug in to survive, but they had realized that counterattack or withdrawal "was impossible under the gun of the furious Coalition attacks." The Iraqis discarded their plans for major operations in the Kuwaiti theater as a result of this experience. Al Khafji was a major effort by Iraq to begin a ground war, the only such attempt Iraq made—hence, the importance of its failure. Iraq's sole hope was to force an early start to a ground war of attrition before it was itself exhausted. At Al Khafji, air power had gained an important victory not fully appreciated at the time.

The lack of determined Iraqi resistance during the ground offensive made close air support by aircraft a peripheral aspect of this war. All the frontline Iraqi divisions crumbled quickly, often with no resistance at all, and as the corps advanced, they reported light resistance throughout the theater. With the exception of isolated instances of determined resistance, possibly two in the Marines' area of operations and several more in clashes by U.S. Army forces with units of the Republican Guards, rarely was the opposition not handled easily by Army or Marine Corps ground weapons alone.[102] In other words, few situations presented themselves of "troops in contact" to test how well close air support by U.S. fixed-wing aircraft or attack helicopters could be synchronized with ground fire-support systems.

As early as the first morning, forward air controllers turned aircraft back to the TACC as unnecessary, and many aircraft returned with their ordnance because they could not be employed anywhere else. The primary close air support aircraft, A-10s and AV-8Bs, saw much less action than planned: A-10s reported 316 of 909 sorties (35 percent) ineffective (that is, they did not drop their bombs), and AV-8Bs had more total missions canceled or with no drops (143) than they had successful missions (131).[103] Even some of the B-52 sorties sched-

---

101. USCINCCENT/J2 Message, Collateral Intelligence Report No. 180, 6 February 1991, GWAPS, CHST 42.

102. A possible exception would be the employment of aircraft (F-16s in one case, A-10s in another) to assist in the protection and extraction of special forces personnel operating behind enemy lines.

103. *Marine Corps Reconstruction Report, Vol. IV,* 77; and Combat Chronology 23/354 TFW(P), entries for 24–28 February 1991, GWAPS, Microfilm Roll 26557. A-10 data are for all sorties; only partial data are available for close air support sorties, but those data indicate the unsuccessful rate was even higher for these sorties.

uled for bombing the breach sites were redirected in flight to other targets because the ground advance had already passed beyond the sites.[104]

Close air support assisted the ground attack but was not considered vital to the attack's success. Because of the nature of the enemy resistance, or the lack of it, pilots flying close air support sorties seldom had to drop munitions close to Coalition ground forces to stop an Iraqi attack. The aircraft employed were capable of much more than was requested of them, but Coalition artillery and rocket launchers, the superior range of Coalition tank guns and other direct fire weapons, and the tremendous advantage of thermal imaging sights that allowed M1A1 tanks to engage Iraqi tanks at ranges nearly double the maximum acquisition range of the Iraqis, allowed the Coalition ground forces to handle those few instances of resistance without substantial assistance from the air. Air power's greater effectiveness was in attacking the forces deeper in the Iraqi defense areas, in the regions where these attacks blended in with the interdiction strikes.

During the ground offensive, Coalition helicopter operations provided great mobility and airborne firepower. Although Army AH-64 Apaches helped destroy Iraqi air defense installations on the first night of the air campaign, only a limited number of helicopters were employed in cross-border attacks before large-scale ground operations began in order to preserve those aircraft for use with the advancing ground forces. Once the ground advance began, helicopters moved logistics support rapidly and repositioned the ground forces themselves. On the first day of the ground offensive, helicopters of the U.S. 101st Airborne Division conducted the largest heliborne operation ever staged by moving a brigade of the 101st to a base ninety-three miles into Iraq and then reaching that far again to cut Highway 8, the Iraqi army's only possible line of retreat west from the theater.[105]

Coalition attack helicopters saw action both in direct support of the attacking Coalition ground forces and in conducting independent, deep attacks behind Iraqi frontline forces, the latter attacks, conducted principally by helicopter units of the XVIII Corps.[106] In several instances, because of low ceilings due to weather, blowing sand, or oil well fires,

---

104. History of the Strategic Air Command, 1 January–31 December 1990, Vol. I (Headquarters, SAC History Office, 1992), 273.

105. *Conduct of the Persian Gulf War*, 261–62.

106. Attack helicopters employed were the Army's AH-64, the Marine Corps' AH-1W, the French Army's Gazelle, and the British Army's Lynx. The Kuwaiti air force also possessed Gazelles, but they were not employed as attack aircraft during Desert Storm. The U.S. Army had AH-1s deployed to the theater, but there is no record of their employment as attack helicopters.

only helicopters could operate successfully. Several deep operations (fifty miles or more) by the AH-64s that accounted for significant destruction of Iraqi equipment took place in the final two days of the war.[107]

A limitation for these deep sweeps proved to be the logistics and planning required to support operations, particularly with the ground forces moving so swiftly. As a result, the first such deep raid did not take place until late on 26 February, with three more multi-battalion attacks taking place during the day and evening of 27 February. The largest raid on that day was conducted by AH-64s on the causeway crossing the Hawr al Hammar, the large lake and marshlands northwest of Basra. (This key exit route from the theater will be discussed later.) During that raid, the Apaches disabled many vehicles caught in the congestion waiting to cross the causeway.[108]

Air interdiction operations during the ground offensive were conducted in two phases. During the first phase, from the initiation of the offensive to the evening of 25 February, aircraft attacked the reserve heavy divisions (and the other Republican Guard divisions as well) in order to destroy their capability to move or maneuver against the Coalition ground forces. The second phase began after intelligence information indicated (and airborne aircraft had confirmed) that a general retreat of Iraqi forces was under way (evening of 25 February). From that time until the cease-fire at 8:00 A.M. local time on 28 February, the focus of air interdiction became one of pursuing and destroying the retreating army.[109]

For the first two days of the ground offensive, air interdiction strikes took place on Iraqi troop concentrations and equipment just beyond the fire support coordination line (the line defining an area on the ground, the close-in battle area, within which air attacks require the approval and coordination of the ground commander). Other aircraft prowled the deeper areas of the theater, often at night, receiving cues from JSTARS aircraft or control/scout aircraft (F-16 Pointer or F/A-18D) to attack any movement of forces. After the general retreat of the Iraqi forces on the evening of 25 February, the interdiction sorties

---

107. Headquarters DA, ODCOPS, Aviation Division, "Apache in Desert Storm," nd, enclosed in a folder, *Army Aviation in Desert Shield/Desert Storm* (U.S. Army Aviation Center, Fort Rucker, AL, 1992), GWAPS, NS 337, 34; and *Marine Corps Desert Storm Reconstruction Report*, Vol. IV, 113.

108. *Army Aviation*, 86–108; "Apache in Desert Storm"; and 8th Air Support Operations Group After Action Review, Operations Desert Shield/Storm, nd, GWAPS, NA 577.

109. No phases were either planned or announced, of course. The term phases is used simply to describe the unfolding events. Word of the general withdrawal came from Iraqi army radio intercepts, communications from the Kuwaiti resistance in Kuwait City, and aircraft in the region. TACC Log, entries of 25 February 1991, GWAPS, NA 215.

What Did the Air Campaign Accomplish?

bore down on the retreating columns of Iraqi forces flowing north in trucks, cars, boats, and any other means available to depart the country. The units in the northern part of the theater had the best chance of escaping intact. The retreating forces that followed them, however, slowed and then stopped at points where many units converged at bridges or roadway chokepoints.

Mutla Ridge, the high ground to the west of Kuwait City and just north of the city of Al Jahra, was the first place air strikes stopped the retreating columns. The major road to Basra passing over the bluffs of the ridge became a natural chokepoint for the traffic retreating from throughout southeast Kuwait. This traffic became combined with that fleeing Kuwait City (see figure 29). Once air attacks halted the forward elements of this traffic, the remaining several miles of vehicles were attacked throughout the evening, leaving a scene of abandoned and burning vehicles approximately two miles long. The news media identified this scene as the highway of death in the immediate aftermath of the war.[110]

A count of destroyed vehicles, made from photos taken on 1 March, put the number at more than fourteen hundred, which included only fourteen tanks and fourteen other armored vehicles. Reporters found somewhere between two- and three-hundred dead Iraqis at the scene; the other occupants presumably either escaped north or became prisoners.

A second chokepoint for the retreating Iraqi forces occurred at the causeway over the Hawr al Hammar. The multilane causeway had been bombed and repaired several times during the war and could sustain only limited traffic. Aircraft, principally F-111Fs, destroyed enough vehicles to block the traffic on the evening of 26 February, and aircraft strikes continued the following day, most notably a deep attack by AH-64s. Aerial photography two days later showed approximately 550 to 600 vehicles abandoned at the location; as at Mutla Ridge, just 10 to 20 of these were armored vehicles.[111]

The final chokepoint for traffic out of the Kuwaiti theater was at the city of Basra. Here, in the final day of the war, with Coalition ground forces moving in from the west and cutting off all escape in that direction, the fleeing Iraqi forces attempted to get through the city and its canals and across the river to the east, the last remaining exit. With all bridges over the canal and river either damaged or destroyed, traffic stopped at the canal on the western side of the city. The backup stretched approximately twenty miles to the west. Into this congestion,

---

110. Steve Coll and William Branigan, "U.S. Scrambled to Shape View of 'Highway of Death,'" *The Washington Post*, 11 March 1991, 1.

111. *Army Aviation*, 86–108; GWAPS Missions Database, sorties of 26/27 February 1991; and briefing, CIA-OIA to GWAPS, 25 June 1992.

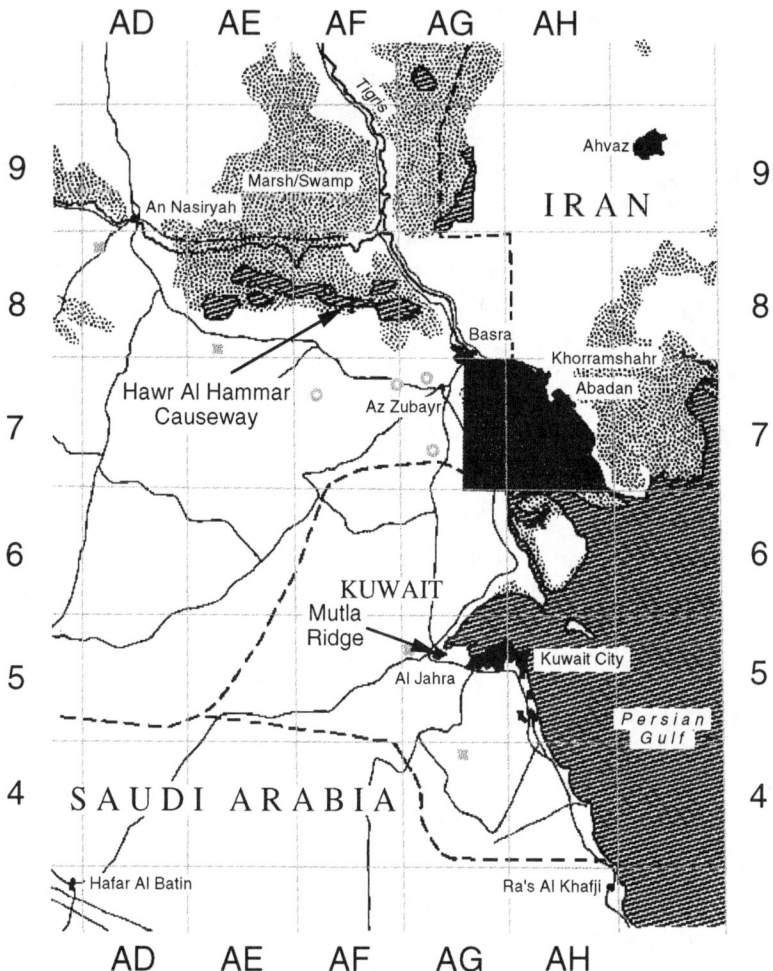

Figure 29 Chokepoints for Retreating Iraqi Troops in the Kuwaiti Theater
Note: Shaded area depicts no-strike areas declared on 27 February.

the remnant of the Iraqi army, including the remaining Republican Guard divisions, had retreated.

No scenes of destruction such as seen at Mutla Ridge or the Hawr al Hammar took place in Basra or at the canal, however, because of conditions that affected the bombing. First, the area west of Basra was not open desert but a more built-up area of farms and small towns. Iraqi tanks and other military vehicles took advantage of this situation by parking on neighborhood streets and generally mixing in with civil-

What Did the Air Campaign Accomplish?

ian buildings in the area.[112] Second, the low weather ceiling in that area, the proximity of the Coalition ground forces on 27 February, and the closeness of the target area to Iranian territory all restricted bombing operations.[113]

Air power had two important effects on the Iraqi army during the four days of the ground war: one imposed during those four final days, the other imposed during the preceding weeks of the campaign. Air strikes during the air war had made the Iraqi forces in some cases unwilling and in other cases unable to maneuver or mount an effective defense. Lack of communications, equipment attrition, and destruction of the theater distribution system had combined to bring about these conditions. The rout of maneuvering Iraqi forces during the engagement at Al Khafji gave those forces a preview of what was in store. During the ground war, concentrated attacks on the Iraqi heavy divisions prevented them from playing any role other than self-defense, and several of these divisions did not even do that. In some instances involving frontline Iraqi divisions, air power had merely to show up to prompt the forces to surrender.[114]

Estimates of air power's worth during the ground war must look beyond the last four days themselves. The most important contribution of air power in the Kuwaiti theater during the ground war, and a prime reason why the ground campaign was so short and so overwhelming, was the success of air interdiction in preventing the heavy divisions from moving or fighting effectively. In other words, the interdiction sorties after 23 February were just a continuation of the campaign that began on 17 January.

Nor were the interdiction sorties dissimilar from the close air support sorties flown; interdiction and close air support sorties often occurred just a few miles apart. What the events on the ground made clear is that air power essentially paralyzed or demoralized the Iraqi heavy divisions on which the Iraqi strategy depended. The remnants of some divisions were destroyed in place or surrendered with little resistance; others fled the theater without much of their equipment, while those farther to the rear were able to make a more orderly departure. Those left with a will to fight were able to do little more than

---

112. Briefing, CIA-OIA to GWAPS, 25 June 1992.

113. CENTAF Historian, "TSgt Barton's Notes from TACC," 25/1020 February 1991, GWAPS, NA 200; TACC Log, entries of 27 February 1991, GWAPS, NA 215; and Airborne Battlefield Command and Control Center LOG, entries of 27 February 1992, GWAPS, NA 287.

114. "Soon as air showed up, Iraqis started surrendering." TACC Log entry for 25 February, recording comments passed by members of 1st Infantry Division, GWAPS, microfilm roll 10263.

Table 4 Operational-Strategic Summary

Target Sets*	Desired/Planned Effects	Actual Results
IADS (SAD) & Airfields (A)	Early air superiority • Suppression medium-high air defenses throughout Iraq • Contain/destroy Iraqi AF	IADS blinded/ intimidated/ suppressed • Low-altitude AAA, IR SAMs remained Iraqi AF bottled up on bases • 2 air-to-surface Iraqi shooter sorties? 375 of 594 HABs destroyed/ damaged • Iraqi AF flees to Iran (starting 25 Jan 91)
Naval (N)	Attain sea control • Permit naval operations in northern Persian Gulf	All Iraqi naval combatants sunk/neutralized • Other vessels sunk Silkworms remained active throughout war
Leadership (L) & Telecomms/C3 (CCC)	Pressure/disrupt governmental functioning Isolate Saddam from Iraqi people, forces in KTO	Unknown degree of disruption • Neither decapitation nor Saddam's overthrow Telecomms substantially reduced • Links to KTO never completely cut • International communications cut
Electricity (E) & Oil (O)	Shut down national grid • Minimize long-term damage Cut flow of fuels/ lubricants to Iraqi forces • No lasting damage to oil production	Rapid shutdown of grid • Down 55% by 17 Jan, 88% by 9 Feb • Lights out in Baghdad Some unintended damage to generators Refining capability down 93% (Day 34) Destroyed about 20% of the fuel/ lubricants at refineries & major depots • 43 day war precluded long-term effects

face the attack and return fire, with no hope of maneuvering or being reinforced or achieving even tactical success. The engagements of the Marines with elements of the Iraqi 3d Armored Division at Kuwait International Airport on 26 February and of VII Corps with elements of the Tawakalna, 12th, and Madinah Divisions on 26 and 27 February were just such desperate actions.

What Did the Air Campaign Accomplish? 103

Table 4 (continued)

Target Sets*	Desired/Planned Effects	Actual Results
NBC (C) &	Destroy chem/bio weapons • Prevent use against Coalition • Destroy production capability Destroy nuclear program • Long term	Some chemical weapons destroyed • But most survived (UN Special Comm) • Chemical use deterred • No biological weapons found (UN) Nuclear program "inconvenienced" (UN) • Most program elements survived
SCUDs (SC)	Prevent/suppress use • Destroy production & infrastructure • Keep Israel out of the war	Firings somewhat suppressed, not salvos • SCUD operations pressured • Aircraft destroyed few, if any, MELs/TELs
Railroads/ Bridges (RR)	Cut supply lines to KTO • Prevent retreat of Iraqi forces	All important bridges destroyed • Many Iraqi workarounds Short duration of war limited effects
Republican Guard (RG) & Other Ground Forces in the KTO	Destroy the RG Reduce combat effectiveness 50% (armor, artillery) by G-Day	RG immobilized • Attrition by G-Day <50% • Some RG units and 800+ tanks escape Front-line forces waiting to surrender or destroyed in place • Attrition by G-Day >50% • Morale destroyed by air

*Military support (MS), Breaching targets (BR), and KTO SAMs are subsumed in the target categories shown.

Ironically, the loss of equipment, a key index of bomb damage assessment used during the war, was not decisive in any direct way. The Iraqi army did not run out of tanks, armored personnel carriers, or artillery; in fact, much of the equipment remaining intact at the start of the ground offensive was abandoned, or was at least unoccupied, when the Coalition ground forces reached it. Reports of AH-64 strikes describing the attacks on armor columns noted that when firing began on the first tank, the crews of the other tanks began abandoning their vehicles.[115] The total number and operability of the tanks had less meaning under those conditions.

Air power had destroyed not only large amounts of equipment, it had also destroyed the confidence of the Iraqi soldiers that the equipment

115. Comment by the XVIII Airborne Corps Aviation Officer, *Army Aviation*, 153.

would do them any good. On the contrary, the equipment was seen as a magnet for air strikes. Whether the Iraqi troops could have held on and for how long, even without a ground attack, are matters for speculation. The demonstrable fact is that the Iraqis simply could not react once the ground attack took place and Coalition forces swept through the theater. One can only guess at possible differences in Iraqi resistance if the Coalition ground forces had had less air support or had there been a shorter air campaign. Certainly, though, air power made that resistance disorganized and totally ineffective.

Summary

Table 4 lists the Iraqi target sets and conclusions, in abbreviated form, reached by the Survey regarding the operational-strategic effectiveness of Coalition air power. For brevity, the table omits much, and the reader should not overlook the subtleties and reinforcing aspects of the air campaign that such condensations inevitably submerge. Although some of the results in the summary table contain quantitative data, the numbers are intertwined with qualitative judgments providing a needed context. As noted throughout this chapter, there are few cases in which quantitative measures alone were sufficient to tell more than a part of the broader operational-strategic story.

Four | What Was the Role of Intelligence?

Few issues from the Gulf War remain more controversial than the performance of American intelligence organizations. Participants have both damned and praised intelligence support of the war effort. In postwar testimony before Congress, for example, General Schwarzkopf stated that while the "intelligence community as a whole did a great job," he felt that he, as a theater commander, was not well served.[1] His specific criticisms were chiefly that one, national intelligence estimates were so heavily qualified as to be "useless" to him in the field and, two, bomb damage assessments done in Washington varied from those done in theater.[2] Paradoxically, he wrote at the same time, "I was blessed with an intelligence staff whose work was so good that the military intelligence community in Washington usually let Central Command take the lead, seconding our assessments of developments in the Middle East."[3]

Part of the difficulty in judging the adequacy of intelligence during Operations Desert Shield and Desert Storm lies in the range and complexity of functions intelligence covers. Another part undoubtedly stems from the uncertainties endemic to intelligence functions such as targeting and bomb damage assessment—uncertainties that are ultimately inherent in any use of military force to achieve political ends. This discussion surveys the various intelligence requirements in the Gulf War and how well they were satisfied; the accuracy and timeliness of information; the variety of purposes served by intelligence and intelligence organizations at various levels; the relations between producers and consumers of intelligence; and the expectations, realistic or otherwise, that commanders and staffs had of intelligence.

---

1. U.S. Congress, House Committee on Appropriations, *Department of Defense Appropriations for 1992*, Hearings before the Subcommittee on the Department of Defense (Washington: Government Printing Office, 1991), Part 2, 288 and 290.

2. Michael Wines, "Gulf Intelligence Draws Complaint by Schwarzkopf," *The New York Times International*, 13 June 1991, A-1 and A-7.

3. Gen. H. Norman Schwarzkopf, *It Doesn't Take a Hero*, written with Peter Petre (New York: Bantam Books, 1992), 293, 430–32, hereafter cited as *Hero*.

Dealing with the role of intelligence in an unclassified format so soon after the events themselves placed limits on what could be discussed here. Many details could not be mentioned, and major pieces of the story such as the roles played by human and signals intelligence in the Gulf War had to be omitted entirely. This chapter should be read with those constraints in mind. At most, it represents a start in understanding the capacities and functions of intelligence in the war.

Estimates

Estimates of Iraq's military capabilities and intentions were not central concerns of the United States until the spring of 1990. U.S. intelligence was just beginning to shift its resources from a focus on the Soviet Union. Moreover, a 1989 national intelligence estimate had conjectured that Iraq was not likely to invade Kuwait. In the fall of that year CENTCOM had begun to orient its regional planning on Iraq, but information on Iraq's military forces, installations, communications, and leadership was far short of that necessary for effective targeting. Moreover, the aggressive security and counterintelligence policies of the Iraqi regime made attempts to collect such information even more complicated.[4] CENTCOM's exercise Internal Look 90 had accelerated the target-development process, but an extensive effort was needed throughout both Desert Shield and Desert Storm to identify and assess the Iraqi target base. Even after the war, much was still unknown.

Before the war, the national intelligence agencies, along with the military services and fighting commands, maintained and updated their installation and order of battle databases as new information became available. Unfortunately, when Baghdad invaded Kuwait, the most comprehensive database—the Automated Installation-Intelligence File (AIF) of the Defense Intelligence Agency (DIA)—was not current, having been caught in the post–Cold War transition from Soviet to regional threats. In preparation for Internal Look 90, however, data collection had begun to rectify this situation, and during the second half of 1990 considerable advances were made. Still, in many areas the information was old and therefore either misleading or useless.

Iraq's deception efforts made the problem of updating information far worse, particularly in the case of its nuclear research program. The Iraqis successfully relocated, dispersed, and, in some cases, buried nuclear processing equipment to avoid attack.[5] As a result of Iraq's hidden facilities and Baghdad's unorthodox procedures undertaken to preserve its nuclear capabilities, the Coalition's understanding of the

---

4. *Conduct of the Persian Gulf War*, 333.

5. David Kay, "Arms Inspections in Iraq: Lessons for Arms Control," 12 August 1992, 3, GWAPS, NA 375.

What Was the Role of Intelligence?

Iraqi program remained slight. From August 1990 and extending through the beginning of the air campaign, the target list contained only two known and two suspected nuclear facilities. This number increased to eight by the end of the war.[6]

After the war, International Atomic Energy Administration inspectors identified more than twenty sites involved in the Iraqi nuclear program, including some sixteen main facilities.[7] These inspections revealed that the Iraqis had a far more extensive and dispersed program than Western intelligence had previously estimated. The intelligence community could not, of course, have produced a picture as comprehensive as the one U.N. special commission inspectors pieced together after recurring and intrusive on-site postwar visits. Nevertheless, certain first-order questions do not appear to have been asked—much less vigorously pursued—about the extent of active deception and concealment measures that Baghdad might take to complicate Coalition targeting.

In addition to protecting its nuclear program, Baghdad went to exceptional lengths to conceal the composition and operation of its Scud missile force. Unlike the case of the nuclear program, intelligence estimates correctly identified most Scud production and support facilities, which Coalition air forces subsequently bombed. Intelligence analysts never knew enough about Iraqi employment procedures, however, to provide the cueing necessary to bring effective air power to bear on the mobile Scuds. Several intelligence teams examined the mobile Scud issue and relayed what appeared to be promising information to DIA and the theater.[8] These teams were schooled in how the Soviets had operated Scuds in Warsaw Pact exercises and the infrared and radar signatures mobile Scud launchers would emit if employed according to previous Soviet practices. The DIA/J-2 intelligence team, in particular, created target materials illustrating how hard it would be for sensors on aircraft to find mobile launchers, especially from medium altitude or higher.[9] When war finally came, this inherent difficulty with target acquisition by fixed-wing aircraft operating at night from medium altitudes was further compounded by major Iraqi divergences from known Soviet practices. The Iraqis would arrive at a mobile launch site, set up within a few minutes, and, dispensing with

6. Master Target Lists, Master Target Folder, GWAPS, BH 53.

7. Security Council Report, S/23215, Seventh IAEA on-site inspection, 11–22 October 1991, 14 November 1991, 63.

8. Report, HQ USAF/IN, "Operation Desert Storm Lessons Learned," 5 May 1991, JULLS Number 41421-92977 (00018), 34–35; and interview, Lt. Gen. Charles A. Horner, transcript dated 28 January 1992, GWAPS, NA 303.

9. Interview, GWAPS with Capt. Edward O'Connell, 23 May 1992. O'Connell was in the DIA targeting branch during the war.

many of the normal calibrations, launch and be on their way within about ten minutes.[10]

Although intelligence identified most, if not all, of the fixed launch sites, analysts could not find mobile launch or intermediate assembly or preparation sites, and so could not predict with any precision the locations from which Scuds might be launched. Moreover, the Scud hunt unfolded in a way that tended to mask this problem from intelligence analysts, strike planners, and commanders alike. The first ten days of the air campaign saw numerous claims of mobile Scud kills by aircrews, backed in some cases with cockpit video, and the lull in launches during the third and fourth weeks seemed, at first, to substantiate pilot reports. In retrospect, however, it appears that many of the Coalition aircraft actually struck decoys, other shorter-range missiles, or traffic such as fuel trucks. Intelligence had not understood the full scope of Baghdad's Scud decoy program and exploitation of "low signature" firing locations.

Intelligence made much more accurate estimates of Iraqi army and air force dispositions and intentions. In the early fall, intelligence estimates correctly noted that the invading Iraqi force had shifted to a more defensive posture. Intelligence knew the locations and intentions of the less capable regular army units digging in near the Kuwaiti/Saudi Arabian border and the more capable Republican Guard being kept as a strategic reserve. By the end of 1990, the national intelligence community believed that Iraq would defend in place, try to force the Coalition (if it were to attack) into a war of attrition on the ground, and attempt to arrive at a stalemate that would undermine U.S. national will.[11]

Of particular interest to air power planners was the appraisal of the Iraqi air force and its supporting air defenses. An October 1990 Central Intelligence Agency assessment correctly surmised that: "The Iraqi Air Force would not be effective because it would either be neutralized quickly by Coalition air action or it would be withheld from action in hardened shelters. Within a few days, Iraqi air defenses would be limited to AAA and hand-held and surviving light SAMs. The [former] would present a significant threat to low-level air operations. . . ."[12]

In the months to follow, other intelligence organizations addressed this issue. The Naval Intelligence Command's Strike Projection Evaluation and Anti-Air Warfare Research (SPEAR) group made a particularly accurate forecast. They held that the Iraqi air force would not put up a determined defense but would rely, instead, on hit-and-run and

---

10. *Conduct of the Persian Gulf War*, 167; and *Hero*, 420.

11. CIA memo of January 1991.

12. CIA assessment of October 1990.

What Was the Role of Intelligence? 109

dispersal tactics to enhance its survival. In addition, the naval analysts (a highly successful mix of operational and intelligence personnel) correctly predicted Baghdad's reliance on radar-guided SAMs as the mainstay of its air defense and accurately assessed the strengths and weaknesses of its KARI integrated air defense system.[13] "The limited amount of [all-weather] fighters compared with Iraq's large number of strategic [radar-guided] SAMs . . . makes the SAM the logical choice as the primary air defense weapon . . . . Iraq probably will not put up a determined, concentrated fighter defense, thus avoiding quick elimination of its interceptor force."[14]

SPEAR's assessment was distributed widely within the theater and briefed to aircrews before Desert Storm; it remains perhaps the best assessment of the Iraqi air force and air defense system.

Intelligence had less success in determining the number of Iraqi troops and equipment in the Kuwaiti theater. Although Coalition leaders knew the general disposition of Baghdad's forces in the Kuwaiti theater before Desert Storm, they understood far less well the *actual* numbers of men and combat equipment in those Iraqi units. As a result, personnel and equipment estimates rested on an assumed full manning. Intelligence attempted to verify that information by imagery.

The resulting numbers, which proved to be a considerable overestimate of the actual Iraqi force in the theater, remained the basis for Coalition action against that force. Intelligence analysts and Coalition planners originally estimated that the Iraqis had about 540,000 troops in the Kuwait theater just before the air campaign and about 450,000 when the ground offensive began.[15] These same estimates put Iraqi equipment totals at nearly forty-three hundred tanks and slightly more than thirty-one hundred artillery pieces in the Kuwaiti theater at the beginning of the air campaign,[16] but the intelligence agencies and theater assessments differed widely on how much equipment remained at the beginning of the ground campaign.

Several factors complicated a more accurate assessment of the true strength of the Iraqi army. First, that army had undergone a reorganization after the Iran-Iraq War, changing the divisional manning and complicating the analysts' task of determining a unit's size and composition once the unit itself was identified. Second, the size of the Iraqi

13. Document, SPEAR, Naval Intelligence Command, *Iraqi Threat to U.S. Forces*, 10 December 1990, 3-53.

14. Ibid., 3-51 and 3-52; also interview, Commander Fitzgerald, SPEAR, with GWAPS, 15 May 1992.

15. *Conduct of the Persian Gulf War*, 254. Also see chapters 1 and 3 for estimates of the strength and equipment totals of the Iraqi army at the beginning of the air campaign and the beginning of the ground offensive.

16. *Conduct of the Persian Gulf War*, 254.

army in the Kuwaiti theater increased throughout the fall of 1990, just as the Coalition forces did, so any estimate of Iraqi strength was soon outdated. Third, the Iraqis made major efforts to thwart accurate preconflict estimates by Coalition intelligence agencies through extensive deception such as constructing numerous unoccupied berms and deploying decoy tanks and artillery. And finally, indications of independent Iraqi brigades and of divisions with additional attached brigades compounded the process of identifying and properly classifying all the units in the theater. Because of these complicating factors, the estimates used figures for the Iraqi units at full strength in men and equipment. Later analysis would indicate that the less-than-full manning made the estimates too high by 20 to 25 percent.[17]

Enough information became available during the air campaign (primarily reports from Iraqi soldiers defecting into Saudi Arabia) to cast doubt on the original strength estimates, but those estimates remained unchanged. Defector reports numbered in the hundreds, but these Iraqi soldiers came almost entirely from the frontline infantry divisions and thus gave little indication of the status of heavy divisions in the rear.[18] Furthermore, the U.S. military command structure refused to comment on or engage in assessments of Iraqi personnel strength, or losses, either during or after the war. Generals Powell and Schwarzkopf, made wary of body counts by their experiences in the Vietnam War, chose what they thought a more important estimate—the numbers and status of maneuver divisions and brigades.[19]

The overestimate of the Iraqi equipment totals induced an unintended consequence in theater targeting. CENTCOM carefully considered equipment totals and used them as a basis for assessing Phase III of the campaign: namely, preparation of the battlefield. Leaders measured their success in terms of *percentages* of equipment destroyed. Considering that postwar analysis credits the Iraqis with eight hundred fewer tanks than were originally estimated, this meant that attaining a 50 percent attrition of the *estimated* number of tanks would have brought approximately 62 percent attrition to the *actual* number of tanks. Just as much uncertainty applies to the amount of equipment *actually* destroyed, though, thereby offsetting the errors.

---

17. Analyses of Iraqi personnel and equipment strengths at the beginning of the air campaign, beginning of the ground offensive, and the end of the war are examined in chapters 1 and 3 of this book.

18. There were possibly well over 100,000 Iraqi deserters; the bulk of these returned to Iraq, not across the line into Saudi Arabia.

19. CENTCOM News Briefing of Gen. H. Norman Schwarzkopf, Riyadh, Saudi Arabia, 27 February 1991; and interview, Mr. Ron Cole, JCS/Historical Staff, and Ms. Diane Putney, Office of Air Force History, with Rear Adm. J. M. McConnell, USN, Deputy Director for Intelligence, Joint Staff, 14 February 1992, GWAPS, NA 261.

Organizational Relationships

Various planning documents written before the war outlined the organizational relationships that would exist between intelligence analysts, targeteers, and operations planners.[20] Those that were developed during Desert Shield and Desert Storm differed considerably from what had been envisioned. At the outset, neither CENTCOM's intelligence nor that of CENTAF staff had adequate manpower to support an air war of Desert Storm's scope.[21]

The plan had always been that skeleton staffs of these organizations would gain augmentees from other organizations during crises or mobilization. The CENTAF intelligence staff was formed from the 9th Tactical Intelligence Squadron and consisted of only eight personnel, six of whom were not fully qualified.[22] Although these personnel participated in CENTCOM's exercise Internal Look 90, which concluded just days before the Iraqi invasion, the exercise was not designed to test intelligence analysis and dissemination.

During the Desert Shield buildup, national and service intelligence organizations did send a limited number of qualified specialists to various intelligence organizations in the theater. Of the 180-some active-duty, fully trained, target-intelligence personnel available throughout the U.S. Air Force, however, merely 40 were deployed to the theater, and, of the active-duty personnel with any target intelligence training, less than 18 percent were deployed.[23] The bulk of the considerable augmentation to in-theater intelligence organizations consisted mainly of relatively untrained augmentees and reservists. It was not so much a lack of intelligence personnel that remained a problem, it was the lack of *qualified* personnel.[24]

Once in the theater, the relationship between the CENTAF operations and intelligence staffs—an uneasy relationship at best in Air Force organizations—was strained even further. When the air staff's officers briefed General Horner in Saudi Arabia on the Instant Thunder

---

20. USCINCCENT OPLAN 1001-90 (Second Draft), 18 July 1990, Annex 7 to Annex B.

21. *Conduct of the Persian Gulf War*, Appendix C, 337; and Report, HQ USAF/IN, "Operation Desert Storm Lessons Learned," 5 May 1991, JULLS Number 41960-26699 (00031), 64, GWAPS, NA 136.

22. Interview, Lt. Col. Frank Kistler, Dr. Mark Mandeles, and Maj. Sanford Terry with Capt. John Glock, USAF, Langley AFB, Virginia, 30 January 1992.

23. Report, HQ USAF/IN, "Operation Desert Storm Lessons Learned," 5 May 1991, JULLS Number 41444-77200 (00024), 50.

24. Interview, Capt. Edward O'Connell with Maj. Robert Heston, USAF, AF/INX, formerly 37th TFW/IN, 4 August 1992; interview, Captain O'Connell with Lt. William Carr, USN, CENTCOM J-2, 11 November 1992; and interview, Barry Watts with Captain O'Connell, 9 April 1993.

concept of a strategic air war, the cool reception they received led CENTCOM and CENTAF intelligence staffs to conclude that the Washington-based plan, along with the officers from Checkmate, would soon recede to irrelevance. The Black Hole (under Glosson) set to work on an air plan for an air offensive.

Due in no small part to the political sensitivity of offensive campaign planning at this early juncture, the Black Hole planners set themselves up as a special access organization and made little effort to inform intelligence personnel of their concept of operations.[25] CENTAF intelligence went ahead with its own target planning and viewed initial requests from Black Hole planners as a nuisance.[26] When intelligence personnel failed to respond expeditiously to their initial requests, the Black Hole regarded them as generally nonresponsive and looked elsewhere for support.[27] Thus began an unfortunate rift between theater intelligence organizations and the Black Hole, a gap that widened as time went on.

The unfortunate physical separation between the two entities exacerbated an already delicate situation. CENTAF's intelligence facility resided in a large tent on a soccer field adjacent to the Royal Saudi Air Force headquarters building, while the Black Hole was located in the basement of that building. Although not vast, this physical separation had its consequences.[28] Theater intelligence personnel did not take part in the many ad hoc discussions that refined the Instant Thunder (Desert Storm Phase I) concept. This meant that they could not anticipate Black Hole requirements. By the time that some of CENTAF's intelligence personnel joined the Black Hole staff, the planners had already forged new links to disparate intelligence and other organizations outside the theater.[29]

Perhaps the single biggest factor that contributed to the rift was the initial inability of theater intelligence to produce imagery of po-

---

25. Interview, Capt. John Glock; and AAR, USCENTAF/IN, "After Action Report and Lessons Learned," 25 May 1991, Colonel Rauschkolb to Colonel Christon.

26. Interview, Dr. Perry Jamison, Center for Air Force History, with Lt. Col. Sam Baptiste, 5 March 1992. Tapes at AFCHO.

27. Report, Lt. Col. J. S. Meyer, Jr., "Operations Desert Shield/Desert Storm," SAC/CC, 9 July 1991, GWAPS, NA 123; interviews, GWAPS with Lt. Col. David Deptula, 20 November 1991, 20 and 21 December 1991, 8 January 1992; and interview, GWAPS with Maj. Gen. Buster Glosson, 9 April 1992.

28. Report, Meyer, "Operations Desert Shield/Desert Storm," SAC/CC, 9 July 1991; AAR, USCENTAF/IN, "After Action Report and Lessons Learned," 25 May 1991, Colonel Rauschkolb to Colonel Christon; and Glock interview.

29. Interview, GWAPS staff with Lt. Col. David Deptula, 20 December 1991; and Glock and Baptiste interview. There were, it should be noted, intelligence officers in the Black Hole, but they could not bridge the gap.

What Was the Role of Intelligence? 113

tential targets for General Glosson's planners in a timely fashion. This failure had a variety of sources, beginning with the generally incomplete and out-of-date national database on Iraq before the crisis.[30] Within the theater, no one told intelligence officers of the evolving target list. The collection management system in theater took time to get started, and since the Black Hole was a compartmented operation with little resident intelligence experience, that organization neither fully appreciated nor properly availed itself of the imagery tasking and prioritization system.[31]

Moreover, few tactical systems in theater could provide the images needed to support planning for a strategic air war.[32] And, once the war began, those that were available were not fully used after Horner and Glosson made a conscious decision "not to waste aircraft to shoot pictures of targets we knew had already been struck."[33]

Early in Desert Shield during one of General Glosson's trips to Washington, he met with Rear Adm. J. M. McConnell, Joint Staff/J-2, who promised to provide whatever intelligence support he could. The relationship blossomed, and soon Glosson spoke to McConnell several times a day on a secure telephone line. McConnell also used secure facsimile to send intelligence materials into theater, mostly one- or two-page analytic reports on recommended targets with accompanying imagery.[34]

Other members of the Black Hole, many of them on assignment from the air staff, turned to friends in Checkmate. By the middle of Desert Shield, Checkmate had become an ad hoc fusion center for intelligence and operational information and maintained contact with national intelligence agencies and a number of specialized planning cells in Washington. It did not take Black Hole personnel long to realize that

30. Interview, Capt. John Glock with Maj. John Heidrick, 9th TIS/INT, 7 January 1992, GWAPS, NA 267.

31. AAR, USCENTAF/IN, "After Action Report and Lessons Learned," 25 May 1991, Colonel Rauschkolb to Colonel Christon; and Report, Intelligence Program Support Group, Office of the Assistant Secretary of Defense (Command, Control, Communications, and Intelligence), *Operation Desert Shield/Storm Intelligence Dissemination Study—Final Report*, Appendix L-CENTAF, 28 May 1992.

32. Report, HQ USAF/IN, "Operation Desert Storm Lessons Learned," 5 May 1991, JULLS Number 41965-98270 (00034), 68; JULLS 32033-32800 (00028), 58–59, GWAPS, NA 136; and Report, Thomas P. Christie, et al., Desert Storm Strategic Air Campaign Bomb Damage Assessment (BDA), IDA Document D-1088, January 1992, 3–5, GWAPS, NA 223.

33. Interview, Captain O'Connell with Major General Glosson, Pentagon, 28 January 1992.

34. Interview, Rear Adm. J. M. McConnell, Joint Staff Intelligence J-2, by Diane T. Putney, AF/HO, and Ron Cole, JCS/HO, 14 February 1992, Pentagon, GWAPS, NA 261. In addition, Checkmate also forwarded such intelligence products to the Black Hole planners.

they could obtain more current information by calling Washington on their STU-III secure telephones and secure faxes than they could get from in-theater intelligence sources.[35] By the time the war started, the Black Hole had become its own intelligence organization: it had its own intelligence sources, and it did its own targeting.

CENTAF, of course, did not operate completely independently of the theater intelligence structure. The CENTCOM Joint Intelligence Center became the senior intelligence organization in the theater, but CENTAF intelligence exercised considerable latitude in weaponeering and other targeting duties. Likewise, CENTAF intelligence reported to a theater battle damage assessment cell on targets attacked in Iraq: the naval component of Central Command (NAVCENT) accomplished damage assessments of Iraqi naval facilities and vessels; the Marine component (MARCENT) provided damage assessments of Iraqi ground force targets within the Marine area of operations; and the Army component (ARCENT) reported the damage inflicted on the remainder of the Iraqi ground forces.[36] Still, at least as far as the air war over Iraq was concerned, theater intelligence organizations played a smaller role than would have been expected.

The ad hoc relationship between Washington and Riyadh intelligence centers challenged the axiom that intelligence developed in theater is better and more timely than intelligence developed in the United States. With the help of the national intelligence agencies in Washington, the steady stream of requests from the Black Hole met with a corresponding response that, over time, turned into a steady dialogue. Many times Washington intelligence analysts knew the target had been struck before in-theater analysts did. Furthermore, developing targets for the strategic air campaign often required levels of expertise unavailable in the theater. For example, a special cell formed under DIA/J-2 in Washington to analyze the Iraqi telecommunications system could not be duplicated in Riyadh. This applied to several other target sets requiring technical analysis.

The Black Hole's ready access to targeting intelligence from national intelligence agencies had the unfortunate effect of cutting CENTCOM J-2 and CENTAF intelligence out of the communication loop. Theater intelligence organizations continued to perform their functions but found that planners rarely heeded their recommendations because they could never advance their proposals rapidly enough to get them into

---

35. For an example of the kind of targeting information being provided to the Black Hole from Admiral McConnell and Checkmate, see Colonel Deptula's targeting folders in GWAPS, CHP, folder 3. In several cases, intelligence reports from CENTAF/IN are dated several days after similar information had been provided by Admiral McConnell or Checkmate.

36. *Conduct of the Persian Gulf War*, 344.

What Was the Role of Intelligence? 115

the fast-paced planning cycle. Even if the Black Hole had worked more cooperatively with theater intelligence, a number of systematic and technical problems that lay beyond the ability of the theater people to solve would have prevented a harmonious relationship. The Washington bypass violated formal channels, but it worked. Operations planners got expert intelligence more rapidly than otherwise might have been the case.

Targeting

The selection of target systems whose neutralization or destruction will achieve the desired operational and strategic objectives has seldom, if ever, been an easy or trivial matter. Uncertainties, gaps, and errors in intelligence about targets and target systems have been the rule, and the Gulf War proved no exception. On the one hand, General Powell has argued that the intelligence available to the Coalition "was probably the best in military history."[37] In light of the array of advanced collection and reconnaissance platforms available to the Coalition, to say nothing of the degree to which the Iraqis were blinded by Coalition air power, there is considerable truth to that generalization.

On the other hand, General Powell has also acknowledged that theater and tactical commanders expressed frustration after the war "over the lack of coordination and timeliness in the dissemination of intelligence collected at the national level."[38] Among other things, a significant percentage of the target materials generated by Washington intelligence agencies and sent to the theater were never disseminated to operational wings.[39]

What air planners in Riyadh came to refer to as the strategic portion of the Desert Storm air campaign focused on Iraq proper. Most of the "strategic" targets in Iraq proper were fixed installations: airfields, naval ports, permanent troop installations, electric power plants, bridges, telecommunications switching facilities, command and control centers, weapons research and development facilities, fixed Scud launch sites, governmental ministries, headquarters for Iraq's military services, ammunition storage depots, and so forth. These installations generally had basic encyclopedia numbers (BENs) and appeared in the AIF.

---

37. Gen. Colin L. Powell, "Report on the Roles, Missions, and Functions of the Armed Forces of the United States" (Washington: CJCS, February 1993), II-13.

38. Ibid.

39. Interview, Captain O'Connell with Major Heston, 4 August 1992; also, interview, Barry Watts with Maj. Lewis Hill, 13 April 1993. Experience by tactical units with the dissemination of targeting materials varied widely from one fighter wing to the next. Some units, such as the F-117 wing, went to extraordinary lengths to obtain needed materials.

The AIF, which included all installations of interest, not merely those suitable for targeting, grew some 38 percent between the invasion of Kuwait and the beginning of the air campaign. Within this growth, the list of installations considered as potential targets increased nearly 50 percent by early January 1991.[40] By and large, the vast majority of the more than 770 strategic targets in Iraq and occupied Kuwait in the Black Hole's final target list had been identified in the AIF before 17 January 1991.[41]

The second major component of the Desert Storm air campaign consisted of attacks against Iraqi ground forces in the Kuwaiti theater of operations (KTO). The forty-three Iraqi divisions and independent brigades deployed in the KTO had some fixed installations associated with them, but the vast majority (more than 90 percent) of the roughly twenty-three thousand strikes by Coalition fixed-wing aircraft and missiles against Iraqi ground order of battle involved potentially mobile forces in the field that did not have BENs and were not listed in the AIF. Targets associated with these forces included tanks, trucks, bunkers, and deployed logistics supplies.

The presence of a target in the DIA's installations and order of battle databases did not mean that pilots had adequate information to conduct an attack. Pilots required photographs and other target materials. Some target folders were prepared in advance and carried into the theater, while others were prepared in the theater, especially as new targets emerged. Combat aircrews at the wing level requested a steady flow of target materials, especially imagery. At one end of the spectrum were systems such as the TLAM and the F-117, both of which had prodigious requirements for specialized information. But even in the case of fighter-bombers, with less exacting requirements for mission planning, the appetite for target imagery and threat information in the units proved well-nigh insatiable.

In this regard, intelligence analysts had a sometimes ill-defined relationship with operational planners during the Gulf War. Normally, target-intelligence officers from CENTCOM and CENTAF nominated targets to be attacked according to their own analyses, those obtained from national intelligence agencies, and their understanding of the overall campaign strategy. They went into the war expecting these nominations to form the basis for each day's ATO. But in Desert Storm, operational planners in the Black Hole, relying on their own intelligence sources, made the basic target selections, especially insofar as the strategic portion of the air campaign was concerned. Inevitably,

---

40. Document, Targets Database, compiled by Capt. John Glock, USAF, GWAPS files.

41. Being in the AIF basically meant that the installation had an encyclopedia number, not that it was one of the 774 unique targets that eventually appeared on the Black Hole's target list.

What Was the Role of Intelligence?   117

this ad hoc arrangement tended to blur and confuse the relations between theater intelligence and operations.

Once targets were selected, CENTAF and CENTCOM targeting officers would begin working with DIA and the Defense Mapping Agency Aerospace Center (DMAAC) in St. Louis, Missouri, to obtain the most precise coordinates for the aimpoints to be used in striking them. Two further problems then emerged: the selection of aimpoints and the precision of the coordinates passed to the units. Sometimes aimpoints were selected at CENTAF, but more often they were chosen at unit level. Who had primary jurisdiction for this responsibility—CENTAF or the wings—became a point of both contention and added confusion.

In addition, the bombing accuracy possible with platforms such as the F-117s required geodetic coordinates. Because of problems with incompatible imagery-dissemination systems in theater, the Black Hole often ended up trying to pass aimpoints to units with geographically rectified imagery whose quality was nowhere near equal to the geodetic DMAAC coordinates that could have passed through intelligence channels.[42] Inevitably, passing less-precise coordinates introduced further friction into the targeting process.

These interconnected problems became particularly acute for certain units that depended on high-quality current imagery for mission preparation. Unfortunately, pilots often flew with outdated pictures of the target or with no imagery at all. For some units, imagery was not critical. But since imagery was a standard part of mission preparation materials, all aircrews had come to expect it. It was not good enough to read a message that described the target and its surroundings; they wanted and expected to see a picture of it. Although the intelligence community had successfully provided imagery for target folders for crews to study in peacetime, the demand in wartime for imagery and imagery-derived products was not met.[43]

From a campaign planning standpoint, one of the most far-reaching decisions of the war was the selection of target categories as contrasted with individual targets. The air staff's Instant Thunder briefing, as presented to General Schwarzkopf on 17 August 1990, identified ten target categories for an offensive air campaign against Iraq proper.[44] With

---

42. Interview, Captain O'Connell with General Glosson, 3 February 1992; and interview, Captain O'Connell with Maj. Jack Gardner, USAF, CENTCOM Target Intelligence Officer, 5 August 1992.

43. *Conduct of the Persian Gulf War*, 338.

44. (1) National leadership facilities, (2) national telecommunications and C-3, (3) oil distribution and storage, (4) electric power, (5) railroads (to which bridges were later added), (6) nuclear/chemical/biological warfare capabilities, (7) military research/production/storage, (8) strategic air defenses, (9) airfields (particularly those containing interceptors and bombers), and (10) Iraq's ballistic missile capabilities.

some minor modifications, the 17 August Instant Thunder target categories were retained by General Glosson's special planning group and used throughout Desert Storm.

It is possible to argue, based on the overall success of the air campaign, that the limited intelligence data available to the air staff in August 1990 were adequate for the selection of target categories. The choices of target categories, however, were shaped at least as much by doctrinal considerations about the proper offensive use of air power at the operational level of war as by detailed intelligence on targets and target systems in Iraq. While air staff intelligence officers did much to fill in the target categories as best they could, the idea of a strategic air campaign rested upon only the most general understanding of Iraq, its society, infrastructure, and military capabilities.[45]

At the most elementary level, certain individual targets were never located prior to the end of the war. The concealed hide sites from which Iraq's mobile ballistic launchers probably operated throughout Desert Storm provide one of the most telling examples of a set of targets that were not pinpointed even by the final day of the conflict. Other targets were, to one degree or another, located, but their full significance or extent was similarly not understood during the war. Al Atheer, for example, was bombed before the end of the war, but not until afterwards did the Coalition learn about its central importance in the Iraqi nuclear program. By the same token, while Ash Sharqat was attacked as a part of Iraq's ballistic missile program during Desert Storm, it was not until after the war that its involvement in isotope separation came to be fully understood.

What these examples suggest is that, notwithstanding the massive amounts of intelligence data produced on Iraqi installations and forces, there were some systemic blind spots. Iraq's nuclear, chemical, and biological warfare programs, along with the extended-range Scuds, were areas that Saddam Hussein wanted to protect as much as possible from Coalition air attacks, and the extent to which the Iraqis were able to do so through concealment, deception, dispersal, redundancy, and mobility does not appear to have been fully appreciated until after war's end. In general, Coalition intelligence located most fixed installations throughout Iraq but did not always appreciate the significance of every installation in relation to target systems any more than did the operational planners and commanders.

Regarding Iraqi ground forces in the Kuwaiti theater, Coalition in-

---

45. John A. Warden III, *The Air Campaign* (Washington: National Defense University, 1988), 51–58; Warden's views may be traced in his series of Instant Thunder briefings, 8–17 August 1990, GWAPS, CHSH 5 and 7; and briefing, Col. John A. Warden III for Gen. John A. Loh, VCSAF, "Iraqi Air Campaign," 8 August 1990, GWAPS, CHSH 7-11; Notes, Lt. Col. Bernard E. Harvey, Checkmate, 7–8 August 1990, GWAPS, CHP 9-1.

What Was the Role of Intelligence?

telligence provided remarkably complete tactical intelligence on the locations and dispositions of the units there. U.S. ground forces involved in the one-hundred-hour ground campaign seem to have encountered no major surprises, especially in the critical breaching operations. "The enemy was exactly where intelligence said he was, disposed as intelligence described . . . ."[46] In retrospect, however, the greatest gaps in intelligence on targets and target sets seem to have occurred with things like Scud launchers that were inherently mobile or elements of the Iraqi nuclear weapons program that could be moved out from under Coalition bombing and concealed.

From an intelligence standpoint, one of the clear success stories in the Gulf War was the Coalition's rapid neutralization of the Iraqi air defenses and air force. The degree to which Coalition intelligence agencies provided not only the relevant installations and associated order of battle, but also furnished the requisite understanding of the Iraqis' operational weaknesses, was truly extraordinary. As a result, Coalition air forces could concentrate their initial efforts precisely against the weaknesses and vulnerabilities of Iraq's air defenses and air force.

By contrast, the Survey did not discern anywhere near the same sophistication on the part of Coalition air efforts against the Iraqi field army in the Kuwaiti theater, which largely became an exercise in incremental attrition. This asymmetry seems to have arisen as much from the historical preferences as from weaknesses in intelligence, but it suggests one area, at least, in which a closer relationship between operations and intelligence could bear fruit in the future.

Bomb Damage Assessment

Few assertions about the Gulf War could command as much agreement as the inadequacy of bomb damage assessment, but there was found no such agreement about the causes of that inadequacy. General Schwarzkopf told Congress that it "was one of the major areas of confusion. . . . It led to some disagreements. As a matter of fact, it led to some distancing on the part of some agencies from the position of CENTCOM, at the time, as to what the bomb damage assessment really was."[47]

Theater planners and intelligence staffs disagreed among themselves and with the Washington intelligence agencies over the levels of damage being achieved by the bombing in Iraq proper and within

---

46. Brig. Gen. John F. Stewart, Jr., "Operation Desert Storm, The Military Intelligence Story: A View from the G-2, 3d U.S. Army," April 1991, 9.

47. Report, Investigations Subcommittee on Armed Services, *Intelligence Successes and Failures in Operation Desert Shield/Storm*, House of Representatives, 102d Congress, 2d session.

the Kuwaiti theater. At the same time, reports from Air Force, Navy, and Marine Corps flight crew members, and those of other Coalition air forces, agreed that they received little or no bomb damage assessment on the targets they attacked during the entire war.[48] Many causes contributed to this, some of them organizational, some procedural, and some technical. Certain limitations were not failings at all; they were simply limits of what could be known or observed. A review of the major impediments to accurate and timely bomb damage assessment can give some understanding of the dimensions of the problem.

The intelligence staffs were not prepared for the enormity of the task, either in numbers of qualified personnel or in established and rehearsed procedures. Those staffs were particularly unprepared to deal with the number of attack sorties that occurred every day of the war. Exercise Internal Look 90, a valuable learning experience for commanders and planners, could not preview the subsequent bomb damage assessment problems since that exercise followed the long-standing practice of simulating the production of bomb damage assessment to simplify and shorten the exercise.[49]

Although regulations and operation plans detailed organizational structures to manage the ordering of national reconnaissance assets, the system did not work well in practice because of inadequate numbers of trained, qualified personnel. To complicate matters further, only a small portion of those assigned to CENTAF intelligence during the crisis had any experience in collection management, while the campaign planners failed to anticipate how massive and time-consuming the bomb damage assessment process would be once the war began.[50] The CENTAF plan for handling such assessments via three computer workstations required modifications during Desert Shield and reduction to a single computer workstation, but the system was still unproven when the air campaign began.[51] The situa-

---

48. The only exceptions to inadequate BDA at the unit level were units flying aircraft equipped to bring back video recordings of their weapons' impacts, or those that had their own reconnaissance assets (e.g., F-14Ds capable of carrying the Tactical Air Reconnaissance Pod System).

49. Report, USCENTAF/IN, "After Action Report and Lessons Learned," 25 March 1991, from Colonel Rauschkolb to Colonel Christon (CENTAF/IN), with seventeen attachments.

50. Document, Majors P. J. Nagy and F. D. Houston, "Intelligence Operations in Southwest Asia," Marine Corps Research Center Research Paper 92-0008, part 1, July 1991, 3, GWAPS, NA 355; AAR, USCENTAF/IN, "After Action Report and Lessons Learned," 25 May 1991, Colonel Rauschkolb to Colonel Christon; and interview, Mr. Lawrence Greenberg, GWAPS with Capt. John Glock, USAF, member of 9th TIS and CENTAF/IN, January 1992, GWAPS, TF V files.

51. Report, Intelligence Program Support Group, Office of the Assistant Secretary of Defense (Command, Control, Communications, and Intelligence), *Operation Desert Shield/Storm Intelligence Dissemination Study—Final Report,* Appendix L-CENTAF, 28 May 1992.

tion was ripe for breakdowns when unexpected circumstances occurred.

The unexpected took place on the first day of the air campaign, when weather presented itself as a formidable obstacle to bomb damage assessment. Heavy overcast during the early days of the war prevented adequate reconnaissance of many strategic targets; most were not covered until 21 January, five days after the beginning of the air campaign. This exigency put intelligence assessments behind from the outset and derailed the prewar planning assumption that imagery of a target would be available to analysts in time for the target to be revisited, if necessary, two days later. When imagery was not forthcoming, the ATO process went ahead anyway, and operations planners looked to other sources—mission reports and video recordings—to judge the effectiveness of the previous day's strikes. Eventually, the imagery flow settled into a regular pattern, but a lag remained between collecting imagery of a target and disseminating it to planners for consideration in the ATO cycle.

Collection managers had to set priorities for the imagery collected from limited assets, but these managers often had not taken part in target planning, nor were they aware of changes to the daily air tasking order. Furthermore, Black Hole planners were unfamiliar with procedures for ordering data collection and did not attend meetings of the coordinating boards that assigned priorities to collection lists. This meant that people not involved in planning the air campaign and unaware of its direction determined each day's reconnaissance requirements.

As in the past, imagery interpretation proved an art, and a rather esoteric and uncertain one at that. It was difficult to assess damage to Iraqi hardened aircraft shelters, command bunkers, and communication buildings attacked by penetrating bombs. Analysts could see a small hole on the target's exterior where the bomb had entered, but most of the effects were contained within the target. Unfortunately, the requisite expertise on structural vulnerabilities and weapons effects largely resided in Washington, and some aircraft shelters ended up being attacked again and again after they had been penetrated and the aircrews had observed large secondary explosions.

The problem of imagery analysis also extended to the Kuwaiti theater, where assessing the operability of Iraqi equipment became an issue. Unless imagery showed a catastrophic kill, it was often impossible, for example, to determine whether a tank intact after a "near-miss" had its engine, aiming devices, or radios disabled by blast or shrapnel.

CENTAF and ARCENT adjusted to the situation. CENTAF's Black Hole had videotaped recordings of F-117, F-111F, and F-15E bombing missions collected and flown daily to Riyadh for analysis. Although these recordings were not of a quality to permit precise bomb damage assessment, they did show bomb detonation on the targets.[52] The Black Hole planners used this evidence, for instance, to determine bomb damage of an aircraft shelter, not the later and often indeterminate intelligence assessment from overhead imagery. ARCENT developed a system that combined pilot reports and video readouts with imagery, but at a discounted rate.[53] The discounting scheme proved a good corrective to pilot reports and even to what appeared on video as a direct hit on an Iraqi tank. Still, the result was another manifestation of the bomb damage assessment problem.

Disagreements over what bombing had accomplished were most manifest in the differences between Washington and theater assessments, the dispute over estimates of Iraqi equipment attrition, explained in the previous chapter, being the most notable. Washington intelligence agencies relied on national-level reconnaissance assets to determine what had been destroyed, while CENTCOM could, in addition, use its limited theater reconnaissance assets and pilot reports. These differences in estimates remained unresolved throughout the war.

All of these factors combined to make bomb damage assessment one of the most controversial issues of the war. Reflecting on his experience in Desert Storm, Maj. Gen. John A. Corder (CENTAF's deputy chief of staff for operations) argued that people expect too much from bomb damage assessment. "At a certain point in time, you're going to have to stand up based on your complete understanding of all sources available. . . . If you wait . . . until you're absolutely sure . . . that the bomb damage assessment problem [is] solved, you might have missed the opportunity."[54]

In the end, General Schwarzkopf moved away from the search for precise assessments and refused to display attrition figures in his daily briefings, preferring, instead, color-coded representations based on the individual enemy division's estimated overall effectiveness.[55] According to General Horner, by the time the ground offensive began, Schwarzkopf was using the *number* of air strikes against a target, not bomb damage assessment, as his prime indicator of enemy combat effectiveness.[56]

52. Some "blooming" on the screen at the instant of the detonation made it difficult to determine the exact point of impact.

53. For example, a 1/3 credit was given an A-10 claim of a kill and a 1/2 credit given an F-111F claim. Message, ARCENT/G2, dtg 170600Z February 1991, GWAPS, CHST 50.

54. Interview, GWAPS with Maj. Gen. John A. Corder, Deputy Commander of Operations, USCENTAF (November 1990 to March 1991), 18 May 1992, GWAPS, NA 361.

55. *Conduct of the Persian Gulf War,* 256.

56. Interview, Perry Jamison, et al., AFCHO, with Lt. Gen. Charles E. Horner, 4 March 1992, GWAPS, NA 322.

But even acknowledging that expectations may have been unrealistically high, the bomb damage assessment system failed to meet the requirements placed upon it because of the pace and scale of the air campaign. Technical systems could not keep pace with demand, much of the requisite expertise was in Washington rather than in the theater, and too many breakdowns apparently occurred in the transmission of information between Washington and the people who needed that information.

The role and record of intelligence in the air war is mixed, with remarkable successes as well as notable (but far from fatal) failures. The accurate strategic assessment of Iraqi intent and capabilities following the August crisis and the mass of detailed information about a wide range of targets acquired from August 1990 through February 1991 contributed immensely to the air campaign. The overall misestimate of Iraqi order of battle and inadequate bomb damage assessment were the largest failures.

Explanations of the former lie, in part, with the relative neglect of Southwest Asia before the Iraqi invasion of Kuwait. CENTCOM's area of responsibility had a far lower priority than other regions during the Cold War, as the post-August scramble for information and staffs to process it clearly shows. Explanations of the latter lie, in part, in a pervasive failure to practice bomb damage assessment regularly on a large scale before the war. This failure—shared by commanders as well as intelligence organizations—set the stage for its inadequacy during the war. Realistic practice would have uncovered large technical, procedural, and organizational problems; such rehearsal may have suggested remedies that could not be improvised during five and a half months of crisis and six weeks of war.

Five | Who Ran the Air War?

One of the more controversial aspects of the air campaign in the Gulf War was the role of the JFACC (pronounced *jay fack*) in the person of General Horner, CENTAF commander. General Schwarzkopf gave him authority to control most Coalition air power, and Horner used that authority with sufficient discretion to get his job done while maintaining good relations with the other services and the allies. Indeed, some would argue (after the war) that his contribution had been to coordinate rather than to command or control.[1]

The idea of a single commander for air goes back at least to World War II. The Air Force position has long been that of "War Department Field Manual 100-20," issued 21 July 1943: "Control of the available air power must be centralized and command must be exercised through the air force commander if [its] inherent flexibility and ability to deliver a decisive blow are to be fully exploited."[2] Centralized control has usually proved hard to implement, however. To illustrate, a convoluted chain of command divided North Vietnam into seven geographic areas, called "route packages," during the Vietnam War. Those packages were then apportioned between the Navy and the Air Force for separate air operations. Strategic Air Command retained control of B-52s flying throughout the theater, while the Marines and the Air Force struggled for control of the former's aircraft in South Vietnam.

Although JFACC became official JCS terminology in the mid-1980s, old tensions between the services over control of theater air power were not completely resolved. The Marine Corps agreed to make sorties available to the JFACC for air defense, interdiction, and recon-

---

1. See, for example, David L. Dittmer, *U.S. Marine Corps Operations in Desert Shield/Desert Storm, Vol. I: Overview and Summary* (Alexandria, VA: Center for Naval Analyses, 1992), 36.

2. This reflected in part the experience of early fighting in North Africa, when aircraft had been parceled out to Army corps—a failure that has influenced Air Force thinking ever since. See Benjamin F. Cooling, ed., *Case Studies in the Development of Close Air Support* (Washington: Office of Air Force History, 1990); and Daniel R. Mortensen, *A Pattern for Joint Operations in World War II, North Africa* (Washington: Office of Air Force History and Army Center of Military History, 1987).

naissance, but the Marines would give up their direct support sorties to JFACC control only *after* Marine Corps requirements had been satisfied. The Navy would continue to control sorties it deemed necessary for fleet defense, and the Army would fly its helicopters with few constraints from the JFACC. Nevertheless, the notion that joint air operations required at least a coordinating authority gained ground.[3]

Meanwhile, CENTCOM began preparing for a JFACC in Southwest Asia. By the time draft OPLAN 1002-90 appeared in the spring of 1990, a fairly conservative definition of the JFACC's functions had taken shape. Those functions were "planning, coordination, allocation, and tasking based upon U.S. Commander-in-Chief Central Command (USCINCCENT) apportionment decisions."[4] Schwarzkopf would use Horner's recommendations to decide how much air power would be apportioned among missions or geographic areas; Horner would then allocate particular forces to particular targets. Horner would have "operational control" of Air Force units but only "tactical control" of aircraft sorties made available by the Navy and the Marine Corps.[5] In the coming months, Schwarzkopf would permit Horner to make the most of that limited authority.

The JFACC and the Tactical Air Control System

General Horner did not have a joint staff. To begin with, he had just the personnel that normally served him in peacetime as commander, Ninth Air Force. In Riyadh, that staff expanded to handle wartime responsibilities both for CENTAF and for the JFACC, but the new members were mostly Air Force, with merely a few liaison officers from the other services and the allies. That arrangement would shape the way Horner exercised his authority as JFACC, and it would cause some lingering suspicion among the other services.

---

3. For an early use of the term "JFACC," see Message, JCS Chairman, subject: Joint Doctrine for Theater Counterair Operations, 4 March 1986. The Air Force and Marine Corps had already reached an "omnibus agreement" in 1980, and this was reaffirmed by JCS Pub 12, Vol. IV, in 1986.

4. Draft CENTCOM OPLAN 1002-90, 18 July 1990, 28. This language had already been used in JCS publications, including Joint Pub 1-02, *Department of Defense Dictionary of Military and Associated Terms*, 1 December 1989, and would be echoed in the operations orders for Desert Shield. Joint Pub 1-02 was careful to point out that the JFACC's functions would "include, but not be limited to" this list.

5. Joint Pub 1-02 (1 December 1989) defined "tactical control" as the "detailed and, usually, local direction and control of movements or maneuvers necessary to accomplish missions or tasks assigned." It defined "operational control" as the "authority to perform those functions of command over subordinate forces involving organizing and employing commands and forces, assigning tasks, designating objectives, and giving authoritative direction necessary to accomplish the mission."

Horner inherited a mechanism for controlling air power called the Tactical Air Control System (TACS). The TACS was designed to control theater-level air operations focusing on the battlefield. In the case of Desert Shield and Desert Storm, however, it would be called upon to conduct an independent strategic air campaign as well. This mechanism included forward air control officers (on the ground with Army units or flying above them) linked to a hierarchy of airborne and ground command posts culminating in the air component commander's Tactical Air Control Center (TACC).

Horner tailored the TACS for the task at hand in ways that made some of his subordinates uncomfortable. Most of those changes centered on a small planning group that began outside the TACC and eventually absorbed many of its functions. Horner brought in General Glosson to run this special planning group, whose original four members came from Washington, where Glosson had also served until his recent transfer to CENTCOM.[6] Horner wanted Glosson's group to work in great secrecy, leading the old CENTAF staff to begin calling this group the "Black Hole." Eventually, the Black Hole grew to about fifty personnel in a CENTAF headquarters staff of more than two thousand.

While the Black Hole quietly planned the campaign that would be executed, the rest of the CENTAF staff was left to plan for daily training missions and to refine the evolving scheme(s) for defending Saudi Arabia should Iraq invade. As August turned into September and the latter prospect became less likely, much of Horner's staff remained isolated from the offensive planning effort. This caused some bitterness that persisted even after December, when the Black Hole was better integrated into the CENTAF staff and Glosson was put in charge of all planning under a new deputy chief of staff for operations, General Corder. Horner preserved a formal direct link to Glosson, however, by putting the latter in command of all CENTAF's fighter wings. As a consequence, both Corder and the rest of the TACC could be bypassed by Glosson, who could talk directly to Horner and Schwarzkopf, on the one hand, and to wing commanders on the other.[7]

The approximately three hundred CENTAF personnel formally responsible for providing intelligence were even more frequently by-

---

6. Glosson was deputy assistant secretary of defense for legislative affairs until July 1990, when he became deputy commander of CENTCOM's Joint Middle East Task Force. The fact that he was already working for Schwarzkopf may have contributed to their good relationship throughout Desert Shield and Desert Storm. Similarly, Horner already knew Glosson before picking him to run the offensive planning effort.

7. Glosson commanded the 14th Air Division (Provisional); Brig. Gen. Glenn A. Proffitt, II, the 15th Air Div (Prov), which included electronic warfare and control aircraft; Brig. Gen. Patrick P. Caruana, the 16th Air Div (Prov), which included B-52 bombers, tankers, and strategic reconnaissance aircraft; and Brig. Gen. Edwin E. Tenoso, the 1610th Airlift Div (Prov).

passed. Glosson decided early in Desert Shield that the CENTAF intelligence staff could not meet his needs fast enough. He and his Black Hole staff developed their own links to the Washington intelligence community, which often sent them information days before it made its way through channels to CENTAF intelligence. Normally, the TACC was the meeting ground where the CENTAF intelligence staff put its products to work for the operations staff. Now, the Black Hole had direct access to its own sources through Checkmate and Admiral McConnell in Washington.[8]

When Glosson took charge of CENTAF planning in December 1990, he also took charge of Horner's principal tool for asserting authority as JFACC: the ATO. Throughout Desert Storm, the daily ATO listed details about almost every Coalition fixed-wing sortie scheduled over the Arabian Peninsula and Iraq.[9] The other services and the allies readily appreciated the importance of being in the ATO, if only to avoid midair collisions with any of the more than two thousand sorties flown daily during the air campaign. Besides, the great distances of the theater demanded air refueling by Air Force tankers, and that was arranged through the ATO.

Nevertheless, the ATO's many critics said that its hundreds of pages were too cumbersome.[10] In earlier wars, the Air Force had handled as many sorties by sending each unit only the fragment ("frag") of the daily order that applied to it. The arrival of networked computers in every unit, however, had encouraged CENTAF to send the complete order to all through its Computer Assisted Force Management System (CAFMS). The units could then scroll through the order on a monitor and print only the relevant portions.

But the volume of communications overwhelmed old transmission equipment and computer terminals. Some units reported that transmission and printing were taking more than five hours. In this context, flying the ATO out to Navy carriers may not have been a bad alternative, even if the carriers had the necessary hardware (which they did not). Partly because Pacific Air Force (PACAF) and U.S. Air Forces in

8. See chapter 4 of this book.

9. Some helicopter sorties were included in the ATO, but most were not. Navy and Air Force cruise missiles were in the ATO, but Army tactical missiles were not.

10. The number of pages in the ATO varied both with the day and with the means of transmission. The peak was Day 40 of Desert Storm, the second day of the ground offensive. When sent through CAFMS, that ATO required 982 screen pages; sent through the AUTODIN message system, it required 261 pages (131 sections). Many units used their STU-IIIs (with modems) for more rapid reception. For a discussion of CAFMS by authors involved in its creation from the late 1970s and in its use during the Gulf War, see John Paul Hyde, Johann W. Pfeiffer, and Toby C. Logan, "CAFMS Goes to War" in Alan D. Campen, ed., *The First Information War* (Fairfax, VA: Armed Forces Communications and Electronic Association, 1992).

Europe (USAFE) did not share CAFMS and had their own systems, Navy carriers resisted using any of their crowded space for a system that might not be the right one.[11] Furthermore, many units had already received the most essential information over the telephone long before the ATO arrived electronically or physically.

Some critics of the ATO complained that it took too long not only to transmit and receive but also to prepare. After the war, one report on the Marine Corps' experience said that the ATO was "an attempt to run a minute-by-minute air war at a 72-hour pace."[12] This criticism was not entirely warranted because most Marine sorties went into the Kuwaiti theater of operations, and many were handled by airborne controllers on a minute-by-minute basis. Indeed, in the case of fixed targets in Iraq, the opposite complaint was made: instead of permitting the ATO process to plan at least two days in advance, Glosson was prone to calling his wing commanders with last-minute changes.

The three-day ATO process began with the creation of a Master Attack Plan in the Iraq target planning cell (the Black Hole) and the KTO target planning cell (drawn from the old CENTAF staff). The Master Attack Plan was much shorter than the ATO because the former included less information and dealt with fewer sorties. The Master Attack Plan dealt solely with sorties that penetrated Iraqi and Kuwaiti air space and did not include air refueling and airlift sorties.

In addition, the Master Attack Plan listed just the times on target, mission numbers, target numbers, target names, aircraft types, and number of aircraft. The ATO added radio call signs, munition loads, identification "squawk" codes, air-refueling guidance (tanker call signs, mission numbers, and tracks), and special instructions (or "spins") on air-refueling procedures, airspace control, rescue, communications, jamming, and so forth. Since the Master Attack Plan listed strike packages chronologically according to time on target, it offered a more comprehensible picture of the air campaign than the ATO, which listed sorties by unit. The Master Attack Plan was a new tool for building a more coherent ATO.

On any day during the war, the Black Hole would be developing the Master Attack Plan for the air campaign to be waged two days ahead, while the ATO shop was preparing the order for the next day, and the rest of the TACC monitored the execution of the current ATO. In practice, of course, this process often appeared chaotic. Myriad details needed coordination, and the JFACC or senior planners could change

---

11. Attempts to install CAFMS at sea during Desert Shield were frustrated by the aircraft carriers' lack of suitable communications equipment.

12. John D. Parson, Benjamin T. Regala, and Orman H. Paananen, *Marine Corps Desert Storm Reconstruction Report, Vol. IV: Third Marine Aircraft Wing Operations* (Alexandria, VA: Center for Naval Analyses, 1992).

targeting at any time on the basis of hot information—intelligence tips, pilot debriefings, or weather shifts. The flying units (which would usually have the night of the second day to complete their planning) also had opportunities to shape the ATO, often through telephone conversations with the Black Hole early in the process. As a result of these ingredients, the ATO sometimes went out late or incomplete (particularly early in the air campaign) and was still subject to change in any case.

The JFACC and the CINC

The role of the JFACC in the Gulf War can be clarified by examining three relationships that General Horner developed during the course of Desert Shield and Desert Storm: with the theater commander, with the other American components, and with allied forces.

In the early days of Desert Shield, General Horner served as CENTCOM's forward commander in the theater, a role that made particular sense in view of the immediate priority given to flying aircraft into the theater. By the end of August, General Schwarzkopf had at his disposal some U.S. ground forces and substantial air power. Iraqi forces had not moved into Saudi Arabia, and the prospect of their doing so seemed increasingly unlikely. General Horner began to pay more attention to the offensive planning responsibility he had assigned General Glosson.

Schwarzkopf now gave Horner a fairly free hand in planning offensive air operations. Standard procedures called for the creation of a joint target coordination board, with representatives from each component to nominate targets for air attack. The Black Hole took over many of the functions normally assumed by such a board. This appears to have been an expedient decision on the part of a command that had few staff members in peacetime and whose augmented but overworked staffs during the Persian Gulf crisis were consumed by the task of deploying hundreds of thousands of troops and thousands of machines to the area of operations. Moreover, to leave planning for an air offensive almost entirely to a cell in the air component would allow for maximum security.

In any case, for months Schwarzkopf remained more comfortable with the work of the Black Hole than with plans prepared for a ground offensive. Especially because he was his own ground commander, Schwarzkopf and his CENTCOM staff gave much more time to ground planning.[13]

Once the war began, Horner briefed Schwarzkopf nightly on target selection, although not on bomb damage assessment. The two com-

---

13. It is noteworthy that Schwarzkopf's memoirs devote relatively few pages to the air war.

manders purposely avoided the bean-counting or body-counting that had plagued commanders during the Vietnam War, although Schwarzkopf's requirement for 50 percent destruction of Iraqi armor and artillery in the Kuwaiti theater before the ground offensive sometimes threatened to degenerate into such an exercise. Schwarzkopf and Horner were interested, of course, in whatever the intelligence community could tell them about bomb damage, using sometimes conflicting reports that came from Washington and from in-theater organizations. Schwarzkopf reviewed the planned air operations and changed them on occasion, although for the most part he consigned the strategic air campaign to Horner and his staff.

Schwarzkopf also served as a conduit for Washington's guidance on waging the war. Such guidance often pertained to escalating the pursuit of Scud missile launchers capable of firing at the Israelis and to restricting bombing in Baghdad following the attack on the Al Firdos bunker.[14]

The story was rather different in the Kuwaiti theater. Here, Schwarzkopf directed the JFACC to concentrate initially on second- and third-echelon Iraqi forces: that is, the heavy divisions and the Republican Guards making up the operational and strategic reserves of the Iraqi army. He also expressed particular concern over the need to prevent Iraqi forces from escaping the theater. Horner adhered to Schwarzkopf's priorities, but corps commanders did not always agree with Schwarzkopf's choices. They were more concerned about the forces immediately to their front and also complained that too much effort was expended on tanks, which were less to be feared than artillery, especially if the Iraqis resorted to chemical shells. Here again, not realizing it was Schwarzkopf's apportionment, some ground commanders blamed Horner or Glosson. The upshot resulted in tension between ground commanders, who felt their needs were not being met, and the JFACC and his staff, who were responding to the theater commander's direction.

The JFACC and the Components

The notion of a single air commander had troubling implications for the U.S. Army, Navy, and Marine Corps. For the Army, the JFACC per se was acceptable, even desirable, but corps commanders feared that their needs would not receive adequate attention from an Air Force that might wish to fight its own war in its own way. As in the past, the Army to some degree wanted an allocation of sorties to use as it saw

---

14. Interview, USAF historians with Lt. Gen. Charles A. Horner, Shaw AFB, 4 March 1992, GWAPS, NA 303.

Who Ran the Air War? 131

fit. The Navy, concerned about fleet defense, had reservations about a JFACC who could control rather than just coordinate. And the Marine Corps, organized on the basis of the Marine Air-Ground Task Force, whose aircraft could remedy relative weaknesses in artillery and tanks, believed that control of its own aviation was essential.

Air Force–Navy relations sometimes reflected procedural and doctrinal differences. The physical location of Vice Adm. Henry Mauz, and later Vice Adm. Stanley Arthur, on board the USS *Blue Ridge* (rather than in Riyadh) made matters worse; the inability of the aircraft carriers to receive the ATO electronically further hindered cooperation. Substantive disagreements occurred as well. The Navy favored more permissive rules of engagement than the Air Force thought prudent. The Navy appealed to General Schwarzkopf to resolve the dispute between Horner and Arthur (with the former's consent); the general supported Horner's more restrictive rules of engagement.[15]

The Navy retained control of air-to-air and air-to-surface sorties for the purpose of fleet defense. The Marine Corps was able to reserve large numbers of sorties for its own use on land—at least half of its F/A-18s and all of its AV-8Bs. Nonetheless, unified command did enable the JFACC to make other use of aircraft from both services, particularly in the first few days of the campaign. As the campaign wore on, Marine Corps aircraft struck fewer fixed targets and concentrated on Iraqi ground forces opposite the Marine sector. Marine fighters were directed to bomb in geographical sectors under the direction of ground and airborne controllers, as were Air Force and other bomber aircraft in the Kuwaiti theater. Some Marines would later say that their planners "gamed" the ATO by overbooking it with sorties to give them flexibility.[16] In fact, the ATO already provided for such flexibility by scheduling as much air power as possible in the Kuwaiti theater and leaving "targeting" to airborne controllers.

Lt. Gen. Walter E. Boomer, the Marine Corps commander, Lt. Gen. John Yeosock, ARCENT's commander, and Lt. Gens. Gary Luck and Frederick Franks, Army corps commanders, expressed major concern over apportionment of air power to support their forthcoming attacks against the Iraqi front. On 31 January, General Schwarzkopf told General Horner that "Target development and nomination during the early phases of the campaign were clearly led by the . . . (JFACC). As we move into battlefield preparation, maneuver commander input into the target selection process becomes even more important. Therefore, the

---

15. See Message from COMUSNAVCENT to USCENTAF, Personal for Lieutenant General Horner from Arthur, subject: Rules of Engagement, 112120Z January 1991.

16. Lt. Gen. Royal N. Moore, "Marine Air: There When Needed," *Proceedings*, November 1991, 63.

opportunity for corps and other subordinate commanders to plan for and receive air sorties to fly against targets of their choosing must increase."[17]

Although he dealt directly with Boomer, Horner handled the Army corps commanders through Yeosock. Indeed, Horner and Yeosock shared an apartment, and the corps commanders could not be sure how much one affected the other's decisions regarding corps target recommendations. Schwarzkopf instructed Horner to meet daily with Lt. Gen. Calvin Waller, Schwarzkopf's deputy, to review the requests by ground commanders for sorties. But Schwarzkopf's own preference for striking Republican Guards sometimes continued to outweigh his corps commanders' preference for striking frontline forces.[18]

Tensions between the Air Force and American ground commanders persisted because the commanders did not understand that many decisions causing them problems were Schwarzkopf's, not Horner's. Sometimes, Schwarzkopf's decisions did please the ground commanders. For example, they liked to see B-52s dropping bombs in front of their positions, and Schwarzkopf often obliged. As General Boomer noted later, ground commanders like himself had been closer to B-52 strikes in Vietnam than any Air Force officer and knew their psychological impact firsthand. Schwarzkopf ordered extensive B-52 bombing of Iraqi troops (who were dispersed and dug in) despite reservations on the part of Air Force officers who preferred to use the big bombers against more vulnerable area targets like supply depots.

In the dispute over the best use of precision bombing in the KTO, however, Schwarzkopf made decisions that displeased his ground commanders and caused grumbling about the JFACC's execution of those decisions. Not only did Schwarzkopf emphasize bombing Republican Guards rather than frontline forces, he also shared Horner's enthusiasm for tank plinking (the destruction of tanks with precision guided bombs), an enthusiasm that was not shared by Generals Franks and Boomer. They were confident that their tanks would easily outmatch Iraqi counterparts and were far more concerned about Iraqi artillery, which could make a Coalition ground attack extremely costly, especially if chemical shells hit Coalition troops during a breach of Iraqi defenses. For their part, the JFACC's air campaign planners complained that targets nominated by ground forces were often out-of-date and had already been disabled by previous air attacks.

Most of the demand for more bombing of Iraqi frontline troops was

---

17. Message, USCINCCENT to COMUSCENTAF, subject: Air Apportionment Planning, 311650Z January 1991, in TACC Current Ops Log, GWAPS, NA 215.

18. Memo, General Waller to commanders of ARCENT, CENTAF, MARCENT, and SOCCENT, subject: Air Apportionment Guidance, 15 February 1991.

Who Ran the Air War?

coming from VII Corps.[19] Since the Marines used much of their own air power for that purpose, they were relatively satisfied. XVIII Airborne Corps hoped to avoid Iraqi front lines entirely by executing a flanking movement into empty desert. As for VII Corps, even its planned thrust was shrouded in enough secrecy to make especially heavy bombing along its front unwise. In the last two weeks before the ground offensive, Schwarzkopf did increase bombing in front of VII Corps almost equal to the bombing intensity elsewhere along the front lines.[20]

The month-long pounding of Iraqi ground forces prior to the Coalition ground offensive was not the kind of warfare Coalition airmen had prepared for before the Persian Gulf crisis. Rather, they had trained to support troops against an enemy offensive. The TACS, designed to do the defensive close support job, had to create new procedures to support Coalition ground forces when they finally launched their offensive. General Horner used a Push CAS technique to feed sorties steadily to the battlefield where ground commanders and airborne controllers could direct strikes in clear weather. Although the battlefield was sometimes obscured by bad weather and smoke from burning oil wells, the groundwork laid by air power in the preceding weeks meant that the ground offensive met little opposition and required little close air support.

During the ground offensive, Horner assumed a more important task, that of helping to block an enemy retreat. The outcry over the so-called highway of death and the early cease-fire conspired with the weather to permit much of the Republican Guard to escape destruction. One aspect of this interdiction failure was a dispute over the proper use of the Fire Support Coordination Line (FSCL, pronounced *fissil*). Ground forces used the FSCL to integrate fire support with their movement and to protect their troops from fratricide by "friendly" air attack. In the area between Coalition ground forces and the FSCL, Coalition aircraft could attack only under direction from ground or airborne controllers. This procedure could cost time to coordinate the actions and required suitable weather conditions and the presence of a controller to execute the attacks; far less weight of fixed-wing air power could be brought to bear under such circumstances. The JFACC corollary to this rule was that helicopters and tactical missiles beyond the FSCL would be controlled by the JFACC.

Because the FSCL definition said little about coordination of weapons employment beyond the FSCL the corps commanders con-

19. Interviews, GWAPS with Gen. Frederick Franks, 3 September 1992, and Maj. Gen. Thomas Rhame, 11 July 1992.

20. See appendix 2, table 23, especially kill boxes AD5 and AE5.

sidered supporting fires beyond the line as "permissive," requiring no further coordination. That is, they resisted any restrictions on employing missiles or helicopters beyond the line and saw attempts to include such strikes in the ATO as efforts to put their organic firepower under JFACC control. To avoid JFACC control, XVIII Airborne Corps advanced the FSCL well north of the Euphrates River on 27 February and thus reserved an area for attack helicopter operations unconstrained by any requirement to coordinate with the JFACC. The effect of this use of the FSCL was to hamper air power's ability to destroy escaping Iraqi ground forces until the FSCL was finally pulled back after several hours.[21]

The dispute over the FSCL during the ground campaign had been building during the air campaign. The corps commanders were dismayed to find that until they launched their offensive, Schwarzkopf would not permit them to move the FSCL beyond the Saudi border. Since the JFACC had the principal responsibility for preparing the battlefield, the corps commanders were not given the air control they had come to expect during the years of preparing for a potential war in Europe with the Warsaw Pact. But visions of that war had never included an enemy army that would sit for weeks while bombing fatally weakened it.

The JFACC and the Allies

General Horner came into the war with several years' experience in dealing with the Persian Gulf nations, including a cordial relationship with the commander of the Royal Saudi Air Force, Lt. Gen. Ahmed Ibrahim Behery. Good working relations helped smooth what might have been a strained relationship. Half a million young American men and women poured into a country with a small population and exotic customs. Since the Americans provided the bulk of the Coalition forces, they dominated the Coalition, and they did so in ways that were usually sensitive to the views of the Saudis and the other allies.

Schwarzkopf and Horner cooperated with the Saudis in putting as many of the Americans as possible well outside the cities. The command solution adopted was not the creation of a truly unified command but rather of a parallel structure that put all Arab forces under a Saudi officer, Lt. Gen. Prince Khalid Bin Sultan al-Saud, who was Schwarzkopf's counterpart. Horner and Behery shared a similar rela-

---

21. TACC log 27 February 1991, GWAPS, NA 215; TACC historian notes, Saluda, GWAPS, NA 200; and interview, GWAPS with Maj. Gen. John A. Corder, 18 March 1992, GWAPS, NA 361. Discussions among the services and joint staff after the war have produced a more workable arrangement for coordinating strikes beyond the FSCL (Joint Staff, "A Doctrinal Statement of Selected Joint Operational Concepts," 23 November 1992, 15–19).

Who Ran the Air War? 135

tionship on paper and exhibited compatible personalities. Both Behery and Khalid had attended the Air War College at Maxwell Air Force Base, Alabama.[22]

From the beginning of the American deployment, Saudi and American personnel cooperated closely on planning the defense of Saudi Arabia and producing the daily ATO. The latter process, with which the Royal Saudi Air Force was familiar, allowed the Saudis a measure of control over the air operations unfolding in their country. The Saudis, for example, initially prohibited low-altitude flying, live-bomb training runs, and breaking the sound barrier.[23] The offensive plan for war with Iraq was developed with less Saudi participation. Nevertheless, by the end of 1990, Saudi planners had joined the Black Hole, where British planners had hitherto provided the only allied involvement.

Other nations also seemed reasonably comfortable with the authority exercised by the JFACC. They could not begin to duplicate his command and control apparatus, and the allied air commanders were eager to do everything they could for him. They were restrained in doing so only by restrictions placed on their activities by their governments. The French government, for example, insisted at the outset that French air be used solely in support of French troops. But the French government came around and eventually permitted French air units to operate far to the east of their ground units. Whenever Coalition governments stood aside, their airmen displayed a practiced capacity for working as allies. NATO forces were especially familiar with American procedures, and the Saudis and other Coalition members had sent pilots to the flying range at Nellis Air Force Base, Nevada, for Red Flag exercises.

Allied cooperation did not simply make Coalition air forces extensions of the U.S. Air Force, however. The governments concerned kept control over the targets that their forces could strike; on the whole, the limitations were neither burdensome to the JFACC nor substantially different from those imposed on American forces. Nonetheless, the weapons systems that foreign air forces favored did, at times, shape Coalition tactics. Most notable was the Royal Air Force's strong preference for JP-233, a runway cratering and mining munition that required low-level flight over Iraqi airfields. Horner's B-52 wings also wanted to execute low-level attacks on runways, but by and large, American fighter commanders did not think that runway attack was all that necessary (given Coalition air superiority) or even productive (given Iraqi capability to repair runways, the extent of their airfields, and the density of antiaircraft gun defenses that made low-level runs particularly hazardous).

22. Interview, GWAPS with General Behery, Riyadh, 11 July 1992, GWAPS, NA 377.

23. Message, CENTAF Situation Report, 191800Z August 1990, GWAPS, CSS 12.

But again, because of the abundance of Coalition aircraft and initial uncertainty about how much of a fight the Iraqi air force would make, there was no strong impetus, at first, to recommend a different use of RAF aircraft. Not until the RAF had lost some aircraft in the opening days of the air campaign did Horner suggest that they might use other bombs on other targets from medium altitude. Even then, the decision was left to the discretion of RAF commanders.

Unified Control of Air Power

The emergence of a single air component commander for Desert Storm attested to an effective control over an exceedingly crowded air space. A single air commander also allowed a degree of coherence in the conduct of air operations that would not have occurred had most air forces been assigned separate operating areas (route packages) as in Vietnam. Horner resorted to something like a route package only for northern Iraq, since European Command's Joint Task Force Proven Force in Turkey could best reach those targets, with its own equipment providing air refueling and escorts. Even in that case, though, the Black Hole provided Proven Force with target lists and included Proven Force strike sorties in the Master Attack Plan.[24]

On the whole, the theater commander wielded air resources as a unified force. Moreover, air forces from many nations operated with a harmony rarely seen at the outset of any large war, and they could conduct combined operations with relative ease. Circumstances overwhelmingly favored this happy outcome. The superabundance of Coalition aircraft, the absence of serious opposition in the air or effective attack against Coalition air bases, and the ability of the Coalition to choose the timing of the war's beginning all meant that neither the theater commander nor the JFACC ever had to make harsh choices in less favorable circumstances. For example, they never had to strip Marines of air support provided by Marine Corps aircraft; they never had to endanger the fleet by leaving it with less than full air defenses in the face an Iraqi air attack; they never had to pull air cover from the soldiers of an ally in the face of enemy attack.

Furthermore, the war did not witness complete control of all air power by the JFACC. In addition to Proven Force's de facto route package in northern Iraq, the Navy controlled fleet air defense sorties, and the Marines controlled direct support sorties. It was not necessary for the JFACC to share much authority with the CENTCOM staff (including the operations deputy). Although a joint target coordination board

---

24. Message, USCINCEUR/ECJ3 to USEUCOM components and USCINCCENT/J3, Order 001, 231243Z December 1990.

Who Ran the Air War?

formally existed, its real authority was limited.[25] In practice, most critical recommendations and decisions about the apportionment and allocation of air power were made by the theater commander, the JFACC, the Black Hole, and the TACC. Certainly, the concepts underlying the air campaign directed against Iraq proper had not come from the CENTCOM staff, although the theater commander himself did personally shape their implementation.

Ultimately, the result was probably a more coherent application of air power than would have resulted from the compromises required by a stronger joint targeting authority. The JFACC's authority in targeting, just as the arrangements settled on for other command and control arrangements for air operations, developed to a great degree in reaction to the situation the Coalition forces faced in the theater. That situation involved organizing air power of tremendous capabilities to fulfill the sweeping objectives planned for its employment. In addition, little experience or guidance concerning the power of the JFACC was available. The JFACC did not play by the book, but it is by no means clear that playing by the book would have achieved more.

---

25. Most of the board's members were below the rank of full colonel. See USCENTAF Combat Plans records and schedules, AFHRC, microfilm roll 23643.

Six | What Were the Conditions in the Theater?

Planners for operations in any theater attempt to anticipate not only the physical conditions of the area in which they must operate but also the political circumstances. In both cases, Desert Shield and Desert Storm presented commanders and staffs with a number of surprises. The political circumstances assumed in prewar plans differed from those that actually applied to deployment to the Arabian Peninsula. The physical conditions of the theater, although anticipated, varied from those experienced by U.S. air forces in the past. Understanding these differences affords a clearer picture of the circumstances under which air power was employed in the Gulf War.

Political Factors

The gulf crisis began during international political conditions uniquely favorable for forming a broad coalition of states to oppose Iraq. The blatant character of the Iraqi aggression, condemned almost universally in the Arab world, promoted local support for a large U.S. force deployment to the region. Iraqi efforts notwithstanding, the crisis remained detached from the Arab-Israeli conflict, which had long complicated American relationships with Arab states in the region. At that same time, the dissipation of the NATO–Warsaw Pact confrontation allowed both NATO and former Warsaw Pact members to support the deployment and contribute forces. Unlike the American experiences in the 1973 Arab-Israeli War and the 1986 raid on Libya, the United States encountered few obstacles in securing overflight rights and obtaining access to bases within and leading to the theater. In all respects, the political circumstances favored the early, massive deployment of air power to the region.

The key countries along the route from the United States to the Arabian Peninsula, and on the peninsula itself, gave swift or blanket approval for the air deployments. The nonstop deployment by fighter and bomber aircraft along an "Atlantic Bridge" to the Persian Gulf required staging aerial tankers at numerous bases from Lajes Air Base in the Azores to Cairo West Airfield in Egypt. Their access was speedily ne-

What Were the Conditions in the Theater? 139

gotiated. Hellenikon Air Base in Greece and Torrejon Air Base in Spain became key locations even though U.S. forces had begun leaving the bases before the gulf crisis at the insistence of the host governments. Later on, several East European countries granted overflight rights, as did Thailand and India for air missions across the Pacific.

The few exceptions to this unprecedented extension of staging and overflight rights were most notably the basing of B-52s requiring bases with extensive runway and ramp operating areas and access to specialized logistical support. The stationing of B-52s overseas raised political concerns for several potential host nations. Throughout the aircraft's history, host foreign governments had allowed B-52 basing only under limited conditions because of the B-52s' link with nuclear weapons and their widely publicized role in the Vietnam War. These restrictions and the concerns that drove them proved resistant to change. General Schwarzkopf ranked the employment of B-52s an important element of the attacks on Iraqi forces, but when the air campaign began, the sole B-52s stationed close to the theater were the twenty aircraft on the British-controlled island of Diego Garcia in the Indian Ocean, approximately three thousand miles from the target areas.

During Desert Shield, the U.S. Air Force proposed B-52 basing in several countries, including Egypt, Saudi Arabia, and Spain, but no moves took place until the air campaign began. It is unclear who was more reluctant: the potential host governments or American officials who did not wish to press them on a potentially delicate issue at a time when weightier matters appeared to be at stake. Certainly the base in Saudi Arabia proposed for B-52 basing raised such concerns, given that Iraq had already accused Saudi Arabia of allowing Westerners to desecrate the Muslim holy places. To minimize the problem, B-52s deployed to their wartime operating bases with no publicity and only *after* the air campaign began. Some B-52s flying from Diego Garcia or Wurtsmith Air Force Base in the United States landed in the theater subsequent to the initial attacks of the air campaign. Soon thereafter, B-52s deployed to Moron Air Base in Spain and later to Fairford Air Base in Great Britain and flew bombing missions from those locations.[1]

While many NATO countries committed their support to the Coalition, Turkey, owing to its unique position as the only NATO country bordering Iraq, played a particularly key role and ran great political risks. Contemplating the prospect of operations from Turkey and increased access by U.S. forces to Turkish air bases, the Turkish government had to weigh carefully its relationships in the Middle East.

At the outset of the crisis in August 1990, U.S. Air Force combat aircraft had deployed to Incirlik Air Base on routine exercise deploy-

---

1. *History of the Strategic Air Command 1 Jan–31 Dec 1990*, Vol. I (Office of the Historian, Strategic Air Command, 1992), 230, 240–41.

ments. The United States sought to augment that force with additional aircraft from Europe, creating an organization called Proven Force to undertake combat operations against Iraq from the north. To gain permission for combat missions from Turkey, and to increase the number of U.S. tactical aircraft deployed there, required careful negotiations with the Turkish government. The U.S.–Turkish Defense and Economic Cooperation Agreement authorized a maximum of forty-eight tactical aircraft, a number the United States sought to double temporarily to ninety-six.[2]

Turkish public and governmental opinion diverged over the country's proper role in the gulf crisis. All agreed on the need for defensive precautions against an Iraqi attack, but many opposed the use of Turkish soil for waging offensive war. During the fall of 1990, both the Turkish defense minister and the chief of Turkey's general staff resigned over the matter. The final agreement, which permitted the use of Turkish air bases, came to fruition literally hours before the opening of the air campaign: on 17 January, the Turkish parliament approved offensive use of their air bases by the aircraft of Proven Force. The additional aircraft, along with the Proven Force commander, arrived at Incirlik that same day; American aircraft began flying combat missions that night.[3]

A further complication arose from the use of the NATO members' AWACS aircraft that were also stationed at Incirlik. Since NATO, as an organization, played no official role in the Persian Gulf War (although individual member nations did), these aircraft could operate in the defense of Turkey but not in support of offensive operations against Iraq. To avoid the problem, the United States deployed American AWACS aircraft in addition to the NATO aircraft. The NATO plane provided defensive surveillance; the American one, offensive command and control.[4]

Excluding Israel from basing or overflight arrangements defused one potential political problem for the Coalition; namely, the linking of the confrontation with Iraq to the Arab-Israeli conflict. Israel had no interest in participating in the war, but Iraq saw—correctly or not—an opportunity to fracture the Coalition by dragging the Israelis in, and so immediately began a series of Scud attacks against the Jewish state. The United States attempted to prevent such a situation by attacking the Iraqi fixed Scud launch sites in western Iraq on the first day of the

---

2. Schroeder and Raab, *History of Joint Task Force Proven Force*, 23–24.

3. Sorties were canceled the next day while the Turkish officials reexamined what they had just signed up to, but operations then restarted less than a day later, with no further interruptions for the remainder of the war; ibid., 30–33.

4. Interview, CMSgt. Jerome E. Schroeder, USAFE History Office, with Maj. Gen. James L. Jamerson, commander Joint Task Force Proven Force, 27 March 1991, Ramstein Air Base, Germany, GWAPS, NA 124.

air war. More than sixteen hundred Coalition strikes (and even more sorties) flew against fixed launch sites, mobile Scuds, Scud-production facilities, suspected hide sites, and communications nodes, all with unknown effect.

The United States also sought to gain Israeli forbearance by actively supporting Israel with Patriot missile defenses and communication links that increased warning time of the Scud launches. At the same time, the United States discouraged any move by Israel to conduct its own air strikes against Iraq.[5] It remains unclear how close the Israelis came to retaliation for Iraqi attacks; one can only speculate about the real damage that would have been done to the Coalition by such a move. Arab Coalition members may not have reacted to an Israeli attack on Iraq in the ways that American decision-makers feared; luckily, the test never came.

Iran, which could have affected Coalition air operations most directly, did not, in fact, play a substantial role militarily during the crisis, but the country did gain much politically. During Desert Shield, Saddam Hussein attempted to secure his eastern flank by allowing territorial concessions to the enemy that Iraq had vanquished only two years before. Although Iran did regain territory during Desert Shield, this did not lead its government to take sides in the Persian Gulf War. During the war, Iranian action indicating potential hostility toward the Coalition or military support for Iraq would have kept aircraft carriers out of the gulf, thereby greatly increasing their aircraft range to the target (adding to the already high demand for air refueling tankers). Also, such action would have made air operations close to the Iranian border, particularly in the Basra area, a subject of great concern.

Iran, recognizing immediately the political advantages accruing from having the Coalition dispose of its ten-year nemesis, however, created no such difficulties. Instead, it provided a service to the Coalition (and even more so to its own interests) by remaining strictly neutral and interning the Iraqi aircraft that fled to Iran beginning in late January. Iran reaped additional benefits by retaining those aircraft and, even more, from the military devastation wreaked on its chief rival for dominance in the Persian Gulf region.

Physical Factors

Distances, Terrain, and Weather

To employ Coalition air power against Iraq, aircraft had to fly extended distances and to operate in conjunction with other aircraft from dis-

---

5. David Makovsky, "Of Friends and Foes," *Jerusalem Post*, 18 January 1992, 14 (excerpts from U.S. News & World Report Staff, *Triumph Without Victory: The Unreported History of the Persian Gulf War*).

Figure 30   Relative Distances in the Area of Operations

tant bases. The flight distances from the air bases to the target areas (see figure 30) made aerial refueling—often multiple refuelings—a nearly standard part of most combat missions. The closest land or carrier basing put aircraft 175 or more miles from the nearest targets in the Kuwaiti theater and more than triple that distance for targets in the Baghdad region. The bulk of the combat aircraft flew from bases in southern Saudi Arabia and the coastal gulf states; for them and the Red Sea carrier aircraft, the targets were seven hundred to one thousand miles away, well beyond the unrefueled combat radius of most aircraft.

Proven Force attacked most of the targets in northern Iraq, but even these aircraft, which could not overfly Syria and therefore had to divert around it, still traveled six hundred miles or more to their targets. For the B-52s, the seven-hundred-mile distances for the aircraft based in the theater were the shortest; most of the B-52s traveled twenty-nine hundred or more miles from Diego Garcia, Moron Air Base, or Fairford Air Base.

Flying from the Saudi Arabian and other gulf state bases meant coordination and flight rendezvous with other aircraft from bases hundreds of miles apart. From Al Minhad in the United Arab Emirates, for example, F-16s would typically join in a "package" of aircraft that could include F-15Cs from Tabuk, Saudi Arabia, EF-111s from Taif, Saudi Arabia, F-4Gs from Shaikh Isa, Bahrain, and KC-135s from Seeb, Oman, along with airborne control aircraft from several additional bases (see figure 31). While the above example names only U.S. Air

What Were the Conditions in the Theater?

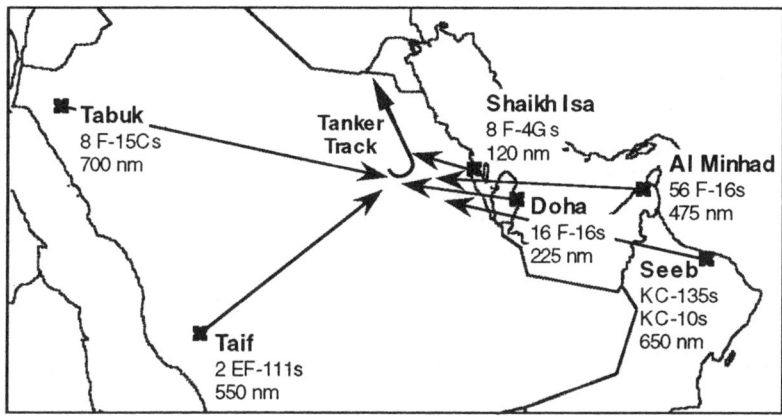

Figure 31 Formation of a "Package" for Attacks into Iraq

Force aircraft, packages also included Navy, Marine Corps, and other Coalition aircraft. The complexity of the coordination and the distances involved added to the scale of operations: the package cited above might involve twenty-four to thirty-six aircraft, and dozens of such packages flew every day.

The basic information for the flights arrived in the daily ATO; delays in publishing the order or late changes forced the flying units to rely on advance information received by telephone from planners at Riyadh. The ATO provided the targets and timing, but the mission commander still determined the routing, tactics, and other procedures and passed this information by secure telephone to the other units in the package. Navy flight crews on board aircraft carriers in the Red Sea or Persian Gulf faced a more difficult time getting the ATOs. Because of equipment incompatibility with Air Force secure communication devices, the tasking order documents were flown daily to the ships. Navy crews, however, had an easier time coordinating the flights since most of the aircraft from the same ship flew together.

In contrast to the complex communications arrangements of CENTCOM forced by the physical dispersion of its air bases, Proven Force crews at Incirlik faced a much simpler task. Here, the U.S. air forces in Europe had set up a composite wing organization composed of attack, air defense, and support aircraft from eight different flying units; the result was that crews could plan the missions and discuss the possible outcomes face-to-face in the same room, minimizing even the need for a published ATO.

Whereas terrain in the target areas presented several advantages to the attacking aircraft, it posed some problems as well. The flat, undifferentiated deserts of the Kuwaiti theater made visual orientation of targets by the attack aircraft quite exacting. The combination of the high altitudes flown by the attacking aircraft, the Iraqi use of decoys and camouflage, obscuring smoke, and conditions of blowing sand (and, particularly late in the war, smoke from oil fires) complicated both visual and infrared observation of vehicles and equipment. Aircrews in Air Force and Navy aircraft equipped with infrared targeting and navigation systems discovered that they could pick out vehicles effectively at night—especially in the early evening—because of the different cooling rates of the sand and the metals of Iraqi vehicles.

The geography of Iraq dictated the paths of resupply to the Kuwaiti theater. Supply routes from the north had to cross a series of bridges over the Euphrates or Tigris Rivers and transit a network of roads that merged as they approached the city of Basra. These bridges and roads provided excellent targets for air-interdiction operations. At the same time, the open and rather hard-packed ground allowed the resupply effort to bypass damaged sections of roads and many bridges.

Perhaps the most dominant terrain feature of the Kuwaiti theater was the large marshy lake, the Hawr al Hammar, beginning west of Basra and extending farther west toward An Nasiriyah (see figure 32). This lake formed a northern barrier for the Iraqi army in the theater, passable at one main causeway. When the Coalition ground forces attacked from the south and west, the Iraqi army's only path of retreat lay north over this causeway or eastward to the damaged and destroyed bridges over the canal west of Basra.[6] On 27 February, the last day of the war, the area bounded by Coalition forces, the Hawr al Hammar, and the canal became the Basra pocket. This area contained most of the Iraqi forces that had not fled the theater earlier or fallen prisoner to the Coalition.

Weather was another of the physical conditions that came to frustrate Coalition operations. Desert Storm air operations encountered the worst January and February weather reported in the theater in fourteen years, conditions that hampered bombing effectiveness considerably. Analysis by the Air Weather Service determined that the Coalition encountered cloud ceilings below ten thousand feet over Baghdad and Kuwait roughly twice as frequently as historical climatology would have indicated.[7]

Particularly in the early days of the air war, as many as half of the sorties did not attack or missed their assigned targets because of poor weather. Some aircraft thus had to employ less accurate radar-aimed

---

6. See chapter 3 for discussions of the attacks on the bridges in Iraq and the retreat of the Iraqi army to Basra.

7. Air Weather Service, Operations Desert Shield/Desert Storm, Report No. 2, "An Analysis of AWS Support to Operations Desert Shield/Desert Storm," 6 December 1991, 125, GWAPS, NA 76. (Henceforth AWS Report 2.)

What Were the Conditions in the Theater?

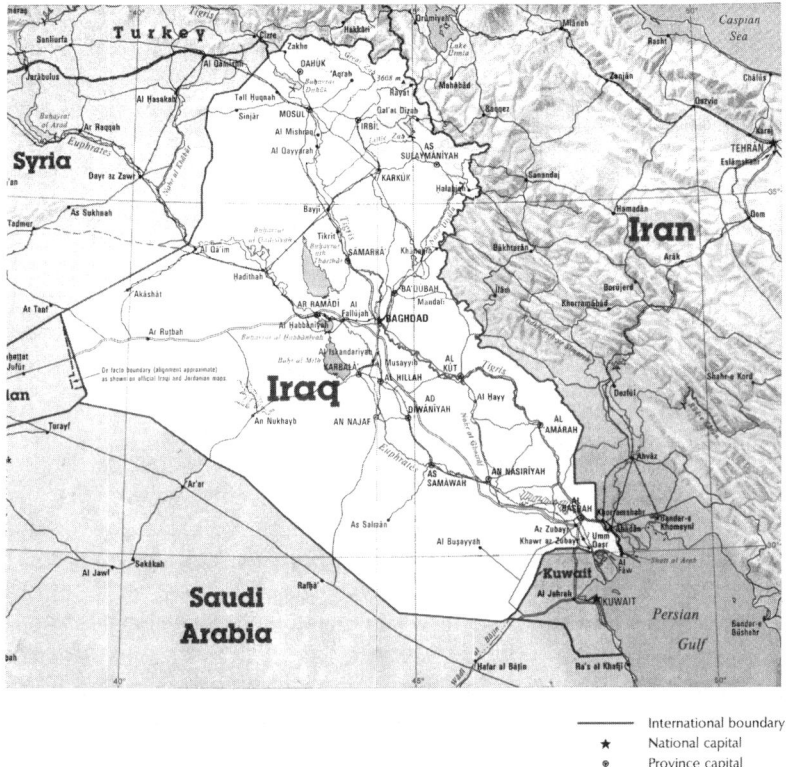

Figure 32 **Map of Iraq and Kuwait**

bomb releases through the clouds; other aircraft, such as A-10s and AV-8Bs, returned with their weapons or did not take off at all. Laser-guided bombs could not be guided if the target lay beneath fog or clouds. On the second and third days of the air war, more than half of the F-117 flights were unsuccessful or canceled because of low clouds over Baghdad; on the following two days in the Kuwaiti theater, A-10s that normally flew a total of more than two hundred sorties a day successfully flew a two-day total of only seventy-five.[8] Weather conditions did not remain as severe for the entire war, but the adverse conditions for the first ten days, and again during most of the ground war, left the most lasting impression on flight crews.

The weather encountered during the air war proved unexpectedly bad, not just because it differed so much from the climatological record but because it differed so sharply from the weather of fall 1990. Dur-

---

8. F-117 Summary Data, GWAPS Missions Database; and 23/354 TFW(P), "Combat Chronology," 20 and 21 January 1991, AFHRA 00885046-51.

ing training for the air campaign, skies remained clear for weeks at a time, and even visibility restrictions from blowing sand were absent in the operating areas.[9] The briefings on the air campaign included a depiction of the anticipated January–February weather patterns, but the expected patterns typically suggested two days of a passing weather front, followed by three to five days of clear skies. Instead, the weather fronts came and stayed, bringing more fog and lower ceilings than expected. Moreover, the decision to bomb from medium altitude multiplied the impact of the weather, for a target visible to an aircraft at an altitude of a thousand feet might escape observation at ten thousand feet.

Two final observations are warranted on the weather encountered. First, while unusually severe for the region, the weather was nonetheless superior to conditions in those same months in most other parts of the northern hemisphere. Flying over Frankfurt, Germany, or Hanoi, Vietnam, for instance, pilots would have experienced low ceilings twice as frequently as those actually encountered in the Persian Gulf region. In other words, visual, medium-altitude bombing tactics would have proven virtually impossible during a typical European winter or Southeast Asia monsoon, during which cloud ceilings at or below ten thousand feet occur 80 or 90 percent of the time.[10]

Second, it is not clear that the Coalition actually encountered unusually poor weather. Planners may have simply been excessively optimistic because of the poor quality of climatological data for the region. U.S. forecasters at several locations in the theater noted disparities between their procedures for recording weather observations and those of the local meteorologists, particularly in reporting ceiling and visibility. The U.S. forecasters, while having insufficient time to make a thorough evaluation, began to doubt that the Persian Gulf data they had used rested on accurate assessments of the previous fourteen years.[11]

The Air Bases

The quality of bases used for Desert Storm varied considerably within and among countries. Saudi Arabia is the most prominent case in point. The Saudis had superb air bases: some were finished, occupied, and offered excess capacity, while others were incomplete, that is, pos-

9. USAF Environmental Technical Application Center Technical Note 92/003, "Gulf War Weather," 2-1 to 2-2-57.

10. USAF Environmental Technical Applications Center Study, "Comparison of Germany, Viet Nam Climatology to Persian Gulf Climatology and Desert Storm—Jan–Mar," 19 May 1992, Capt. R. P. Arnold and TSgt. R. C. Bonam.

11. AWS Report 2, 117–18, 123.

What Were the Conditions in the Theater?

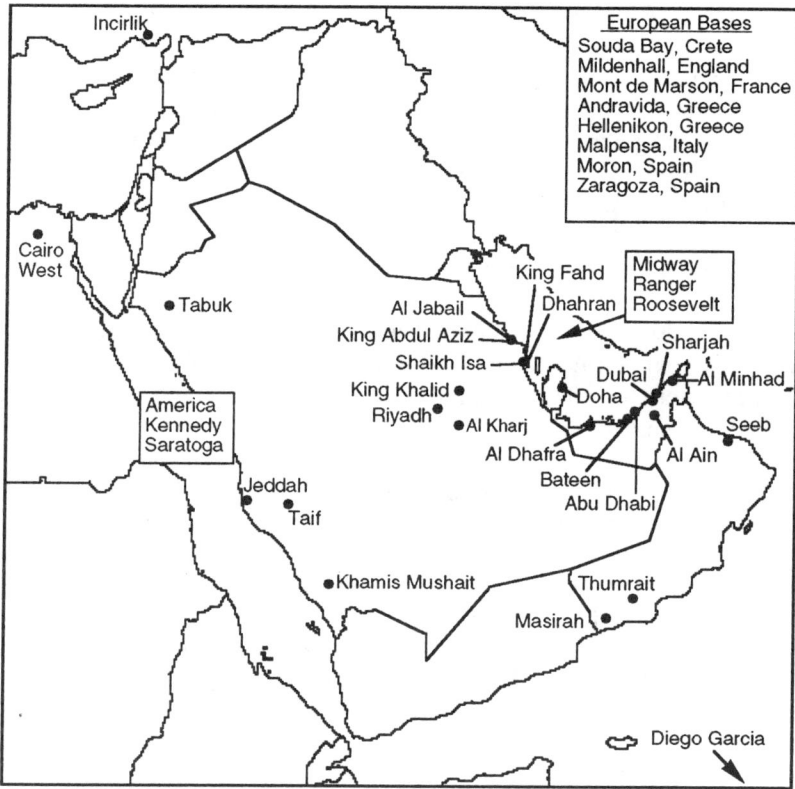

Figure 33   Map of Region Depicting Major Air Bases Used by Coalition Air Forces during Desert Storm

sessing runways and ramps, but little else. The facilities occupied by the Coalition air forces varied from those at Khamis Mushait, which had ample aircraft shelters and modern living and working conditions, to those at Al Kharj, a site still under construction. Al Kharj had merely runways and taxiways, and the nearest source of water was twelve miles away (see figure 33).

Even with excess capacity, however, the bases could not handle the size of the air forces deployed there during the Gulf War—particularly after the second phase of deployments in November 1990—without additional engineering support and temporary construction. The Saudi bases were just part of the story, though. The U.S. operations plan that served as the basis for the original deployment directed flying units to fourteen air bases in five countries. U.S. aircraft actually operated out of twenty-three bases, eleven of which were in Saudi Arabia. The remainder were in the other gulf states, which lacked the Saudi base infrastructure to support air operations.

The Saudi air bases owed much to long-standing security assistance relations with the United States. Dhahran served during World War II as a resupply point for U.S. forces in Asia, and the U.S. Army Corps of Engineers rebuilt Dhahran Airfield in 1956. In the 1960s and 1970s, U.S. Army and Air Force engineers designed and constructed several more bases, including the major ones at Taif, King Khalid Military City, and Khamis Mushait. These bases and support facilities, which accounted for three-quarters of U.S. military sales to Saudi Arabia over the past forty years, provided the needed infrastructure to help absorb a deployment of the size and speed of Desert Shield.[12]

The American military organized base support on the run. Not only was the Desert Shield deployment larger than anticipated, almost none of the units (2 percent) deployed to a base originally assigned to them in the operations plan. General Boomer, commander of I Marine Expeditionary Force, commented that the deployment seemed to be "first come, first served" in acquiring airfields.[13]

Most bases required a vast array of services for the early deploying units that arrived ahead of most of their logistical support, a calculated risk assumed by CENTCOM in the interest of deterring an early Iraqi attack. Logistical personnel scrambled to improve functions such as fire fighting, feeding arrangements, water purification, sanitation, fuel supply, and secure communications, all of which created vulnerabilities or could have impeded operations. Fortunately, the bases could expand, and at many locations local businesses could provide rental equipment or services to ameliorate shortages. In some cases, Coalition forces found it necessary to build the bases almost from scratch. In less than two months, for example, Al Kharj changed from a base with no buildings to one with tents, dining halls, hangar space, a hospital, electric power generators, and other services to support a population of nearly five thousand Air Force personnel.

The rapid growth from August 1990 to January 1991 did not happen, of course, without shortcuts in procedures and turbulence on the bases themselves. People, for lack of quarters, slept in hallways and in hangars; pilots flew extended missions without adequate rest; aircraft were parked in open rows without protection; tent cities adjoined munitions storage areas; and the leadership at each base cut whatever deals they could with local merchants for food, transportation, and

---

12. Remarks by Henry S. Rowen, ASD (ISA), at the Defense Institute of Security Assistance Management's (DISAM) Fourth International Military Assistance Symposium, 17 July 1991. Excerpted from *DISAM Journal*, Vol. 13, No. 4, Summer 1991, 4.

13. Lt. Gen. Walter E. Boomer, "Special Trust and Confidence Among the Trail-Breakers," U.S. Naval Institute *Proceedings*, November 1991, 47.

What Were the Conditions in the Theater?

other services. It was only after months of such improvisation that more orderly routines and support structures came to the bases.

Proven Force operations at Incirlik faced different circumstances. Incirlik had long served as a host base for U.S. Air Force operations and, in addition to Air Force personnel, housed more than two thousand Air Force family members and other U.S. civilians. Because of the Scud and terrorist threats in the area during the gulf conflict, the Air Force evacuated these people between 15 and 21 January, providing room for more than three thousand additional deploying forces. Thus, although a tent city arose to house many of the personnel, maintenance and support facilities and office space were already in place and operating.

Base security personnel alone could not protect the air bases. The principal threat in August and September was expected to come from an Iraqi army attack south into Saudi Arabia, with the most dangerous thrust along the coast to the oil fields. Early-arriving U.S. Army and Marine Corps forces moved in to hold the key enclaves around Al Jubayl and Dhahran, from which the Coalition aircraft would launch to meet the attack. By September, the threat of a direct attack by the Iraqi army had receded, but the danger of terrorism remained a primary concern throughout the deployment period and the war.

Both Generals Schwarzkopf and Horner pushed to get the American forces out of the communities, especially high-rise hotels, and onto the bases in dispersed quarters as rapidly as possible. When the air campaign began, the U.S. forces on Dhahran Air Base even moved from base facilities to bunkers and makeshift quarters near the aircraft. At peak strength, just forty-five hundred Air Force security police were available throughout the theater. On the whole, they had to confine their activities to providing security within base perimeters and limited exterior screening but not to defense of the base itself.

Most often, security outside the base remained with the host nation's security forces, and this proved effective. Despite Iraqi threats to unleash terrorists against U.S. forces in the theater and around the world, only one confirmed terrorist incident occurred in the theater during the entire period of the deployment: shots were fired at a bus carrying American servicemen and women near Jeddah Air Base, inflicting minor injuries. Saudi security forces apprehended four Palestinians and two Yemenis.[14] The efficiency of the Saudi police force, the lack of preparation and perhaps coordination by the Iraqis and their allies, and the protection inherent in the vast distances secured the bases from attack. This proved extremely fortunate since many bases had little in the way of passive protection—bunkers for ammunition and fuel, extensive perimeter defenses, and aircraft shelters.

14. Air Force Office of Special Investigation Briefing, nd, presented to OSI Commanders Conference 1991, 3; and USCENTAF/SP Battle Cell Log, 3 February 1991.

A final threat to the bases came from Scud missiles, possibly armed with chemical warheads. Launched from Iraq, they could reach bases on the Arabian Peninsula—Bahrain, Dhahran, and Riyadh—and Incirlik Air Base in Turkey. Patriot missile batteries protected the bases, but a Scud alert meant that military personnel had to take shelter and don gas masks and other protective gear. Multiple Scud alerts dulled the reactions of personnel to these measures, but the threat of a Scud-delivered chemical weapons attack persisted, a threat that CENTCOM took with increasing seriousness as the war went on and Iraq's position became more desperate.

Base personnel had minimal contact with the local population, both for security reasons and, particularly in Saudi Arabia, to ease Saudi fears of disruptive Western influence on their culture. CENTCOM prohibited possession of alcohol or sexually explicit material, set off-base dress codes for members, and did not allow chaplains to wear religious insignia off base. While the Saudis were sensitive to the actions of U.S. personnel off base, they made no moves to curb religious services on U.S. sites, and chaplains conducted Catholic, Protestant, and Jewish services. Easing the relationship was the extensive Saudi experience in coping with large numbers of Westerners assigned to work on vast development projects in or near the oil fields. The physical isolation of most bases also helped.

Life on the bases meant a combination of hectic round-the-clock schedules, boredom on off-duty time, and Scud alerts after the air campaign began. As the supply system became established, recreational equipment arrived, base stores opened, and local commanders pushed to improve living conditions. Bases could operate on more normal routines, but with many restrictions. Because the objectives and time of the deployment were uncertain initially, CENTCOM began planning in October 1990 for rotations of forces after six months; the command abandoned that policy within several weeks when the second deployment was announced. Everyone would remain for the duration.

Life for the aircrews during the air campaign involved little beyond sleep and the flight schedule. Crew routines varied with the type of aircraft they flew. Fighter and support aircraft missions often lasted five to ten hours, and these crews flew every day (or night), with an occasional day off. Crews for longer missions flew every other day. For example, crews on B-52 missions from Diego Garcia or from bases in Europe spent fifteen hours or more in the air; AWACS or JSTARS aircraft missions lasted more than twelve hours. And flight times did not include the hours of preparation and debriefing on either side of the missions. Additional crews augmented the flying squadrons, but commanders of every type of aircraft unit requested still more crewmen and women to support the number of sorties flown daily. Flight surgeons cited fatigue as the most pervasive problem facing aircrews, attributing at least two noncombat fatalities to it. A study of Tactical Air Command crew members reported that two-thirds used medical stimulants and sedatives during the deployment, and 57 percent did so during the war.[15]

Theater Conditions and the Preparation of Air Power

As noted, the overall political and physical conditions of the theater proved uniquely suitable to the deployment and application of air power. Even the often great distances from base to target worked to the Coalition's advantage: Iraqi Scuds alone proved capable of bringing Coalition bases under attack, but only some of them—most bases were out of range of the Scuds. Once the war began, Coalition aircraft could pummel the enemy without serious fear of disruption from enemy ground forces, artillery, SAMs, or aircraft.

The desert has always proven the most favorable environment for the application of air power, and in this war it afforded the additional important benefit of removing most concerns about collateral damage throughout much of the Kuwaiti theater. And, despite the deficiencies of some of the austere bases inhabited by Coalition forces, never has an expeditionary force deployed to a region so well endowed with air and seaports,[16] first-class roads, and a wealthy local economy to provide various support services. Above all, Coalition forces benefited from the passivity of an opponent who had, at least in theory, the capability to make the deployment a harrowing and costly military ordeal, rather than the exhausting and chaotic but nonetheless peaceful operation it was.

---

15. Report, HQ USAF/SGPA, *Aerospace Medicine: Consolidated After-Action Report—Desert Shield/Desert Storm,* January 1992.

16. Of these, Dhahran and the associated port at Ad Dammam were by far the most important, serving as they did as the main points of debarkation for both air- and sealift. An Iraqi attack on the port and associated airfields could have complicated the deployment tremendously.

Seven | **What Were the Instruments of Air Power?**

Removing Iraqi forces from Kuwait required the efforts of many nations, but the United States provided the bulk of the military resources, concepts for their employment, and the command and control structure to implement those concepts. These truths apply to the air campaign as well as to all other aspects of the war. On closer study, it becomes apparent that in some areas the American effort constituted close to 100 percent of the whole; in others, considerably less. Moreover, the American armed services provided different kinds of air power that reflected the practices, concerns, and equipment characteristic of each individual branch of those armed services. The following pages examine the composition of those forces to provide the reader with a better understanding of the instruments of air power and their complexity.

From outside the Middle East, four countries besides the United States (Great Britain, France, Canada, and Italy) sent combat flying units. Several more nations (South Korea, New Zealand, and Argentina) provided a nominal number of transport aircraft (C-130s) and crews; while others (the Netherlands, Belgium, Luxembourg, and Germany) sent air units to Turkey to take part in the NATO defense of that country against Iraq but not to participate in Desert Storm. Gulf state air forces were from Saudi Arabia, Kuwait, Bahrain, Qatar, and the United Arab Emirates.[1] U.S. air assets were spread among the Air Force, Navy, Army, and Marine Corps, including Army and Air Force Special Operations Command aircraft, which flew more than one thousand fixed- and rotary-wing sorties during Desert Storm.

Coalition air power also included cruise missiles, drones for reconnaissance and decoys, and satellites for communications, reconnaissance, and weather observation. Elements of that air power moved the forces to the region, reconnoitered the target areas, controlled the employment of air forces, defeated the Iraqi air force in the air and on the

---

1. Plus, Japan, South Korea, Kuwait, and Italy donated (paid the cost of) a total of two hundred airlift flights into Saudi Arabia. Appendix 2 outlines the numbers and types of aircraft supplied by each member of the Coalition.

ground, and struck targets throughout Iraq and Kuwait. This chapter discusses each of these elements.

American crews flew more than 85 percent of the sorties during the war. Many countries supplied air-to-air fighters, air-to-ground attack aircraft, and cargo aircraft, but the United States provided all or almost all of the Coalition's command and control systems, electronic warfare aircraft, heavy bombers, cruise missiles, and stealth capability. Overall, the key contributions of the United States came not just in numbers of systems but in *capabilities* of the various elements of air power (see figure 34). Some were based on *quality* (for example, stealth), others on a *quantity* so great that it brought a quality of its own (for instance, aerial refueling and airlift).

An array of high-technology American systems gave the Coalition a devastating advantage. The F-117s, Tomahawk missiles, and conventional air-launched cruise missiles delivered conventional warheads with great precision, unchecked by Iraqi defenses. Airborne warning and control aircraft monitored Iraqi and Coalition flight activity, and the JSTARS aircraft monitored and targeted Iraqi ground forces throughout the Kuwaiti theater.

In addition, satellites and airborne platforms provided communications, precise navigation, and reconnaissance information to air and ground forces. But it was the *combination* of U.S. capabilities, not all of which were based on advanced technologies, that made Coalition air power so predominant. F-111s, A-6s, and thirty-year-old B-52s, for example, took part in air strikes, effectively using advanced technology weapons as well as unguided bombs. To counter the vulnerability of strike aircraft to Iraqi defenses, Coalition pilots flew into the heavily defended areas of Iraq escorted by aircraft firing missiles that homed in on enemy radars (F-4Gs, EA-6Bs, or A-7s), and by aircraft that blinded enemy radars by electronic jamming (EF-111s or EA-6Bs).

The success of the aerial attacks also depended on the ability to mass formations of aircraft, made possible by an extensive network of aerial refueling aircraft. High-technology systems played a crucial role, but just as essential was the ability to employ nearly two hundred tankers at a time, to organize and maneuver large attack formations, to stage large airlifts routinely, and to conduct continuous aircraft carrier flight operations, all based on an underpinning of intense and realistic training. These American air power capabilities cannot easily be expressed in numbers.

Coalition air power may be depicted in several ways. Table 5 gives one common measure, the number of sorties flown by type of aircraft during Desert Storm. Any one measure tells just part of the story, however. Sortie counts do not include the space systems constantly in use or the hundreds of helicopters attached to ground and naval forces. The depiction of sorties flown gives an indication of the weight of effort

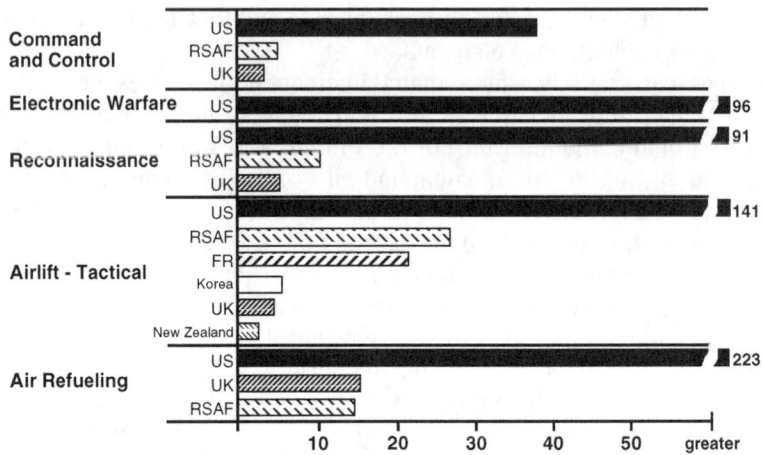

Figure 34 Coalition Aircraft Totals in Key Elements of Air Power Support

by each country but does not differentiate an A-4 embarked on a sortie of three hundred miles, carrying five, five-hundred-pound bombs, from a B-52 sortie of more than three thousand miles, carrying fifty, five-hundred-pound bombs.

The contributions to air power of air-to-ground sorties are captured in the January–February statistics. Nevertheless, those statistics do not reflect the total contributions to air power made by air refueling and airlift aircraft during Desert Shield. Since no one measurement can be all inclusive, the contributions are best examined by focusing on seven air power elemnts, with merely a brief mention of other comparative measures.

Airlift

The airlift that brought the forces, along with the supplies to sustain them, to the region was the greatest such airlift in history. On the basis of a common measure for airlift capacity, millions of ton-miles per day (MTM—the product of aircraft cargo weight in tons and the distance flown), Desert Shield/Desert Storm activity far surpassed earlier airlifts.[2]

- Peak period of Desert Shield/Desert Storm: 17 MTM/day
- 1973 airlift to Israel during Arab-Israeli War: 4.4 MTM/day

2. Briefing, Headquarters USAF/XOXWG, "Logistics in the Air Power Campaign," 16 May 1991, GWAPS, NA 584B. See tables 7 through 9 of appendix 2.

What Were the Instruments of Air Power? 155

- Operation Just Cause, to Panama, 1989: 2.0 MTM/day
- Berlin airlift, 1948–1949: 1.7 MTM/day
- "Hump" airlift of WW II: .9 MTM/day

The size of the effort is even more impressive considering the short-term nature of the next two largest airlifts compared with the Desert Shield and Desert Storm effort of more than nine months.

C-5s, C-141s, and commercial cargo and passenger aircraft mobilized for military service as part of the Civil Reserve Air Fleet (CRAF) carried out the U.S. strategic, or inter-theater, airlift.[3] The C-141s flew most of the missions (53 percent), the C-5s carried the most cargo (42 percent), and the CRAF aircraft carried most of the passengers (64 percent). From bases in the United States, these aircraft flew to air bases in Europe in transit to bases in the Southwest Asia theater. European bases served as both stopover points and terminals; Rhein-Main in Germany and Torrejon in Spain saw the heaviest use (27 and 44 percent, respectively, of the total traffic). In the theater, Dhahran, Saudi Arabia, served as the main terminus. This base alone handled half of the arriving traffic; during December 1990, for example, forty cargo and passenger aircraft arrived every day.[4]

The strategic airlift aircraft carried nearly all the people and more than 5 percent of the cargo shipped to the theater (approximately 15 percent, if fuel is excluded from the total cargo figures).

Aerial refueling tankers, KC-10s and KC-135s (assigned to Strategic Air Command [SAC]), also took part in the airlift. While employed on refueling missions to the theater, these aircraft brought both their own and other units' personnel and support equipment. In this way, SAC became relatively self-sufficient in its aircraft deployment.[5] The plans called for twenty KC-10s to serve strictly as cargo aircraft, but the need for aerial refueling sorties placed a particularly heavy demand on the tanker fleet. Ultimately, SAC supported this exclusive airlift requirement partially and reluctantly. The KC-10s flew 379 such cargo-only missions from August 1990 through January 1991.[6]

3. The Civil Reserve Air Fleet consists of civil aircraft committed to augmenting the Military Airlift Command fleet in certain emergency conditions. The aircraft are mobilized in stages, or increments, based on presidential order. Since institution of the program in 1952, however, CRAF mobilization had never been invoked until Desert Shield.

4. Data derived from the Military Air Integrated Reporting System and recorded in report, John Lund and Ruth Berg, *Strategic Airlift in Operation Desert Shield and Desert Storm: An Assessment of Operational Efficiency* (Santa Monica, CA: Rand WD-5956-AF, 1992), 36.

5. Briefing, SAC staff to GWAPS personnel, 10 February 1992.

6. Military Airlift Command, MAC History 1990 (Scott AFB, IL: Hq MAC/HO, 1991), 79; SAC History, 335–36; and GWAPS *Statistical Compendium*, Table 22.

Table 5 Total Sorties by U.S. Service/Allied Country by Aircraft Type

Service	Aircraft Type	Flown	Service	Aircraft Type	Flown
USAF	A-10	8,084	USSOCCENT	AC-130	104
USAF	B-52	1,741	USSOCCENT	AH-6	3
USAF	C-12	8	USSOCCENT	C-130	13
USAF	C-130	13,971	USSOCCENT	CH-47	14
USAF	C-141	1,766	USSOCCENT	EC-130	155
USAF	C-21	256	USSOCCENT	HC-130	107
USAF	C-29	20	USSOCCENT	HH-3	63
USAF	C-5	740	USSOCCENT	HH-3E	112
USAF	C-9	64	USSOCCENT	HH-60	9
USAF	E-3	379	USSOCCENT	MC-130	84
USAF	E-8	42	USSOCCENT	MH-3	19
USAF	EC-130	450	USSOCCENT	MH-47	2
USAF	EC-135	24	USSOCCENT	MH-53	282
USAF	EF-111	1,105	USSOCCENT	MH-6	1
USAF	F-111E	458	USSOCCENT	MH-60	284
USAF	F-111F	2,423	USSOCCENT	UH-60	10
USAF	F-117	1,299	Total		1,262
USAF	F-15C	5,685			
USAF	F-15E	2,172			
USAF	F-16	13,087			
USAF	F-4E	4	USN	A-6	4,824
USAF	F-4G	2,683	USN	A-7	737
USAF	KC-10	1,465	USN	E-2C	1,183
USAF	KC-135	9,559	USN	EA-6B	1,126
USAF	OA-10	660	USN	F-14	4,005
USAF	EP-3	4	USN	FA-18	4,449
USAF	RC-135	197	USN	P-3	23
USAF	RF-4	719	USN	S-3B	1,674
USAF	RF-4C	103	USN	TLAM	282
USAF	TR-1	89	Total		18,303
USAF	U-2	149			
Total		69,406			
			USA	C-12	183
			USA	C-23	3
USMC	A-6	795	USA	OV-1D	161
USMC	AV-8	3,359	USA	RC-12	216
USMC	C-12	9	USA	RU-21	242
USMC	EA-6B	504	USA	RV-1D	111
USMC	F/A-18	4,936	Total		916
USMC	KC-130	598			
USMC	OV-10	482	CRAF	CRAF	800
Total		10,683	Total		800

The entire strategic airlift fleet worked steadily throughout the deployment period, with two peak periods: during the initial response in August–September 1990 and again in December, after the order for the second stage of deployments (a surge that lasted through the end of Desert Storm). The C-5s and C-141s curtailed all other commitments but often ran short of aircrews, especially in the early days of the crisis before the activation of crews from the reserves. Military Airlift Command estimated, in fact, that its crew force would run out of allowable flying hours by the end of August, when the reserves were

What Were the Instruments of Air Power?

Table 5 (continued)

Service	Aircraft Type	Flown	Service	Aircraft Type	Flown
Saudi Arabia	Tornado/ADV	451	Canada	B-707	163
Saudi Arabia	BAE-125	110	Canada	C-130	124
Saudi Arabia	C-130	1,606	Canada	CC-144	54
Saudi Arabia	E-3	303	Canada	CF-18	961
Saudi Arabia	F-15C	2,088	Total		1,302
Saudi Arabia	F-5	1,129			
Saudi Arabia	H-212	113			
Saudi Arabia	Tornado/IDS	667			
Saudi Arabia	KC-130	267	Kuwait	A-4	651
Saudi Arabia	RF-5	118	Kuwait	F-1	129
Total		6,852	Total		780
France	C-130	271	Bahrain	F-16	166
France	C-160	582	Bahrain	F-5	122
France	F1-CR	92	Bahrain	H-212	5
France	Gabriel	4	Total		293
France	Jaguar	571			
France	KC-135	223			
France	M-20	2			
France	M2000	512	Italy	G-222	13
France	SA-330	1	Italy	Tornado	224
Total		2,258	Total		237
UK	BN2T	35			
UK	BNIS	517	UAE	C-130	35
UK	Buccaneer	226	UAE	C-212	10
UK	C-130	832	UAE	M2000	64
UK	F-3	705	Total		109
UK	Tornado/GR-1	1,644			
UK	Jaguar	600			
UK	Nimrod	147			
UK	Tristar	75			
UK	VC-10	359	Qatar	Alpha	2
UK	VCTR	277	Qatar	F-1	41
Total		5,417	Total		43

Source: Composite Sorties Database

activated. Military Airlift Command used the reserves in peacetime regularly, but such an extensive use of reservists was new. Approximately half of that command's airlift flight crews and maintenance personnel resided in the reserves, and even before the crisis, at any one time an estimated 20 percent of the reserve associate crews were flying on a regular basis.[7]

7. Lt. Gen. Vernon J. Kondra, *Operation Desert Shield-Desert Storm: The Vernon J. Kondra Notes, 24 Aug 1990–31 May 1991*, transcribed by Clayton Snedecker, 21st Air Force Historian (McGuire AFB, NJ: 1992), 6–8; John Lund and Ruth Berg, *Strategic Airlift in Operation Desert Shield and Desert Storm*, 27, 28; and Letter, MAC DCS Plans and Programs/XPX to MAC History Office, "Review of Chapter III of 1990 MAC History, Operation Desert Shield," 6 September 1991.

The Civil Reserve Air Fleet had been a long-standing contingency force but had never been used; some adjustments were needed. The first stage of CRAF augmentation, an authorization for thirty-eight aircraft and crews, including twelve Boeing 747s, occurred on 17 August 1990; it provided an increase of just ten aircraft, however, since the other twenty-eight had already begun working under contract with the airlines. The second stage, authorizing seventy-six more aircraft, took place on 17 January 1991, but merely nine cargo aircraft were added; the remainder were already contracted and flying.[8]

The CRAF augmentation provided a vital addition to the airlift, particularly in passenger-carrying ability, but with some attendant limitations. During the war, because of the concerns of some of the aircraft owners, CRAF aircraft could not stay on the ground at bases within range of Scud missiles during hours of darkness. This was problematic, since the main debarking base of Dhahran was within this range. In addition, the aircraft insurance policies specified geographical exclusion zones in which rates increased 2,000 percent, making each trip extraordinarily expensive.[9] An earlier activation of CRAF II, dedicated to transporting personnel (one-third of whom flew on military transports), might have eased the initial deployment.

Intra-theater airlift distributed the supplies and people throughout the Arabian Peninsula after they arrived in the theater. C-130s—149 from the U.S. Air Force (one-third of the total Air Force fleet) and smaller numbers from across other Coalition nations (Saudi Arabia, the United Kingdom, France, Canada, United Arab Emirates, South Korea, New Zealand, and Argentina), bore the brunt of this work.[10] These aircraft flew regular routes to all regional bases and supported large ground unit transfers within the theater. Where their routes ended, smaller transports or cargo helicopters continued the lift. The size of the theater and the number of bases made extensive intra-theater airlift essential. Of the twelve reporting categories, intra-theater airlift (22,064 sorties) ranked second only to interdiction (38,277 sorties) in total number of sorties flown during the war.[11]

In addition to moving passengers, spare parts, fuel, mail, and other items, intra-theater airlift accomplished tasks that road transport or communications could not. The C-130s were among the first aircraft

---

8. MAC History, 65; and *Conduct of the Persian Gulf War*, 420.

9. *Kondra Notes*, 84, 111, 114; *Strategic Airlift in Desert Shield and Desert Storm*, 22–23; and Stacy Shapiro and Meg Fletcher, "War Tensions Heat Up Market: Insurers Restrict Cover for Gulf Area," *Business Insurance*, 14 January 1991, 45.

10. These aircraft augmented the U.S. AC-, MC-, EC-, HC-, and KC-130s that also took part in operations.

11. See appendix 2, table 20.

What Were the Instruments of Air Power? 159

deployed to the theater (ninety-six had arrived by 9 September) to move the initial munitions, tents, and other support needed to stock the bases being established. The intra-theater airlift aircraft not only were scheduled on the ATO, they also physically *delivered* the ATO every day to locations that were without communications equipment for receiving classified information and to aircraft carriers that did not have the equipment for receiving the ATO electronically.

Throughout Desert Storm, daily flights to Riyadh delivered film from reconnaissance aircraft and videotape from attack aircraft. When the XVIII Airborne Corps repositioned four hundred miles to the west for the ground attack, C-130s flew scheduled landings at the repositioning site every seven minutes, twenty-four hours a day, for nearly fourteen days. During the ground war, airlifted logistics followed the ground advance, including an air drop by C-130s of more than one hundred tons of food and water to the 101st Airborne Division on the Euphrates River: the large number of prisoners taken had depleted the supplies of that division.[12] This aspect of airlift, less visible than the large transportation network leading to the theater, proved no less vital to the war's smooth prosecution.

Aerial Refueling

Aerial refueling facilitated two different aspects of the Gulf War: the speedy deployment of large air forces to the region, and the use of those forces in large and complex air combat operations. Five countries using twelve different types of aircraft provided this refueling capability. Participating aircraft included nearly three hundred U.S. Air Force KC-10s and KC-135s—almost half of the USAF fleet. Others included twenty Marine Corps and Special Operations Command KC-130s, sixteen Navy KA-6s (plus other A-6s and S-3s configured for aerial refueling), fifteen British aircraft (VC-10/Victor/Tristar), twelve Saudi KE-3s/KC-130s, six French KC-135s, and three Canadian Boeing 707s.

Non–U.S. tankers mainly refueled aircraft from their own nation, but they were capable of refueling others and often did. All were needed because so many air defense fighters and airborne control aircraft remained aloft for extended periods, and numerous attack aircraft needed to refuel both en route to the targets and on the return leg to their bases because of the distances involved. The tanker aircraft proved a critical resource, but a heavier commitment of the U.S. fleet would not have helped; the limitation was airspace, not numbers (see figure 35). With a daily average of 360 tanker sorties, the refueling

---

12. Briefing by Col. Maxwell C. Bailey, commander, 317th Tactical Airlift Wing, to the chief of staff of the Air Force, 19 July 1991.

tracks saturated the available airspace; the number of refueled aircraft is uncertain, but SAC tankers alone refueled an average of 1,433 aircraft a day.[13]

Some 60 percent of all attack sorties required aerial refueling. Of the total number of Desert Storm sorties by category, aerial refueling ranked third, behind airlift. U.S. aircraft accounted for 90 percent of that total, with the U.S. Air Force fleet of KC-10s and KC-135s assuming the preponderant share.

Aerial refueling capability enabled fighter squadrons and bombers to deploy—even loaded with armaments—nonstop from the United States to the Southwest Asia theater. More than one thousand U.S. aircraft deployed in this way. It took nearly one hundred tankers operating out of en-route bases to create an Atlantic air refueling bridge and a less frequently used bridge across the Pacific. Fighter aircraft deployments from the United States to the theater traversed sixty-nine hundred nautical miles, took fifteen to sixteen hours' flying time, and required from seven (for F-15Es) to fifteen (for F-4Gs) refuelings en route. The ability to fly nonstop enabled F-15Cs to be on alert in Saudi Arabia within a day after notification to deploy and five U.S. Air Force fighter squadrons to arrive in the region within five days.[14] Similarly, aerial refueling not only extended the range of attack aircraft, it allowed massive concentrations of strikes and continuous airborne control and surveillance of battle areas.

Command and Control

U.S. forces almost had a monopoly on airborne command and control systems, although NATO and Saudi Arabian AWACS aircraft performed supporting roles. Roughly half of the U.S. Air Force's AWACS fleet took part. Flying from Saudi Arabia, a contingent of eleven Air Force E-3 AWACS aircraft maintained continuous coverage of the air picture from the Red Sea to Persian Gulf throughout the war. At any given time, three AWACS planes covered Saudi Arabia, while on the flanks of the E-3 orbits, U.S. Navy E-2C aircraft augmented the AWACS coverage (working principally with Navy aircraft), and a Saudi E-3 flew in a rear orbit over central Saudi Arabia. Flying from Incirlik, a contingent of three U.S. Air Force E-3 AWACS provided airborne control for the Proven Force missions into Iraq. NATO E-3 AWACS defended Turkey, but they were not authorized to take part in offensive operations

---

13. GWAPS *Statistical Compendium*, Tables 109–113; and Desert Storm/Desert Shield Tanker Assessment, Headquarters, Strategic Air Command, Plans and Requirements (XP), 23 September 1991, 2-3, 9-3.

14. Two aircraft carriers were also on station in the region by this time.

What Were the Instruments of Air Power?

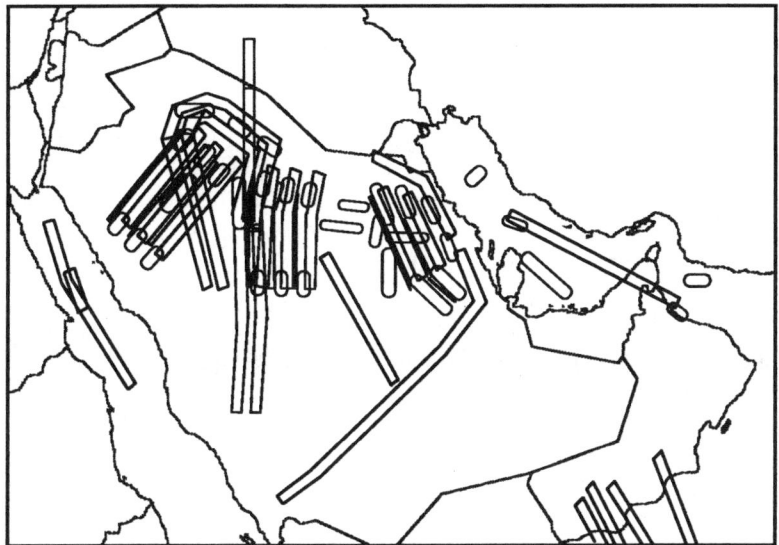

Figure 35   Aerial Refueling Tanker Tracks over Saudi Arabi and Nearby Regions

against Iraq. Both systems played their part: NATO for defensive purposes only and U.S. AWACS for controlling offensive strikes.[15]

AWACS aircraft organized the air battle, and airborne battlefield command and control center (ABCCC) aircraft—specially equipped Air Force EC-130s—took part in controlling air attacks against Iraqi ground forces. Several other systems acted with them. U.S. Air Force EC-135s served as radio relays for the ABCCC aircraft (antenna placement on the ABCCC aircraft hindered communications with aircraft at higher altitudes). Air Force OA-10s and Marine Corps OV-10s and F/A-18Ds served as forward air controllers to direct strike aircraft on close air support missions. Additionally, the JSTARS aircraft, latecomers to the theater, detected moving Iraqi forces.[16]

The JSTARS aircraft were not designed to perform command and control, but they did, in part, serve in that role. The JSTARS system

---

15. Memo, Capt. Guy Cafiero to GWAPS, Task Force 4, "E-3 Employment Desert Storm," AWACS File, GWAPS; and interview, CMSgt. Jerome E. Schroeder with Maj. Gen. James L. Jamerson, commander, JTF Proven Force, Ramstein AB, Germany, 27 March 1991, GWAPS, NA 124.

16. Other aircraft, such as the U.S. Navy's S-3s and British Nimrods, also assisted with command and control connectivity, a particularly difficult task for the Coalition, given the great distances to the target area and the broad dispersion of the strike aircraft. (See tables 5 and 6 of appendix 2.)

had advanced radars to detect and track ground targets, but in 1990 it was still in a developmental stage and had not undergone operational testing by the Air Force and Army. Nevertheless, two of these aircraft were pressed into use, and with civilian technicians to operate the equipment, the planes arrived in the theater just days before the beginning of the air war. One of the two aircraft flew every night of the war, performing reconnaissance of Iraqi ground formations (and suspected Scud sites), passing targeting information to the ABCCC and AWACS aircraft and even coordinating target information directly with the strike aircraft.[17]

Sixteen military and five commercial communications satellites made the command and control of Coalition forces possible. Fourteen U.S. military communications satellites were in orbit when the crisis began, and they were augmented by two others, one British (SKYNET) and one NATO spacecraft. Five leased commercial satellites and communications circuits were also added. Taken together, these systems provided a transmission rate of two hundred million bits per second, or about thirty-nine thousand simultaneous telephone calls. Military systems provided approximately 75 percent of this total capacity.[18] These space systems carried 90 percent of the inter-theater communications and an undetermined, but substantial, portion of the intra-theater.[19]

Reconnaissance

Reconnaissance assets included an array of air and space systems. Spacecraft included a total of six meteorological satellites, three Defense Support Program satellites that scanned for and reported bright infrared "events"—the exhaust glow from Scud launches (the satellites were put in orbit originally to warn of a Soviet ballistic missile attack

---

17. USCENTAF, "Joint Surveillance and Target Attack Radar System (JSTARS) Employment Concept," GWAPS, Microfilm Roll 10238. Target location and navigation by both aircraft and ground forces were tremendously assisted by a constellation of sixteen Global Positioning System satellites, intended for operational capability in 1991 but pressed into service ahead of schedule [US Space Command Assessment, 25–32; and Andrew Wilson, ed., *Interavia Space Directory 1991–92* (Alexandria, VA: Jane's Information Group, 1991), 203–5].

18. Joint Staff/J-6Z briefing, "Use of Satellite Communications Desert Shield/Desert Storm," undated; *Interavia Space Directory 1991–92*; and Report, Paul High, Jr, "Assessment of USCENTCOM Intelligence Communications Support (draft)," April 1992, S-127/IPSG-INCA, 8884-28.

19. The entire Desert Storm communications architecture was a collection of interconnected land-line, radio, and satellite systems. Since satellites were used for trunking of local distribution (indigenous systems could not handle the volume of Coalition communications traffic), phone conversations between units within a few miles of each other, sometimes even on the same base, could be connected via satellite.

What Were the Instruments of Air Power?

against the United States). Two civil satellites—the U.S. LANDSAT and the French SPOT—also provided imagery.[20]

A second category of U.S. reconnaissance assets were the strategic airborne reconnaissance platforms, a group of nine RC-135 Rivet Joint aircraft and nine U-2/TR-1 aircraft operated by SAC.[21] These aircraft had sophisticated sensors for collecting imagery and electronic intelligence, but they were vulnerable while flying in Iraqi airspace. Therefore, while the Coalition had a large array of strategic airborne and space systems, greater capability was needed for observing Iraqi forces and obtaining targeting data and bomb damage assessment, particularly during periods of cloud cover. For these tasks the Coalition needed a third category of tactical reconnaissance: aircraft capable of flying under the clouds and penetrating Iraqi-defended airspace.

This third category, tactical reconnaissance aircraft, proved deficient. The U.S. Air Force employed twenty-four RF-4Cs (six of them flying from Incirlik), and even these were a late addition to the force. The six aircraft at Incirlik did not arrive until February 1991, and twelve of the other RF-4Cs did not arrive in the theater until just before the beginning of the air war. More were not sent, reportedly because of a lack of ramp space.[22] This "lack of ramp space" argument suggests that these assets were assigned an extremely low priority that resulted in a shortage of tactical reconnaissance during the war. The Marine Corps had retired its own version of this aircraft, the RF-4B, only months prior to the war and before an operational replacement was available.[23]

Other measures compensated for part of the shortfall in tactical reconnaissance. Six of the British Tornado aircraft (GR1As) and ten Saudi RF-5Cs flew reconnaissance missions throughout the war. A variety of fighter aircraft (F-16s, French and British Jaguars, F-14s, A-6s, and F/A-18s, the latter three mainly in maritime reconnaissance) flew reconnaissance missions in an attempt to overcome the shortage.[24] Finally, Pioneer unmanned aerial vehicles (UAVs), used by the U.S. Army, Navy, and Marine Corps, flew almost three hundred sorties during Desert Storm, predominantly by the Marines. The UAVs had both in-

---

20. Report, United States Space Command Operations Desert Shield and Desert Storm Assessment, January 1992, 10–24, 39–46; and *Interavia Space Directory 1991–92*, 467–69, 474–77. See table 5 of appendix 2.

21. The AWACS and JSTARS aircraft, mentioned in the first category of command and control, also had an immense reconnaissance capability: AWACS of airborne aircraft and JSTARS of ground traffic.

22. *Conduct of the Persian Gulf War*, T-139-41.

23. Lt. Gen. Royal N. Moore, Jr., "Marine Air: There When Needed," *Proceedings*, November 1991, 63–70.

24. GWAPS Missions Database.

frared and television capability for day and night reconnaissance and were used for battleship gunfire support, identifying ships, finding missile sites, command bunkers, and Iraqi equipment, and assessing bomb damage.[25]

But remotely piloted vehicles had neither the range nor the capabilities for large-scale reconnaissance. Inadequate numbers of aircraft that could penetrate enemy air space and take pictures of targets reflected a belief that national systems could take up the slack, a confidence that proved misplaced.

Electronic Warfare

Electronic warfare aircraft played a central role in the neutralization of the Iraqi air defense system, one of the most dramatic successes of the war which, in turn, made possible the type of air campaign that followed. Electronic warfare assets included airborne and space systems designed to collect electronic intelligence and aircraft devoted primarily to suppressing Iraqi electronic capabilities (communications, radars, and missile control centers).

Given the importance of keeping Coalition aircraft attrition low, electronic warfare aircraft were of greater importance to overall air operations than ever before. Unavailability of electronic warfare aircraft, in fact, was a reason to abort an attack mission. Of the one hundred mission packages flown from Incirlik during the war, only one was flown without such aircraft—the first night, before these aircraft had arrived at the base—and in that case, planners changed targets to a lower threat area than originally chosen.[26] Of the manned attack aircraft, just the F-117s did not require careful integration of electronic warfare aircraft support into mission planning. The United States dominated this mission area: of the approximately three thousand electronic warfare sorties flown in Desert Storm, U.S. air forces conducted all but eighty of them.[27]

U.S. capabilities in electronic warfare included aircraft that destroyed Iraqi air defense radars. The sixty-one Air Force F-4Gs (almost the entire U.S. inventory, stationed in Bahrain and Incirlik) and twelve F-16s (specially configured versions of that aircraft), flown from Incirlik, were dedicated to this mission. These aircraft attacked Iraqi SAM and warning radars, most often with AGM-88 HARMs that sought out and destroyed air defense radar systems by homing in on their

---

25. *Conduct of the Persian Gulf War*, 723–24.

26. Schroeder and Raab, *History of Joint Task Force Proven Force*, 59.

27. Those eighty sorties were by British Nimrod aircraft. GWAPS *Statistical Compendium*, Table 64.

emissions. U.S. Navy and Marine Corps F/A-18s, EA-6Bs, and—to a lesser extent—A-7s carried HARMs (although none of these aircraft could equal the missile programming capability of the F-4G). The British had six Tornados capable of launching a similar type of missile.[28]

Some aircraft could destroy radar systems, and many other aircraft had electronic jamming equipment to blind Iraqi radars and block radio communications. Often, this jamming equipment was in a pod attached to the wing or fuselage, along with bombs and missiles, for self-protection of the aircraft. Such configurations were common, not just for U.S. aircraft but for other Coalition and Iraqi planes and helicopters as well. Decoy drones deceived Iraqi radars, diverting attention from the Coalition aircraft and exciting the Iraqi radars, which then became HARM targets.[29]

The most capable jamming equipment, however, was carried in aircraft dedicated to electronic jamming that masked the presence of the attack aircraft. Those so dedicated were the Air Force's twenty-four EF-111s and eight EC-130s and the Navy's twenty-seven and the Marine Corps' twelve EA-6Bs. For these types, the Air Force component was a relatively small one. The numbers reflect the Navy and Marine Corps preference for relying more on dedicated electronic jamming aircraft than on attack aircraft carrying their own jamming pods. In this war, everyone sought the dedicated aircraft, and the EA-6Bs became the key non–U.S. Air Force resource that CENTAF employed to accompany Air Force attack aircraft.

Air-to-Air Combat Capability

The Coalition shared more widely the mission of controlling the air. The aircraft of six different countries took part in that mission, and of the total number of air defense sorties during Desert Storm, the U.S. share was roughly 66 percent, rather than the 85- to 90-percent share of most other mission types. The Air Force F-15C and Navy F-14 (circa one hundred of each) and eighty-nine dual-role (air-to-air and air-to-ground) U.S. Navy F/A-18s served as the primary air-to-air fighters.[30] Saudi Arabia made the largest non–U.S. contribution, with sixty-nine F-15Cs and another twenty-four Tornados (air defense variant), fol-

---

28. Robert W. Ward, et al., *Desert Storm Reconstruction Report, Vol. VIII: Space and Electronic Warfare* (Alexandria, VA: Center for Naval Analyses, 1992), 3-30 to 3-35; and "Despatch by Air Chief Marshal Sir Patrick Hine, RAF, Joint Commander of Operation Granby, Aug 1990–Apr 1991," second supplement to *The London Gazette*, Number 52589, 29 June 1991, 40.

29. *Conduct of the Persian Gulf War*, 158.

30. The USAF F-16 is also a dual-role fighter, but it was not used in the air-to-air role during Desert Storm.

lowed by Canada (eighteen CF-18s), Great Britain (eighteen Tornados), France (twelve Mirage 2000s), and Bahrain (twelve F-16s).[31]

More aircraft could have been available, since many of the air-to-ground aircraft were also capable of air-to-air missions (F-16s, for example), but the lack of incursions by Iraqi aircraft during the war made it unnecessary. On the contrary, some of the air defense fighters switched to dropping bombs during the war (the Saudi F-15s and Canadian CF-18s are two examples). The Kuwaiti F-1 squadron was an air-to-air unit, but because Iraq also flew F-1s (thus causing an aircraft identification problem), Kuwaiti F-1s were not allowed to fly air defense missions. They did fly bombing missions, however, escorted by Kuwaiti A-4s so they could be readily identified.[32]

Air defense missions, and others such as reconnaissance, aerial refueling, and airlift, began in earnest in August 1990, not January 1991. The number of combat air patrol missions during Desert Shield was similar to the defensive counterair missions of Desert Storm—13,887 and 13,075, respectively.[33] During Desert Shield, the U.S. portion of combat air patrol was similar to the portion flown in Desert Storm, approximately 67 percent, but the service contributions were much different: the Marine Corps F/A-18s flew 4,461 combat air patrol sorties during Desert Shield, far out of proportion to the number of F/A-18s in the Corps and more than the Air Force sorties flown (3,580). Part of the reason for this discrepancy is that U.S. Navy carriers were not yet in the gulf, and Marine Corps aircraft in Bahrain were well placed to fly these sorties over the gulf. The Marine Corps flew some escort missions during Desert Storm but no defensive counterair sorties, dedicating its effort instead to interdiction and close air support. The U.S. Navy essentially took over flying the defensive counterair sorties flown earlier by the Marines.[34]

Attack

The largest air power mission in terms of numbers of sorties and of aircraft involved was surface target attack. The assets involved in this task included many types of aircraft and several disparate weapons

---

31. There were also the ground components of air defense, such as Hawk and Patriot missiles and other ground and ship defense systems not addressed here.

32. When the Kuwaiti F-1s flew, word was passed to the air defense network that F-1s in the company of the A-4s were not hostile. (Discussions, GWAPS personnel with Kuwaiti pilots, 15 July 1992, Kuwait City, Kuwait, GWAPS, NA 377.)

33. There were, in addition, another fourteen thousand air-to-air training missions during Desert Shield. GWAPS *Statistical Compendium*, Tables 47, 54, 58, and 64. (See table 10 of appendix 2.)

34. GWAPS *Statistical Compendium*, Tables 47, 68, and 69.

What Were the Instruments of Air Power?

Table 6 Desert Storm Attack Aircraft

Organization	Type*	Number
U.S. Air Force	A-10	132
	B-52	66
	F-15E	48
	F-16	244
	F-111E	18
	F-111F	64
	F-117	42
U.S. Navy	A-6	95
	A-7	24
	F/A-18	89
U.S. Marine Corps	A-6	20
	AV-8B	86
	F/A-18A/C/D	84
	AH-1W	50
U.S. Army	AH-64	274
U.S. Special Operations Command	AC-130	4
Saudi Arabia	Tornado	24
	F-5	87
Great Britain	Tornado	39
	Jaguar	12
	Buccaneer	12
Kuwait	A-4	20
	F-1	15
France	Jaguar	24
Bahrain	F-5	12
Italy	Tornado	10

*Numbers are approximate, and only those aircraft flying at least one-hundred sorties are included. Numbers of aircraft varied somewhat during the war because of attrition, replacement, and routine movements and include attack aircraft based out of the theater at Incirlik, Moron, Fairford, and Diego Garcia.

systems. Tables 6 and 7 give some idea of the variety of instruments used.[35]

U.S. aircraft flew some 88 percent of the more than forty-six thousand attack sorties conducted during Desert Storm (counting just

35. USAF F-4Gs and USN and USMC EA-6Bs, discussed under electronic warfare, could be included in this listing as well, based on their HARM employment. CENTAF Combat Plans Handout, "Desert Shield Beddown/Sortie Rates," as of 15 January 1991, GWAPS Microfilm Roll 10264, AFHRA 00269612; and *Conduct of the Persian Gulf War*, 666–70, 787.

Table 7 Missiles Employed in Desert Storm Strikes

Organization	Type	Number launched
U.S. Navy	Tactical Land Attack Missile (TLAM)	282 (last one launched on 1 Feb)
U.S. Army	Army Tactical Missile System (ATACMS)*	21 missions (some missions had two missiles employed)
U.S. Air Force	Conventional air-launched cruise missile (CALCM)	35 (all launched the first day of the air war)

*The ATACMS is included in this section on air strikes simply because its range—more than fifty miles—sets it apart from other rocket systems and naval gunfire.

fixed-wing aircraft); the Air Force alone flew 60 percent of that figure.[36] Nearly all attack helicopter missions were executed by U.S. forces. Numbers of sorties alone do not give the dimensions of the contributions of each type of aircraft, however; for that one has to look more closely.

Though air attacks took place around the clock, few units flew on twenty-four-hour-a-day operations: the F-117s, F-111(E and F)s, A-6s, and F-15Es flew almost entirely at night; TLAM attacks on Baghdad, after the first night, took place mostly during the day in order to keep the pressure on day and night (the only other strikes on downtown Baghdad were by the night-flying F-117s); some aircraft (AV-8Bs, Jaguars, A-4s) flew almost entirely day missions because of limited night capability; the A-10s, F-16s, and F/A-18s flew mostly during the day but had some aircraft or crews dedicated to night flying; and B-52s attacked both day and night, creating the impression of continuous bombing, thus maximizing the psychological aspects of those attacks (see figure 36).

The Coalition placed a premium on aircraft with the self-contained capability to laser-designate targets for laser-guided bombs, and those aircraft were more valuable than sortie count alone would indicate. They were the F-117s, F-111Fs (but not the F-111Es), F-15Es, A-6s, French Jaguars, Saudi F-5s, British Buccaneers, and some British Tornados.[37] While not a particularly new capability (laser designation ap-

---

36. Attack sorties counted are those of interdiction, close air support, and airfield attack (under the offensive counterair category). GWAPS Composite Sorties Database; Lt. Col. Steven L. Head, "Briefing on the Conduct and Performance of the Air Campaign in Operation Desert Storm," 21 March 1991, GWAPS, CHO 1–2.

37. The Buccaneers, F-5s, and Jaguars had this capability during daylight only.

What Were the Instruments of Air Power?

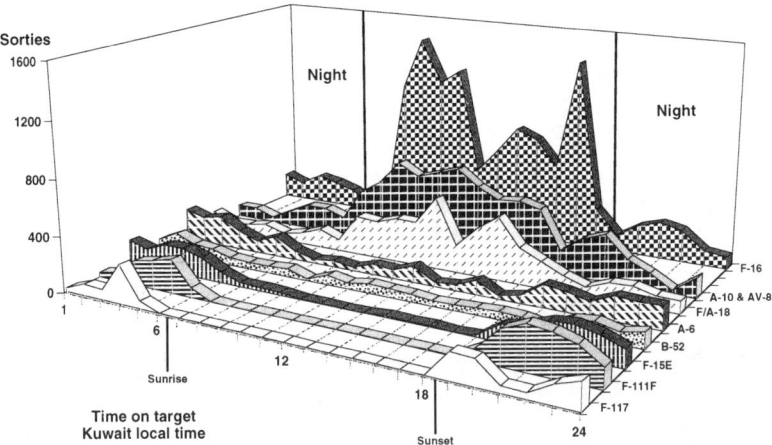

Figure 36   Coalition Attack Aircraft Sorties by Time on Target, 17 January–28 February 1991

peared late in the Vietnam War), many of the newest aircraft—F-16s and F/A-18s, for instance—lacked it. The F-15Es received laser-targeting capability only *after* the aircraft had deployed to the theater.

While the Air Force had a surplus of capabilities in some areas, nearly every aircraft capable of laser designation went to the theater, and more were needed. The Proven Force wing at Incirlik attempted to secure at least some capability by bringing in F-4E aircraft from Clark Air Base in the Philippines, but those aircraft did not arrive until just before the war ended.

The Buccaneers were another late addition to the war, brought in by the British when the laser-designating capability was deemed particularly valuable. The Buccaneers laser-designated their targets during daytime while flying with the bomb-carrying British Tornados. Later in the war, the British expedited to the theater a day and night laser-designating capability, then still under development, for use on some of the British Tornados.[38]

During the war, the U.S. Air Force made the greatest use of precision munitions—both missiles and laser-guided bombs—on attack aircraft. Table 8 compares Air Force, Navy, and Marine Corps use of the three types of precision weapons expended and presents additional information on British and French capabilities.[39]

38. "Despatch by Air Chief Marshal Sir Patrick Hine," 42.

39. The Directorate of Supply, Headquarters, USAF/LGS, Combat Support Division (LGSP), also contained in GWAPS *Statistical Compendium*, Tables 188, 189, and 190 (see tables 29 to 31 of appendix 2); and G. J. Onslow, Operational Research Branch.

The Air Force, in flying 60 percent of the attack missions, expended far higher percentages of guided bombs and air-to-surface missiles than the Navy or Marine Corps. The expenditure of guided bombs reflected the Air Force's heavy bombardment of Iraqi aircraft shelters and employment of F-111Fs and F-15Es in attacking Iraqi armor in the Kuwaiti theater.[40] The employment of Maverick missiles, almost entirely by A-10s, showed the dedication of those aircraft to Iraqi equipment attrition in the Kuwaiti theater. The use of the Maverick by A-10s stands in stark contrast to the slight use of the same by other aircraft, most notably the F-16s, which used only 116—far fewer than the planners had anticipated.

The Navy and Marine Corps used relatively few guided bombs and air-to-surface missiles. A shortage of these weapons in the stocks available to the Navy and Marine Corps provides the best explanation for the lack of employment. In addition, the supply of precision munitions was being husbanded for possible use during the ground offensive. As it turned out, the rate of employment of precision munitions during the ground war by all fixed-wing aircraft was far less than expected, a result of both the weather and the tactical conditions at the time.[41]

The attack helicopters of the U.S. Army and Marine Corps belong in any description of air power employed in the Gulf War. The numbers shown in table 6 account for only the most capable of the attack helicopters, the ones primarily used to attack Iraqi armor.[42] The war put heavy demands on the U.S. helicopter fleet; the number of AH-64 Apaches represented nearly half of the Army's fleet of that aircraft, and four of the six Marine Corps AH-1W squadrons were in the theater.[43]

Note for the Record 01/91: Analysis of Attack and Reconnaissance Operations During Operation Granby (Headquarters Strike Command, Royal Air Force, ORB NFR 1/91, July 1991), A-2, C-2, GWAPS, NA 515.

40. GWAPS Missions Database, as displayed in GWAPS *Statistical Compendium*, Tables 183 and 184.

41. Frank Schwamb, et al., *Desert Storm Reconstruction Report, Vol. II: Strike Warfare* (Alexandria, VA: Center for Naval Analyses, 1991), 6-1 through 6-11; and John D. Parsons, Benjamin T. Regala, and Orman H. Paananen, *Marine Corps Desert Storm Reconstruction Report, Vol. IV: Third Marine Aircraft Wing Operations* (Alexandria, VA: Center for Naval Analyses, 1992), 27, 79.

42. In addition to the Army AH-64 and Marine Corps AH-1W, the French Army Gazelle and the British Lynx helicopters were employed in attack roles. The Royal Navy Lynx helicopters firing Sea Skua air-to-surface missiles, for instance, were one of the most effective weapons systems against Iraqi ships (Jeffrey Lutz, et al., *Desert Storm Reconstruction Report, Vol. VI: Antisurface Warfare* [Alexandria, VA: Center for Naval Analyses, 1991], 3-14 through 3-17). There were several hundred other helicopters that performed missions of armed reconnaissance, escort, and maritime surveillance (AH-1J/F/T, OH-58D, and MH-53E Light Airborne Multipurpose System [LAMPS] helicopter).

43. *Conduct of the Persian Gulf War*, 666, 669.

What Were the Instruments of Air Power?

Table 8 Desert Shield/Desert Storm U.S. Weapons Expenditures (and Percent of Total U.S. Expenditures)

Munition types:	Guided bombs, all types	Anti-radiation missiles (principally HARMs)	Air-to-surface missiles (Maverick for AF; principally Walleye for N and MC)
Air Force	8,456 (90%)	1,120 (55%)	5,255 (96%)
Navy	623 (7%)	679 (33%)	147 (3%)
Marine Corps	263 (3%)	240 (12%)	46 (1%)
Totals	9,342	2,039	5,448
Royal Air Force (UK)	1,126	112 Air-Launched Anti-radiation Missiles (ALARMs)	N/A
French Air Force	N/A	N/A	approx 60 AS-30s (laser-guided missiles)
Grand Totals	10,468 (U.S. 89%)	2,151 (U.S. 95%)	5,508 (U.S. 99%)

Most strikes by these attack helicopters took place during the ground war, as they advanced with, and sometimes ahead of, the ground forces. Marine Corps and Army VII Corps attack helicopters operated close to the front lines, but in the areas of the XVIII Airborne Corps operations, the AH-64s engaged in several independent deep attacks, apart from the ground elements, against withdrawing Iraqi troops. The main weapon these aircraft used in antiarmor operations was the Hellfire missile. During the war, the U.S. Army expended 2,876 such missiles; the Marine Corps expended 159.[44]

Summary

Coalition air power was overwhelming in both numbers and quality. Whereas that predominance applied to the more typical elements of air power—air-to-air fighters, air-to-ground attack aircraft, and airlift aircraft—it applied even more to the Coalition's special capabilities in air power—aerial refueling, airborne and satellite reconnaissance, electronic warfare, airborne command and control, stealth, and precision munitions. These special capabilities, ones that Iraq could not

---

44. See chapter 3, table 3.

even begin to cope with, were the province of U.S. forces; while other Coalition air forces possessed some of them (except for stealth), their contribution was nowhere near that of the United States.

How much of its total air power capability did the United States employ? The answers vary, but in the unique capabilities mentioned above, the United States was close to fully committed: effectively all of the stealth capability and airborne designators for laser-guided bombs; the predominant amount of reconnaissance and electronic warfare aircraft; and more than half of aerial refueling and command and control assets. Furthermore, better than half of the U.S. Air Force aircraft normally stationed in Europe participated in the Gulf War.

The high percentages of U.S. air power devoted to the Gulf War does not necessarily mean that the United States would have been unable to apply air power in another contingency elsewhere at the same time. The emergence of a second contingency would have called for a reappraisal of the air power needed for the Gulf War and of the options for air employment. Clearly, some flexibility was possible. That flexibility would have entailed adjustments of aircraft sortie rates, target or mission priorities, and the tempo of the air campaign.

In addition, while the Air Force, Navy, and Marine Corps used a large part of their reserve components in airlift and aerial refueling, only three tactical fighter squadrons (two F-16 and one A-10) from the reserves took part. The flexibility lay at the lower-technology end of the available air power, however, not in the higher technology, specific capabilities. All that can be reasonably said is that facing multiple contingencies, the United States would have fought a markedly different war with air power in the gulf.

Eight | **What Supported the Air Power?**

The air power described in the previous chapter was the combat potential or operational instruments of air power, and as such represented only the end product of the organizations, doctrine, training, supplies, and support structure required to make aircraft or satellites militarily significant. This chapter focuses on other elements necessary for employing air power, dividing them into two categories: the tangible and the intangible.

The tangibles are the vast support structure of supply, maintenance, communications, and people to which all aircraft and other operational systems are tethered. The intangibles include aspects of doctrine, predispositions to the use of air power, and the role of air power in military operations (some would say mind-set) that affected air planning and operations. They also include the expectations of the various services concerning the integration of air power in land or sea operations, the effect of the orientation by Great Britain and the United States to NATO employment concepts for using air power, and the effects of the Vietnam experience on senior American leadership.

The Tangibles

On the eve of the gulf conflict, the United States had an extensive system of bases and lines of communication for projecting and sustaining air power, but that support structure—a product of the Cold War—was centered in the United States and Europe and required further extension to support a Southwest Asian conflict. Matériel prepositioned in the theater, in addition to the number of bases available in the gulf states, provided U.S. military planners with a great advantage, as did the amount of preparation time between the August 1990 invasion and the start of Desert Storm in January 1991.

The key to success, however, was a willingness to innovate and adapt when plans changed and automated systems failed. Despite some early chaos and a continuing lack of precise accountability for much of the equipment and supplies that flooded into the theater, the air campaign was never constrained by a lack of fuel, parts, or maintenance capability, truly a remarkable accomplishment. Airlift forces proved vital to the success of this support and, by enabling other U.S. forces, to the entire Coalition effort. By war's end, strategic airlift had moved more than 500,000 people and 540,000 tons of cargo (an unprecedented amount) to the theater. Once in the region, tactical airlift moved more than half that amount again within the theater.[1]

Moving units and supplies to the Persian Gulf involved not only spanning great distances but also adapting to an unusual deployment concept. For most logistics planning, the Air Force aircraft squadron had been the basic combat unit that would deploy from operational bases in the United States to operational bases overseas. Such a concept did not fit the situation in the Southwest Asian theater, though, where the entire operational base itself had to be deployed. Saudi Arabia was by no means lacking in operational bases for its own use, but neither it nor the other gulf states had ever experienced a deployment the size and speed of Desert Shield. Many units deployed to newly built, bare bases with no available support structure and about which little was known. Most of the early deploying units did not even know where they were being sent until just before or, in some cases, during the deployment itself.[2]

Since no approved time-phased deployment schedule existed for Desert Shield, units quickly had to estimate equipment tonnage, passengers, cargo size, and destinations. The resulting errors made projecting airlift requirements highly problematic. For example, estimated lift requirements for the first seven deploying units increased 60 percent between 11 and 13 August and forced MAC to schedule additional, unforeseen sorties and to delay airlift for follow-on support units.[3] It was not until 14 August that CENTCOM published the first complete deployment schedule, only to learn that it exceeded MAC's capability by 200 to 300 percent. As a result, deploying fighter squadrons did not receive necessary airlift support, the major problem from which many smaller problems flowed.

The Joint Operations Planning and Execution System (JOPES) automated deployment system was incapable of tracking partial shipments of equipment and, as a result, quickly lost accountability of more than half of all the shipments rushed to the gulf. Moreover, since des-

---

1. GWAPS *Statistical Compendium*, Table 23.

2. On 9 and 10 August 1990, squadrons of F-15Es and F-16s had their destinations changed while they were in mid-flight (William T. Y'Blood, *The Eagle and the Scorpion; and The USAF and the Desert Shield First-Phase Deployment, 7 August–8 November 1990* [Washington: Center for Air Force History, 1992], 51–52; and "4th Tactical Fighter Wing in Southwest Asia," 18).

3. RAND, *Assessment of Desert Shield Deployment*, 10 October 1991, 57–58.

What Supported the Air Power? 175

tinations and associated units were classified, cargo was often shipped to "Desert Shield" and invariably ended up at Dhahran, unmarked as to its final destination or priority.[4]

When CENTCOM assigned priority to move combat power to the theater, sustaining supplies became backlogged, awaiting shipment along with partial sets of unit equipment. A second difficulty arose at this juncture because the separate supply and transportation systems, while having independent tracking mechanisms, had poor connectivity. Therefore, supply items became "invisible" during shipping and could not be tracked down, much less expedited. Invariably, an item delayed meant an item reordered, further clogging the system. Moreover, the backlogs of equipment and supplies in the United States awaiting shipment were insignificant when compared to the situation at Dhahran, where the backlog of arriving supplies awaiting further sorting and distribution soon reached crisis proportions.

With such an unpromising start, it was all the more remarkable that supplies flowed as well as they did and that the Air Force could later claim that no Desert Storm sortie was lost because of unavailability of repair parts. Those results came from new procedures instituted on the fly. First, the Air Force supply system envisioned for the theater had to be completely abandoned: its computer system was inadequate, and the designed telecommunications capability never worked properly. As a result, at the end of August 1990 all Air Force Desert Shield supply accounting was transferred to a mainframe system at Langley Air Force Base, Virginia. This system included almost all aircraft supplies but only 50 to 60 percent of all other supplies. Still, with an astounding 288,000 item records, it was the largest Air Force retail supply account ever assembled.[5]

When the supply system began to resemble a water pipe crimped at both ends, the transportation system went to work eliminating the backlogs. MAC personnel reviewed cargo at the aerial ports in the United States and found that in excess of half of it was coded as top priority, but much of it did not need to go by air at all. Consequently, teams periodically went through the cargo and redesignated some for sea transport.[6] At the other end of the pipeline, units did the best they could to get the material out of Dhahran. "Deployed tactical airlift units would fly the first sortie of the day to Dhahran and leave several peo-

---

4. Ibid., 10.

5. CENTAF Supply Support Activity briefing viewgraphs, undated, provided to GWAPS during 4–5 August 1992 interviews, GWAPS, NA 584.

6. JULLS Number 31952-58451 (00218), submitted by Jerry Rife; RAND, *Assessment of Desert Shield Deployment*, 68; and *Kondra Notes*, 16–17.

ple (from units deployed to the various operating locations) there to roam about the yard looking for their shipments and return on the last sortie of the day with whatever they had found."[7]

MAC addressed weaknesses in the priority system by setting up a special airlift route, Desert Express, to move critical parts to the gulf quickly. By the end of October 1990, a MAC cargo aircraft flew daily to the theater from Charleston Air Force Base, South Carolina, with the most critical parts needed for wartime readiness. Commercial air express services brought critical supplies to Charleston, where they were transloaded to Desert Express and delivered to the theater usually within seventy-two hours of requisition (previously, it had taken as long as two weeks). A similar system, European Express, brought parts to the gulf from Europe.

Results were dramatic: grounding actions for Air Force aircraft decreased from 500 (for the 750 aircraft being maintained) on 1 October 1990 to 219 (for 1,229 aircraft) on 17 January 1991. No comparative data are available for the other services, but they received similar service. (Half of the shipments, in fact, were destined for Army units.) During Desert Storm, the overall rate for Air Force aircraft being unready to fly because of supply shortages was less than 4 percent, better even than the standard for peacetime and far less than the projected war standard of up to 25 percent after thirty days of combat.[8]

Supplying jet fuel for Coalition aircraft could have been an even greater problem than spare parts had it not been for fuels support by the host nations and requisitioning refueling equipment from Air Force units around the world. The amounts needed were staggering: the Air Force alone used fifteen million gallons of jet fuel *a day* at the height of the war. Except for some specialized jet fuels, Saudi Arabia, Oman, and the United Arab Emirates contributed all fuel for land, sea, and air operations—approximately two billion dollars' worth—and negated the need for a substantial sealift effort by an inadequate U.S. sealift tanker fleet.

Storing, transporting, and issuing this fuel remained a significant obstacle that was surmounted by a combination of new pipelines and the Air Force's supply of fuel bladders, hydrant systems, refueling vehicles, and trained personnel gathered from all over the United States, Europe, and the Pacific. To meet this requirement, however, the Air Force deployed 92 percent of its entire refueling assets to the theater, leaving other combatant commands with limited ability to establish any kind of bare-base aircraft refueling capability had that been necessary. This would not have been the only shortfall, since the Air Force

---

7. MAC/LERX staff paper, undated, provided during an interview with Mr. Orson Glover, HQ MAC/LGSW, 11–12 August 1992.

8. Background Paper, "CENTAF Logistics Story," CENTAF/LG, April 1991.

What Supported the Air Power? 177

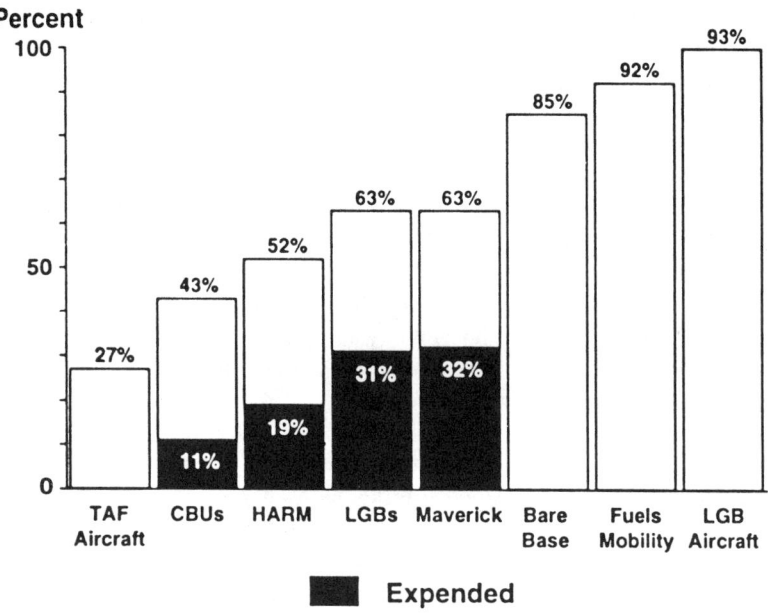

Figure 37   Deployment of Selected USAF Assets

had also deployed to the gulf 85 percent of all its equipment for operating from bare bases—tents, dining facilities, and so forth (see figure 37).

Problems with supplying aircraft munitions were similar to those for sustainment supplies and might have brought significant degradations to air operations in August or September of 1990. They were overcome, however, by the start of the air campaign. Here, accurate accounting of munitions was necessary because the Air Force employed more than thirty kinds, the Navy nine varieties, and Army aviation thirteen. The other Coalition air forces added some twenty-six unique types of their own munitions. Furthermore, CENTAF had anticipated a forty-five day transit time for munitions from the United States, but the actual time was fifty-five to seventy-two days, and in many cases, that transit time was to a Persian Gulf port, not to the intended destination.[9]

Munitions shipments also faced other complications. Specific transportation restrictions limited the number of roads, railroads, and ports (just two in the United States) that could be used. In addition, shortages of qualified drivers and explosives handlers exacerbated accounting problems for inventories of munitions components. Despite

---

9. Report, USAF/ACP to General Accounting Office, "Munitions Activity in SWA," January 1992.

the nearly one hundred million dollars spent on the Air Force's Combat Ammunition System since its inception in 1982, it was not prepared to handle the task. Certain munitions in the transportation system could not be tracked, leaving logisticians the unenviable task of determining what exactly had arrived on ammunition ships as they were unloaded.[10]

Inventories had to be created and maintained manually, a process that continued throughout Desert Shield and Desert Storm and resulted in significant inaccuracies in reported inventories. Senior Air Force planners never could be confident of what munitions were actually available. One saving grace came from the Air Force Combat Ammunition Center located at Sierra Army Depot, California. Established in 1985, the center sought to develop a cadre of trained personnel skilled in managing munitions production. Graduates of this training constituted the backbone of the production teams in the theater.

While inventory accounting problems had the potential to create munitions shortages, those uncertainties were offset by the large quantities of munitions shipped. By the cease-fire, nearly 350,000 tons of munitions had been shipped by air and sea for use by Air Force units (including forty-eight ships en route); of this amount, 69,000 tons were actually expended. The percentages listed in figure 37 depict the major munitions employed in the war. As the figure indicates, stocks of all munitions remained at the end of the war, but some rationing took place in special munitions such as the CBU-87 and laser-guided bombs, particularly by the Navy and Marine Corps, in anticipation of a longer ground war or higher expenditures of those munitions.[11]

Prepositioned stocks of munitions and equipment in the theater helped enormously. The Air Force had stocked approximately one billion dollars' worth of fuel, munitions, and equipment in the gulf states and aboard three maritime prepositioned ships. These stocks represented approximately thirty-five hundred airlift cargo missions for Air Force stocks alone and a total of more than ten thousand sorties for all services. The importance of this prepositioning can be grasped by noting that the total of all inter-theater airlift sorties during the first phase of the deployment (August to November 1990) amounted to just over six thousand sorties.[12]

10. Interview, Lt. Col. William Swezey, ASD/ALZ, 15 April 1992 (Colonel Swezey was the senior munitions manager in CENTAF during Operations Desert Shield and Desert Storm).

11. David L. Dittmer, *U.S. Marine Corps Operations in Desert Shield/Desert Storm, Vol. I: Overview and Summary* (Alexandria, VA: Center for Naval Analyses, 1992), 36; and Ronald Nickel, et al., *Desert Storm Reconstruction Report, Vol. IX: Logistics* (Alexandria, VA: Center for Naval Analyses, 1991), 3–11.

12. For much of this material, airlift would have been inefficient use of the aircraft, but the material could not have been available as soon in any other way.

Prepositioned munitions accounted for about half of the tonnage eventually dropped in the war, but the proportions of specific munitions varied. The prepositioned stocks represented a mix of conventional ordnance: Mk-80 series general-purpose bombs, Vietnam-vintage cluster bombs, and some laser-guided bomb components. For security and safety reasons, however, the munitions ashore did not contain the latest technology weapons.[13] As a result, many more precision munitions were brought to the theater than were included in the prepositioned stocks.

Early in the deployment, CENTAF had to rely on whatever munitions were available in the prepositioned stocks, but matching those munitions with aircraft was a difficult and time-consuming problem, with some units having access only to the munitions with which they deployed. CENTAF established a priority of critical munitions—primarily items for the conduct of defensive operations—but these priority munitions did not arrive in the theater for up to six weeks.

On a more positive note, aircraft maintenance achieved excellent results. One factor leading to this success was the attention given to securing needed supplies and spare parts described earlier. A second major factor was the Air Force's innovative concept for establishing centralized maintenance support centers. Engines, for example, were serviced in Europe and on Guam rather than at the individual bases in the theater, giving better efficiency to the entire process. Establishing such centers on the theater's sparsely outfitted bases would have overstrained the base support structure.

Even so, theater maintenance was a major effort: practically 38 percent (seventeen thousand) of all Air Force personnel deployed in the theater were maintenance personnel.[14] All indications were, moreover, that there were not too many maintenance personnel in the theater; in fact, the number of personnel was one-third fewer than Air Force planners had anticipated would be needed to support the aircraft deployed and to provide the kinds of maintenance required under combat conditions.[15]

Maintenance in-commission rates for Air Force aircraft also were excellent, but whether they were better than in peacetime, as is some-

---

13. Interview, AF/LGSP personnel, 2 April 1992.

14. Briefing, AFMEA/MEMS, "Desert Shield vs Europe Force Projection/Support," January 1991; USAF Wartime Manpower and Personnel Readiness Team Desert Shield/Desert Storm Electronic Database; and USAF Statistical Digest: Fiscal Year 1991 Estimate, D-38 and D-48.

15. No judgments are implied about the "correct" tooth-to-tail ratio. The ratios of specialties of Air Force personnel would vary considerably depending on numbers of engineering, security, or other personnel, based on the operating environment, host nation support, and so forth.

times claimed, is open to question. Differences between the peacetime and (the largely ad hoc) Desert Shield/Desert Storm reporting systems make comparisons inexact. Whatever the comparison, the rates achieved were superb, considering repairs to battle-damaged aircraft and the harsh desert environment. Other services achieved similar in-commission rates with their flying units, with simply a few isolated problems. The desert environment appears to have had little persistent effect on reliability, except for the T-64 and T-700 helicopter engines (used on the CH/MH-53 and MH/SH-60 helicopters, respectively), which experienced sand-erosion problems that brought reliability to only one-tenth of rates anticipated.

Another tangible element of support was communications. Providing ground and air communications and control throughout the theater of operations forced CENTCOM to deploy entire systems. CENTCOM immediately deployed satellite communication terminals and eventually employed in excess of seventy-two hundred terminals and pieces of equipment that were linked electronically to more than sixty-three communications, intelligence, navigation, and weather-monitoring satellites.[16] In comparison, just three terminals existed on land in the theater before 2 August 1990.

This communications explosion typified the increases taking place in several areas. The use of the STU-III became a vital link in every operational element. The Saudis, into whose telephone system these instruments were linked, asked for access to the secure system. Since the STU-IIIs were based on sensitive technology, the National Security Agency modified a commercial version of the STU-III and distributed sets to the Arab forces. These modified sets could communicate only with others of their type, could not link with a STU-III, and could not link with the STU-IIs used by NATO forces. As a result, U.S. commanders had to use multiple phone lines to talk to all the members of the Coalition.[17]

Even with these shortcomings, CENTCOM established more communications links in the first ninety days of Desert Shield than U.S. forces had assembled in Europe in the previous forty years. Forty Au-

---

16. Report, United States Space Command Operations Desert Shield and Desert Storm Assessment, January 1992, 6, 16, 27, 34; Joint Staff/J6Z Briefing, "Use of Satellite Communications Desert Shield/Desert Storm," undated; and Col. Alan D. Campen, USAF (Ret.), "Gulf War's Silent Warriors Bind U.S. Units Via Space," *Signal*, August 1991, 83. The above sources put the number of communications terminals at between twelve hundred and two thousand.

17. Col. Randy Witt, "Air Force Tactical Communications in War, the Desert Shield/Desert Storm Comm Story," Headquarters, USCENTAF, Riyadh, March 1991, 2-38, GWAPS, NA 49.

tomatic Voice Network trunks were in Europe; 265 were functioning in Saudi Arabia by March 1991.[18]

As with land communications, the number of aircraft arriving in the theater quickly overwhelmed the capabilities of the air traffic control system. Large gaps in radar and radio coverage created flight safety problems and magnified the enormous task of providing adequate air defense. The complex airspace structure created to handle the three thousand sorties a day during Desert Storm grew to 122 airborne refueling orbits, 195 Army aviation flight routes, 76 strike routes, 36 training areas, 60 Patriot engagement zones, and a host of other areas, routes, and orbits. CENTAF deployed approximately 320 controllers to handle the U.S. facilities and to augment the number of host nation air controllers. The Army, Navy, and Marine Corps also deployed their own air control equipment and controllers to support their operations.[19]

Handling the volume of aircraft airborne at any one time required an extensive network even in peacetime; adding communications and control procedures in a wartime environment compounded problems in all systems and networks. With more than nine hundred frequencies in the daily ATO by January, which virtually saturated the frequency spectrum, the CENTAF staff formed a planning group to manage radio frequency allocation. The group had to take note of the frequencies used by the Saudis, who did not have an assignment policy, and those of Army units on the ground; in such an environment, the chances for communications interruptions and radio interference were enormous. For security purposes, the frequencies during wartime were usually changed daily, but CENTAF had to abandon this practice.[20]

In short, creating and staffing this control system was a tremendous effort and could be done only in steps. Although the system was put together piecemeal, beginning in August 1990, it was operating as an entire system within a month and was multinational by the end of December. To do this, however, the Air Force depleted command and control units in the U.S. and Europe to the point where it exhausted effective tactical air command and control reserves.

One of the most misleading but accurate statistics was that less than 10 percent of active-duty Air Force personnel deployed to the

---

18. Defense Science Board, *Lessons Learned during Operation Desert Shield & Desert Storm*, "For Comment" draft (Washington, 1992), 5; and "Lessons from the First Space War," *Interavia Space Markets*, April 1991, 10.

19. Memo, Major Howdeshell, AFCC, Air Traffic Service, to Major Leary, GWAPS, subject: Air Traffic Support of Desert Storm, 27 May 1992; and Defense Science Board, *Lessons Learned during Operations Desert Shield & Desert Storm*, 20–21.

20. "Air Force Tactical Communications in War," 2-16.

gulf.[21] It is misleading because so much more of the Air Force's total capability was dedicated to that theater. In addition, without considering the deployed units themselves, the numbers give no indication of the total number of Air Force units affected. A review of the identities of the Air Force wings and air divisions in the theater would reveal a "(P)" following their designations, meaning "provisional." That is, the unit combined personnel and squadrons from more than one existing unit. Thus, no Air Force wing deployed in toto to the gulf; rather, it dispatched flying squadrons that would join other squadrons in the gulf to form new, provisional wings.

The composition of wings took on many variations for Desert Shield and Desert Storm. One pattern was to deploy two of a wing's three flying squadrons, usually sending with them the most experienced crews, best aircraft, and an augmented crew force and support staff. What remained on the home station was something less than one-third of a wing. The two squadrons joined in the theater at some later date (during the second phase of the deployments) with one or more squadrons from other wing(s)—from Europe, for instance—and formed a provisional wing. As an example, the 4th Tactical Fighter Wing (TFW) at Al Kharj consisted of the two squadrons it deployed, the 335th and 336d Tactical Fighter Squadrons (TFS) flying F-15Es, plus the 53d TFS (of the 36th TFW, Bitburg Air Base, Germany) flying F-15Cs, and the 157th TFS and 138th TFS (from the reserves) flying F-16s.

Exceptions did occur, however, such as when all of a wing's squadrons deployed to the same provisional wing, but even then that wing contained elements of several other flying units. The B-52s were even more fragmented, deploying in only partial squadrons because the squadrons also maintained a nuclear alert commitment in the United States.

Nonflying Air Force personnel deployed in far more fragmented units than did flying personnel. These personnel, both active and reserve, were selected to deploy by *functional,* not *organizational,* designation. A maintenance squadron in the United States or Europe, for example, would be ordered to deploy six jet-engine mechanics; this group could then be further split and deployed to different provisional units in the gulf. While a provisional wing was composed of two, three, or even four flying units, the balance of the wing could come from an array of units. This practice was criticized widely in at least two respects.

First was unit cohesion. Support organizations created in the theater were composed of officers and enlisted personnel who did not know and had not worked with one another. This situation became even more chaotic since individuals were assigned temporarily to provi-

---

21. Approximately 5 percent of the Air Force Reserve and 4 percent of the Air National Guard were deployed. GWAPS *Statistical Compendium,* Table 40.

sional units, so their administrative control (for pay, accountability, promotions, and the like) remained with their original units. The difficulties for reservists in this situation were even greater since they often fell under different accounting rules.[22]

A second problem involved the depletion of resources from the parent units, making them less able to respond to a crisis or further deployment. Here too the reserves were most affected because they first lost personnel who volunteered and, later, personnel called up to fill other requirements. Their absence could have affected the unit's readiness and ability to meet unit requirements.[23]

Air Reserve Components (Air Force Reserve and Air National Guard) made up roughly 20 percent of total Air Force personnel in the gulf and proved absolutely essential in certain specialties. For example, one-third of all of the air reservists mobilized were medical personnel. While fewer in number, the reserves comprised large percentages of both strategic and tactical airlift and air refueling crews and two-thirds of the Air Force communications personnel deployed. Three of the fighter squadrons in the gulf were from the reserves: two F-16 squadrons and one A-10 squadron.

There probably would have been greater reliance on the reserve components had there not been an end to the Cold War. When the second phase of deployment took place in November 1990, the substantial forces in Europe—both Air Force and Army—were available for redeployment because no Soviet threat existed. By January 1991, better than half of the aircraft of U.S. Air Forces Europe were in the gulf region or Turkey, ready to support Desert Storm. As a result, fewer reservists were needed than would have been the case several years earlier for a similar deployment. Thus, the Air Force elected to call up only about 65 percent (thirty-four thousand) of the total number (fifty-two thousand) authorized by the president, percentages similar to those of the other services.

Finally, the call-up of reservists and selection of Air Force personnel to deploy tended to mask rates of those not able to deploy. Since entire units were not deployed, commanders could pick from volunteers and select those most fit for combat duty. The Air Reserve, for instance, reported no nondeployable personnel. Also, based on Air Force surveys conducted in September 1990 and February 1991, a mere 1.7 percent of the military couples with dependents were deployed, but a far higher percentage of single member sponsors (of de-

---

22. *Operation Desert Shield Problems Encountered by Activated Reservists*, "Report to the Assistant Secretary of Defense for Reserve Affairs," United States General Accounting Office, September 1991 (GAO/NSIAD-91-290), 1–2.

23. "The Contribution of the Reserve Components to the Persian Gulf War," in *The Reserve Components of the United States Armed Forces*, June 1992, 40.

pendents) deployed—13.3 percent. Women made up 15 percent of the Air Force, but only 7 percent deployed. The most likely explanation is that Air Force functional specialties that did deploy (crew members, maintenance, and security police, for instance) had a lower percentage of women in their roles than overall Air Force percentages. In the early stages of the deployment, it appeared that women were not being deployed on the first aircraft, waiting for clearer indications of the Saudi position regarding the presence of U.S. servicewomen in theater, but that concern was soon dismissed.

The Intangibles

American air commanders brought to the theater experience and expectations that shaped the war as powerfully as any material piece of equipment. Two wars in particular had shaped their attitudes. One, the Southeast Asia conflict, seemed to offer cautionary lessons to colonels and higher-ranking officers who had participated in it two decades earlier. The second was a war with the Soviet Union that never took place but that nearly all members of the armed forces had trained for assiduously, preparing air forces in various and generally useful ways for the air campaign against Iraq.

During Desert Shield, U.S. planners and commanders thought a great deal about their previous warfare experiences. They cautioned one another about the mass housing of U.S. troops in Saudi Arabia, fearing a repeat of the Beirut bombing of 1983. They refrained from fixating on the removal of Saddam Hussein as a war objective, bearing in mind the frustrating hunt for Manuel Noriega in 1989.

No experience from their collective past, however, compared with the lessons from Vietnam. Colonel Warden and his Checkmate staff in the Pentagon referred to their draft plan for a campaign against the Iraqis as Instant Thunder—a not-so-subtle repudiation of "Rolling Thunder," an early air campaign in Vietnam. Vietnam-era commanders had taken part in a campaign of gradual escalation tied to theories of diplomatic bargaining that stretched out over months; Gulf War commanders hoped to strike decisive blows in a war that might last only a week or two. Warden's code name for the plan did not survive, but many planners in Washington and the theater accepted this concept wholeheartedly.

Civilian decisionmakers, no less than soldiers, had in mind a host of Vietnam-era lessons; in particular, they willingly let the military design the campaign in accordance with broad political guidance from the White House.[24] Throughout the Vietnam War, U.S. politicians directed

---

24. *Hero*, 320; and Bob Woodward, *The Commanders* (New York: Simon and Schuster, 1991), 324, 339, 347.

What Supported the Air Power?

the military to use force incrementally, in a restricted fashion, and for ambiguous political objectives. Against Iraqi forces, civilians allowed the massive use of force, with few constraints (aside from those dictated by the laws of war and common sense) and for clear purposes. Washington headquarters did not micromanage the Gulf War; targeting suggestions were sent to the theater, but theater commanders ran the war.

Such, at any rate, was the view among the civilian and military leadership. In truth, the distinction between the conduct of the Gulf and Vietnam Wars was in certain respects overstated. The restrictions imposed on the use of air power in North Vietnam, for example, were shaped considerably by a fear of igniting a broader war, with Chinese or Soviet intervention, a concern wholly absent in the gulf. Political guidance for the use of air power in South Vietnam created considerably fewer constraints than in the North. Furthermore, targeting downtown Baghdad in the Gulf War changed after the bombing of the Al Firdos bunker on 13 February. In the two weeks preceding that incident, F-117s hit twenty-five targets in downtown Baghdad; in the two weeks after, they struck only five—which had been very carefully chosen.

The political objectives in the Gulf War were, in important respects, ambiguous as well. The presidential goal of securing a stable Persian Gulf, for example, could mean many things. Commanders could not know for certain just how much value they should place and how much effort they should direct on the destruction of the Ba'athist regime and the rule (if not the person) of Saddam Hussein. These qualifications notwithstanding, however, planners were undoubtedly correct to see a tremendous difference from the way the Vietnam War was conducted.

If memories of Vietnam explain some of the predilections of commanders—to strike massively and for limited but clear political objectives—those memories also explain some of the commanders' aversions. Commanders would not countenance, for example, body counts of Iraqi soldiers killed, an unwillingness that persisted in postwar reporting. Recollections of Vietnam may help explain as well the intention of air campaign planners to deny the enemy any sanctuaries, at any rate in his own territory: the Coalition waged war throughout the length and breadth of Iraq from the first night. And memories of Vietnam help account for the unwillingness of General Horner and his subordinates to endorse anything that might resemble the route package system used in Indochina, which divided the enemy country into sectors assigned to particular air forces.

Decades of intense preparation for war in Europe also shaped operations in the gulf. Such practices as low-level attack, which had been standard in Europe, were partially reflected in prewar training and in the first several days of operation in the gulf. More important, the entire tactical system—the assembly of force packages, escorted by specialized SEAD (suppression of enemy air defense) aircraft—reflected American practice in Europe. So too did the definition of key missions; CENTAF planners referred to attacks against strategic targets as "interdiction," in keeping with the absence of any other category of deep targets in Central Europe. Many of the personnel and units assigned to CENTAF came to the theater from Europe, and, of course, European-based units operated out of Turkey during the war.

Above all, the constant international cooperation required for a European war had prepared American forces well to lead an international coalition and to operate within it. All of the major Coalition partners had trained extensively with American units, which had become accustomed, in turn, to dealing with other nationalities. Such practices as the creation of a common ATO were routine for all concerned, and pilots used English as the common language. Commanders and staffs had rehearsed many large-scale air operations, and although Desert Storm was far larger than any exercise, it resembled the kind of effort that would have taken place in a European war. On a more tangible level, Coalition air forces, to a great degree, flew the same types of aircraft and used similar munitions and spare parts.

Not all the commonalities offered advantages, however. Because France, Kuwait, and Iraq all flew French F-1 aircraft, identification procedures seemed chancy, and the Coalition restricted their use during the war.

In some important respects, Desert Storm posed a different challenge than did the Soviet threat to Europe. The Warsaw Pact had many small air bases in Eastern Europe; the Iraqis had far fewer but much larger bases, which complicated runway cutting operations, for example. Weather posed far greater problems in Europe than in the gulf. NATO planners anticipated far more resistance from Warsaw Pact air forces and air defense units than the Iraqis would eventually offer, and the terrain in the gulf favored air power far more than did Eastern Europe. Above all, air forces in Europe anticipated a mission vastly different from what they would undertake in the gulf, where the Coalition was able to initiate the air campaign. In Europe, air power would delay and disrupt onrushing Warsaw Pact attacks; in the gulf, it would serve two disparate purposes: to conduct strategic attacks against an enemy's homeland, and to destroy a dug-in army on the defensive, not moving forward.

Coalition air forces contended with some difficulties adapting to the different circumstances. American munitions had been acquired primarily for a European war, and some of the initial estimates of Iraqi attrition rested on calculations of what might happen, for example, to moving armor that was attacked using aircraft-delivered mines—

What Supported the Air Power?

munitions less effective against a static opponent. Few units had practiced extensively for medium-altitude attacks, with the result that efficiency dropped when such attacks became the norm after the third day of the war. On the whole, however, Coalition forces used the five and a half months of crisis before the war well, adjusting, for instance, to technical challenges posed by the use of infrared navigation and targeting systems over the peculiar terrain and the special climactic conditions of the Persian Gulf.

Perhaps the greatest intangible attribute brought to the gulf by American commanders, in the air as on land, was supreme confidence in the ability of their troops and the quality of their equipment. They had spent the two decades prior training for a far sterner test than the one they would now face, and although few individuals outside the military (and not all that many within it) understood the full extent of Coalition superiority vis à vis the Iraqis, few doubted that the war would end other than with a crushing Coalition victory. This mood of confidence mixed with a deep sense of determination (the TACC logs show this vividly) that this war would wipe clean the memory of the half-hearted efforts and mishaps of Vietnam and other occasions on which air forces had achieved less than their advocates had hoped. Many officers expected and desired that this war would, in some fashion, settle an open account in the history of air power.

Nine | **Was Desert Storm a Revolution in Warfare?**

Many circumstances in the Gulf War favored the United States and its Coalition allies. The end of the Cold War meant that they could concentrate their vast military forces almost exclusively on the war against Iraq. The terrain and Iraqi force structure favored the effective application of air power. Underestimating American capabilities and resolve, Saddam Hussein conceded the initiative and gave the U.S.–led Coalition the time to marshal and prepare forces for battle.

Notwithstanding these strongly favorable circumstances, the extraordinarily lopsided quality of the war, in general, and of the air campaign, in particular, has led a number of observers to conclude that the war augured a revolution in the conduct of war, a transformation of warfare itself. This line of argument interprets Desert Storm as confirming the decade-old Soviet prediction of an impending "military-technical revolution" driven by advances in microelectronics, automated decision-support systems, telecommunications, satellite and other advanced sensors, lasers, and, especially, nonnuclear munitions so accurate and lethal that they could wreak levels of military damage comparable to those attainable with tactical nuclear weapons.[1]

In his introduction to the Department of Defense's official study of the war, Secretary of Defense Richard Cheney agreed. "This war demonstrated dramatically the new possibilities of what has been called the 'military-technological revolution in warfare.'"[2] Others, outside the Bush administration, expressed this view no less enthusiastically. To illustrate: William Perry, secretary of defense in the Clinton administration, wrote in *Foreign Affairs,* "a new class of military sys-

---

1. Mary C. Fitzgerald, "The Soviet Image of Future War: 'Through the Prism of the Gulf War,'" Hudson Institute HI-4145, May 1991, 4, 66–67; and interview with Marshal N. V. Ogarkov, "The Defense of Socialism: Experience of History and the Present Day," *Krasnaya Zvesda [Red Star],* 9 May 1984, English trans. FBIS, *Daily Report: Soviet Union,* 9 May 1984, Vol. II, No. 091, Annex No. 054, R-19. See also Benjamin S. Lambeth, "Desert Storm and Its Meaning: The View from Moscow," RAND R-4164-AF (Santa Monica, CA: RAND, 1992) and Mary C. Fitzgerald, "The Soviet Military and the New 'Technological Operation' in the Gulf," *Naval War College Review,* 44:4 (Autumn 1991), 16–43.

2. *The Conduct of the Persian Gulf War,* xx, 164.

tems . . . gave American forces a revolutionary advance in military capability."[3]

At first, then, the question of revolutionary change appears to hinge on technology. In his memoir of World War II, Gen. Dwight D. Eisenhower and his staff identified what they believed were the five most important pieces of equipment contributing to success in Africa and Europe. "[T]he 'duck,' an amphibious vehicle . . . proved to be one of the most valuable pieces of equipment produced by the United States during the war. . . . [F]our other pieces of equipment . . . [that] came to (be) regarded as among the most vital to our success . . . were the bulldozer, the jeep, the 2-1/2 ton truck and the C-47 airplane. Curiously enough, none of these is designed for combat."[4]

The uniqueness of the Gulf War can be approached in a similar way by looking at five kinds of technology—not always single pieces of equipment—that seem to best characterize the air campaign. The number five is, of course, arbitrary; we could have easily added space systems or tactical airlift, among others, to the list. Unlike Eisenhower's list, however, the Gulf War listing focuses solely on the execution of the air campaign, not on the entire war. Note too that our selections are not intended to suggest that these technologies are the best or most important items of U.S. air power but only that they worked best and most distinctively in the Gulf War. The five topics chosen for discussion are stealth/low observability, laser-guided bombs, aerial refueling, the high-speed antiradiation missile, and the STU-III.

Five Key Technologies

Stealth/Low Observability

Stealthy, low-observable platforms were the keystones of Coalition attacks against the Iraqi air defense system, leadership, and communications targets early on the first day of the war, even in heavily defended areas. Throughout the war, they attacked with complete surprise and were nearly impervious to Iraqi air defenses. These platforms needed minimal support from other aircraft but were able to provide stealth to a much larger force by disabling the enemy's air defense system, thus making all Coalition aircraft harder to detect and attack.[5]

3. William Perry, "Desert Storm and Deterrence," *Foreign Affairs* (Fall 1991):66.

4. Dwight D. Eisenhower, *Crusade in Europe* (New York: Doubleday and Company, 1948), 163–64.

5. Low observability as a design and engineering goal involves the systematic reduction of observable signatures in various spectra, including, but not limited to, radar. The design of stealthy aircraft like the F-117 focused on reducing radar signatures because radar-based air defenses have long posed the greatest threat to air operations. Strictly speaking, it is the combination of low observability and tactics that produces stealth in

Stealth thus not only restored a measure of surprise to air warfare, it also provided air forces some freedom of action that otherwise would not have been attainable.

U.S. forces used three platforms during the Gulf War that were in the stealth/low-observability category: the F-117 stealth fighter[6] and two long-range cruise missiles, the TLAM and the conventional air-launched cruise missile (CALCM). Neither cruise missiles nor the stealth fighter figured in the deployment plans envisioned in OPLAN 1002-90, issued prior to Desert Shield, but they did become vital parts of the strategic air campaign. The F-117, which flew only 2 percent of the total attack sorties, struck nearly 40 percent of the strategic targets, and it remained the centerpiece of the strategic air campaign for the entire war. Two hundred and eighty-eight TLAMs were launched during the war: 64 percent in the first two days of the air war and none after 1 February. Merely thirty-five CALCMs were employed, all launched from B-52s on the first day of the war.

Low observability allowed for direct strikes at the heart of the Iraqi air defense system at the very outset of the war. In the past, air forces fought through elaborate defenses and accepted losses on their way to the target or rolled those defenses back. In the Gulf War, the Coalition could strike Iraqi air defenses immediately, and they never recovered from these initial, stunning blows. With the combination of stealth and accuracy possessed by the F-117 and cruise missiles, these two platforms carried out all of the attacks against downtown Baghdad; the F-117 operated at night and the TLAMs during the day.

Given the American sensitivity to casualties—their own and those among Iraqi civilians—these were two ideal weapons systems for attacking targets in the heart of a heavily defended, populous city. Moreover, the F-117 had a psychological utility that is probably shared solely by the B-52. Both are aircraft of a kind that only a superpower could have, and both can deliver destruction with no advanced warning. Small wonder, then, that both figured prominently in psychological operations pamphlets that were showered upon Iraqi troops.

On the other hand, the F-117 and long-range cruise missiles also have limitations: both are less flexible and considerably more expensive than most conventional systems. Throughout Desert Storm, the F-117, a subsonic, light bomber, had to operate at night to maximize stealthiness, and nearly 19 percent of the strikes attempted by F-117s

---

an operational sense. During this discussion, however, these terms will be used somewhat interchangeably.

6. In some ways it is incorrect to call the F-117 a fighter—it is really a single-seat bomber.

were adversely affected by weather (misses or no drops).[7] While not as sensitive to weather conditions as the F-117, cruise missiles had a smaller payload, required a lengthy targeting process, and could not be retargeted after launch. Even without the flexibility of other aircraft, however, these platforms were able to set the terms for air operations over Iraq and to bring the reality of the war home to the residents of Baghdad.

Laser-Guided Bombs

Few scenes were as vivid on television as the picture of a guided bomb going through a ventilation shaft in an Iraqi office building. From all appearances, a new age of precision bombing had supplanted years of employing less accurate, unguided bombs. In fact, the new age had only partly arrived: laser-guided bombs (LGBs) achieved dramatic success in the war—in some measure because of the early neutralization of Iraqi air defenses—but overall, they comprised just a small fraction of the munitions expended in the war.

Laser-guided bombs are simply general-purpose bombs with guidance kits added: that is, sensors in the front to detect laser energy and to give steering commands and a wing assembly in the rear to provide lift. Laser-guided bombs are part of a larger family of precision-guided munitions (PGMs), many of which (air-to-air missiles, for instance) have been around for well over thirty years. Radio-guided bombs were used in World War II and Korea, and the Air Force dropped more than four thousand LGBs on North Vietnam between April 1972 and January 1973, targeted almost exclusively against bridges.[8]

In the Gulf War, more than 17,000 PGMs were expended, of which 9,342 were LGBs, 5,448 were air-to-surface missiles (predominantly Mavericks), 2,039 were antiradiation missiles (predominantly HARMs, discussed later), and 333 were cruise missiles (see above). By way of comparison, approximately 210,000 unguided bombs were dropped in the Gulf War.

What, then, explains the wartime prominence of LGBs, a not-so-new weapon that comprised less than 5 percent of the total weapons employed? There are three reasons, one of which has already been noted—the marriage of LGBs and imaging infrared target sensors with stealth in the F-117. The stealth characteristics of the F-117 made the normally high-risk tactic of directing the path of an LGB while flying

---

7. See appendix 4. The F-117 database contained more than four hundred weather-related misses or no-drops. Equivalent data were not available for other aircraft.

8. Headquarters, Pacific Air Forces *Summary, Air Operations Southeast Asia*, monthly reports for May 1972 through January 1973.

in a heavily defended area a much more routine affair. Any target in Iraq became open to destruction by the F-117's GBU-27, a two-thousand-pound bomb designed to penetrate hardened facilities.

A second reason for the importance of LGBs was Iraq's extensive system of bunkers and aircraft shelters that were vulnerable only to a precision bomb with a penetrating warhead. It was vital that these targets be destroyed, and the LGBs were the one means of doing so.

Third, LGB attacks were needed to attain attrition of the heavily revetted Iraqi armor in the Kuwaiti theater.

Laser-guided bombs were particularly effective because their employment came as something of a surprise to the Iraqis. That reaction is completely understandable, for the LGB performance also surprised the United States. The one new U.S. weapon system prepared to drop LGBs was the F-117, an aircraft whose existence had been kept secret until just a year or two before the gulf crisis and whose capabilities were largely unknown. Its one publicized employment had been in Operation Just Cause in Panama; in that conflict, the F-117's main notoriety came from a dispute about whether its LGBs, deliberately aimed to miss a building, missed by the correct amount. The U.S. fighter bombers designed in the 1970s, the F-16 and F/A-18, could not laser-designate, and the first squadron of F-15Es received laser-designating equipment only after deploying to the theater, as did the Royal Air Force Tornados.[9]

Laser-guided bombs carried principally by F-117s and F-111Fs were planned for precision air attacks on nearly the entire Iraqi target structure: air defense operations centers; national leadership and military headquarters; communications nodes; nuclear, chemical, and biological weapons research and storage facilities; and bridges were the most prominent. Beyond this planned use, much of the LGB employment was unplanned, growing out of adaptations made in the midst of the air campaign.

Originally, the Coalition intended to destroy the Iraqi air force when its aircraft rose to meet the Coalition attacks. When the Iraqi aircraft remained instead on the ground in hardened shelters, Coalition aircraft shifted the attacks to the nearly six hundred shelters themselves. Only weapons with the accuracy of LGBs and with hardened warheads, often dropped two at a time, were able to penetrate the reinforced concrete of those shelters. The results of these attacks were the flight of much of the Iraqi air force to Iran and the dispersal or destruction of the rest.

In the Kuwaiti theater, CENTAF turned to the use of LGBs when the planned air attacks on Iraqi armor, using cluster munitions or unguided bombs, proved to be largely ineffective. Iraqi revetted armor

---

9. See chapter 7 for a discussion of all aircraft capable of laser designation.

was simply less vulnerable to these munitions, particularly at the bombing altitudes used by the Coalition. The use of F-111Fs, F-15Es, and A-6s carrying five-hundred-pound LGBs against the dug-in Iraqi armor was one of the major innovations of the war and marked a major turning point in the attrition operations against the Iraqi army. This episode was an excellent example of the flexibility of the weapon, the aircraft, and the organization in dealing with the unexpected.

Laser-guided bomb employment also had its limitations. Laser designation was not possible through overcast skies, fog, or smoke. The designating aircraft also had to remain in the target area and within line of sight of the target until bomb detonation. On the one hand, LGBs opened up new targeting possibilities. First, without them, systematic attacks on a communications system would have been unlikely simply because the probability of disabling a telephone switch or an antenna would have been too low without an excessive number of sorties. Second, targets that would have been considered lucrative and vulnerable but too costly to attack were now open to assault. On the other, LGBs were of less value against large-area targets such as supply depots or deployed forces without a vital point to attack.

Nevertheless, against the primary Iraqi targets in this war, LGBs were as devastating to the Iraqis as they were unexpected.

Air Refueling

Air refueling between aircraft took place well before World War II and has been a part of normal U.S. air operations since the 1950s. During the gulf crisis, it was absolutely essential both to the deployment and to the war itself. Some aircraft required as many as seventeen refuelings to deploy from the United States to the gulf region. More than one hundred tankers operated the Atlantic and Pacific air refueling bridges, permitting the rapid deployment of some one thousand fighters, bombers, and support aircraft. Throughout the course of the war, Air Force tankers alone flew almost seventeen thousand sorties, usually with multiple receiver aircraft per tanker sortie.[10]

Nearly 60 percent of the wartime sorties by aircraft capable of being refueled in the air actually required tanker support. An elaborate network of air refueling tracks and anchors extended from the Red Sea across the Arabian Peninsula and into the Persian Gulf to support these requirements. This complex arrangement produced more than sixty air refueling tracks in which 275 tanker sorties per day operated, responding to the changing demands of the receiver aircraft. Liaison officers placed on board the E-3 airborne warning and control aircraft

10. Headquarters SAC, Plans and Requirements (XP), "Desert Shield/Desert Storm Tanker Assessment," 23 September 1991, 2-13.

managed the dynamic air refueling process, changing tankers from track to track to fill gaps as plans changed or emergencies developed.

The distances between Coalition air bases and targets meant that aircraft attacking deep into Iraq frequently had to refuel at least twice: once en route to the target and again on the return to home base. In some cases, refueling was conducted over Iraqi territory, an indication of the extent to which the Coalition controlled the air. Coalition air forces also relied on refueling to help them control the skies over the battlefield and strike into the enemy heartland. A list of representative aircraft and target areas shows the extent of the dependence.

Aircraft	Combat Radius	Target Distance
F-117	550 nm	to Baghdad 905 nm
F-15E	475 nm	to Western Scud areas 680 nm
F/A-18	434 nm	Red Sea Carrier to Kuwait City 695 nm
B-52G	2,177 nm	Diego Garcia to Kuwait 2,500 nm

In addition to supporting Coalition attack aircraft, aerial tankers refueled combat air patrol aircraft and an entire array of airborne warning, reconnaissance, targeting, and control aircraft that had to provide twenty-four-hour coverage during both Desert Shield and Desert Storm. Only aircraft such as A-10s and AV-8Bs, flying from the more forward operating bases and attacking targets in the Kuwaiti theater, could fly back and forth without in-flight refueling.

Air operations without the extensive support of aerial tankers would have changed the character of the war; by how much can only be guessed. Initial deployments to the theater would have been delayed, making more use of en-route bases and requiring considerable logistical support at those bases. Because of the ranges to the targets, all dimensions of the air campaign would have been altered: the number of sorties a day as well as operating bases used. In short, the air campaign was designed under the assumption that all necessary tanking would be available, and a change in that assumption would mean a change in the design. Aerial tankers facilitated the speed and mass of the attacks and provided a margin of safety in air operations. Moreover, against an enemy capable of attacking air bases close to the border, the ability to refuel extensively permitted operations from distant, secure bases and provided a buffer of inestimable worth.[11]

---

11. Chapter 7 has further discussion on aerial refueling operations.

HARM

Several air power weapons contributed to the Coalition's command of the air over Iraq and the Kuwaiti theater, but no single weapon was as significant as the HARM. The use of HARMs effectively neutralized both elements of Iraqi ground-based defenses—antiaircraft artillery (AAA) and SAMs—by suppressing the SAMs and thereby allowing Coalition aircraft to fly above the lethal range of AAA. Other forms of countermeasures to Iraqi radars (jamming, in particular) were important, but the HARM was the chief lethal component of the effort to suppress enemy air defenses.[12]

The HARM homed in on Iraqi radar emissions and destroyed the emitter, and it was launched from a variety of platforms, most notably the F-4G Wild Weasel aircraft. The U.S. Air Force fired some 1,067 HARMs, and the U.S. Navy and Marine Corps fired 894. Combined with the destruction of Iraqi air defense control centers and of Iraqi aircraft in the air and on the ground, overall air defense suppression resulted in an attrition rate for Coalition aircraft of less than a tenth of that incurred by the United States operating over North Vietnam during the Linebacker II campaign of 18 to 29 December 1972.[13]

Although most of the HARMs were fired during the first week of the war—two hundred on the first night—they continued their influence throughout the war. On the first night of the air war, an elaborately choreographed combination of stealth aircraft, specialized electronic warfare aircraft, decoys, cruise missiles, and attack aircraft delivered a sudden, paralyzing blow to the integrated air defense system from which the Iraqis never recovered.

The HARM's role was to take out the Iraqi SAM radars, activated by the decoys and attack aircraft. Its deterrent effect was just as important as its ability to actually destroy Iraqi radars. After the first day of the war, Iraqi radar activity declined precipitously because of the unwillingness of operators to turn on their radars for anything more than brief periods of time. Iraqi operators would, in fact, turn off their radars if they knew a HARM-carrying aircraft was in the vicinity. This was a classically indirect effect of a weapon; a measure of HARM's physical destruction of enemy targets tells only part of the story. By the third day of the war, the radar threat had been so reduced by the Iraqi fear of HARMs that the Coalition could fly at altitudes of ten thou-

12. Other lethal missiles that homed in on Iraqi radars included the British ALARM and the older American Shrike system, of which fewer than two hundred were launched.

13. Linebacker II losses were twenty-five aircraft out of about thirty-two hundred combat sorties, compared to thirty-eight losses out of about seventy thousand combat sorties in the Gulf War.

sand feet or higher, where radar-guided SAMs would have posed an unacceptable threat.

The experience of the 35th Tactical Fighter Wing (Provisional), whose F-4G aircraft were the main employers of HARM, indicates how the dominance over SAMs came about. The 35th Wing fired 905 HARMs and recorded 254 radars destroyed, for a 28 percent success rate. More significant, however, was that the radars, if not destroyed, had virtually ceased to operate. During the first week of the war, F-4Gs accompanying strike packages invariably fired all of their missiles; later on, some of these aircraft returned from missions having fired none.

In the Kuwaiti theater, the F-4Gs began a patrol, the "Weasel Police," so that they no longer accompanied each strike package, but each element of the F-4Gs could cover thirty to forty attack formations. Still later in the war, the dominance became so complete that tanker aircraft could accompany the F-4Gs farther north, allowing them to remain on-station even longer. Throughout the entire war, only five Coalition aircraft were lost to Iraqi radar-guided SAMs, and four of those five did not have F-4G support.[14]

STU-III

The STU-III was an essential item of support equipment for the units that deployed to the Persian Gulf region. More than 350 STU-IIIs were used in the area of operations alone. This unit, and the family of secure facsimile machines and field phones associated with it, enabled air campaign planners and staffs to preserve operational secrecy and still establish the informal and ad hoc organizations that sprang up to conduct the campaign.[15]

Campaign planners communicated regularly with agencies in Washington and with deployed wings, frequently bypassing intermediate theater-level organizations. The STU-III and secure fax created the potential for a tremendous volume of communication between parallel groups in the theater and the United States, dealing with everything from the selection of targets to the status of various spare parts or key munitions. Traditional hierarchies and cumbersome procedures were circumvented, which led to improvisation and creativity, on the one hand, and confusion on the other.

14. TSgt. Charles L. Starr, *History of the 35th Tactical Fighter Wing (Provisional), Operations Desert Shield and Desert Storm, 2 August 1990–2 August 1991*, Vol. I (35th Fighter Wing Special History), 148–50, 179–83, 190.

15. Col. Randy Witt, et al., "Air Force Tactical Communications in War: The Desert Shield/Desert Storm Comm Story," Headquarters CENTAF, March 1991, GWAPS, NA 49; and Headquarters TAC DCS Communications-Computer Systems, "Desert Shield/Desert Storm After Action Report," 16 July 1991, GWAPS, NA 180.

Was Desert Storm a Revolution in Warfare?

Targeting and sortie production were affected in many ways. On numerous occasions the Checkmate organization in the Pentagon worked with Washington intelligence organizations to develop prospective targets, then called or faxed the target identification—often including building or site diagrams—to the strategic planning cell in Riyadh. If the target was a high priority one, General Glosson might call a fighter unit on the same day and divert aircraft to this new target. The next day, another call from Washington could bring the first information on target damage. Significantly, the entire intelligence organization in Riyadh could be left unaware of these actions until later, if at all. Similarly, adequate coordination with tanker, electronic countermeasures, and reconnaissance aircraft was at times omitted in these late targeting changes, with a resulting loss in sorties and effectiveness.[16]

Conditions in the theater made extensive use of secure telephones a necessity. In the early days of the deployment, the STU-III tied into the local commercial telephone system was one of the few communications capabilities available. Later, pre-mission communications by a mission commander with elements of an attack package at distant bases still took place by secure telephone; so too did subsequent coordination on changes to call signs, times, radio frequencies, and so forth.

The daily ATO grew to hundreds of pages and was laboriously transmitted over the CAFMS, but most units had already received the ATO information that pertained to them via secure telephone from Riyadh long before the ATO was sent electronically. Some units avoided CAFMS entirely by arranging for electronic transmission of the ATO from personal computer to personal computer over the intrinsic voice network of the STU-III system. The Black Hole also used this technique to transmit master attack plans to Checkmate. The negative side of using STU-IIIs for data communications was the pressure put on voice circuits.[17]

Although callers (who would have liked more secure phones and lines) often had trouble "going secure," the STU-III came to symbolize the aspects of computers and telecommunications that worked best. The great promise of these intertwined technologies was only partly realized in this war. CAFMS was by no means the only computer-communications system to prove inadequate under the demands of Desert Shield and Desert Storm. While the American military led other armed forces in its use of computers, the rapidity of technical change had left many of its systems obsolescent even before they were fully developed. Older mainframe systems were just beginning to acquire

---

16. See chapters 2, 4, and 5.

17. See chapter 5.

the hardware and software necessary for integrated databases and distributed processing.

Problems with mainframe systems, exposed immediately at the beginning of the crisis in August 1990, required even more extensive use of secure phones to overcome efficiency breakdowns. Because the Iraqi invasion came while CENTCOM was still developing an operations plan for that contingency, JOPES did not have the necessary data to help commanders schedule the deployment. JOPES itself was undergoing hardware and software development and was not ready to manipulate rapidly changing deployment data fast enough to meet CENTCOM's demands.

JOPES ran on the Worldwide Military Command and Control System's old Honeywell mainframe computers acquired in the 1970s; it was supposed to integrate separate databases for peacetime planning and crisis planning. JOPES's problems extended beyond its transitional condition, however, to a shortage of personnel trained to operate in this evolving system. For weeks, manual calculations, personal computers, and telephones had to work around JOPES to get American forces deployed to Southwest Asia.[18]

Computer system after computer system followed the sorry pattern of JOPES's performance. MAC did not have enough time to schedule missions using its Flow Generation (FLOGEN) model, and so it resorted to personal computer spreadsheets.[19]

The Combat Ammunition System was still under development, and the version used by TACAIR, U.S. Air Forces in Europe and Pacific Air Forces, did not have sufficiently accurate data to be helpful. As for the larger problem of tracking supplies in general, the interim solution of having each deployed unit linked to the supply computer at its host base in the United States never worked well. The pre-crisis plan to deploy mainframes to the theater for supply accounting gave way eventually to linking as many deployed units as possible to Tactical Air Command's Unisys computer at Langley Air Force Base, Virginia. Achieving that arrangement, however, took the better part of Desert Shield's five months and innumerable STU-III calls.[20]

The STU-III, like the other four technologies featured in this chapter, hit its stride in the Gulf War. But for the most part, these technologies were not really new and were available in less sophisticated forms during the Vietnam War. Thousands of laser-guided bombs were dropped

---

18. JULLS 91055-65325 (00141), Headquarters MAC CAT Director; and JULLS 91154-50811 (00109), USCENTAF Rear/LG.

19. *Kondra Notes.* Kondra was at Headquarters MAC DCS Plans and later DCS Operations.

20. Interviews, GWAPS with Col. Mike Christensen, 18–20 November 1992; Col. Van McCrea, 4–5 April 1992; and Frank Spruce, 22 October 1992, all at Langley AFB.

on North Vietnam, together with even more numerous radar-seeking missiles; bombing missions from Thailand depended on air refueling to reach the Hanoi-Haiphong region; and the bases scattered around Thailand coordinated strike packages over the telephone.

Still other technologies went through more dramatic changes after the Vietnam War. Airborne radar, for example, came into its own first with AWACS and then (just in time for the Gulf War) with JSTARS. If Iraq's air force and army had been more active, these radar systems would have played a more central role. Nonetheless, the *fundamental* technologies of the Gulf War do not appear to have been terribly new.

Beyond Technology: Defining Revolutionary Change

Technology by itself, though, may be only a small part of revolutionary change in the conduct of war. The Soviet argument for a dawning revolution focused less on military hardware catching up with long-standing doctrinal promises than on technological advances making qualitative transformations in nonnuclear, or "conventional," warfare. Soviet theorists have argued that so-called reconnaissance-strike complexes would enable commanders to detect targets and attack them effectively—at long ranges and within minutes. These combinations of sensors and weapons would blur traditional distinctions between offensive and defensive fires and allow the conduct of war over far greater distances than ever before. Given the use of advanced reconnaissance systems and precision munitions in the Gulf War, it was natural for Soviet observers, as well as like-minded American commentators, to conclude that "the integration of control, communications, reconnaissance, electronic combat, and delivery of conventional fires into a single whole" had been realized "for the first time."[21]

Close examination of the evidence, however, suggests that this conclusion went too far. Although many of the pieces of reconnaissance-strike complexes were present in Desert Storm, Coalition forces did not, in fact, integrate them on a large scale. For example, to direct the use of precision bombs, Coalition commanders relied on an air-tasking system whose cycle times and use of advanced reconnaissance sensors had not changed appreciably from the Vietnam era. Episodes such as using JSTARS to detect Iraqi forces moving up for the attack on Al Khafji at the end of January were important exceptions, but exceptions nonetheless. Despite the presence of airborne, space, and ground sen-

21. "Soviet Analysis of Operation Desert Storm and Operation Desert Shield," LN 006-91, trans. Defense Intelligence Agency, Washington, 28 October 1991, 32. For an example of American defense analysts who reached much the same conclusion regarding the realization of "recce-strike complexes" in Desert Storm, see Ashton B. Carter, William J. Perry, and John D. Steinbruner, "A New Concept of Cooperative Security," Brookings Occasional Paper (Washington: Brookings Institution, 1992), 3.

sors, many mobile Scud launchers still managed to elude the Coalition's best attempts at their destruction.

Yet even if the technologies of Desert Storm turn out to be not quite as revolutionary as they appeared to be on American television sets, the facts of Desert Storm do require further consideration. If nothing else, the one-sided character of the war demands explanation. Why was the Coalition able to smash an army of hundreds of thousands of men and thousands of tanks, artillery pieces, and vehicles at a cost of fewer than two hundred troops killed and fifty aircraft lost? Why, moreover, did so few expert observers in the United States and elsewhere anticipate such lopsided results? And why did the war look so different from the conflicts of the past few decades, in which air action served as a prelude and accompaniment to a bloody struggle on the ground?

The notion of periodic and radical changes in the conduct of war is an old one. Scholars have written of the military revolution of the seventeenth century and of the revolution brought about by the advent of the railroad, rifle, and telegraph in the middle of the nineteenth century. During the twentieth century one can identify at least two such dramatic changes in warfare. The first culminated in the period 1939–1942, with the appearance of blitzkrieg (lightning warfare), strategic bombardment, offensive carrier aviation, and amphibious warfare. These developments depended in various ways on the technologies involved in mechanization, aviation, and radio communication.

The second change, which centered on the marriage of nuclear weapons and intercontinental ballistic missiles, covered the period from the late-1940s to the mid-1960s and culminated in the fielding of large arsenals of ballistic missiles with nuclear warheads that were never used in anger.

A useful definition of a revolution in war might be a quantum change in the means of waging war and in its outcome, such that the very face of battle—its lethality, pace, and geographical scope—is transformed. In most cases, a revolution in war involves the rise of new warrior elites, new forms of organization, and new dominant weapons.[22]

In each case, revolutionary change in the conduct of war required the advent or maturation of new military technologies (the internal combustion engine, armor, etc.), their integration into new military systems (the tank or the long-range bomber), the adoption of appropriate operational concepts (the armored breakthrough and its ex-

---

22. Eliot A. Cohen, "On Revolutions in Military Affairs," unpublished manuscript. October 1994.

ploitation), and finally, the requisite organizational adaptation (the panzer division and the Clausewitzian approach to war embedded in the German troop regulations of that era).[23]

Technology alone does not a revolution make; how military organizations adapt and shape new technology, military systems, and operational concepts matter much more. In France and the low countries in May 1940, the British and the French had technology and military systems at least comparable to those of the Germans, and British tank enthusiasts such as J. F. C. Fuller and B. H. Liddell Hart had articulated the requisite operational concepts. But without the necessary organizational adaptation, the British and French were unable to withstand the German blitzkrieg. More than the inventions of clever technologists or the reflections of insightful theorists would be needed to make armored warfare successful; doctrine and organization played their part as well. Furthermore, politics—the purposes of war and the domestic pressures on its conduct—can also shape a revolutionary change in warfare.

It is therefore insufficient to look merely at the technologies of precision weapons, airborne radars, and data links and to declare the existence of a "military-technical revolution." If history is any guide, the technologies necessary for such dramatic change may require much time and trial before armed forces can use them as effectively as theory might predict. Because the conditions under which Desert Storm was conducted were so special, the question posed earlier in this chapter will elude a definitive answer. We can, however, ask whether the *precursors* of a revolutionary change in the conduct of war appeared in this conflict. To answer that question, it makes sense to ask which elements of the conflict appeared to have precedents in earlier experience and which seemed new or radically different.

Older Forms of Air Warfare

With few exceptions, the planners of Desert Storm used the same target categories as in previous wars. In World War II, Korea, and Vietnam, aircraft attacked air defenses, fielded armies, oil refineries, electrical power grids, and even command, control, and communications. In the Gulf War, the Coalition achieved successes against some of these target systems (especially strategic air defenses and electric power)

---

23. See Gen. Ludwig Beck, Truppenführung *(Troop Leading): German Field Service Regulations,* Part I, trans. U.S. Army, report no. 14, 507, 18 March 1936, 1–2. This way of thinking about military revolutions is based on work that has been done on the subject in recent years by Mr. Andrew Marshall, the Director of Net Assessment, Office of the Secretary of Defense.

extraordinarily quickly: what took a day or two to accomplish in this conflict might have taken months in others.

But the concept of what to attack to disorganize and paralyze an enemy nation did not differ substantially from previous air campaigns. A partial exception to this generalization was the emphasis on targeting national-level leadership and telecommunications from the outset, rather than vital elements in enemy war production as had been the focus of the Combined Bomber Offensive of World War II. Only a relatively small proportion of the Coalition effort (fewer than one thousand strikes out of a total of about forty-two thousand), however, went against this set of targets. Leadership attacks also had precedents, most notably in the fatal aerial ambush of Adm. Isoroku Yamamoto in April 1943.

Suppression of Enemy Air Defenses (SEAD)

The Coalition successfully shut down the Iraqi air defense system within days of the war's beginning. The operational achievement was impressive, but again, very little was new *in principle* about this aspect of the air campaign. Since 1943, American air forces have undertaken the achievement of air superiority as their first priority. As defenses (particularly SAMs) have grown more sophisticated, the suppression of enemy air defenses has become an increasingly important part of that task.[24]

The measure-countermeasure struggle of World War II included electronic and physical means of jamming or confusing enemy radars, and radar-homing missiles have long been part of the arsenals of the United States and its allies. Direct attacks on enemy ground-based air defenses (as distinct from airfields) became common in the Vietnam War, when the advent of radar-guided SAMs led to the creation of dedicated radar-hunter-killer aircraft, the Wild Weasels. In 1972, Linebacker II achieved considerable successes against North Vietnamese air defenses, albeit at a far greater cost than in the gulf.

Since then, virtually all large air operations have featured some SEAD operations. The Israeli operation in the Beka'a Valley in 1982 combined SEAD and air-to-air combat to defeat the Syrian Air Force and its ground-based air defense. Although on a much smaller scale than the Gulf War (the Beka'a is roughly half the size of one of the thirty-odd kill boxes in the Kuwaiti theater), it exemplified the sophisticated use of a variety of means to take down an air defense system.

24. War Department, "Command and Employment of Air Power," Field Manual 100-20, 21 July 1943, 1; and "Basic Aerospace Doctrine of the United States Air Force," Air Force Manual 1-1, Vol. I, March 1992, 10.

Was Desert Storm a Revolution in Warfare?

The Gulf War operation departed from others in its speed, scope, and relative cheapness in terms of casualties. Coalition forces did not conduct SEAD as an isolated effort to protect a specific mission or area but rather as an integrated attack designed to disable the entire Iraqi national-level air defense system. The intimate cooperation of aircraft from different services and nations in this effort also represented something of a departure from the past and testified to the benefit of centralized planning under a JFACC.

Precision Munitions

For many noncombatant observers, the most vivid images from the Persian Gulf War came from videotapes of laser-guided bombs hitting particular points on buildings and bridges with seemingly unerring accuracy. Yet, the use of precision munitions in general and laser-guided bombs in particular was not new. The *intensity* of the operation, however, did represent a departure. Desert Storm saw in six weeks the dropping of more than double the number of laser-guided bombs released over North Vietnam in nine months. Aircraft attacked a much broader range of targets than in the Linebacker operations, prosecuted the bulk of the attacks with these munitions at night rather than in the daytime, and used precision-guided missiles (most notably some fifty-four hundred Maverick antiarmor missiles and more than two thousand HARM antiradar missiles) more extensively than ever before. The war saw a combination of qualitative *and* quantitative changes in weapons employment.

Functional Effects

In the Gulf War, planners consciously sought functional effects; that is, they measured their success in terms other than pure destruction. It mattered little, for example, if bombs had leveled a sector operations center in the Iraqi air defense system. It would suffice if a couple of accurate and damaging hits had so intimidated the occupants that they abandoned the site. Similarly, if the pervasive presence of F-4G Wild Weasel aircraft deterred enemy radar operators from turning on their equipment, the physical destruction of those radars mattered little. Functional-effects thinking led planners to assign fewer aircraft and fewer bombs to many targets, which, in turn, meant that they could attack more targets simultaneously rather than a few repeatedly and in depth.

Although the capability to hit a wide range of targets simultaneously was new, seeking functional effects was not. Daylight bombing attacks on German aircraft production in the spring of 1944 to force the *Luftwaffe*'s fighter arm into the skies to fight reflected a similar approach.²⁵ Here too the effect sought was a functional one that was, to some extent, insensitive to the amount of physical destruction actually inflicted on German aircraft production.

Paralysis as a Goal

Finally, theorists had long argued that air power could disorganize and paralyze an enemy's military industries and operations, as Allied bombing of Germany sought to do in World War II. In the Gulf War, the Coalition's strategic-operational goal of the air campaign, particularly during the elaborately planned first two days, was more ambitious: to paralyze Iraqi national leadership by destroying its telecommunications, strategic air defenses, and air force. As described in chapter 3, the Coalition achieved impressive successes, especially against Iraqi strategic air defense.

Operational Thresholds

The majority of the military systems and operational concepts central to the Desert Storm air campaign, then, had historical antecedents. Most of the technologies had seen service in earlier wars.²⁶ Even the low-observability (or stealth technology) of the F-117 was not new. The plane had first taken part in combat during Operation Just Cause in Panama on the night of 20 December 1989,²⁷ and stealth technology aimed at eluding radar-based air defenses had helped to protect the SR-71 for decades.²⁸

But even if the technologies and concepts were not new, the ways in which Coalition air forces applied them often were. Moreover, as Soviet military theorists had long observed, quantitative changes in the conduct of war have a way of becoming qualitative transformations. It is not surprising, then, that knowledgeable observers, including a number of officers involved in the planning and conduct of the Desert Storm air campaign, concluded that they had witnessed something "revolutionary" in the Gulf War. In this war, air power crossed some operational thresholds that, if not as obvious as the initial use of a new

---

25. William E. Kepner, *Eighth Air Force Tactical Development: August 1942–May 1945* (England: Eighth Air Force and Army Air Forces Evaluation Board, July 1945), 76–77.

26. JSTARS was an important exception.

27. "Out of the Black," *Lockheed Horizons*, May 1992, 51. This issue of *Lockheed Horizons*, subtitled "We Own the Night," was devoted entirely to the F-117 program.

28. "Early F-117 Program Set Pattern for B-2, A-12, A-X; No Prototypes," *Aerospace Daily*, 11 June 1992, 411; also Bill Sweetman, *Stealth Aircraft: Secrets of Future Airpower* (Osceola, Wi.: Motorbooks International, 1986), 14–21.

Was Desert Storm a Revolution in Warfare? 205

weapon or operational concept, did suggest a transformation of war. The following examples illustrate this proposition.

Target/Sortie Ratios

Mission planners normally calculate the number of aircraft that would have to be sent against a given target to have a specified probability of destroying it with a particular munition. Assuming unguided, or dumb, bombs, they might have to send dozens or even hundreds of sorties to achieve a 90 percent or higher probability of destroying many kinds of targets. To cite an extreme example, the Thanh Hoa bridge in North Vietnam withstood literally hundreds of attacks from U.S. Air Force and Navy fighter-bombers during Rolling Thunder without sustaining major structural damage.[29]

In examining the sorties flown by F-117s and F-111Fs during Desert Storm, however, it quickly becomes evident that target/sortie ratios were dramatically different even from the Linebacker era, when large numbers of laser-guided bombs first saw combat use. To provide a sense of just how different, one can compare (table 9) twelve representative sorties by F-117s and F-111Fs delivering laser-guided bombs with twelve flown by Proven Force F-111Es delivering unguided Mk-82s (five-hundred-pound bombs). The twelve Proven Force sorties covered two targets (an AM radio transmitter and a sector operations center in Kirkuk) with 168 Mk-82s; by contrast, the dozen F-117 and F-111F sorties covered some twenty-six precision targets with a total of twenty-eight bombs (mostly two-thousand-pound weapons, but including some five-hundred-pound GBU-12s for two tank-plinking sorties).

The target/sortie ratio for the dozen dumb-bomb sorties was 1:6, whereas it was approximately 2:1 for the twelve precision sorties. Thus, the differential between the precision and non-precision cases was $26/2 = 13:1$, or better than an order-of-magnitude difference. Moreover, the low-light laser-guided bombs of the sort dropped during Desert Storm by the F-117s and F-111Fs had substantially higher probabilities of hitting individual point targets than dozens of unguided Mk-82s.

---

29. The more than 350 U.S. Air Force and Navy strike sorties flown against the Thanh Hoa bridge from 1965 to 1968 failed to drop a single span of this overbuilt structure, even though it was often rendered temporarily unusable (Col. Glenn Griffith, et al., "The Tale of Two Bridges," *The Tale of Two Bridges and the Battle for the Skies over North Vietnam*, edited by Maj. A. J. C. Lavalle [Washington: Government Printing Office, 1976], 31, 38, 42–43, 46, 55–56, 59, 62–63). USAF losses against the bridge over this period included F-105s, F-4s, and a C-130. During Linebacker I, two attacks involving a total of twenty-six F-4 sorties delivering laser-guided bombs finally succeeded in dropping the Thanh Hoa bridge without any aircraft losses (ibid., 84–86).

Table 9 Precision versus Non-Precision Target Coverage

Number/Type Aircraft	Number/Type Ordnance	Target/Location:
12 Precision Sorties = 26 Targets:		
F-117	1 GBU-27 1 GBU-27	AT&T. Building, Baghdad Intercept Operations Center, Al Taqaddum
F-117	1 GBU-27 1 GBU-27	Presidential Quarters, Abu Ghurayb Hardened Command Post, Al Taji NW
F-117	1 GBU-10 1 GBU-27	Chemical/Biological Facility, Salman Pak Ammunition Depot, Fallujah
F-117	1 GBU-27 1 GBU-27	Ammunition Depot, Karbala Al Jumhuriya Fiber-optic Bridge, Baghdad
F-117	2 GBU-27	TV Transmitter, Baghdad
F-117	1 GBU-10 1 GBU-10	Isis 1 reactor, Al Tuwaitha Iraqi AWACS, Saddam International
F-117	2 GBU-10	Iraqi Air Force Headquarters, Baghdad
F-111F	4 GBU-12	4 T-72 Tanks, Medina Division
F-111F	3 GBU-12 1 GBU-12	3 Tanks Building along N. Kuwait/Iraq border
F-111F	2 GBU-24	2 Aircraft Shelters, Al Asad airfield
F-117	1 GBU-10 1 GBU-10	Highway bridge over Euphrates Highway bridge over Nahr Desma
F-117	1 GBU-10 1 GBU-27	Ba'ath Party Headquarters, Baghdad Possible Air Defense Operations Center, Balad SE
12 Non-Precision Sorties = 2 Targets:		
4 F-111E	14 Mk-82	AM Radio Transmitter, Kirkuk
8 F-111E	14 Mk-82	Sector Operations Center, Kirkuk

Precision-guided weapon technology had improved considerably since the Vietnam War, a fact reflected in the superb performance of the GBU-27 guided bomb dropped by the F-117s. The success of air defense suppression by specialized aircraft such as the F-4G, the EF-111, and the EA-6B reinforced this capability, because now aircraft could fly at medium altitudes and designate their targets with more care than in the past (see table 9; see also expanded tables on F-117 and F-111 strike data in appendix 4).

Changes in the Vulnerability of Certain Target Classes

Throughout the history of air warfare, targets have had markedly different degrees of vulnerability to air attack. The speed of an attacking aircraft, the sophistication of its navigation and target identification systems, and the accuracy of its ordnance determined what aircraft could and could not do. It would not have occurred to air planners during World War II, for example, to think that one might systematically attack an enemy's entire telephone system, even if one could, on extraordinary occasions, conduct isolated precision attacks against pieces of it.

The Gulf War saw at least two classes of difficult targets—armored vehicles in revetments and impenetrable aircraft shelters—become vulnerable to air attack from medium altitude at night. Many experts assumed before Desert Storm that, save for an occasional lucky bomb, both hardened aircraft shelters like the Iraqi "Yugos" and main battle tanks in revetments would be virtually invulnerable to bombing attacks from fixed-wing aircraft.

The integration of forward-looking infrared (FLIR) sensors with laser targeting devices aboard individual aircraft provided the accuracy and ease of employment necessary for systematic attacks against both classes of targets. The combination of the I-2000 hard-target-penetrating warhead and laser guidance kits meant that bombs could penetrate structures as hard as the Iraqi Yugos and destroy any aircraft inside. Given the degree of air superiority achieved early in Desert Storm by Coalition air forces, coupled with an Iraqi reluctance to risk destruction of the Iraqi air force by contesting control of the air, Coalition airmen could conduct systematic campaigns of attrition against Iraqi aircraft shelters and the armored vehicles of Republican Guard and other Iraqi ground units.

Whether combinations like the F-117 and GBU-27 will exert comparable dominance in future wars with different terrain or a more mobile adversary remains unclear. Only a more demanding test than the Gulf War could establish without question the supremacy of the precision-guided air-delivered bomb as the dominant weapon of war. Nevertheless, the shelter busting and tank-plinking that occurred in

Desert Storm were qualitatively different from and superior to the laser-guided bombing effort of the last phase of the Vietnam War.

Stealth, Air Superiority, and Campaign Options

The F-117, in conjunction with unmanned precision weapons such as the TLAM, gave Coalition air forces, from the outset of operations, the wherewithal to attack a wide range of targets systematically. Above all, the Coalition could prosecute these attacks without first "rolling back" Iraq's air defenses. The "air superiority" built into the F-117 also allowed it to attack key elements of Iraq's strategic air defenses as an integral part of Coalition efforts to gain early control of the air. In effect, platforms like the F-117 provided low-risk attack options that required neither traditional air superiority as a prerequisite nor electronic-warfare and fighter-escort support.

As a result, planners had a far greater array of options available to them than would have been the case with conventional aircraft. In this connection, the difference between the operations of Proven Force—which relied exclusively on conventional aircraft using unguided munitions—and the operations during the rest of the air campaign—from areas south, west, and east of Iraq—is instructive. The Proven Force attacks looked more like the traditional roll-back efforts of previous campaigns, in which attacks on air defenses proceeded from the enemy's perimeter inward.

Beyond Visual Range (BVR) Shots

Desert Storm was the first major air campaign in which a sizable portion (more than 40 percent) of the air-to-air engagements that produced kills began with BVR missile shots. Here, the limit was less technology (although improved long-range radar-guided missiles helped) than command and control. In the past, fears of air-to-air fratricide had inhibited the use of long-range missiles fired BVR. The overwhelming superiority of Coalition air and Iraq's conservative air doctrine meant that the Iraqi air force did not rise to fight very much. When it did, however, Coalition aircraft making use of information gathered by AWACS aircraft could shoot safely at opponents that they could not see, or not see well.

Air Power's Dominance of the Iraqi Field Army

The duration, intensity, and military effectiveness of the thirty-nine days of air operations that preceded the Coalition ground offensive on 24 February undoubtedly exceeded anything that the Iraqi leaders foresaw, based on their experience during the Iran-Iraq War. The Iraqi army's one attempt, in late January 1991, to move out into the open and precipitate the kind of bloody, close combat on the ground that Iraqi strategists believed would achieve important political, if not military, results succumbed swiftly to Coalition air power. Unlike in previous wars, air power operated almost as effectively at night as during the day, and in some cases more so. Unable to attack or retreat in the face of Coalition air power, the Iraqi army in the Kuwaiti theater after Al Khafji could only hunker down and continue to suffer mounting punishment, both physical and psychological, from the air.

When the Coalition's ground attack finally came, the ground forces of the U.S.–led alliance were able to destroy or expel from Kuwait the Iraqi divisions there in a scant one hundred hours of operations with extraordinarily low combat casualties. Indeed, the magnitude of what General Schwarzkopf asked Coalition air power to accomplish against Iraq's army in the Kuwaiti theater was astonishing by virtually any standard: to destroy 50 percent of the Iraqi armor and artillery in the Kuwaiti theater *before* Coalition ground forces engaged. The fact that Coalition air forces fell somewhat short of this ambitious goal in the case of some Republican Guard and other units should not detract from what they accomplished overall in that theater. In the case of Iraqi frontline divisions, the 50 percent attrition in equipment levels were not only met but, in some areas, exceeded.

Whether this remarkable outcome presages a new relationship between air forces and ground forces will, no doubt, be debated for years to come. Certainly, the success of air power ran contrary to the expectations of many experts in the United States before the war. The kill rates achieved against dug-in armor proved unprecedented. Air power had had successes against armor on the move in past wars, but in Desert Storm, the combination of rotary- and fixed-wing aircraft operating against forces on the move proved devastating.

To be sure, given the mitigating effects of political circumstances, training, technology, geography, and force ratios that heavily favored the Coalition, some caution is indicated. We may require a sterner test against a more capable adversary to come to a conclusive judgment. But if air power again exerts similar dominance over opposing ground forces, the conclusion will be inescapable that some threshold in the relationship between air and ground forces was first crossed in Desert Storm.

Conclusion: A Nascent Revolution

The general absence of new operational concepts for the use of air power in the Gulf War suggests that if a revolutionary change in the conduct of war is under way, the harder parts of its implementation may still lie in the future. To a surprising extent, the master attack plan/air tasking order process used by the air planners and commanders in Riyadh merely modified an approach long used within NATO. It also bore a striking family resemblance to the way in which American planners had constructed and executed air campaigns as far back as World War II. Although staffs made improvised use of computers for word processing, construction of databases, and record keeping, planners appear to have made surprisingly extensive use of pencils and yellow legal pads for their work. On the whole, the Coalition had not automated the extremely complicated tasks of developing force packages and ATOs and monitoring bomb damage nearly as much as those who speak of a military technical revolution would expect.

Concerning organizational innovation, the Black Hole planning group in Riyadh was an ad hoc organization staffed largely by outsiders. It disappeared at the end of the war, as did the wartime version of Checkmate. No organizational structure capable of operating as a genuine reconnaissance-strike complex existed, even though, as has been noted, most of the military systems needed for such a complex were present in the theater, and some swift attacks based on JSTARS information did occur. Imagining the kind of organization and doctrinal context necessary for a true reconnaissance-strike complex is not easy. In fact, our present situation regarding such strike complexes may be analogous to trying to imagine a 1940 panzer division and its associated operational culture from the vantage point of 1922 or 1923.

One large organizational innovation that did occur—unforeseen and by force of circumstances—was the dispersion of much command and control activity outside the theater. Officers in the basement of the Pentagon helped pick targets and plan attacks; staffs at Langley Air Force Base managed CENTAF's spare parts accounts; Space Command provided warning of missile attacks against Israel and Saudi Arabia; meteorologists in the United States processed weather information for use within the theater. From the outset, the civilian and military leadership of the American high command declared its strong desire that direction of this war should rest in the hands of the theater commander in chief.

By and large it did, but the dependence of modern military organizations on vast amounts of information, and the relative ease with which communications technology could disseminate that information, meant that supporting authority would, in some measure, trickle out of the theater. Now, commanders could tap the expertise of large staffs and organizations thousands of miles away to formulate decisions on courses of action to take during the next few hours. The formal scheme of organization did not acknowledge this, but the command system soon depended on informal arrangements and ad hoc groupings. The prevalence of such organizations may prove to be part of a broader trend, not merely an aberration.

The rapid collection, processing, and exploitation of information is likely to become even more important in a future war than it has been in the past. In this regard, access to space-based sensors and location/navigation systems provided the Coalition yet another one-sided advantage throughout Desert Shield and Desert Storm, a condition that may not necessarily be repeated in future conflicts. This may, for example, be the last war in which only one side will have ready access to precise location information from satellites. It may also be the last occasion on which air supremacy could shield a moving army from an enemy's prying eyes; observation from space and the proliferation of remotely piloted vehicles could deny the benefit that XVIII Airborne Corps and VII Corps had in their swing to the west of Iraqi positions.

Similarly, in future warfare the struggle for information may play a central role, taking the place, perhaps, that the contest for geographical position has held in previous conflicts. In Desert Storm, the effective operational-strategic employment of precision systems such as the F-117–GBU-27 combination required correspondingly precise target information, whereas the areas in which the strategic portion of the air campaign was least effective were precisely those in which fundamental gaps in Coalition understanding of entire target systems existed. While the Coalition unquestionably achieved the requisite "information dominance" against electricity, the nervous system of Iraq's air defense system, and the Iraqi air force in air-to-air combat, the evidence suggests that the Iraqis were able to deny the Coalition crucial information about their nuclear weapon and ballistic missile programs.

Did Desert Storm constitute a revolution in the nature or conduct of war? At a distance of four years, and after careful scrutiny of the evidence, some of the aspects of the war that seemed most dramatic at the time appear less so than they did in the immediate afterglow of one of the most one-sided campaigns in military history. Despite the talk of Iraq possessing the fourth largest army in the world, the fact remains that in this war a minor power found itself confronted by the full weight of the world's sole superpower, amply and ably aided by the forces of its key allies. While the overall outcome—the ejection of Iraqi forces from Kuwait—was likely from the moment the war began, the cost and longer-term consequences were not.

True revolutions in war may take decades and require not merely new technologies but new forms of organization and behavior to mature. It is probably too soon to conclude without reservation that we have entered a new era of warfare. But as we consider the war, some signposts of change surely stand out. Military planners and organizations will wish to reflect on the undoubted departures made during the

Gulf War for some time to come. But whether the signposts identified here really point down paths consideraly different from those the armed forces of the United States have been down before will depend on the future actions of the travelers themselves. The ingredients for a transformation of war may well have become visible in the Gulf War, but if a revolution is to occur, somcone will have to make it.

Ten | What Does Desert Storm Tell Us about the Future of Air Power?

Desert Storm and American Attitudes toward Air Power

Air power is an unusually seductive form of military strength because, like modern courtship, it appears to offer the pleasures of gratification without the burdens of commitment. Francis Bacon wrote of command of the sea that he who has it, "is at great liberty, and may take as much and as little of the Warre as he will," and a similar belief occasionally possesses the more passionate advocates of air power. Statesmen may think that they can titrate doses of air power in a way that they cannot do with ground combat. Furthermore, it appears that the imminent arrival of so-called nonlethal or disabling technologies may offer an even more appealing prospect—war without friendly *or* enemy casualties. The experience of Desert Storm enhanced the attractiveness of air power by making it appear spectacularly cheap in terms of lives expended and effective in results achieved.

It is small wonder, then, that one of the consequences of the Gulf War was a miracle of political ornithology: doves turning themselves overnight into hawks. When the American foreign policy establishment began debating the use of military power in Yugoslavia in 1992, more than one distinguished commentator who had had reservations about the use of force in the gulf expressed a newfound belief in the utility of bombing as a tool of foreign policy. Thus, Anthony Lewis of the *New York Times* wrote during the Gulf War in disgust at the ruin wrought by aerial bombardment. "We should never again tolerate anyone who talks about 'surgical strikes.'" Since then, however, he has developed a keener appreciation of air power. "A few air strikes in Dubrovnik" would have stopped the Yugoslav horrors in 1991. There is a "straightforward way to apply force" in Bosnia that involves "minimum risk" and provides a course that is not merely right but "clear and doable": namely, precision air attacks.[1]

---

1. See his columns in the *New York Times* of 8 February 1991, 14 June, 3 August, and 7 December 1992, and 12 April 1993.

One of the great attractions of air power after Desert Storm was its promise of low casualties. During the crisis of August 1990 through January 1991, a long parade of military experts and historians had trudged to Capitol Hill to warn senators and members of Congress that bombing merely stiffened an opponent's morale. Such *obiter dicta* took liberties with the historical record, but no one during that tense autumn had much interest in a careful review of the relevant scholarship. Competent observers and responsible statesmen believed them, and in some cases (to their subsequent embarrassment) warned of a bloody stalemate should the United States go to war. They were proven wrong, but the issue remained alive, even after the war's completion.

Just as important as the operational thresholds crossed in this war were the political thresholds, among them heightened Western sensitivity to casualties, both friendly and enemy. The phrase "no target is worth an airplane" (a dictum that did not hold if it came to supporting troops in contact with the enemy on the ground or rescuing a downed pilot) captured an attitude toward losses that prevailed during the war. The cessation of daylight attacks against Baghdad targets following the loss of two F-16s on 19 January, and the withdrawal of A-10s from attacks against the Republican Guard following the loss of two on 15 February, revealed a sensitivity to loss having few precedents in American military history.[2]

The degree of concern about enemy losses, though less strong, was nonetheless pronounced. Including some three hundred deaths reported by the Iraqis to have occurred when the Al Firdos bunker was bombed, the Iraqis themselves claimed fewer than twenty-three hundred civilian dead despite the intensity and scope of the forty-three-day air campaign.[3] Regarding collateral damage, American peace activists who visited Iraq immediately after the war looking for evidence that Baghdad had been razed by Coalition bombing found, instead, "a city whose homes and offices were almost entirely intact, where electricity was coming back on and the water was running."[4]

In fact, even Iraqi combat deaths seem to have been remarkably low. While the total Iraqi combat fatalities over the forty-three days of Desert Storm may have been higher than the estimate of ninety-five

---

2. In interview after interview conducted by GWAPS personnel with military participants in the Gulf War, the "lesson" that the low casualties experienced in Desert Storm established a "norm" that the U.S. military will have to meet in future wars was virtually universal.

3. William M. Arkin, Greenpeace International, briefing to GWAPS, 31 October 1991.

4. Erika Munk, as cited in John G. Heidenrich, "The Gulf War: How Many Iraqis Died?" in *Foreign Policy,* Spring 1993, 118. Munk's conclusion that "Baghdad wasn't razed" is from an article in the May 1991 issue of *Nation.*

hundred that one observer has recently made,[5] it seems clear that although Coalition forces waged high-intensity combat, including extensive bombing of strategic targets throughout Iraq and heavy attacks against Iraqi ground forces, enemy casualties remained relatively low.

The trend toward "bloodlessness" as a desideratum in the conduct of war may have gained impetus from the growth in television coverage of combat operations via satellite. Cable News Network reporting of the initial Coalition attacks on Baghdad while they were in progress remains one of the most vivid images from the Gulf War. Television coverage may have influenced political-military decision makers during the Gulf War, although some senior participants in White House decision making discount this.[6]

Careful review of the timing of media coverage of Coalition air attacks against Iraqi forces fleeing northward from Kuwait City along Highway 6 at the end of the war, for example, indicates that most of it appeared after President Bush had announced his decision to end hostilities on the evening of 27 February 1991 (Washington time). Transcripts indicated that there was no television coverage of the highway of death on the evening news programs from the three broadcast networks on the evenings of 25, 26, or 27 February. In fact, the only public indication preceding Bush's announcement that the Coalition might be inflicting "wanton" slaughter on fleeing Iraqi forces consisted of print coverage such as the "'Like Fish in a Barrel,' US Pilots Say" article that appeared in *The Washington Post* on the morning of 27 February.[7]

---

5. Heidenrich, "The Gulf War: How Many Iraqis Died?" 123. The best estimate, based primarily on enemy prisoner of war reports, is that Coalition air power killed some ten- to twelve-thousand Iraqi military in the Kuwaiti theater prior to the ground war. Available data did not permit a serious estimate of the number of Iraqi soldiers killed there during the 100-hour ground war. That total, however, which could easily have been as high as ten thousand, would have to be added to the total for the first thirty-nine days of the campaign. Iraqi personnel losses in the KTO are also covered in sections 4-6 of a forthcoming RAND report, by Stephen T. Hosmer, MR-305-AF, "Effects of the Coalition Air Campaign against Iraqi Ground Forces." Much evidence gathered after the war has consistently indicated that relatively few Iraqi soldiers died during the 100-hour ground war (see, for example, George Kuhn, "Numbers from Combat," *Phalanx*, June 1993, 22).

6. See Walter Goodman, "How Bad Is War? It Depends on the TV Pictures," *The New York Times*, 5 November 1991, C-18.

7. Richard Randall, "'Like Fish in a Barrel,' US Pilots Say," *The Washington Post*, 27 February 1991, A-28. The Randall article, which was based on reporting from aboard the USS *Ranger*, provided perhaps the most vivid account of air attacks against retreating Iraqi ground forces. One of *The Washington Post*'s front-page articles on the war that morning, however, also echoed Randall's reporting from the *Ranger*. This front-page piece depicted Coalition air attacks on Iraqi armor and truck columns as "a combat frenzy variously described as 'a turkey shoot' and 'shooting fish in a barrel.'" (Rick Atkinson and William Claiborne, "Allies Surround Republican Guard, Say Crippled Iraqis Are Near Defeat," *The Washington Post*, 27 February 1991, A-1).

On the other hand, General Schwarzkopf reported that late in the afternoon of 27 February (Riyadh time, which would have been early in the morning of the same day in Washington, D.C.), General Powell called to say that the two of them needed to discuss a cease-fire because people in Washington were getting nervous about all of the damage that CENTCOM's forces were inflicting on the Iraqis.[8] The episode suggests the ways in which decision makers may find themselves considering not only actual media coverage of events—such as the air attacks on Iraqis trying to flee the Kuwaiti theater—but *anticipated coverage of such activities.* In the final analysis, Americans did not trouble themselves greatly about Iraqi casualties; but the war did demonstrate clearly that concern to keep casualties among American fighting men and women to an absolute minimum, and to keep those of the enemy civilians relatively low, had become a distinctive feature of the new American way of war.

War in the Information Age

Conventional warfare depends, increasingly, on the skillful manipulation of electronically transmitted information. In the gulf it did not always prove possible to deliver the necessary information to the right place at the right time, however, and so on too many occasions crews flew without proper target graphics, and ground commanders lacked adequate quantities of updated maps and photographs. As the quantity of information available to armed forces increases, so too does the need to process it quickly: that is, to pass it to units capable of doing something about it. The advantage goes overwhelmingly to combatants who can bring together information from many sources, updating old databases (removing from the target list, for example, the radar station that was destroyed two days ago) and acting on perishable information. Countries such as the United States or, in a smaller way, Israel, have enormous and growing advantages in these areas. Indeed, it is fair to suggest that information has become the high ground of modern warfare, and for the moment the United States occupies it.

But the information explosion does not mean, as a casual observer might think, that war will now become more transparent to those who conduct it. Clausewitz's fog of war may now rise not so much from a paucity of good information as a plethora of half-knowledge. A fog it remains, nonetheless, and it lay heavily over the Persian Gulf in early 1991. Any editor knows that the advent of the personal computer and facsimile machine prompts authors to fiddle with articles constantly and to submit them just before the deadline. Similarly, the flood of combat information prompts commanders to change targets or tactics at

---

8. *Hero*, 468.

the last moment. As we have seen, commanders in the Gulf War changed one-fifth of all missions during the few hours between the time staffs printed the centralized ATO and the time aircraft took off. Those same commanders made many more changes before the ATO had gone into production *and* after aircraft had departed their bases.

Proverbs to the contrary notwithstanding, pictures sometimes lie, or at least deceive. Air planners in Riyadh attempted to do their own bomb damage assessment by looking at videotape footage of laser-guided bomb strikes. Lacking time (and in some cases experience in photo interpretation), they sometimes misinterpreted what they saw, mistaking an exploding fuel truck or decoy for a mobile missile launcher, for example, or thinking that a bomb bursting on a concrete roof meant that the contents of the building had been destroyed. Short decision times created by modern weapons can also force quick decisions on the basis of electronically gathered and displayed information whose underlying ambiguity may not appear to those who use it. The shooting down of an Iranian airliner on 3 July 1988 by an American cruiser provides a case in point.

Time pressure created by data abundance breeds longer-term problems as well. The constant pressure of the data stream, together with the growth of nighttime operations, means that leaders try to keep on top of events at the cost of sleep, with all the loss of acuity that that practice entails. Combat information increasingly takes the form of abstract representations of reality compiled from multiple (but, from the point of view of the consumer, anonymous) sources. It becomes harder to discriminate among different types of information when a distant, anonymous expert, or even a machine, has done the sifting. Increasingly attractive information displays, easily manipulated by computer-literate commanders, can create a dangerous sense of omniscience on the part of those sitting in bunkers or on flying command posts.

For decades, now, American generals have decried civilian micromanagement of military operations in the Vietnam War, an indictment only partly warranted but accepted uncritically by politicians as well as soldiers at the outset of the Gulf War. Today, however, the danger of military micromanagement looms much larger. A general in Washington, an admiral in a command ship, a theater commander in rear headquarters may have access to almost the same information as a forward commander, and in some cases more. Commanders will often succumb to the temptation to manipulate tactical units accordingly.

And, of course, dependence on vast quantities of electronic information poses certain risks. Ingenious hackers (and most countries have a few) have repeatedly penetrated even supposedly secure governmental computer systems. The payoff for falsification of combat-relevant information looms so large that one must assume that securing against information sabotage takes a high priority amid many military organizations. In this area, perhaps, the genius of a few talented individuals may compensate for the overall qualitative and quantitative weakness of a small country.

Moreover, insofar as information collection and transmission systems are large, complex, and small in number (true for specialized aircraft such as JSTARS and AWACS), they become lucrative targets for attack by specialized weapons (homing missiles or, in the future, more exotic weapons such as devices that create a disruptive electromagnetic pulse).

During the war, pilots complained repeatedly of having to fly against targets without the kind of target graphics to which they had become accustomed in peacetime. In the future, soldiers may become overly dependent on the routine presence of detailed, well-presented, and, above all, accurate information that simply may not exist in wartime. As the verisimilitude of computer simulators and war games increases, these warriors of the future may, paradoxically, find themselves all the more at a loss when the real world departs sharply from the "cyberworld" they have come to know well.

The abundance of reliable and secure voice, data, and facsimile communications between the theater and the rest of the world, as well as within the theater, transformed command and control. Modern communications technology subverted hierarchies and made abundant linkages between the theater and the United States both inevitable and desirable. True, the dependence of the theater on agencies half a globe away from the theater reflected, in part, the meager staffing of this command, generally viewed as a backwater until 1990. Had the war taken place in a more prominent theater (Europe, for example), such poaching by Washington organizations and such ad hoc command arrangements would not have evolved.

As the American overseas presence recedes, however, and as the large theater commands shrink in size, it will become necessary for central staffs to backstop expeditionary headquarters. CENTCOM, in other words, may prove the model, not the exception, for future theater staffs. The new technologies (in some cases, merely the maturation of old technologies) threaten age-old principles such as "unity of command" and delegation of authority. Such pieces of military folk wisdom have so much authority that they will persist in peacetime even if they must disappear in war. A new concept of high command—in which, inevitably, authority diffuses because of modern technology—will have to take root.

Information-gathering and processing technology can help but not solve the problem of bomb damage assessment. For much of the war, commanders sent out sorties, uncertain whether the targets assigned had already received adequate attention. Part of the problem stemmed from excessive reliance on intelligence derived from national intelligence-gathering systems that the theater staff—itself small in number and not always adequately trained—had had little experience in working with.

As we have seen, bomb damage assessment is an intrinsically difficult problem. From an overhead photograph, for example, it may prove impossible to figure out whether a small black hole on top of a hardened aircraft shelter indicates a hit by a dud bomb, an explosion in the thick, rubble-filled space between the shelter's inner and outer walls, a satisfactory explosion within the shelter, or an artful paint job by Iraqi camouflage specialists. The blooming ball of fire on a videotape frame of a missile hitting a tank may conceal an absence of damage; or, conversely, a picture of an apparently intact tank fifty meters from a shell hole may mislead interpreters who do not realize that a near-miss had so badly jolted its optics, fire computer, and radio that none of those critical items could work. When a weapon does not simply blow a hole in the ground, it may prove impossible to come up with any interpretation of a photograph. And unless reconnaissance units can keep targets under near constant surveillance—from many angles, and using different kinds of sensors—intelligence analysts may not know which projectile did what kind of damage.

The existential problem of bomb damage assessment means that the fog of war will persist, although clever intelligence services will work to develop ever more sophisticated means of interpreting imagery, and cross-checking damage through different sources of information. These individual uncertainties can create much higher aggregate levels of confusion: hard as it may be to figure out what a particular target consists of and how to strike it, figuring out a target system may prove even more arduous. The story of the Iraqi nuclear program is a cautionary one in this regard.

But the war also revealed a less excusable American lack of attention to the problem of bomb damage assessment. Prewar exercises and simulations usually included unrealistically good and prompt information on the results of notional strikes; reconnaissance assets appeared late in the theater and under low priorities. All services were short of reconnaissance aircraft, relying (excessively, as it turned out) on satellite photography. Moreover, most aircraft could not take pictures of where their bombs or missiles had landed. These shortfalls revealed an institutional failure to accept the notion that knowing what a bomb has done is almost as important as delivering it in the first place. In future conflicts, where commanders might have less time or much smaller forces, such an inability to track battle damage to an enemy could prove crippling.

Indeed, even in retrospect it has proven extremely difficult to decipher the air war's effects. Part of the reason for this comes from the unreadiness of the Department of Defense to conduct a comprehensive and immediate battlefield survey; part comes from the intemperate unwillingness of General Schwarzkopf to permit teams to enter the theater for that purpose. A few teams did eventually conduct surveys, but over limited and unrepresentative portions of the battlefield. The armed forces have easily spent hundreds of millions of dollars in recent years to simulate battle; they (and Schwarzkopf in particular) made no comparable effort in this war to capture its reality.[9]

Of course, official historians assiduously collected documents and conducted oral histories, and analysts from the Navy's Center for Naval Analyses did an excellent job of recording electronic data. But the American armed forces could—and should—have done a far more thorough job of recording and analyzing real battle even as it unfolded, and certainly after its occurrence.

Quality and Quantity

Two other technological developments appeared in this war and merit further reflection. First, it became apparent that the entry costs into some kinds of military capability have become enormous. In some cases (stealth aircraft is one, highly specialized electronic warfare aircraft is another) only a superpower can afford to play the game. In other cases (air-to-air aviation, for example) no country will find it easy—within this decade at any rate—to match American capabilities, even if it can hold its own against a regional competitor.

Behind such technology lies an array of training facilities and organizations (the vast, instrumented Nellis ranges near Las Vegas, for example) that make American training extremely difficult to match. Furthermore, the sheer size of supporting forces such as the American airlift and air-refueling fleets gives the United States a unique strength. Almost two-thirds of all combat missions in the gulf required midair refueling, and almost all of that came from American aircraft. Only the United States could build aerial bridges across the Atlantic that allowed some short-legged planes to refuel in midair as often as necessary to fly nonstop from the East Coast to Saudi Arabia. Even after the cuts of the Bush-Clinton years, the strength in-depth of American air power will remain unique.

All countries, however (including the United States), will feel the effects of a broader trend toward what one might call the "speciation of munitions." The new munitions can, in theory, and often in practice, achieve affects unthinkable with the simple gravity bomb of earlier years. Without extremely accurate laser-guided bombs, for example, American aircraft could not have hit the manifolds pumping oil into the

---

9. Dr. Abram Shulsky made this point to us with particular force.

Persian Gulf in the second week of the war. The most modern cluster bombs kill and maim soldiers in open or in soft-skinned vehicles more efficiently than do conventional bombs.

But as conventional air-delivered munitions have become increasingly specialized in their effects, they have become more vulnerable to unintentional misuse during the normal confusion of war. The Royal Air Force, for instance, made use of JP-233, a hugely expensive system (whose development cost hundreds of millions of pounds) that spat cratering munitions into and scatterable mines over airstrips. Not only could JP-233 have no other use, in this war it had only a minor and moderately useful role to play, because Iraqi aircraft that did take off had little chance of surviving Coalition top cover. And yet the Royal Air Force had spent years training to use JP-233, had shaped its doctrine and tactics to its delivery, and could not very well refrain from using it, despite the risks entailed in flying low and straight over enemy installations.

To take another case, Coalition air planners projected, before the war, that in nine days of intensive operations their forces would kill 90 percent of the Republican Guard's armor; in eighteen days, a similar percentage of Iraqi armor overall would succumb to air attack. To arrive at these projections analysts used assumptions about loss rates drawn, among other things, from the projected use of large quantities of CBU-89—air scatterable mines. The expected lethality of this munition, in turn, derived from assumptions about use against Soviet forces marching west in a European scenario. Against dug-in, immobile Iraqi armor, of course, such mines would not do nearly so much damage. The made-to-order GBU-28 (a special, deep-penetrating bomb that weighed more than two tons) would do nothing against a mobile Scud missile. The speciation of munitions can bring unusual capabilities, but it poses an equal risk of creating forces so specialized that they lose their flexibility.

When the United States goes to war it rarely counts the cost of bullets. But the high price of munitions affects the peacetime buys that determine the size of wartime stocks, stocks which cannot grow appreciably during a few months of fighting. During the Gulf War the Air Force shipped no less than two-thirds of its stock of laser-guided bomb kits to the war, and it expended approximately half of those. Or to take a more recent example, the January and June 1993 attacks on Baghdad, which used up sixty-nine TLAMs, ate up seventy-five million dollars' worth of ordnance, or more, for uncertain effects.[10]

---

10. The 17 January 1993 attack used up forty-five missiles, thirty-seven of which hit; the 26 June attack used twenty-four, sixteen of which hit. Of the others, some exploded harmlessly, but others careened into residential areas and killed a number of civilians on both occasions.

The trend toward the increasing specialization and expense of weapons evidenced in this war merely confirmed earlier trends that date back to Vietnam and before. Once again, the need for high-quality intelligence will go up—perhaps beyond what commanders may reasonably expect. Military organizations may find it impossible to find the precision intelligence to match their precision weapons, even as their political masters succumb to the attractive (but, on the evidence of the Gulf War, tenuous) notion that a few artfully placed thousand-pound warheads can cripple an enemy beyond repair. Students of the war will note that the massive bombardments by B-52s raining down dumb bombs played a large part in crushing the morale of Iraqi soldiers and smashing the large military facilities that figured so prominently in Saddam's aspirations for power.

Quantity, then, still counts. In a whimsical but instructive science fiction story, Arthur C. Clarke recounts the tale of an advanced civilization that loses because, in the rueful words of the defeated chief of staff, "of the inferior science of our enemies."[11] This goes too far, but the story bears reading. Smart weapons have much to offer American planners, but in weapon acquisition, as in life more broadly, brilliance can take one only so far.

The War and American Influence

America's reliance on air power has set the American way of war apart from all others for well over half a century. Other countries might field doughty infantrymen, canny submariners, or scientific artillerists comparable in skill and numbers to our own. The United States alone, however, has engaged in a single-minded and successful quest for air superiority in every conflict it has fought since World War I. Air warfare remains the distinctively American form of warfare—high tech, cheap in American lives lost, and (at least in theory) quick. From the point of view of America's enemies, past, current, and potential, air power seems the distinctively American form of military intimidation.

Air warfare plays to to the machine-mindedness of a machine-oriented civilization. Aircraft can bring massed and accurate destructive force to bear at key points without having to maneuver cumbersome organizations on land or sea. Air power can indeed overawe opponents, who know quite well that they cannot hope to match or directly counter American air power.

On the other hand, these enemies will find indirect responses. The Saddam Husseins of this world have surely learned from the Al Firdos episode that they need not take American children hostage to deter

---

11. Arthur C. Clarke, "Superiority," *Expedition to Earth* (New York: Harcourt, Brace, and World, 1970), 93.

bombardment; they can take their own citizens' young no less effectively. Mobility, when abetted by camouflage and tight communications security, can also shield a potential opponent from harm, as the apparent failure to destroy mobile Scud launchers from the air indicates. It does not appear that the Iraqis made any serious efforts to attack Coalition air bases, although in some cases these would have had little defense against commando forces or long-range missiles. In the future, however, an opponent may attempt to score at least propaganda points—and perhaps do more serious damage—by striking the sprawling fixed bases on which land-based aviation depends.

The soldier or Marine will surely say to the air power enthusiast that nothing can substitute for the man with the bayonet. True, but some politically desired effects (elimination of electrical power in Baghdad, for example) required no use of ground forces at all. And, in some cases, the United States has proved unwilling to use ground forces to achieve its objective (as in, for instance, achieving the overthrow of Saddam Hussein). Air power may not decide all conflicts or achieve all of a country's political objectives, but neither can land power.

Here, perhaps, we have the most dangerous legacy of the Persian Gulf War, for although all of the above propositions have some truth to them, the fantasy of near bloodless uses of force in support of policy is just that—fantasy. Set aside, for the moment, the question of so-called nonlethal weapons. No military technology (indeed, no technology at all) works all of the time. Inevitably, even the best-aimed laser-guided bomb will lose its fix on a target because of a passing cloud or a failure in its steering mechanism, and it will hurtle into an orphanage or hospital. Other considerations—the barely perceptible jitter of the laser beam, relatively minor errors in altimeters or other devices—can and do lead to failures to hit targets precisely. As one wise engineer puts it, "the truly fail-proof design is chimerical."[12]

As for so-called nonlethal weapons, the term does not correspond to reality. The occupants of a helicopter crashing to earth after its flight controls have fallen prey to a high-power microwave weapon would take little solace from the knowledge that a nonlethal weapon had sealed their doom. Some of these weapons (blinding lasers, just to mention one) may not kill, but surely have exceedingly nasty consequences for their victims. In the end, a disabling weapon works only if it renders an opponent vulnerable to the real thing.

But the simple and brutal fact is that force works by destroying and killing. In the Gulf War the commanding generals ostentatiously, indeed, obsessively, abjured Vietnam-style body counts, but that did not diminish the importance of terrifying enemy soldiers through the fear

12. Henry Petroski, *To Engineer Is Human* (New York: Vintage, 1992), 217.

of violent death from tons of ordnance raining down upon them. And fear of violent death comes solely from the possibility, indeed, the imminence, of the real thing.

True, in the Gulf War relatively small numbers of Iraqis died before the ground war, although others suffered indirectly from the combined effects of air attack and the Coalition embargo. That so few died reflects, among other things, the potential of the new technologies and the scrupulous regard for civilian life shown by Coalition planners. The essential ingredient of fear remained constant, though.

Sometimes even fear does not suffice. The objectives of conflicts such as the war with Iraq will frequently mandate killing. The destruction or permanent disabling of some 50 percent of the armor of the Republican Guard (in roughly equal proportions by air and ground action) made little difference outside the Kuwaiti theater. The Republican Guard remained, at war's end, an organized force, and after drawing upon ample stocks of weapons in Iraq proper, they put down the Kurdish and Shiite uprisings that followed the war. To stop that, and to undermine Saddam Hussein's regime (which the Bush administration most certainly wished to do), would have required the killing or wounding of these men, who constituted the bulwark of the regime. The escape of Republican Guard soldiers paved the way for the horrors inflicted upon the peoples of Iraq during the spring and summer of 1991.

Similarly, the only effective antiproliferation program in the long run will target the truly important elements of any arms program—the technicians who make it possible. This uncomfortable fact, long known to the Israelis, who have had few scruples about killing German rocket scientists in Egypt or rogue supergun designers in more recent years, sits poorly with Americans. When Gen. Michael Dugan, U.S. Air Force chief of staff, hinted to journalists in September 1990 that the most effective use of air power might consist of attacks on the persons of Saddam Hussein, his intimate associates. and key members of the Iraqi general staff and Ba'ath Party, he no more than pointed to the truth, impolitic as his outraged superiors found it.

Furthermore, it appears likely that in modern conditions civilian populations, or large portions of them, will, as in the past, become the objects of terror. That grim warrior, Gen. William Tecumseh Sherman, described the purpose of his 1864 march through Georgia and South Carolina thusly: "My aim then was to whip the rebels, to humble their pride, to follow them to their inmost recesses, and make them fear and dread us. 'Fear of the Lord is the beginning of wisdom.'"[13] Sherman's troops did not massacre the inhabitants of the South: they merely

---

13. William Tecumseh Sherman, *Memoirs of General William Tecumseh Sherman* (New York: Library of America, 1990), 729.

ruined their private and public possessions, attacking (as a contemporary strategic analyst might antiseptically observe) "the economic infrastructure" of the South.

In many cases today, war means bringing power—particularly air power—to bear against civil society. Those who hope for too much from air power desire to return to a mode of warfare reminiscent of the mid-eighteenth century in western Europe: war waged by mercenary armies, isolated from society, and with (by modern standards, at any rate) remarkable efforts to insulate civilians from their effects. Sherman, reflecting the character of armed struggle in his century as well as ours, believed that in modern conditions civil society must *inevitably* become a target of military action.

As leaders attempt to use their civilians as hostages against American air power, this will become ever more true, whether we like it or not. Moreover, throughout the nineteenth and twentieth centuries military power has become increasingly intertwined with society. The electrical generators that keep a defense ministry's computers running and its radars sweeping the skies for opponents also provide energy for hospitals and water purification plants. The bridges indispensable to the movement of military forces support the traffic in food, medicine, and all other elements of modern life for large civilian populations. Sherman faced a similar situation when he besieged Atlanta in 1864. "You cannot qualify war in harsher terms than I will," he told the hapless leading citizens of that city. "War is cruelty, and you cannot refine it."[14]

Many Americans cling to the idea that wars result from the malice of the occasional evil leader, not the ardent fears and ambitions of clans, classes, or entire peoples. The Bush administration's obsession with Saddam Hussein, and the Clinton administration's more recent fixation on Gen. Mohamed Farah Aidid in Somalia, illustrate the point. In the case of the war with Iraq, for example, American military planners may indeed have underestimated the extent to which the entire Ba'athist Party, and not just Saddam Hussein, accounted for the troubles they faced. Insofar as war remains a social phenomenon, societies, and not simply their armed forces, will remain the targets of military action.

American air power dominated the Gulf War as has no other conflict since World War II. Special circumstances helped account for this achievement, but in the end, airmen were probably correct in their belief that this war marked a departure. No other nation on earth has power comparable to this, nor will any country accumulate anything like it, or even the means to neutralize it, for at least a decade and probably several. American air power has a mystique to it which it is

---

14. Ibid., 601.

in the American interest to retain. When presidents use it, they should either hurl it with devastating lethality against a few targets (say, a full-scale meeting of an enemy war cabinet or general staff) or extensively enough to cause sharp and lasting pain to a military and a society.

Both uses of force pose problems, however. The first type represents, in effect, the use of air power for single or multiple assassination: a procedure not without precedent (American pilots stalked and slew Japan's Admiral Yamomoto in 1943), but which sets troubling precedents and invites more primitive but nonetheless effective forms of revenge. The second involves the use of air power in ways bound to offend American elites and some of the broader public, no matter what pains commanders take to avoid the direct loss of human life. To strike hard, if indirectly, at societies by smashing communication or power networks will invite the kind of wrenching television attention that modern journalists excel at providing.

Still, to use air power in penny packets is to disregard the importance of a menacing and even mysterious military reputation. "The reputation of power is power," Hobbes wrote, and that applies to military power as well as to other kinds. The sprinkling of air strikes over an enemy will harden him without hurting him and deprive the United States of an intangible strategic asset. American leaders at the end of this century have indeed been vouchsafed a military instrument of a potency rarely known in the history of war. But glib talk of revolutionary change obscures the organizational impediments to truly radical change in the conduct of war, and, what is worse, the inherent messiness and brutality of the business altogether. In the end, students of air power will serve the country well by putting the Gulf War in a larger context, one in which the gloomy wisdom of Sherman tempers the brisk enthusiasm of those who see air power as a shining sword, effortlessly wielded, that can create and preserve a just and peaceful world order.

Appendix One

Gulf War Chronology, April 1990 to February 1991

(*Note:* Dates used are according to Riyadh time.)

April 1990

Central Command initiates planning to meet a major Iraqi attack into Saudi Arabia and Kuwait. The planning reflects a reorientation in U.S. military planning for the Southwest Asia theater away from its previous Soviet-threat focus. The draft plan, USCINCCENT OPLAN 1002-90, proposes three phases: deterrence; interdiction and defensive operations; and a counteroffensive campaign, to be undertaken in concert with friendly Arabian Peninsula states. Lt. Gen. Charles Horner, COMUS-CENTAF, briefs Gen. Norman Schwarzkopf on a three-phase air plan in support of this new operations plan. The air plan's first phase (deterrence) emphasizes an immediate air defense capability while building up combat capabilities in the region. The next two phases (delay/attrition and counteroffensive) call for air attacks on airfields, transportation chokepoints, chemical weapons storage and production sites and delivery means (Scud missiles), and, if the Iraqis used chemical missiles, key refineries, power plants, and the Baghdad nuclear research center at Tuwaitha.

Central Command J-2 initiates an "Iraq Regional Warning Problem" to increase the priority of intelligence on Iraq.

23 July

As Iraq increases its military activity near the northern border of Kuwait, Central Command begins a command post exercise, Internal Look 90, that examines the draft OPLAN 1002-90.

The United Arab Emirates request assistance from the United States in providing air refueling support for the UAE's air defense aircraft. The United States deploys two KC-135s to Al Dahfra in an operation code named Ivory Justice.

2 August

Iraq invades Kuwait. The U.S. National Military Command Center orders the USS *Independence* carrier battle group to the North Arabian Sea and two USAF KC-10s to Diego Garcia.

Kuwaiti A-4s and F-1s fly attack and air defense missions from their bases in Kuwait, then land in Saudi Arabia and Bahrain.

4 August

Generals Schwarzkopf and Horner meet with President Bush, Secretary Cheney, and Gen. Colin Powell at Camp David to conduct a briefing on military options. General Horner outlines a conceptual plan for a limited strategic air campaign against high-value targets in Iraq that the president could use to retaliate against Baghdad if the Iraqis use chemical weapons against Coalition troops. Horner maintains that American aircraft operating from Saudi bases and from aircraft carriers in the Red Sea and Persian Gulf could establish air superiority in the region within a period of days.

7 August

President Bush orders deployment of U.S. forces to Saudi Arabia and other Gulf States. Forces include the 82nd Airborne Division, the *Eisenhower* carrier battle group, two F-15C squadrons, sufficient AWACS for twenty-four-hour combat air patrol, and supporting air refueling assets.

USS *Independence* arrives on station in the Gulf of Oman. Members of the Headquarters USAF, Deputy Director of Air Force Plans for Warfighting staff gather at the Pentagon to build a conceptual plan for a strategic air campaign against Iraq.

8 August

Twenty-three USAF F-15Cs and accompanying KC-10s arrive at Dhahran Air Base, while five AWACS aircraft arrive at Riyadh Air Base.

General Schwarzkopf asks Gen. John M. Loh, USAF vice chief of staff, for help in drawing up a strategic air campaign.

10 August

General Schwarzkopf names General Horner as the Joint Force Air Component Commander.

Twenty-four each of USAF F-16Cs and F-15Es arrive in theater,

Gulf War Chronology, April 1990 to February 1991   229

along with two RC-135 Rivet joint aircraft and twelve Royal Air Force Tornado F-3s. Other combat and support aircraft will arrive on a near daily basis until early September.

17 August

General Schwarzkopf receives briefing of the Instant Thunder air campaign plan from Col. John Warden (Warden had briefed an earlier version to Schwarzkopf on 10 August).

Stage I of the Civil Reserve Air Fleet is activated for the first time, committing thirty-eight airliners to the Desert Shield airlift.

20 August

Iraqi flight activity observed at all three primary Kuwaiti airfields.

Colonel Warden briefs General Horner on Instant Thunder plan.

The first U.S. Marine aircraft (AV-8Bs) arrive in the theater, with a squadron of F/A-18s, six A-6Es, and twelve EA-6Bs arriving in the theater by 24 August.

22 August

President Bush invokes his authority to call up to 200,000 personnel and units of selected reserves. A day later, Secretary of Defense Cheney sets the maximum numbers to be called: Army, 25,000; Navy, 6,300; Marine Corps, 3,000; and Air Force, 14,500.

Republican Guard units move northward after they are replaced on the Kuwait-Saudi Arabia border by less well-equipped regular army units, decreasing the likelihood of a no-warning attack.

General Horner assigns Brig. Gen. Buster Glosson as CENTAF director of the Special Planning Group. This group includes Army, Navy, and Marine Corps officers, as well as representatives from the British Royal Air Force and, later, the Royal Saudi Air Force.

24 August

General Schwarzkopf briefs General Powell on a four-phase plan, code named Desert Storm, to eject Iraqi fores from Kuwait.

26 August

General Glosson briefs General Horner on a proposed air campaign plan. General Horner directs the first twenty-four hours of the plan to be put into air tasking order format by the next day.

2 September

The CENTAF Special Planning Group completes a CENTAF operations order for Phase I, a strategic air campaign against Iraq. This Phase I plan is briefed to General Schwarzkopf (3 September), General Powell (13 September), Secretary of Defense Cheney, the Joint Chiefs of Staff, and the president and members of the National Security Council (10 and 11 October).

6 September

One month into the deployment, General Schwarzkopf reports his fixed-wing combat air assets as 109 air-to-air, 243 air-to-ground, 227 dual-role, and 317 support aircraft. The first munitions ship arrives in the theater.

12 September

With the arrival of five AC-130 "gunships," all Phase I combat aircraft are in the theater. Strength is 962 fixed-wing (600 combat) and approximately 1,100 rotary wing aircraft. Five Patriot SAM batteries now deployed in the theater, with thirty-two PAC II missiles.

2 October

The aircraft carrier *Independence* enters the Persian Gulf, only the second time that a carrier battle group has passed through the Straits of Hormuz (the other time occurred in 1974).

13 October

Upon completion of a NATO exercise, USAFE postpones actions on deployment of twenty-four F-16s and fourteen F-111Es from Incirlik, Turkey, awaiting a response from the Turkish government on a request to retain these aircraft at Incirlik.

8 November

President Bush orders more than 150,000 additional air, sea, and ground forces to the Persian Gulf region to provide "an adequate offensive option" to drive Iraqi forces from Kuwait (Phase II forces). The subsequent deployment order calls for most of the USAF air units to arrive not later than 15 January; some air units (A-10s) to arrive by 30 January; and other air units to deploy after commencement of hostilities. Supplementary forces include three additional carrier battle groups (*Ranger, Roosevelt,* and *America*).

29 November

UN Security Council votes to use force against Iraq unless that country fully complies with previous council resolutions calling for its unconditional withdrawal from Kuwait and release of foreign nationals by 15 January 1991.

2 December

Iraq test launches three or four Scud missiles.

5 December

CENTAF forms the 14th and 15th Air Divisions (Provisional) (ADPs) to exercise control over all CENTAF-assigned tactical fighter wings and combat support aircraft (electronic warfare, reconnaissance, AWACS, etc.), respectively. General Glosson is named commander, 14th ADP, putting him in the position of both planning the coming air campaign and commanding the USAF fighter wings that will execute it. Brig. Gen. Glenn A. Profitt, II, is appointed commander of the 15th ADP.

16 December

Desert Storm Operations Plan is published.

19 December

U.S. secretary of defense and chairman of the Joint Chiefs of Staff arrive in Riyadh for briefings.

23 December

Combined Joint Task Force Proven Force established by U.S. commander, European Command, in order to support Coalition forces from bases in Turkey. Maj. Gen. James L. Jamerson, USAF, is named as commander, JTF Proven Force. On 15 January 1991, the Turkish government approves the temporary deployment of an additional forty-eight fighter aircraft to Incirlik Air Base (added to the forty-eight aircraft that had remained there following a NATO exercise), as part of JTF Proven Force.

28 December

Iraq test launches a single short-range ballistic missile (probably an Al-Abbas Scud) between points in southeastern and western Iraq. US-CINCCENT reports that the Iraqis protect their Scuds by dispersing their mobile erector launchers (MELs), moving them mainly at night for launches near sunset, and concealing the MELs and Scuds in buildings or in camouflaged, earth-covered trenches.

15 January 1991

President Bush authorizes military actions to bring about Iraq's withdrawal from Kuwait.

At the UN deadline for Iraq, the Coalition in-theater aircraft force from twelve countries includes 195 air-to-air, 477 air-to-ground, and 426 dual-role combat aircraft, backed by 749 support aircraft and more than 1,500 helicopters (383 are attack helicopters). USCENTCOM forces in the theater total 422,041.

Intelligence estimates are that the Iraqi force defending Kuwait include twenty-four committed and eleven reinforcing divisions (numbers later upgraded to twenty-five committed, nine reinforcing, and eight theater reserve divisions), fielding 540,000 personnel, 4,200 tanks, 2,800 armored fighting vehicles, and 3,100 artillery pieces.

17 January

Desert Storm air campaign begins with more than 2,700 fixed-wing aircraft sorties, including nearly 700 sorties entering Iraqi airspace the first night, and the launch of 116 TLAMs. The first strikes concentrate on Iraqi leadership, command and control facilities, electrical power generation, and the air defense system.

18 January

Shortly after the Turkish Parliament authorizes the use of Turkish airspace to carry out UN Security Council resolutions, Task Force Proven Force sorties launch first strikes into Iraq from Turkey.

Iraq fires seven Scuds missiles at Tel Aviv and Haifa, Israel, and one at Dhahran, Saudi Arabia. A total of eighty-eight Scud missiles are fired at Israel, Saudi Arabia, or Bahrain during the war, thirty-three of them during the first week. Coalition aircraft immediately begin intensive operations to find, destroy, or simply suppress the operations of the mobile missile launchers.

President Bush declares a national emergency and authorizes partial mobilization, allowing mobilization of 360,000 members of the

Ready Reserve (selected reserve units, individual mobilization augmentees, and individual ready reserve) for a period of twelve months. The Air Force share was fifty-two thousand, including those members called up earlier. More than thirty-two thousand members of the Air Reserve Component are activated by the end of the war, more than ten thousand of whom serve in the theater of operations.

Secretary Cheney activates Stage II of Civil Reserve Air Fleet, making a total of 79 passenger aircraft and 108 cargo aircraft.

20 January

Bombing quickly reduces Iraqi electric power generation, down by more than two-thirds its capacity within three days, and the national electric grid is shut down. These effects are not immediately known by the Coalition, and it will be a week later until Central Command estimates this level of destruction.

Commanders restrict all bombing missions to medium altitude (ten- to fifteen-thousand feet) in order to have the aircraft remain above the reach of antiaircraft artillery and infrared surface-to-air missiles. This action increases the survivability of the aircraft at some expense to bombing accuracy.

22 January

General Horner assesses that coalition forces have established air superiority over Iraq. Air supremacy is declared on 27 January.

C-130 airlift forces begin moving the 82nd and 101st Airborne Divisions to attack positions.

23 January

After the first week of operations, the Iraqi Air Force had lost thirty-nine aircraft, fourteen of them to air-to-air combat. Coalition air losses have been seventeen (eleven U.S. aircraft and six other Coalition, including four RAF GR-1 Tornados), all but one to ground-based defenses. As air-to-air engagements between Coalition and Iraqi aircraft decline to near zero, air attacks begin against protective shelters of Iraqi aircraft.

24 January

A Saudi pilot in an F-15C shoots down two Iraqi F-1s over the Persian Gulf as the Iraqi aircraft proceed south toward Coalition ships.

Twenty-six Iraqi aircraft fly to Iran and are interned. These flights continue on a sporadic basis over the next two weeks. While some of the escaping aircraft are shot down, by war's end more than a hundred Iraqi aircraft will be in Iran.

United States announces that Iraq is releasing crude oil into the Persian Gulf. A special attack mission by F-111s on 27 January against the Al Ahmadi refinery and oiling buoy stop the oil flow into the gulf.

26 January

Central Command announces a shift in emphasis in air attacks, placing priority on attacking the Republican Guard divisions.

30 January

Beginning late in the evening of 29 January and continuing the next day, Iraqi ground forces launch at least four separate battalion-size attacks along the eastern Saudi-Kuwait border, including one attack that succeeds in capturing the Saudi town of Al Khafji. For the next two days, Coalition air and ground forces drive back and destroy many of these forces. In addition, Coalition air forces attack and turn back Iraqi armored units within Kuwait as these armored units attempt to reinforce the attacks. An AC-130 gunship is shot down on 31 January during this action, with the loss of all fourteen crew members.

1 February

The last six TLAMs of the 282 employed during the war are launched.

Precision munitions delivering aircraft are directed to attacking bridges, and the degradation of the Iraqi bridge system and highway structure mounts steadily throughout the war. By G-Day, thirty-seven highway bridges and nine railroad bridges in Iraq will be unusable, two-thirds of them along the lines of communication between Baghdad and the Kuwaiti theater.

2 February

All of Iraq's missile boats are damaged or destroyed, except for one that escapes to Iran. The threat of these missile boats is not assessed as removed until 17 February because of the lack of adequate bomb damage assessment.

5 February

F-16Cs are employed as "Killer Scouts," aircraft that remain in the target area and provide direction to succeeding flights of aircraft in order to improve target identification and attack efficiency in the theater's kill boxes.

7 February

U.S. carrier *America* leaves station in the Red Sea en route to the Persian Gulf, in preparation for the ground attack.

8 February

Secretary of Defense Cheney and Joint Chiefs Chairman, General Powell, visit Riyadh for briefings on the coming ground campaign.

F-111F aircraft begin using infrared equipment to find and direct laser-guided bombs onto Iraqi armor. Throughout the remainder of the war, these aircraft, along with F-15Es and A-6Es with similar equipment, conduct these bombing missions, substantially increasing the rate of destruction of Iraqi armor.

12 February

General Schwarzkopf further directs the focus of air combat operations to preparing the battlefield, shifting the emphasis to Iraqi frontline units.

13 February

Two laser-guided bombs from a USAF aircraft strike the Al Firdos district bunker in Baghdad, causing hundreds of civilian casualties. Future targeting of air attacks in downtown Baghdad comes under increasing scrutiny, and the numbers of these strikes diminish until the final days of the war.

15 February

Two A-10s are shot down over Republican Guard units. Henceforth, A-10s are restricted to the kill boxes close to the southern border within the Kuwaiti theater until the ground offensive begins.

Controversy arises between the Washington intelligence agencies (CIA and DIA) and Central Command concerning the accuracy of the command's estimates of Iraqi armor and artillery losses. CIA contends there has been far less attrition than Central Command estimates.

16 February

Central Command intelligence assesses Iraqi navy as incapable of conducting offensive operations and Iraqi air force as posing only a minimal threat to Coalition air operations.

18 February

ARCENT raises complaints about the low number of sorties made available to VII and XVIII Airborne Corps and the policy for determining targeting in the Kuwaiti theater. These complaints reflect a continuing perception that Air Force planners were not giving due weight to Army target requests.

22 February

With the closure of the XVIII Airborne Corps' 196th Artillery Brigade, the last of Central Command's combat forces in the region are in place for the ground offensive.

23 February

On the eve of the ground offensive, Central Command estimates that the Iraqis have 2,669 tanks, 1,961 armored vehicles, and 1,660 artillery pieces in the theater.

For the first time, more than three thousand Coalition sorties are scheduled during Desert Storm in preparation for the ground offensive, with primary emphasis given to supporting friendly ground forces.

24 February

Coalition ground attack begins at 0400 local time. Air campaign shifts into Phase IV. Close air support provided by "Push CAS" system. Attack altitude restrictions for aircraft are removed. Stringent target identification measures announced in an effort to eliminate "friendly fire" incidents.

Low ceilings and rain showers hamper air operations in Kuwait.

Iraqi ground forces begin surrendering in large numbers.

25 February

Scud missile lands in a barracks in Dhahran, killing twenty-eight U.S. Army reservists and wounding more than a hundred.

26 February

As a general retreat of Iraqi forces in southern Kuwait begins, Coalition aircraft destroy large numbers of Iraqi vehicles along a four-lane road over Mutla Pass, just west of Kuwait City. These attacks throughout the night of 25–26 February create what becomes known as the "highway of death."

VII Corps begin to engage Republican Guards (Tawakalna Division).

27 February

VII and XVIII Airborne Corps engage Iraqi armored units, including the Madinah and Hammurabi Republican Guard Divisions.

F-111Fs drop GBU-28s, forty-seven-hundred-pound ground-penetrating bombs, on a deep underground command bunker at Taji.

28 February

Offensive air operations cease at 0800 local time.

Appendix Two

Statistical Appendix

Section 1. U.S. Fixed-Wing, Strike, and Combat Support Aircraft, Strength in the Theater

Note: This information supplements the data in chapter 7. Except for CENTAF strength figures (weekly summaries), aircraft strengths represent maximum achieved during Desert Storm. Precise number of aircraft varied somewhat during the war from the numbers presented because of attrition, replacement, routine movements for maintenance, etc.

Table 1A: CENTAF Strike Aircraft Strength (by week)

Date	A-10	AC-130	B-52	F-4G	F-15	F-15E	F-16	F-111	F-117	Combat Aircraft Total
8-Aug-90	0	0	0	0	24	0	0	0	0	24
15-Aug-90	0	0	14	0	46	22	44	0	0	126
22-Aug-90	48	0	20	20	48	24	46	0	18	224
29-Aug-90	48	0	20	24	48	24	46	18	18	246
4-Sep-90	96	0	20	24	72	24	120	32	18	406
11-Sep-90	96	4	20	36	72	24	120	32	18	422
18-Sep-90	96	5	20	36	72	24	120	32	18	423
25-Sep-90	96	5	20	36	72	24	120	32	18	423
2-Oct-90	96	5	20	36	72	23	120	32	18	422
9-Oct-90	96	5	20	36	72	24	120	32	18	423
16-Oct-90	96	5	20	36	72	24	120	32	18	423
23-Oct-90	96	5	20	36	72	24	120	32	18	423
30-Oct-90	96	5	20	36	72	24	120	32	18	423
6-Nov-90	96	5	20	36	72	24	120	32	18	423
13-Nov-90	96	5	20	36	72	24	120	32	18	423
20-Nov-90	96	4	20	36	72	24	120	32	18	422
27-Nov-90	96	4	20	36	72	24	120	32	18	422
4-Dec-90	102	4	20	36	72	24	120	52	36	466
11-Dec-90	102	4	20	36	72	24	120	64	36	478
18-Dec-90	102	4	20	36	72	26	120	64	36	480
25-Dec-90	102	4	20	36	96	28	120	64	36	506
1-Jan-91	120	4	20	48	96	46	168	64	36	602
8-Jan-91	144	4	20	48	96	48	210	64	36	670
15-Jan-91	144	4	20	48	96	48	208	64	36	668
22-Jan-91	144	4	36	49	96	48	210	63	36	686
29-Jan-91	144	3	37	49	96	48	212	64	42	695
5-Feb-91	143	6	36	49	96	48	212	64	42	696
12-Feb-91	142	7	65	49	96	48	215	64	42	728
13-Feb-91	146	7	66	49	96	48	215	64	42	733
14-Feb-91	146	7	66	49	96	48	215	64	42	733
15-Feb-91	143	7	66	49	96	48	214	64	42	729
16-Feb-91	143	7	65	49	96	48	214	64	42	728
17-Feb-91	143	7	65	49	96	48	214	64	42	728

Statistical Appendix

Table 1A (continued)

Date	A-10	AC-130	B-52	F-4G	F-15	F-15E	F-16	F-111	F-117	Combat Aircraft Total
18-Feb-91	143	7	64	49	96	48	213	64	42	726
19-Feb-91	143	7	64	49	96	48	215	64	42	728
20-Feb-91	143	7	65	48	96	48	215	66	42	730
21-Feb-91	146	7	65	48	96	48	215	66	42	733
22-Feb-91	145	8	65	48	96	48	215	66	42	733
23-Feb-91	146	8	65	48	96	48	215	66	42	734
24-Feb-91	146	8	66	49	96	48	215	66	42	736
25-Feb-91	146	8	66	49	96	48	215	66	42	736
26-Feb-91	146	8	65	49	96	48	215	66	42	735
27-Feb-91	145	8	66	49	96	48	214	66	42	734
28-Feb-91	145	8	66	49	96	48	212	66	42	732

Table 1B: CENTAF Combat Support Aircraft Strength (by week)

Date	C-20	C-21	C-29	C-130	E-3	EC-130E	EF-111	HC-130	KC-10
8-Aug-90	–	–	–	–	5	–	0	–	–
15-Aug-90	–	–	–	32	5	–	0	–	6
22-Aug-90	–	–	–	51	5	–	0	2	–
29-Aug-90	1	4	–	66	5	–	10	4	–
5-Sep-90	1	4	–	70	6	6	10	4	–
12-Sep-90	1	4	–	96	6	6	13	4	–
19-Sep-90	1	4	–	96	6	6	14	4	–
26-Sep-90	1	4	–	96	6	6	14	4	6
3-Oct-90	1	8	–	95	6	6	14	4	6
10-Oct-90	1	8	–	95	6	6	14	4	6
17-Oct-90	1	8	1	95	6	6	14	4	6
24-Oct-90	1	8	1	95	6	6	14	4	6
31-Oct-90	1	8	1	95	6	6	14	4	6
7-Nov-90	1	8	1	96	6	6	14	4	6
14-Nov-90	1	8	1	96	6	6	14	4	6
21-Nov-90	1	8	1	96	6	6	14	4	6
28-Nov-90	1	8	1	96	6	6	14	4	6
5-Dec-90	1	8	–	96	6	6	14	4	6
12-Dec-90	1	8	–	96	6	4	14	4	6
19-Dec-90	1	8	–	96	4	4	14	4	6
26-Dec-90	1	8	–	96	7	4	18	4	6
2-Jan-91	1	8	–	96	7	4	18	4	6
9-Jan-91	1	8	–	128	9	6	18	4	7
16-Jan-91	1	8	–	128	10	6	18	4	24
23-Jan-91	1	8	–	132	11	6	18	4	30
30-Jan-91	1	8	–	149	11	7	18	4	30
6-Feb-91	1	8	2	151	11	8	18	4	28
13-Feb-91	1	8	2	151	11	8	20	4	28
20-Feb-91	1	8	2	150	11	8	20	4	29
27-Feb-91	1	8	2	150	11	8	20	4	29

Table 1B (continued)

Date	KC-135	MC-130	MH-53	MH-60	RC-135	RF-4C	TR-1	U-2	J-STARS	Total
8-Aug-90	2	–	–	–	–	–	–	–	–	7
15-Aug-90	53	–	–	–	3	–	–	–	–	99
22-Aug-90	70	–	4	–	3	–	–	2	–	137
29-Aug-90	79	4	4	–	4	6	2	2	–	191
5-Sep-90	79	4	8	–	4	6	2	2	–	206
12-Sep-90	89	4	8	8	4	6	2	2	–	253
19-Sep-90	91	4	8	8	4	6	2	2	–	256
26-Sep-90	91	4	8	8	4	6	2	2	–	262
3-Oct-90	94	4	8	8	4	6	2	2	–	268
10-Oct-90	94	4	8	8	4	5	2	2	–	267
17-Oct-90	102	4	8	8	4	6	2	3	–	278
24-Oct-90	111	4	8	8	4	6	2	3	–	287
31-Oct-90	114	4	8	8	4	6	2	3	–	290
7-Nov-90	116	4	8	8	4	6	2	3	–	293
14-Nov-90	116	4	8	8	4	6	2	3	–	293
21-Nov-90	115	4	8	8	4	6	2	3	–	292
28-Nov-90	115	4	8	8	4	6	2	3	–	292
5-Dec-90	116	4	8	8	4	6	2	3	–	292
12-Dec-90	126	4	8	8	4	6	2	3	–	300
19-Dec-90	127	4	8	8	4	6	2	3	–	299
26-Dec-90	127	4	8	8	4	6	2	3	–	306
2-Jan-91	164	4	8	8	4	6	2	3	–	343
9-Jan-91	179	4	8	8	5	6	4	3	–	398
16-Jan-91	202	4	8	8	7	18	4	5	2	457
23-Jan-91	199	4	13	8	7	18	4	5	2	470
30-Jan-91	196	4	13	4	7	18	4	5	2	481
6-Feb-91	196	4	13	4	7	18	4	6	2	485
13-Feb-91	193	4	15	4	9	18	4	6	2	488
20-Feb-91	191	4	17	4	9	18	4	6	2	488
27-Feb-91	192	4	17	4	9	18	6	6	2	491

Note: Air Force Component, Central Command (CENTAF) aircraft totals derived from Central Command situation reports and "USAF Deployment Status Reports" published by the AF/XO Operations Center at the Pentagon.

CENTAF aircraft strength for A-10s also includes OA-10s; B-52s strength includes those aircraft flying from Diego Garcia, Moron Air Base, Spain, and Fairford Air Base, Great Britain. EC-130Es include both EC-130 Compass Call and EC-130 Volant Solo.

Table 2: Joint Task Force Proven Force (U.S. Air Force, Europe, aircraft operating from Incirlik Air Base, Turkey)

F-16	36	EC-130	3
F-15C	28	RF-4C	6
F-111E	18	KC-135	13
F-4G	12	E-3B	3
EF-111	6		

Note: Information from U.S. Department of Defense, *Conduct of the Persian Gulf War*, Final Report to Congress, April 1992, 106, 108.

Statistical Appendix

Table 3: U.S. Navy Carrier-Based Aircraft

Red Sea Force		Persian Gulf Force	
USS *America*		USS *Midway*	
F-14	20	F/A-18	30
F/A-18	18	A-6E	14
A-6E	14	EA-6B	4
E-2	4	E-2	4
S-3B	8	KA-6D	4
KA-6D	4	SH-3H	6
SH-3H	6		
USS *Kennedy*		USS *Ranger*	
F-14	20	F-14	20
A-7E	24	A-6E	22
A-6E	13	EA-6B	4
EA-6B	5	E-2	4
E-2	5	S-3B	8
S-3B	8	KA-6D	4
KA-6D	3	SH-3H	6
USS *Saratoga*		USS *Roosevelt*	
F-14	20	F-14	20
F/A-18	18	F/A-18	19
A-6E	14	A-6E	18
EA-6B	4	EA-6B	5
KA-6D	4	KA-6D	4
E-2	4	E-2	4
S-3B	8	S-3B	8
SH-3H	6	SH-3H	6

Note: Information from *Conduct of the Persian Gulf War*, 110.

USS *America* transferred from the Red Sea Force to the Persian Gulf Force between 7 and 15 February.

Table 4: U.S. Marine Corps Fixed-Wing Aircraft

AV-8B	62, with another 26 afloat
F/A-18A/C/D	84
A-6E	20
EA-6B	12

Note: Information from U.S. Department of Defense, *Conduct of the Persian Gulf War, Final Report to Congress*, April 1992, 106, 109.

Section 2. Space Systems and Support

The following tables depict the U.S. space assets that were available to support coalition air operations during the Gulf War.

Table 5: Space Order of Battle

Function	Satellite System	2-Aug-90	16-Jan-91	Military	Civilian
Communications	FLTSATCOM	2	2	X	
	LEASAT	2	2	X	
	GAPFILLER	1	1	X	
	DSCS II	2	2	X	
	DSCS III	4	4	X	
	Skynet	2	2	X	
	NATO-3	1	1	X	
	INTELSAT	4	4		X
	INMARSAT	1	1		X
	LES-9	1	1		X
	DARPA MACSAT	1	1	X	
Meteorology	DMSP	2	3	X	
	NOAA TIROS	2	2		X
	METEOSAT	1	1		X
Multi Spectral Imagery	LANDSAT	2	2		X
	SPOT	2	2		X
Navigation	GPS	13	16	X	
	TRANSIT	7	7	X	
Early Warning	DSP	2	3	X	
Surveillance	Classified	Classified	Classified	X	

Table 6: Navigational Satellite Support for the Gulf War

Aircraft Supporting the Gulf War with GPS Installed

Air Force	Army	Navy
F-16C/D	RU-21H	P-3E
MH-53		RP-3
RC-135		HH-60H
B-52G		MH-53E
E-8		HH-65A

Statistical Appendix 243

Table 6 (continued)

Aircraft Equipped with Portable Receivers

Air Force	Army	Navy	Marines
H-3	UH-1 H/V	H-3	AH-1
C-130	AH-1F	P-3	CH-46
MH-60	UH-60 A/L		UH-1
	UH-60		CH-53
	EH-60A		
	AH-64A		
	OH-58A/C/D		
	CH-47D		

GPS Receivers Deployment as of March 1991

	Air Force	Army	Navy	Marines
Military	190	557	85	10
Commercial	150	3710	130	500

U.S. Space Command component commands operated the military communication satellites, Global Positioning System (GPS) satellites, Defense Meteorological Satellite Program (DMSP) satellites, and the Defense Support Program (DSP) satellites for the detection of missile launches. Coalition air forces were also able to draw on the services of other U.S. civil satellite systems as well as European satellites.

The data in the tables were drawn from various sources: USSPACECOM Operations Desert Shield and Desert Storm Assessment, Air Weather Service Support to Operations Desert Shield/Desert Storm Report #2, the Navy ultra-high frequency (UHF) Satellite Communication System Description FSC-200-83, and Interavia Space Directory.

Defense Satellite Communication System (DSCS), the military-wide band super high frequency (SHF) satellite communication system, was the principal multichannel satellite transmission means for U.S. Central Command forces for both strategic and tactical operations. When the massive deployment of U.S. forces to the Gulf area was in progress, the growing communications needs necessitated the addition of a third DSCS satellite in December 1990. This reserve DSCS II was repositioned from its Pacific orbit, augmenting the primary Indian Ocean DSCS II and the East Atlantic DSCS III satellite.

Meteorological satellites were the only reliable source of weather information over denied territory in Iraq. The launch of a Defense Meteorological Satellite Program (DMSP) satellite was accelerated to December 1990 to augment two other DMSPs and two National Oceanographic and Atmospheric Administration (NOAA) Television and Infrared Observation Satellites (TIROS) in orbit.

Multi-spectral imagery satellites such as the U.S. land satellite (LANDSAT) and the French Satellite Probatoire d'Observation de la Terre (SPOT) were used to create up-to-date maps of the area of responsibility (AOR), plan amphibious and airborne operations, and track the movement of Iraqi forces.

The Navigational Satellite Timing and Ranging (NAVSTAR) Global Positioning System (GPS) proved to be an assured method of navigating in the featureless desert. In particular, GPS was important for the mid-course guidance of the Stand-off Land Attack Missile (SLAM) and Conventional Air Launched Cruise Missiles (CALCMs), navigational accuracy of F-16s and B-52s, improvement of emitter source location by RC-135s, and rescue operations. In addition, ground forces and helicopter units relied on GPS navigation to coordinate troop movements, execute rendezvous, locate and mark mines, and position artillery equipment.

Scud launch detection was conducted by three Defense Support Program (DSP) satellites. Launched in December of 1990, the third DSP satellite was positioned to improve Scud launch detection and reporting accuracy.

Statistical Appendix

Section 3. Airlift Summaries

Table 7: U.S. Cumulative Strategic Airlift Missions (weekly)

Date	C-5	C-141	C-9	KC-10	Civil	Total
31-Aug-90	415	1,041	–	17	195	1,668
7-Sep-90	544	1,263	–	28	271	2,106
14-Sep-90	679	1,527	–	48	357	2,611
21-Sep-90	776	1,784	–	72	429	3,061
28-Sep-90	861	1,965	–	93	494	3,413
5-Oct-90	948	2,101	–	111	560	3,720
12-Oct-90	1,040	2,278	–	121	630	4,069
19-Oct-90	1,137	2,458	–	132	700	4,427
27-Oct-90	1,234	2,599	–	144	755	4,732
3-Nov-90	1,331	2,705	–	154	796	4,986
10-Nov-90	1,407	2,843	–	164	834	5,248
17-Nov-90	1,540	2,996	–	174	892	5,602
25-Nov-90	1,646	3,142	–	183	961	5,932
2-Dec-90	1,790	3,386	–	195	1,046	6,417
9-Dec-90	1,943	3,688	–	216	1,164	7,011
16-Dec-90	2,123	4,040	–	244	1,312	7,719
24-Dec-90	2,327	4,435	–	281	1,458	8,501
31-Dec-90	2,481	4,794	–	310	1,606	9,191
7-Jan-91	2,603	5,115	24	333	1,764	9,839
14-Jan-91	2,769	5,485	40	340	1,939	10,573
21-Jan-91	2,966	5,895	75	340	2,099	11,375
2-Feb-91	3,187	6,290	90	340	2,286	12,193
12-Feb-91	3,342	6,693	99	340	2,473	12,947
19-Feb-91	3,467	7,037	99	340	2,667	13,610

Note: Data prepared by U.S. Transportation Command's History Office or extracted from Transportation Command situation reports. Weekly airlift data were not always available.

Table 8: U.S. Airlift Shipment

Date	Resupply/ Sustainment Cargo	Passengers	Cargo	Resupply/ Sustainment Cargo	Passengers to Date	Cargo to Date
24-Aug-90	–	21,554	11,428	–	34,207	29,475
31-Aug-90	–	17,206	12,443	–	55,761	40,903
7-Sep-90	3,688	10,635	23,165	6,188	72,967	53,346
14-Sep-90	3,373	29,119	24,210	9,876	83,602	76,511
21-Sep-90	3,966	12,009	13,453	13,249	112,721	100,721
28-Sep-90	6,029	12,967	11,541	17,215	124,730	114,174
5-Oct-90	5,177	14,454	14,669	23,244	137,697	125,715
12-Oct-90	3,961	14,699	18,310	28,421	152,151	140,384
19-Oct-90	4,788	7,500	4,942	32,382	166,850	158,694
26-Oct-90	3,805	5,880	8,402	37,170	174,350	163,636
2-Nov-90	5,437	7,056	9,418	40,975	180,230	172,038
9-Nov-90	8,558	6,834	11,030	46,412	187,286	181,456
16-Nov-90	10,225	4,417	12,104	54,970	194,120	192,486
24-Nov-90	10,052	2,568	12,563	65,195	198,537	204,590
1-Dec-90	8,141	14,390	22,562	75,247	201,105	217,153
8-Dec-90	8,539	19,149	17,773	83,388	215,495	239,715
15-Dec-90	8,671	25,952	24,820	91,927	234,644	257,488
22-Dec-90	9,355	34,680	16,899	100,598	260,596	282,308
29-Dec-90	6,306	47,137	26,647	109,953	295,276	299,207
5-Jan-91	6,254	35,379	22,841	116,259	342,413	325,854
12-Jan-91	6,454	26,275	24,064	122,513	377,792	348,695
19-Jan-91	10,771	22,509	28,832	128,967	404,067	372,759
26-Jan-91	6,726	15,064	26,886	139,738	426,576	401,591
2-Feb-91	15,883	14,726	27,091	146,464	441,640	428,477
9-Feb-91	9,796	13,110	25,576	162,347	456,366	455,568
16-Feb-91	10,440	11,060	22,810	172,143	469,476	481,144
23-Feb-91	–	–	–	182,583	480,536	503,954

Note: Data prepared by U.S. Transportation Command's History Office or extracted from Transportation Command situation reports. Weekly airlift data were not always available.

Cargo totals of airlift represent approximately 15 percent of the total dry cargo shipped by air- and sealift. Passenger totals represent more than 99 percent of total passengers traveling by air- and sealift.

Statistical Appendix

Table 9: Strategic Airlift Summary, by Aircraft Type

Aircraft Type	Category	Aug	Sep	Oct	Nov	Dec	Jan	Feb	Mar	Total
C-141 DS/DS	Missions	996	983	691	727	1,400	1,674	1,533	318	8,322
	Short Tons	19,663	18,772	12,445	12,519	26,147	32,398	29,434	4,577	155,955
	Passengers	19,353	7,860	2,138	4,041	18,988	28,664	6,661	5,421	93,126
C-141 DE	Missions	–	–	2	30	31	33	29	10	135
	Short Tons	–	–	2	235	399	580	637	213	2,066
	Passengers	–	–	–	–	–	–	–	–	0
C-141 EE	Missions	–	–	–	–	24	31	28	9	92
	Short Tons	–	–	–	–	375	488	442	136	1,441
	Passengers	–	–	–	–	–	–	–	–	0
C-141 subTotal	Missions	996	983	693	757	1,455	1,738	1,590	337	8,549
	Short Tons	19,663	18,772	12,447	12,754	26,921	33,466	30,513	4,926	159,462
	Passengers	19,353	7,860	2,138	4,041	18,988	28,664	6,661	5,421	93,126
C-5	Missions	417	510	438	424	574	697	585	128	3,773
	Short Tons	23,437	31,698	25,895	21,945	34,335	43,108	34,035	7,571	222,024
	Passengers	20,956	13,259	7,753	3,138	13,541	16,443	8,133	1,162	84,385
KC-10	Missions	17	89	58	49	120	46	0	0	379
	Short Tons	407	3,491	1,816	1,586	3,520	1,309	0	0	12,129
	Passengers	102	112	102	141	519	135	0	0	1,111
Civilian	Missions	198	305	259	237	577	793	807	213	3,389
	Short Tons	8,948	14,001	10,727	9,362	27,425	33,502	33,603	7,657	145,225
	Passengers	32,559	37,274	39,779	13,111	85,126	69,874	29,699	13,583	321,005
Total	Missions	1,628	1,887	1,448	1,467	2,726	3,274	2,982	678	16,090
Total	Short Tons	52,455	67,962	50,885	45,647	92,201	111,385	98,151	20,154	538,840
Total	Passengers	72,970	58,505	49,772	20,431	118,174	115,116	44,493	20,166	499,627

Source: MAIRS Database (MACOS/DOCR).

Note: Abbreviations: DS/DS, Desert Shield/Desert Storm; DE and EE, Desert Express and European Express, special airlift missions flown from the United States and Europe, respectively, dedicated to delivering crucial spare parts as rapidly as possible (usually within seventy-two hours of requisition).

Totals for the civilian category are for U.S. carriers. More than 63 percent of the cargo and passengers in this category were carried by Boeing 747s.

Section 4. Desert Shield Sorties

The grand totals in each column of tables 10 through 18 require some explanation. The totals given are aggregate totals for Desert Shield, 7 August 90 through 15 January 91, but they are not the sums of the columns. Entries for each date show trends in flight activity; they represent sorties on *that date* only, not weekly totals.

Table 10: Combat Air Patrol by U.S. Aircraft

Representative Date	USAF Scheduled	USAF Flown	USMC Scheduled	USMC Flown	USN Scheduled	USN Flown	Mission Total Scheduled	Mission Total Flown
7-Aug-90	0	0	0	0	0	0	0	0
14-Aug-90	6	6	0	0	0	0	6	6
21-Aug-90	18	18	0	0	8	8	26	26
28-Aug-90	20	20	14	18	4	4	38	42
4-Sep-90	20	20	40	38	4	4	64	62
11-Sep-90	24	26	50	45	4	4	78	75
18-Sep-90	20	20	48	46	4	4	72	70
25-Sep-90	16	16	48	42	4	4	68	62
2-Oct-90	16	16	36	36	0	0	52	52
9-Oct-90	24	24	30	26	4	4	58	54
16-Oct-90	20	20	30	30	4	4	54	54
23-Oct-90	24	26	24	24	6	6	54	56
30-Oct-90	20	24	26	26	4	4	50	54
6-Nov-90	14	14	28	28	4	4	46	46
13-Nov-90	22	22	28	28	4	4	54	54
20-Nov-90	22	24	34	28	2	2	58	54
27-Nov-90	18	18	24	24	6	6	48	48
4-Dec-90	14	14	24	24	30	30	68	68
11-Dec-90	14	14	24	24	6	6	44	44
18-Dec-90	18	20	24	24	6	6	48	50
25-Dec-90	50	50	24	24	14	14	88	88
1-Jan-91	38	44	24	24	10	10	72	78
8-Jan-91	26	28	24	24	24	24	74	76
15-Jan-91	72	71	24	44	38	38	134	153
Grand Total	3,486	3,580	4,553	4,461	1,269	1,269	9,308	9,310

Source: USCINCCENT SITREPs

Statistical Appendix

Table 11: Strategic Reconnaissance Sorties (U-2, TR-1, RC-135)

Representative Date	USAF Scheduled	Flown	USN Scheduled	Flown	Mission Total Scheduled	Flown
13-Aug-90	2	2	0	0	2	2
20-Aug-90	3	2	0	0	3	2
27-Aug-90	4	4	0	0	4	4
3-Sep-90	4	4	0	0	4	4
10-Sep-90	4	4	0	0	4	4
17-Sep-90	4	4	0	0	4	4
24-Sep-90	4	3	0	0	4	3
1-Oct-90	4	4	0	0	4	4
8-Oct-90	4	4	0	0	4	4
15-Oct-90	4	4	0	0	4	4
22-Oct-90	4	3	1	1	5	4
29-Oct-90	5	5	1	1	6	6
5-Nov-90	5	5	1	1	6	6
12-Nov-90	3	3	1	1	4	4
19-Nov-90	5	5	2	2	7	7
26-Nov-90	2	2	1	1	3	3
3-Dec-90	5	5	1	1	6	6
10-Dec-90	2	2	1	0	3	2
17-Dec-90	4	3	1	1	5	4
24-Dec-90	5	4	1	1	6	5
31-Dec-90	5	4	0	0	5	4
7-Jan-91	3	4	0	0	3	4
14-Jan-91	5	4	0	0	5	4
15-Jan-91	5	7	0	0	5	7
Grand Total	628	620	74	68	702	688

Source: USCINCCENT SITREPs

Table 12: Tactical Reconnaissance Sorties by U.S. Aircraft

Representative Date	USAF Scheduled	Flown	USN Scheduled	Flown	Mission Total Scheduled	Flown
7-Aug-90	0	0	0	0	0	0
14-Aug-90	0	0	0	0	0	0
21-Aug-90	0	0	0	0	0	0
28-Aug-90	0	0	0	0	0	0
4-Sep-90	6	6	0	0	6	6
11-Sep-90	6	6	0	0	6	6
18-Sep-90	6	6	0	0	6	6
25-Sep-90	6	6	0	0	6	6
2-Oct-90	6	6	0	0	6	6
9-Oct-90	6	3	0	0	6	3
16-Oct-90	6	6	0	0	6	6
23-Oct-90	7	7	0	0	7	7
30-Oct-90	8	8	0	0	8	8
6-Nov-90	8	8	0	0	8	8
13-Nov-90	8	8	0	0	8	8
20-Nov-90	8	8	0	0	8	8
27-Nov-90	7	7	0	0	7	7
4-Dec-90	4	4	0	0	4	4
11-Dec-90	4	6	0	0	4	6
18-Dec-90	3	3	0	0	3	3
25-Dec-90	6	4	2	2	8	6
1-Jan-91	6	6	2	2	8	8
8-Jan-91	6	6	1	1	7	7
15-Jan-91	14	13	1	1	15	14
Grand Total	**738**	**684**	**36**	**34**	**774**	**718**

Source: USCINCCENT SITREPs

Statistical Appendix

Table 13: Support Sorties by U.S. Aircraft

Representative Date	Air Refueling								Airlift	
	USAF		USMC		USN		Mission Total		USAF	
	Scheduled	Flown	Scheduled	Flown	Scheduled	Flown	Scheduled	Flown	Scheduled	Flown
7-Aug-90	0	0	0	0	0	0	0	0	0	0
14-Aug-90	16	16	0	0	0	0	16	16	96	59
21-Aug-90	23	26	0	0	0	0	23	26	92	116
28-Aug-90	45	29	12	12	4	4	61	45	114	121
4-Sep-90	42	38	4	10	9	7	55	55	163	134
11-Sep-90	46	41	4	20	4	4	54	65	171	186
18-Sep-90	58	47	4	6	12	14	74	67	173	171
25-Sep-90	42	40	5	12	4	5	51	57	204	216
2-Oct-90	47	42	0	0	2	3	49	45	215	218
9-Oct-90	44	42	2	2	0	0	46	44	188	190
16-Oct-90	52	53	4	4	8	9	64	66	186	189
23-Oct-90	52	50	4	4	9	9	65	63	156	145
30-Oct-90	57	59	3	2	13	13	73	74	152	151
6-Nov-90	44	42	4	5	12	12	60	59	150	153
13-Nov-90	51	52	1	1	11	11	63	64	119	129
20-Nov-90	61	64	5	3	15	14	81	81	130	136
27-Nov-90	53	53	4	4	4	4	61	61	167	151
4-Dec-90	68	61	3	4	15	15	86	80	187	184
11-Dec-90	62	60	4	3	8	7	74	70	217	228
18-Dec-90	69	66	4	4	9	9	82	79	202	214
25-Dec-90	47	41	7	7	4	4	58	52	206	214
1-Jan-91	55	58	3	3	7	7	65	68	199	204
8-Jan-91	98	99	3	3	12	13	113	115	218	210
15-Jan-91	84	76	3	3	15	15	102	94	289	283
16-Jan-91	50	42	3	2	21	21	74	65	266	272
Grand Total	8,383	7,935	562	715	1,081	1,068	10,026	9,718	27,930	27,982

Source: USCINCCENT SITREPs

Table 14: Electronic Combat Sorties (F-4G, EF-111A, EA-6B, EC-130)

Representative Date	USAF		USMC		USN		Mission Totals	
	Scheduled	Flown	Scheduled	Flown	Scheduled	Flown	Scheduled	Flown
7-Aug-90	0	0	0	0	0	0	0	0
14-Aug-90	0	0	0	0	0	0	0	0
21-Aug-90	6	4	0	0	25	25	43	41
28-Aug-90	15	15	2	2	23	23	47	47
4-Sep-90	24	24	6	4	26	22	65	57
11-Sep-90	31	30	8	6	13	13	56	53
18-Sep-90	32	31	8	6	33	36	89	88
25-Sep-90	32	32	10	8	34	26	84	74
2-Oct-90	35	33	10	8	14	14	66	62
9-Oct-90	36	31	10	8	11	11	61	54
16-Oct-90	34	37	6	6	23	23	71	74
23-Oct-90	38	36	8	8	14	15	67	67
30-Oct-90	38	37	3	4	18	18	69	69
6-Nov-90	38	29	0	1	19	18	70	60
13-Nov-90	38	36	0	0	16	15	65	61
20-Nov-90	43	48	10	7	13	13	75	77
27-Nov-90	38	39	5	5	4	3	51	50
4-Dec-90	40	41	0	0	22	20	79	76
11-Dec-90	34	34	0	0	7	6	48	46
18-Dec-90	39	37	0	0	5	4	49	45
25-Dec-90	28	28	7	7	0	0	35	35
1-Jan-91	46	41	0	0	4	4	54	49
8-Jan-91	50	51	0	0	22	23	84	87
15-Jan-91	29	28	5	3	24	23	67	63
Grand Total	4,555	4,339	962	880	2,175	2,155	8,822	8,478

Source: Sortie Recap Data

Table 15: Airborne Command and Control (AWACS, ABCCC)

Representative Date	USAF Scheduled	USAF Flown	USN Scheduled	USN Flown	ALLIES Scheduled	ALLIES Flown	Mission Totals Scheduled	Mission Totals Flown
7-Aug-90	0	0	0	0	1	1	1	1
14-Aug-90	2	1	0	0	3	3	5	4
21-Aug-90	2	2	5	5	2	2	9	9
28-Aug-90	2	3	8	8	2	2	12	13
4-Sep-90	2	2	10	10	3	3	15	15
11-Sep-90	2	2	3	3	3	3	8	8
18-Sep-90	3	3	13	14	3	3	19	20
25-Sep-90	2	2	9	8	3	3	14	13
2-Oct-90	3	3	7	6	3	3	13	12
9-Oct-90	2	2	3	3	3	3	8	8
16-Oct-90	2	2	9	9	3	3	14	14
23-Oct-90	2	2	10	10	3	3	15	15
30-Oct-90	2	2	6	6	3	3	11	11
6-Nov-90	1	1	12	8	4	4	17	13
13-Nov-90	1	1	8	6	4	6	13	13
20-Nov-90	2	2	8	8	4	4	14	14
27-Nov-90	2	2	3	3	3	3	8	8
4-Dec-90	1	1	16	16	4	4	21	21
11-Dec-90	2	2	6	6	4	4	12	12
18-Dec-90	4	4	4	4	4	4	12	12
25-Dec-90	3	3	6	6	4	4	13	13
1-Jan-91	4	4	4	4	3	3	11	11
8-Jan-91	4	4	18	18	3	3	25	25
15-Jan-91	5	5	18	18	3	3	26	26
16-Jan-91	3	1	21	21	4	2	28	24
					0	0		
Grand Total	377	385	1,142	1,132	519	514	2,038	2,031

Source: USCINCCENT SITREPs

Table 16: Air-to-Air Training Sorties

Representative Date	USAF Scheduled	USAF Flown	USMC Scheduled	USMC Flown	USN Scheduled	USN Flown	Mission Totals Scheduled	Mission Totals Flown
10-Aug-90	15	7	0	0	0	0	15	7
17-Aug-90	16	16	0	0	0	0	16	16
24-Aug-90	10	10	20	19	0	0	30	29
31-Aug-90	8	10	8	4	30	29	46	43
7-Sep-90	26	28	24	28	34	33	84	89
14-Sep-90	16	13	16	8	14	14	46	35
21-Sep-90	24	24	28	19	43	41	95	84
28-Sep-90	8	10	18	2	42	41	68	53
5-Oct-90	12	16	28	24	26	27	66	67
12-Oct-90	12	8	30	24	48	52	90	84
19-Oct-90	4	4	32	24	33	31	69	59
26-Oct-90	0	0	1	1	18	19	19	20
2-Nov-90	4	4	29	28	43	42	76	74
9-Nov-90	3	9	30	24	52	52	85	85
16-Nov-90	22	22	40	38	9	9	71	69
23-Nov-90	6	5	0	13	0	0	6	18
30-Nov-90	0	0	22	13	10	10	32	23
7-Dec-90	20	20	15	15	20	18	55	53
14-Dec-90	12	12	14	27	30	30	56	69
21-Dec-90	8	8	29	28	28	26	65	62
28-Dec-90	12	14	44	38	20	20	76	72
4-Jan-91	30	30	96	96	10	9	136	135
11-Jan-91	12	2	24	26	40	33	76	61
Grand Total	2,950	2,720	2,553	2,110	3,631	3,578	9,134	8,408

Statistical Appendix

Table 17: Air-to-Ground Training Sorties

Representative Date	USAF Scheduled	USAF Flown	USMC Scheduled	USMC Flown	USN Scheduled	USN Flown	Mission Totals Scheduled	Mission Totals Flown
14-Aug-90	28	24	0	0	0	0	28	24
21-Aug-90	31	25	0	0	67	67	98	92
28-Aug-90	56	56	22	14	36	35	114	105
4-Sep-90	156	148	40	25	67	64	263	237
11-Sep-90	192	182	44	33	26	26	262	241
18-Sep-90	218	213	40	35	111	135	369	383
25-Sep-90	217	214	40	33	68	70	325	317
2-Oct-90	226	225	52	34	42	41	320	300
9-Oct-90	234	226	44	24	31	33	309	283
16-Oct-90	220	219	46	40	54	59	320	318
23-Oct-90	229	228	36	38	75	76	340	342
30-Oct-90	246	239	27	29	72	71	345	339
6-Nov-90	236	230	28	21	70	70	334	321
13-Nov-90	226	217	32	32	63	56	321	305
20-Nov-90	238	239	86	33	61	61	385	333
27-Nov-90	230	224	40	8	21	20	291	252
4-Dec-90	252	252	38	37	92	88	382	377
11-Dec-90	264	263	45	37	41	37	350	337
18-Dec-90	273	269	20	16	34	27	327	312
25-Dec-90	56	55	9	9	4	4	69	68
1-Jan-91	75	75	38	34	29	26	142	135
8-Jan-91	346	560	75	66	86	85	507	711
15-Jan-91	130	122	12	10	65	64	207	196
Grand Total	27,266	26,178	5,188	4,238	7,451	7,389	39,905	37,805

Source: USCINCCENT SITREPs

Table 18: Allied Sorties by Mission (Royal Air Force, Royal Saudi Air Force, Royal Canadian Air Force, French Air Force, and Italian Air Force)

Representative Date	CAP Sched	CAP Flown	Air-To-Ground Sched	Air-To-Ground Flown	Air-To-Air Sched	Air-To-Air Flown	AWACS Sched	AWACS Flown	Air Refueling Sched	Air Refueling Flown
7-Aug-90	16	16	0	0	0	0	1	1	0	0
14-Aug-90	60	59	0	0	4	0	3	3	0	0
21-Aug-90	8	8	12	12	4	4	2	2	2	2
28-Aug-90	18	18	23	14	4	7	2	2	6	4
4-Sep-90	16	16	32	28	4	2	3	3	8	8
11-Sep-90	20	20	39	37	9	6	3	3	7	7
18-Sep-90	28	28	36	35	4	4	3	3	11	11
25-Sep-90	24	24	38	32	4	8	3	3	8	8
2-Oct-90	20	20	47	36	13	12	3	3	9	9
9-Oct-90	24	24	22	20	28	28	3	3	8	8
16-Oct-90	36	36	66	65	17	17	3	3	11	11
23-Oct-90	34	30	60	57	21	22	3	3	12	12
30-Oct-90	26	26	138	143	74	55	3	3	11	8
6-Nov-90	28	28	121	109	75	62	4	4	12	10
13-Nov-90	28	28	122	114	82	59	4	6	12	11
20-Nov-90	42	42	149	139	71	64	4	4	11	11
27-Nov-90	24	22	147	139	88	68	3	3	12	11
4-Dec-90	30	30	164	153	75	79	4	4	21	21
11-Dec-90	28	28	142	130	84	75	4	4	13	16
18-Dec-90	28	28	146	119	92	89	4	4	22	20
25-Dec-90	28	28	71	69	39	39	4	4	14	17
1-Jan-91	36	34	115	106	80	67	3	3	20	19
8-Jan-91	28	28	182	183	83	72	3	3	21	24
15-Jan-91	58	56	123	105	42	31	3	3	20	20
Grand Total	4,542	4,532	12,045	11,045	6,250	5,522	515	512	1,721	1,719

Table 18 (continued)

Representative Date	Tactical Recce		Airlift		Strategic Recce		Total	
	Sched	Flown	Sched	Flown	Sched	Flown	Sched	Flown
7-Aug-90	4	4	40	40	0	0	61	61
14-Aug-90	4	4	47	47	0	0	118	113
21-Aug-90	0	0	37	37	0	0	65	65
28-Aug-90	2	2	26	26	0	0	81	73
4-Sep-90	2	2	42	42	0	0	107	101
11-Sep-90	0	0	26	26	0	0	104	99
18-Sep-90	2	2	35	35	0	0	119	118
25-Sep-90	0	0	25	25	0	0	102	100
2-Oct-90	0	0	0	0	0	0	92	80
9-Oct-90	2	2	20	20	0	0	107	105
16-Oct-90	2	2	22	22	0	0	157	156
23-Oct-90	4	4	22	22	2	2	158	152
30-Oct-90	8	8	66	66	0	0	326	309
6-Nov-90	2	2	70	70	1	1	313	286
13-Nov-90	7	5	52	52	1	1	308	276
20-Nov-90	10	6	54	52	1	1	342	319
27-Nov-90	9	8	75	76	0	0	358	327
4-Dec-90	8	8	73	81	1	1	376	377
11-Dec-90	9	7	56	53	1	1	337	314
18-Dec-90	8	8	76	86	2	2	378	356
25-Dec-90	7	6	56	57	0	0	219	220
1-Jan-91	8	8	85	83	0	0	347	320
8-Jan-91	7	7	60	61	1	1	385	379
15-Jan-91	5	5	114	110	2	2	367	332
Grand Total	711	653	6,996	7,093	102	100	32,069	30,423

Source: USCINCCENT SITREPs

Table 19: Iraqi Air Activity during Desert Shield (numerical tally not always available)

Date	Sorties Detected	Activity Level as Indicated in SITREP
9-Aug-90	—	Activity noted
10-Aug-90	—	Increase in activity noted
11-Aug-90	—	Activity noted
12-Aug-90	—	Activity noted
13-Aug-90	—	Activity noted
14-Aug-90	47	Between 0100–1400Z
15-Aug-90	19	Midday hours
16-Aug-90	—	Activity continues at normal levels
17-Aug-90	—	Activity continues at normal levels
18-Aug-90	—	Activity continues at normal levels
19-Aug-90	—	Activity continues at normal levels. Higher than normal activity in the vicinity of Baghdad.
20-Aug-90	—	Activity continues at normal levels. Higher than normal activity in the vicinity of Baghdad.
21-Aug-90	—	Increase in activity noted
22-Aug-90	—	Activity noted
23-Aug-90	—	Activity noted
24-Aug-90	—	Activity noted
25-Aug-90	25 +	Higher than normal activity
26-Aug-90	70 +	Higher than normal activity
27-Aug-90	—	Activity continues at normal levels
28-Aug-90	—	Activity continues at normal levels
29-Aug-90	171	Highest activity to-date
30-Aug-90	197	Highest activity to-date
31-Aug-90	173	Change to normal
1-Sep-90	—	Decrease in activity noted
2-Sep-90	68	Activity noted
3-Sep-90	37	Transport + Other
4-Sep-90	—	Activity noted
5-Sep-90	79	Lower than normal activity
6-Sep-90	—	Lower than normal activity
7-Sep-90	—	Activity noted
8-Sep-90	—	Lower than normal activity
9-Sep-90	—	Lower than normal activity
10-Sep-90	90	Activity continues at normal levels
11-Sep-90	82	Activity continues at normal levels
12-Sep-90	—	Activity continues at normal levels
13-Sep-90	80	Activity continues at normal levels
14-Sep-90	—	Activity continues at normal levels
15-Sep-90	—	Activity continues at normal levels
16-Sep-90	—	Activity continues at normal levels
17-Sep-90	—	Activity continues at normal levels
18-Sep-90	—	Activity continues at normal levels
19-Sep-90	—	Higher than normal activity
20-Sep-90	—	Higher than normal activity
21-Sep-90	—	Higher than normal activity

Statistical Appendix

Table 19 (continued)

Date	Sorties Detected	Activity Level as Indicated in SITREP
22-Sep-90	—	Higher than normal activity
23-Sep-90	—	Higher than normal activity
24-Sep-90	—	Activity continues at normal levels
25-Sep-90	—	Higher than normal activity
26-Sep-90	—	Higher than normal activity
27-Sep-90	—	Higher than normal activity
28-Sep-90	—	Higher than normal activity
29-Sep-90	115	Higher than normal activity
30-Sep-90	123	Higher than normal activity
1-Oct-90	92	Lower than normal activity
2-Oct-90	105	Activity continues at normal levels
3-Oct-90	127	Higher than normal activity
4-Oct-90	120	Higher than normal activity
5-Oct-90	117	Higher than normal activity
6-Oct-90	127	Higher than normal activity
7-Oct-90	112	Activity continues at normal levels
8-Oct-90	107	Activity continues at normal levels
9-Oct-90	—	Activity continues at normal levels
10-Oct-90	140	Higher than normal activity
11-Oct-90	148	Higher than normal activity
12-Oct-90	52	Lower than normal activity
13-Oct-90	130	Activity continues at normal levels
14-Oct-90	123	Activity continues at normal levels
15-Oct-90	114	Lower than normal activity
16-Oct-90	173	Higher than normal activity
17-Oct-90	112	Lower than normal activity
18-Oct-90	153	Higher than normal activity
19-Oct-90	93	Lower than normal activity
20-Oct-90	93	Lower than normal activity
21-Oct-90	75	Lower than normal activity
22-Oct-90	112	Lower than normal activity
23-Oct-90	106	Lower than normal activity
24-Oct-90	90	Lower than normal activity
25-Oct-90	150	Higher than normal activity
26-Oct-90	176	Higher than normal activity
27-Oct-90	67	Lower than normal activity
28-Oct-90	130	Activity continues at normal levels
29-Oct-90	94	Lower than normal activity
30-Oct-90	163	Higher than normal activity
31-Oct-90	158	Higher than normal activity
1-Nov-90	—	Activity noted
2-Nov-90	98	Lower than normal activity. Activity continues at normal levels for Islamic Holy Day.
3-Nov-90	138	Higher than normal activity
4-Nov-90	133	Activity continues at normal levels
5-Nov-90	129	Activity continues at normal levels

Table 19 (continued)

Date	Sorties Detected	Activity Level as Indicated in SITREP
6-Nov-90	186	Higher than normal activity
7-Nov-90	170	Higher than normal activity
8-Nov-90	109	Lower than normal activity
9-Nov-90	96	Lower than normal activity
10-Nov-90	76	Lower than normal activity
11-Nov-90	94	Lower than normal activity
12-Nov-90	130	Activity continues at normal levels
13-Nov-90	160	Higher than normal activity
14-Nov-90	170	Higher than normal activity
15-Nov-90	40	Lower than normal activity
16-Nov-90	128	Activity continues at normal levels
17-Nov-90	—	Activity noted
18-Nov-90	172	Higher than normal activity
19-Nov-90	135	Activity continues at normal levels
20-Nov-90	129	Activity continues at normal levels
21-Nov-90	147	Higher than normal activity
22-Nov-90	117	Activity continues at normal levels. Decrease in activity noted.
23-Nov-90	90	Lower than normal activity
24-Nov-90	152	Higher than normal activity
25-Nov-90	117	Activity continues at normal levels. Decrease in activity noted.
26-Nov-90	105	Lower than normal activity
27-Nov-90	45	Lower than normal activity
28-Nov-90	117	Activity continues at normal levels.
29-Nov-90	129	Higher than normal activity
30-Nov-90	122	Activity continues at normal levels. Higher than normal activity for Islamic holy day.
1-Dec-90	161	Higher than normal activity
2-Dec-90	209	Higher than normal activity
3-Dec-90	137	Activity continues at normal levels
4-Dec-90	—	Activity continues at normal levels
5-Dec-90	100	Lower than normal activity
6-Dec-90	—	Activity noted
7-Dec-90	134	Higher than normal activity for Islamic holy day.
8-Dec-90	—	Activity noted
9-Dec-90	186	Higher than normal activity
10-Dec-90	—	Activity noted

Table 19 (continued)

Date	Sorties Detected	Activity Level as Indicated in SITREP
11-Dec-90	—	Activity noted
12-Dec-90	213	Higher than normal activity
13-Dec-90	188	Higher than normal activity
14-Dec-90	98	Lower than normal activity
15-Dec-90	174	Higher than normal activity
16-Dec-90	—	Higher than normal activity; 3rd highest for December.
17-Dec-90	154	Activity continues at normal levels
18-Dec-90	208	Higher than normal activity
19-Dec-90	191	Higher than normal activity
20-Dec-90	210	Higher than normal activity
21-Dec-90	174	Higher than normal activity
22-Dec-90	138	Activity continues at normal levels
23-Dec-90	—	Activity noted
24-Dec-90	98	Decrease in activity noted
25-Dec-90	176	Higher than normal activity
26-Dec-90	156	Activity continues at normal levels
27-Dec-90	191	Higher than normal activity
28-Dec-90	115	Lower than normal activity
29-Dec-90	231	Higher than normal activity. Highest since invasion of Kuwait.
30-Dec-90	219	Higher than normal activity
31-Dec-90	129	Activity continues at normal levels
1-Jan-91	36	Lower than normal activity
2-Jan-91	37	Lower than normal activity
3-Jan-91	93	Lower than normal activity
4-Jan-91	—	Decrease in activity noted because of bad weather.
5-Jan-91	60	Decrease in activity noted because of bad weather.
6-Jan-91	88	Lower than normal activity because of bad weather.
7-Jan-91	59	Decrease in activity noted because of bad weather.
8-Jan-91	33	Decrease in activity noted because of bad weather.
9-Jan-91	81	Lower than normal activity because of bad weather.
10-Jan-91	130	Increase in activity noted
11-Jan-91	—	Activity noted
12-Jan-91	221	Increase in activity noted. Higher than normal activity (Good KTO weather)
13-Jan-91	142	Decrease in activity noted because of bad weather.
14-Jan-91	—	Activity noted
15-Jan-91	64	Activity noted (Only Transport Flights noted)

Source: CINCCENT SITREPs

Section 5. Desert Storm Sorties and Strikes

Table 20: Total Sorties by U.S. Service/Allied Country by Mission Type

Mission Type	USAF	USN	USMC	SOCCENT	USA	CRAF	Saudi Arabia
Interdiction	23,756	5,060	4,015	32	0	0	1,133
BAI	536	0	249	0	0	0	523
Total AI	24,292	5,060	4,264	32	0	0	1,656
CAS	1,438	21	2,937	31	0	0	0
FAC	682	0	1,019	0	0	0	0
Total CAS	2,120	21	3,956	31	0	0	0
DCA	4,097	24	0	0	0	0	2,391
CAP	461	4,221	0	0	0	0	0
Total CAP	4,558	4,245	0	0	0	0	2,391
OCA	2,490	44	184	0	0	0	153
SEAD	3,045	1,263	18	0	0	0	0
Escort	887	629	555	0	0	0	124
Total OCA	6,422	1,936	757	0	0	0	277
Admin Lift	0	0	0	1	0	0	0
Airlift	11,620	0	9	2	0	800	1,788
Airland	16	0	0	0	0	0	41
Courier	7	0	0	0	0	0	0
Air Evac	3,741	0	0	2	0	0	0
Helo Support	0	0	0	14	0	0	0
Tactical Airlift	1,244	0	0	0	201	0	0
Total Airlift	16,628	0	9	19	201	800	1,829
Recce	869	1,190	3	2	0	0	118
SLAR	0	0	0	0	147	0	0
Observation	442	241	0	0	0	0	0
Total Recce	1,311	1,431	3	2	147	0	118
Refueling	11,024	0	453	56	0	0	485
Tanker	0	2,782	8	0	0	0	0
Total Refueling	11,024	2,782	461	56	0	0	485
Psych Ops	26	0	0	82	0	0	0
Rescue	96	3	1	238	0	0	0
SOF	12	0	0	488	0	0	0
Total SOF	134	3	1	808	0	0	0
VIP Support	197	0	0	0	0	0	0
Support	6	41	714	64	0	0	9
Total Support	203	41	714	64	0	0	9
ECM	0	5	0	0	6	0	0
ESM	190	260	17	0	547	0	0
EW	1,388	0	326	84	15	0	0
Total EW	1,578	265	343	84	568	0	0
ABCCC	201	1,143	157	0	0	0	0
ABN Early Warning	379	0	0	0	0	0	85
C3	24	0	0	0	0	0	0
Total C3	604	1,143	157	0	0	0	85
Training	173	262	14	76	0	0	2
Utility	1	0	0	0	0	0	0
Total Training	174	262	14	76	0	0	2
Surface CAP	0	198	0	0	0	0	0
Total Surface CAP	0	198	0	0	0	0	0
Other	165	916	4	68	0	0	0
Special	193	0	0	22	0	0	0
Total Other	358	916	4	90	0	0	0
Grand Total	69,406	18,303	10,683	1,262	916	800	6,852

Statistical Appendix

Table 20 (continued)

UK	France	Canada	Kuwait	Bahrain	Italy	UAE	Qatar	Total
1,256	491	48	568	122	135	58	43	36,717
0	40	0	212	0	0	0	0	1,560
1,256	531	48	780	122	135	58	43	38,277
0	0	0	0	0	0	0	0	4,427
0	0	0	0	0	0	0	0	1,701
0	0	0	0	0	0	0	0	6,128
696	340	693	0	152	0	0	0	8,393
0	0	0	0	0	0	0	0	4,682
696	340	693	0	152	0	0	0	13,075
890	58	0	0	0	0	0	0	3,819
0	0	0	0	0	0	0	0	4,326
0	172	144	0	14	0	0	0	2,525
890	230	144	0	14	0	0	0	10,670
0	0	0	0	0	0	0	0	1
1,279	835	277	0	0	13	19	0	16,642
70	18	0	0	0	0	24	0	169
0	0	0	0	0	0	0	0	7
0	0	0	0	0	0	0	0	3,743
0	2	0	0	4	0	0	0	20
35	0	0	0	0	0	2	0	1,482
1,384	855	277	0	4	13	45	0	22,064
156	62	0	0	0	0	6	0	2,406
0	0	0	0	0	0	0	0	147
0	0	0	0	0	0	0	0	683
156	62	0	0	0	0	6	0	3,236
711	223	64	0	0	89	0	0	13,105
0	0	0	0	0	0	0	0	2,790
711	223	64	0	0	89	0	0	15,895
0	0	0	0	0	0	0	0	108
0	1	0	0	0	0	0	0	340
0	0	0	0	1	0	0	0	500
0	1	0	0	1	0	0	0	948
0	0	0	0	0	0	0	0	197
40	0	0	0	0	0	0	0	874
40	0	0	0	0	0	0	0	1,071
0	0	0	0	0	0	0	0	11
80	0	0	0	0	0	0	0	1,094
0	0	0	0	0	0	0	0	1,813
80	0	0	0	0	0	0	0	2,918
0	0	0	0	0	0	0	0	1,501
0	0	0	0	0	0	0	0	464
0	0	0	0	0	0	0	0	24
0	0	0	0	0	0	0	0	1,989
0	4	64	0	0	0	0	0	685
90	0	0	0	0	0	0	0	1
90	4	64	0	0	0	0	0	686
40	0	0	0	0	0	0	0	238
40	0	0	0	0	0	0	0	238
7	8	12	0	0	0	0	0	1,180
67	4	0	0	0	0	0	0	286
74	12	12	0	0	0	0	0	1,466
5,417	2,258	1,302	780	293	237	109	43	118,661

Source: Composite Sorties Database

Table 21: Strike Counts by Automated Installation-Intelligence File (AIF) Category

Aircraft Type	OCA	NBC	C3	Elect	Governmt Control	Navy	POL	Lines of Comm	GOB
A-10	175	2	133	0	2	0	20	2	3,367
A-6	169	38	83	33	0	183	22	91	1,519
AV-8	8	2	6	4	0	0	4	2	2,421
B-52	99	42	38	66	0	0	42	17	1,175
F-111E	104	16	14	40	0	0	47	11	40
F-111F	496	38	30	0	6	0	4	184	1,804
F-117	419	357	382	3	124	2	8	163	49
F-15E	278	6	140	14	2	0	16	171	949
F-16	895	324	340	73	24	10	123	296	8,258
F-4G	279	0	0	0	0	0	0	0	1
F/A-18	217	83	188	7	0	137	16	113	1,898
GR-1	597	19	30	22	0	0	207	104	232
TLAM	12	33	48	63	45	0	20	0	0
Subtotal	3,748	960	1,432	325	203	332	529	1,154	21,713
Other Aircraft	220	9	62	20	0	41	10	14	1,077
Total	3,968	969	1,494	345	203	373	539	1,168	22,790

Aircraft Type	Scuds	SAM	Military Industries	Subtotal	Other	Total
A-10	135	49	2	3,887	2,947	6,834
A-6	56	52	18	2,264	353	2,617
AV-8	2	18	0	2,467	118	2,585
B-52	58	21	106	1,664	42	1,706
F-111E	30	10	71	383	40	423
F-111F	69	9	30	2,670	132	2,802
F-117	64	49	158	1,778	10	1,788
F-15E	391	40	23	2,030	94	2,124
F-16	421	218	422	11,404	294	11,698
F-4G	0	630	0	910	10	920
F/A-18	96	157	71	2,983	1,568	4,551
GR-1	18	35	22	1,286	31	1,317
TLAM	58	0	2	281	0	281
Subtotal	1,398	1,288	925	34,007	5,639	39,646
Other Aircraft	61	79	49	1,642	21	1,663
Total	1,459	1,367	974	35,649	5,660	41,309

Source: Missions Database

Statistical Appendix

Notes for table 21:
1. "Other" category of aircraft includes A-7s, F-5s, Mirage 2000s, AC-130s.
2. "Other" column of target categories denotes those sorties that could not be identified on the missions database as striking a particular target category.
3. AIF categories included the following targets:

Offensive Counter Air (OCA)

Airfields
  Air Bases
  Reserve Fields
  Helicopter Bases
Noncommunications Electronic Installations
  Radar Installations
  Radars Collocated with SAM Sites
  ATC/Nav Aids
  Meteorological Radars
Air Logistics, General
  Air Depots
Air Ammo Depots
  Maintenance and Repair Bases
  Aircraft and Components Production and Assembly

Nuclear, Biological, Chemical (NBC)

Atomic Energy Feed and Moderator Materials Production
Chemical and Biological Production and Storage
Atomic Energy-Associated Facilities Production and Storage
Basic and Applied Nuclear Research and Development, General

Command, Control, and Communications (CCC)

Telecommunications
Offensive Air Command Control Headquarters and Schools
Air Defense Headquarters
Electronic Warfare
Space Systems
Missile Headquarters, Surface to Surface
National, Combined, and Joint Commands
Ground Force Headquarters
Naval Headquarters and Staff Activities

Electricity

Electric Power Generating, Transmission, and Control Facilities

Government Control

Government Control Centers
Government Bodies, General
Government Ministries, and Administrative Bodies, Nonmilitary, General
Government Detention Facilities, General
Unidentified Control Facility
Trade, Commerce, and Government, General
Civil Defense Facilities (in Military Use)

Naval

Mineable Areas
Maritime Port Facilities
Cruise Missile Support Facilities, Defensive
Shipborne Missile Support Facilities
Cruise Surface to Surface Missile Launch Positions
Naval Bases and Installations
Naval Supply Depots

Petroleum, Oil, and Lubricants (POL)

POL and Related Products Production, Pipeline, and Storage Facilities

Lines of Communication (LOC)

Highway Transportation
Railroad Transportation
Inland Water Transportation

Statistical Appendix

Scuds

Guided Missile and Space System Production and Assembly
Fixed Missile Facility, General
Fixed, Surface to Surface Missile Sites
Offensive Missile Support Facilities
Medium Range Surface to Surface Launch Control Facilities
Fixed Positions for Mobile Missile Launchers
Tactical Missile Troops Field Position

Surface to Air Missile (SAM)

Missile Support Facilities, Defensive, General
Surface to Air Missile Sites/Complexes
Tactical Surface to Air Missile Sites/Installations
SAM Support Facilities

Military Industrial Base

Basic Processing
Basic Equipment Production
End Products (Chiefly Civilian)
Technical Research, Development, and Testing, Nonnuclear
Covered Storage Facilities, General
Material (Chiefly Military)
Industrial Production Centers
Defense Logistics Agencies

Miscellaneous/Other

All installation not in above list
This category could arguably fit into OCA

Table 22: Strike Counts by Master Target List Categories

Aircraft Type	A	C	C3	E	L	N	O	RR	RG	SAD
A-10	6	0	6	0	0	0	0	0	0	146
A-6	103	20	67	37	0	184	19	53	0	38
AV-8	0	0	0	0	0	0	0	0	0	0
B-52	85	19	27	62	0	0	26	15	0	3
F-111E	57	60	4	24	0	0	43	0	0	8
F-111F	462	40	10	1	2	0	0	67	0	2
F-117	219	373	209	1	173	2	2	120	10	111
F-15E	164	13	28	6	0	0	5	37	0	55
F-16	636	285	105	49	28	0	91	28	12	80
F-4G	7	0	0	0	0	0	0	0	0	2
F/A-18	158	59	104	5	0	94	8	90	11	108
GR-1	603	0	3	24	0	0	197	100	0	14
TLAM	12	91	14	63	61	0	20	0	0	16
Subtotal	2,512	960	577	272	264	280	411	510	33	583
Other Aircraft	184	28	3	12	0	25	9	7	0	43
Total	2,696	988	580	284	264	305	420	517	33	626

Aircraft Type	Scuds	SAM	MS	Subtotal	Other	Total
A-10	2	4	0	164	6,670	6,834
A-6	11	6	93	631	1,986	2,617
AV-8	0	0	0	0	2,585	2,585
B-52	12	0	291	540	1,166	1,706
F-111E	20	0	111	327	96	423
F-111F	14	0	84	682	2,120	2,802
F-117	168	2	246	1,636	152	1,788
F-15E	306	0	6	620	1,504	2,124
F-16	281	27	757	2,379	9,319	11,698
F-4G	5	0	6	20	900	920
F/A-18	46	37	180	900	3,651	4,551
GR-1	32	0	135	1,108	209	1,317
TLAM	0	0	2	279	2	281
Subtotal	897	76	1,911	9,286	30,360	39,646
Other Aircraft	50	17	67	445	1,218	1,663
Total	947	93	1,978	9,731	31,578	41,309

Source: Missions Database

Statistical Appendix

Notes for table 22:

1. The Master Target List designations mainly identify the strategic target sets attacked. The RG column includes some of the targets within the Republican Guard areas but gives an incomplete picture of attacks on the Republican Guard divisions. The "other" target category includes strikes against ground order of battle targets, including additional strikes against the Republican Guard beyond those shown in the RG column. See the Kill Box Strike Counts (tables 23 and 24) for more accurate information of total strikes against the Republican Guard divisions.

2. Master Target List categories are defined as follows:
- Airfields (A)
- Breaching (not counted)
- Chemical (C)
- Command and Control (CCC)
- Electricity (E)
- Leadership (L)
- Military/Support (MS)
- Naval (N)
- Oil (O)
- Republican Guard (not able to fully track) (RG)
- Railroads and Bridges (RR)
- Strategic Air Defense (SAD)
- Surface to Air Missile Sites (SAM)
- Scud Sites (Scuds)

See further discussions in chapter 2.

Strikes Targeted by Kill Box
17 January–28 February 1991
Map/grid applies to tables 23 and 24.

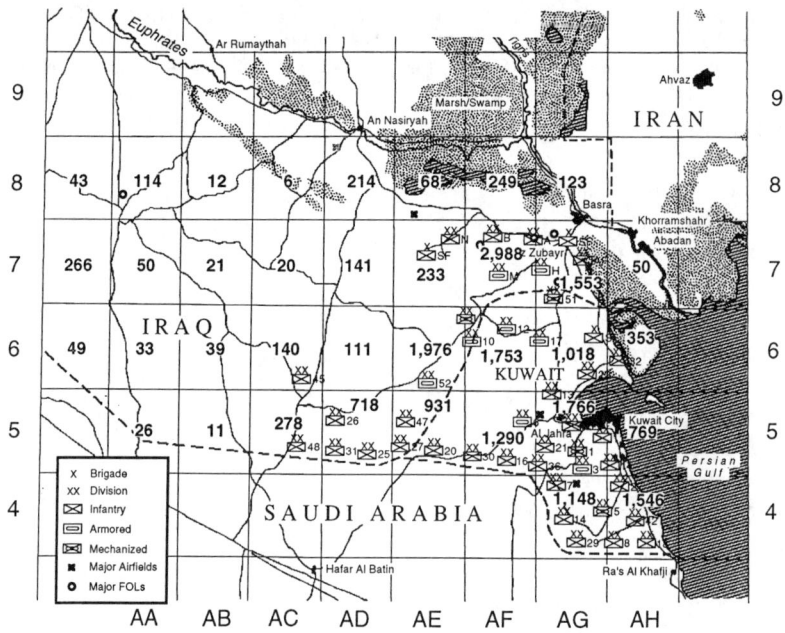

Notes: 1. The twenty-two kill boxes shown contained the major ground formations of the Iraqi army.

2. Counts do not include strikes on fixed (permanent) installations that were counted as one of the AIF categories described in table 21. Approximately 7 percent of the strikes within kill boxes met this criteria.

3. The "Other" category denotes those strikes within the Kuwaiti theater, but with mission data that did not allow identification of a specific kill box.

4. The "Other" category of aircraft includes A-7s, F-5s, Mirage 2000s, and AC-130s.

Statistical Appendix

Table 23: Strikes by Day by Kill Box

Day	AE8	AF8	AG8	AE7	AF7	AG7	AH7	AC6	AD6	AE6	AF6	AG6	AH6
1	1	0	0	0	1	20	0	0	1	23	5	3	1
2	1	0	4	0	17	4	0	1	0	22	2	1	0
3	2	0	0	2	20	0	0	6	0	34	5	7	0
4	0	0	0	0	10	0	0	0	0	9	10	0	9
5	4	0	0	0	4	0	0	3	0	3	1	0	2
6	0	0	0	4	1	3	0	4	0	17	0	0	0
7	0	0	0	2	0	4	0	4	0	48	0	0	6
8	4	5	1	0	66	45	1	0	6	8	0	2	5
9	0	4	0	8	83	80	0	0	0	6	102	8	0
10	4	5	0	25	109	16	0	0	0	10	91	11	0
11	2	46	0	8	95	4	0	0	0	5	6	2	0
12	0	46	0	0	150	10	0	0	0	84	5	2	0
13	0	6	2	0	240	91	0	2	1	127	3	2	0
14	0	0	2	3	62	160	0	0	1	186	21	17	5
15	0	0	2	0	64	98	2	0	0	111	6	9	0
16	0	0	4	6	120	16	0	0	0	71	31	20	0
17	4	0	5	0	18	11	0	0	0	67	51	19	2
18	6	2	2	10	49	5	0	0	14	36	52	26	0
19	0	0	4	26	121	53	4	0	0	21	39	20	0
20	0	0	4	6	120	80	0	0	8	42	130	47	0
21	0	13	3	0	120	42	0	0	0	17	80	13	0
22	0	0	2	0	69	26	0	0	20	18	86	26	15
23	2	0	0	0	8	12	0	6	2	72	56	49	4
24	0	2	0	0	46	55	0	4	0	29	84	21	0
25	0	0	0	4	115	42	0	0	0	30	88	36	1
26	4	3	9	0	191	30	0	0	18	8	70	24	1
27	0	0	8	1	196	62	0	3	4	57	129	23	7
28	0	7	2	14	141	52	1	14	2	29	86	18	0
29	0	0	6	1	136	36	0	0	3	15	69	19	1
30	2	0	14	14	95	52	0	0	4	60	107	22	30
31	0	6	0	0	63	56	0	14	0	30	33	10	4
32	0	0	4	4	21	9	0	10	2	4	29	2	0
33	0	2	0	0	94	19	0	23	5	28	26	15	6
34	0	8	0	0	91	45	0	7	2	117	33	78	9
35	4	4	0	4	19	26	0	4	0	58	32	6	15
36	0	15	1	27	98	106	42	5	0	13	76	60	8
37	0	16	4	25	15	0	0	18	0	160	32	47	7
38	0	6	0	4	12	9	0	4	12	121	17	38	19
39	0	11	12	14	21	21	0	6	2	140	25	47	8
40	0	12	4	4	56	85	0	2	4	16	15	87	63
41	17	30	13	13	15	40	0	0	0	24	20	163	93
42	12	0	6	4	16	28	0	0	0	0	0	18	32
43	0	0	5	0	0	0	0	0	0	0	0	0	0
Total	69	249	123	233	2,988	1,553	50	140	111	1,976	1,753	1,018	353

Table 23 (continued)

Day	AB5	AC5	AD5	AE5	AF5	AG5	AH5	AG4	AH4	Other Kboxes	Sub-total	Other	Total
1	0	0	54	42	35	28	2	8	18	65	307	916	1,223
2	0	0	20	47	6	5	2	8	28	84	252	559	811
3	0	0	28	4	3	6	0	0	4	56	177	483	660
4	0	10	0	15	8	2	3	9	24	76	185	369	554
5	0	0	24	1	2	4	14	0	0	56	118	432	550
6	0	4	8	8	8	2	0	0	19	97	175	384	559
7	0	6	29	23	10	3	9	14	0	71	229	447	676
8	0	0	8	20	52	17	6	28	72	72	418	468	886
9	0	0	0	1	25	2	11	2	11	39	382	404	786
10	0	0	0	26	10	3	0	4	37	52	403	458	861
11	0	0	2	0	35	0	0	4	8	34	251	392	643
12	0	0	3	4	47	2	2	17	30	31	433	490	923
13	0	0	0	27	14	10	2	31	13	29	600	317	917
14	0	0	4	2	14	2	8	38	41	24	590	368	958
15	0	4	9	24	9	23	8	26	36	41	472	452	924
16	0	4	4	24	17	26	0	53	107	16	519	415	934
17	2	0	4	30	42	133	20	60	28	20	516	386	902
18	0	0	16	52	69	110	23	49	38	36	595	386	981
19	0	4	2	24	76	34	1	20	60	25	534	396	930
20	0	2	14	6	34	16	12	28	56	43	648	442	1,090
21	0	4	10	18	25	8	5	33	18	45	454	432	886
22	0	0	25	0	28	40	7	16	147	49	574	526	1,100
23	0	10	5	41	52	89	7	91	21	61	588	533	1,121
24	0	0	11	11	46	64	33	76	38	61	581	547	1,128
25	0	20	26	6	29	38	21	17	76	60	609	600	1,209
26	0	8	28	2	19	78	26	70	29	75	693	515	1,208
27	0	0	10	22	12	6	29	16	45	68	698	571	1,269
28	0	2	16	16	11	66	62	22	42	73	676	574	1,250
29	0	6	57	20	60	57	33	55	23	173	770	492	1,262
30	0	6	69	48	92	84	49	28	63	92	931	403	1,334
31	0	36	40	28	20	31	41	65	50	121	648	363	1,011
32	0	2	21	37	9	8	76	16	22	57	333	349	682
33	0	21	15	19	109	136	76	50	74	96	814	500	1,314
34	0	8	22	21	34	103	37	33	53	106	807	465	1,272
35	1	14	13	26	14	53	29	24	44	74	464	404	868
36	4	4	17	6	20	59	40	38	55	84	778	457	1,235
37	4	61	58	109	48	110	31	49	7	56	857	467	1,324
38	0	29	37	85	48	113	14	34	47	106	755	474	1,229
39	0	11	7	33	56	83	2	14	20	164	697	553	1,250
40	0	2	2	3	40	73	23	2	22	134	649	346	995
41	0	0	0	0	2	39	5	0	20	80	574	449	1,023
42	0	0	0	0	0	0	0	0	0	94	210	332	542
43	0	0	0	0	0	0	0	0	0	4	9	20	29
Total	11	278	718	931	1,290	1,766	769	1,148	1,546	2,900	21,973	19,336	41,309

Source: Missions Database

Note: Days 1 through 43 correspond to calendar dates 17 January through 28 February.

Statistical Appendix

Table 24: Strikes by Aircraft by Kill Box

Aircraft Type	AE8	AF8	AG8	AH6	AB5	AC5	AD5	AE5	AF5	AG5	AH5	AC6	AD6	AE6	AF6	AH4
A-10	0	0	0	0	0	174	289	336	347	57	0	31	24	424	314	44
A-6	0	8	8	117	11	0	12	11	28	195	278	2	6	77	78	182
AV-8	0	0	0	18	0	0	0	0	110	461	22	0	0	0	0	550
B-52	0	18	0	0	0	12	32	93	127	61	6	15	0	86	34	20
F-111E	0	0	6	0	0	0	0	0	0	0	0	0	0	0	0	0
F-111F	4	15	0	0	0	1	47	129	0	1	0	0	0	273	124	0
F-117	0	0	0	0	0	0	0	0	0	7	0	0	0	0	0	0
F-15E	11	6	8	0	0	3	77	0	37	24	8	2	0	137	146	2
F-16	50	191	97	0	0	135	1,731	1,012	399	542	27	73	47	886	910	99
F-4G	4	5	1	0	0	8	29	24	42	64	10	1	4	21	35	0
F/A-18	0	6	3	0	0	2	38	82	151	291	328	7	18	33	64	317
GR-1	0	0	0	0	0	0	10	0	4	4	0	0	0	0	0	4
TLAM	0	0	0	0	0	0	0	0	0	0	0	0	0	0	0	0
Subtotal	69	249	123	0	0	221	2,955	1,545	1,245	1,707	679	131	99	1,937	1,709	1,218
Other Aircraft	0	0	0	0	0	12	33	8	45	59	90	9	12	39	44	328
Total	69	249	123	0	0	233	2,988	1,553	1,290	1,766	769	140	111	1,976	1,753	1,546

Aircraft Type	AG6	AH6	AB5	AC5	AD5	AE5	AF5	AG5	AH5	AC6	AD6	AE6	AF6	AH4	Other Kboxes	Subtotal	Other	Total
A-10	30	0	11	174	289	336	347	57	0	31	24	424	314	44	364	2,533	4,301	6,834
A-6	196	117	0	0	12	11	28	195	278	2	6	77	78	182	119	1,473	1,144	2,617
AV-8	26	18	0	0	0	0	110	461	22	0	0	0	0	550	30	1,704	881	2,585
B-52	24	0	0	12	32	93	127	61	6	15	0	86	34	20	133	1,030	676	1,706
F-111E	0	0	0	0	0	0	0	0	0	0	0	0	0	0	0	0	423	423
F-111F	4	0	0	0	47	129	0	1	0	0	0	273	124	0	15	1,680	1,122	2,802
F-117	0	0	0	0	0	0	0	0	0	0	0	0	0	0	7	15	1,773	1,788
F-15E	56	0	0	4	40	40	37	24	8	2	0	22	146	2	580	1,286	838	2,124
F-16	517	19	0	87	285	269	399	542	27	73	47	64	910	99	938	8,426	3,272	11,698
F-4G	22	1	0	0	1	9	42	64	10	1	4	13	35	0	437	732	188	920
F/A-18	133	197	0	0	18	18	151	291	328	7	18	156	64	317	105	1,949	2,602	4,551
GR-1	8	0	0	0	0	0	4	4	0	0	0	8	0	4	48	86	1,231	1,317
TLAM	0	0	0	0	0	0	0	0	0	0	0	0	0	0	0	0	281	281
Subtotal	1,016	352	11	278	706	905	1,245	1,707	679	133	99	933	1,937	1,218	2,776	20,914	18,732	39,646
Other Aircraft	2	1	0	0	12	26	45	59	90	9	12	215	39	328	124	1,059	604	1,663
Total	1,018	353	11	278	718	931	1,290	1,766	769	140	111	1,148	1,976	1,546	2,900	21,973	19,336	41,309

Source: Missions Database

Section 6. Aircraft Attrition

Table 25: U.S. Aircraft Attrition during Desert Shield

Date	Unit/Service	Aircraft Type	Mission	Location	Cause	Remarks
20-Aug-90	82ND ABN DIV, USA	OH-58D	Nvg training	King Fahd	Ground impact during gun jink	No injuries
28-Aug-90	U.S. Air Force	C-5	Transport	Ramstein AFB	-	13 fatalities
3-Sep-90	363 TFW, USAF	F-16C	Training	2400N0530OE	Engine fire	Minor injuries; pilot picked up by UAE SAR
6-Sep-90	I MEF, USMC	AH-1W	-	Near Dhahran	-	2 minor injuries
7-Sep-90	101ST AVN BDE, USA	OH-58C	Nvg training	King Fahd	Impacted sand dune while noe	1 minor injury
13-Sep-90	I MEF, USMC	CH-53E	-	King Abdul Aziz	Crashed on take-off	Minor injuries - smoke inhalation, burns
23-Sep-90	USS Kennedy, USN	SH-3	-	Red Sea	-	Crashed in water 100 yd from USS Kennedy
29-Sep-90	U.S. Army	UH-60	Nvg training	-	Impacted sand dune	Crashed in terrain flight mode - 5 injuries
30-Sep-90	4 TFW, USAF	F-15E	Training	Oman	Ground impact vicinity Thumrayt	Low altitude training - 2 fatalities
2-Oct-90	U.S. Army	OH-58C	Training	-	Lost reference to ground	Impacted during approach - no injuries
8-Oct-90	HMM-164, USMC	UH-1N	Nvg training	2014N05948E	Mid-air collision	SAR discontinued 090730z oct- 8 fatalities
8-Oct-90	106 TRS, USAF	RF-4C	Training	-	Ground impact during gun jink	2 fatalities - deployed to Al Dhafra, UAE
10-Oct-90	48 TFW, USAF	F-111	Training	40 NM SE Taif	Impact during low level train	2 fatalities
24-Nov-90	U.S. Marine Corps	CH-53E	-	-	Fire in #2 engine	A/C landed - crew exited - no injuries
5-Dec-90	-	AH-1	-	-	Lost power on takeoff	Crashed - no injuries
7-Jan-90	U.S. Army	AH-64	-	-	APU fire	Extensive damage to aircraft
9-Jan-91	U.S. Air Force	F-16C	Night Cannon	-	-	1 fatality
11-Jan-91	101ST AVN BN, USA	CH-47D	-	-	Engine failure and fire	No fatalities
13-Jan-91	138 TFS, USAF	F-16	-	-	Aircraft malfunction	Pilot successfully ejected

Source: USCINCCENT SITREPs and "USCENTAF Mishap Rate Charts" published 11 January 1991 by CENTAF/SE.

Table 26: Desert Storm Total Combat Losses by Cause

Service/ Country	Aircraft	AAA	IR SAM	RDR SAM	Direct Enemy Action- Other	MIG 25	Unknown	Total
USAF	A-10	0	4	0	0	0	0	4
	AC-130	0	1	0	0	0	0	1
	EF-111	0	0	0	1	0	0	1
	F-15E	1	0	1	0	0	0	2
	F-16	1	0	2	0	0	0	3
	F-4G	1	0	0	0	0	0	1
	OA-10	0	2	0	0	0	0	2
Total		3	7	3	1	0	0	14
USN	A-6E	2	0	1	0	0	0	3
	F-14	0	0	1	0	0	0	1
	F/A-18	0	0	0	0	1	1	2
Total		2	0	2	0	1	1	6
USMC	AV-8B	2	3	0	0	0	0	5
	OV-10	0	2	0	0	0	0	2
Total		2	5	0	0	0	0	7
Saudi Arabia	F-5	0	0	0	0	0	1	1
	Tornado GR-1	1	0	0	0	0	0	1
Total		1	0	0	0	0	1	2
UK	Tornado GR-1	1	1	4	0	0	1	7
Italy	Tornado GR-1	0	0	0	0	0	1	1
Kuwait	A-4	0	0	1	0	0	0	1
Grand Total		9	13	10	1	1	4	38

Source: Air Force Studies and Analysis Agency/Regional Forces Division, Maj. Bill Troy.

Table 27: Desert Storm: Coalition Aircraft Combat Attrition Rates

Service/ Country	Aircraft Type	Combat Sorties Flown	Aircraft Damaged		Aircraft Lost	
			Damaged Aircraft	Number Damaged per 1,000 Sorties	Lost Aircraft	Number Lost per 1,000 Sorties
USAF	A-10	7,983	13	1.6	4	0.5
	AC-130	101	1	9.9	1	9.9
	B-52G	1,741	5	2.9	0	0
	EF-111	1,105	0	0	1	0.9
	F-111F	2,420	3	1.2	0	0
	F-15C	5,674	1	0.2	0	0
	F-15E	2,142	0	0	2	0.9
	F-16	13,066	4	0.3	3	0.2
	F-4G	2,678	0	0	1	0.4
	OA-10	657	1	1.5	2	3.0
	Total	37,567	28	0.7	14	0.4
USN	A-6E	4,800	4	0.8	3	0.6
	F-14	3,916	0	0	1	0.3
	F/A-18	4,316	0	0	2	0.5
	Total	13,032	4	0.3	6	0.5
USMC	A-6E	793	1	1.3	0	0
	AV-8B	3,349	2	0.6	5	1.5
	F/A-18	4,934	8	1.6	0	0.0
	OV-10	482	0	0	2	4.1
	Total	9,558	11	1.2	7	0.7
Allies	A-4	651	0	0.0	1	1.5
	F-5	1,129	0	0.0	1	0.9
	Jaguar	571	4	7.0	0	0.0
	Tornado GR-1	2,482	1	1	9	10
	Total	4,833	5	8	11	13

Principal sources: Desert Storm Coalition Aircraft Attrition Worksheet, Air Force Studies and Analysis/Regional Forces Division, Maj. Bill Troy, and Composite Sorties Database.

Statistical Appendix

Table 28: Coalition Air-to-Air Kill Matrix

No	Date	Shooter	Bandit	Kill By
1	17-Jan-91	F-15C	MiG-29	AIM-7
2	17-Jan-91	F-15C	Mirage F-1	AIM-7
3	17-Jan-91	F-15C	Mirage F-1	GRND
4	17-Jan-91	F-15C	Mirage F-1	AIM-7
5	17-Jan-91	F-15C	MiG-29	AIM-7
6	17-Jan-91	F-15C	MiG-29	AIM-7
7	*17-Jan-91	F/A-18	MiG-21	AIM-9
8	*17-Jan-91	F/A-18	MiG-21	AIM-7
9	19-Jan-91	F-15C	MiG-25	AIM-7
10	19-Jan-91	F-15C	MiG-25	AIM-7
11	19-Jan-91	F-15C	MiG-29	GRND
12	19-Jan-91	F-15C	MiG-29	AIM-7
13	19-Jan-91	F-15C	Mirage F-1	AIM-7
14	19-Jan-91	F-15C	Mirage F-1	AIM-7
15	**24-Jan-91	F-15C	Mirage F-1	AIM-9
16	**24-Jan-91	F-15C	Mirage F-1	AIM-9
17	26-Jan-91	F-15C	MiG-23	AIM-7
18	26-Jan-91	F-15C	MiG-23	AIM-7
19	26-Jan-91	F-15C	MiG-23	AIM-7
20	27-Jan-91	F-15C	MiG-23	AIM-9
21	27-Jan-91	F-15C	MiG-23	AIM-9
22	27-Jan-91	F-15C	MiG-23	AIM-7

Table 28 (continued)

No	Date	Shooter	Bandit	Kill By
23	27-Jan-91	F-15C	Mirage F-1	AIM-7
24	28-Jan-91	F-15C	MiG-23	AIM-7
25	29-Jan-91	F-15C	MiG-23	AIM-7
26	02-Feb-91	F-15C	IL-76	AIM-7
27	06-Feb-91	F-15C	MiG-21	AIM-9
28	06-Feb-91	F-15C	MiG-21	AIM-9
29	06-Feb-91	F-15C	Su-25	AIM-9
30	06-Feb-91	F-15C	Su-25	AIM-9
31	06-Feb-91	A-10A	OBS HELO	30 MM
32	*7-Feb-91	F-14 (2)	Mi-8	AIM-9M
33	07-Feb-91	F-15C	Su-7/17	AIM-7
34	07-Feb-91	F-15C	Su-7/17	AIM-7
35	07-Feb-91	F-15C	Su-7/17	AIM-7
36	07-Feb-91	F-15C	ATTACK HELO	AIM-7
37	11-Feb-91	2 x F-15C	ATTACK HELO	AIM-7
38	15-Feb-91	A-10A	Mi-8 Hip	30 MM
39	20-Mar-91	F-15C	Su-22	AIM-9
40	22-Mar-91	F-15C	Su-22	AIM-9
41	22-Mar-91	F-15C	PC-9	GRND

Source: HQ TAC/DOT (A-Team)
* Association of Naval Aviation. "The Shield and the Storm."
Falls Church, VA. 1991. pp 8-9.
** Deur, John M., Wall of Eagles Aerial Engagements and
Victories in Operation Desert Storm, p. 22

Statistical Appendix

Section 7. Weapon Cost Data

Table 29: Desert Shield/Storm: USAF Weapons Cost and Utilization (FY 90$)

Air-To-Air Missiles	Expended	Unit Cost	Total Cost
AIM-7M	67	$225,700	$15,121,900
AIM-9M	48	$70,600	$3,388,800
Total	115		$18,510,700

General Purpose Bombs	Expended	Unit Cost	Total Cost
MK-82 LD (500 lb Low Drag General Purpose Bomb)	51,932	$498	$25,862,136
MK-82 HD (500 lb High Drag General Purpose Bomb)	7,952	$1,100	$8,747,200
MK-84 LD (2000 lb Low Drag General Purpose Bomb)	7,856	$1,871	$14,698,576
MK-84 HD (2000 lb High Drag General Purpose Bomb)	2,611	$2,874	$7,504,014
M117 (750 lb Low-Drag Demolition Bomb)	43,435	$253	$10,989,055
UK-1000 (1000 lb General Purpose Bomb)	288	$16,222	$4,671,936
CBU-52/58/71 (Fragmentation Bomb)	17,831	$2,159	$38,497,129
CBU-87 (Combined Effects Munitions, Anti-Armor, Anti-Personnel)	10,035	$13,941	$139,897,935
CBU-89 (Gator/Anti-Personnel/Anti-Tank)	1,105	$39,963	$44,159,115
MK-20 (Rockeye II/Anti-Materiel/Anti-Tank Cluster)	5,345	$3,449	$18,434,905
Total	148,390		$313,462,001

Guided Bombs	Expended	Unit Cost	Total Cost
GBU-10 (Laser/Mk-84)	2,377	$22,000	$52,294,000
GBU-12 (Laser/Mk-82)	4,086	$9,000	$36,774,000
GBU-15 (Electro-optical and Infrared/Mk-84)	71	$227,600	$16,159,600
GBU-24 (Low-level Laser/Mk-84)	284	$65,000	$18,460,000
GBU-24 (Low-level laser/BLU 109 2000 lb penetrating warhead)	897	$85,000	$76,245,000
GBU-27 (Laser/BLU-109 2000 lb penetrating warhead)	739	$75,539	$55,823,321
*GBU-28 (Laser/4000 lb penetrating warhead)	2	$100,000	$200,000
Total	8,456		$255,955,921

Anti-Radiation Missiles	Expended	Unit Cost	Total Cost
AGM-45 (Shrike)	53	$89,000	$4,717,000
AGM-88 (HARM/ High-speed, anti-radiation missile)	1,067	$257,000	$274,219,000
Total	1,120		$278,936,000

Air-To-Surface Missiles	Expended	Unit Cost	Total Cost
AGM-65B (Maverick/EO guided missile, shaped charge)	1,673	$64,100	$107,239,300
AGM-65D (Maverick/IR guided missile, shaped charge)	3,405	$111,000	$377,955,000
AGM-65G (Maverick/IR guided missile, penetrator/blast frag)	177	$269,000	$47,613,000
Total	5,255		$532,807,300

CALCMS	Expended	Unit Cost	Total Cost
*CALCM (Conventional Air-Launched Cruise Missile)	35	$1,500,000	$52,500,000
Grand Total			$1,452,171,922

* These costs are in FY 91$

Sources: The Directorate of Supply HQ USAF/LGS, Combat Support Division (LGSP); 1990 Weapons File

Table 30: Desert Shield/Storm: USN Weapons Cost and Utilization (FY 91$)

Air-To-Air Missiles	Expended	Unit Cost	Total Cost
AIM-7M	14	$225,700	$3,159,800
AIM-9M	26	$70,600	$1,835,600
Total	40		$4,995,400

General Purpose Bombs	Expended	Unit Cost	Total Cost
MK-82 (500 lb General Purpose Bomb)	10,941	$498	$5,448,618
MK-83 (1000 lb General Purpose Bomb)	10,125	$1,000	$10,125,000
MK-84 (2000 lb General Purpose Bomb)	971	$1,871	$1,816,741
MK-20 (Rockeye II / Anti-Materiel/Anti-Tank Cluster)	6,814	$3,449	$23,501,486
CBU-78 Gator (Anti-Personnel/Anti-Tank)	148	$39,963	$5,914,524
Total	28,999		$46,806,369

Guided Bombs	Expended	Unit Cost	Total Cost
GBU-10 (Laser/Mk-84)	202	$22,000	$4,444,000
GBU-12 (Laser/Mk-82)	205	$9,000	$1,845,000
GBU-16 (Laser/Mk-83)	216	$150,000	$32,400,000
Total	623		$38,689,000

Anti-Radiation Missiles	Expended	Unit Cost	Total Cost
AGM-45 (Shrike)	18	$89,000	$1,602,000
AGM-88 (HARM/ High-speed, anti-radiation missile)	661	$257,000	$169,877,000
Total	679		$171,479,000

Air-To-Surface Missiles	Expended	Unit Cost	Total Cost
AGM-123A Skipper (II)	9	$31,240	$281,160
AGM-62B Walleye (II)	131	$70,000	$9,170,000
AGM-84B SLAM (Stand-Off Land Attack Missile)	7	$346,000	$2,422,000
Total	147		$11,873,160

TLAMS	Expended	Unit Cost	Total Cost
BGM-109 TLAM (Tomahawk Land Attack Missile)	298	$1,100,000	$327,800,000

Helicopter Munitions	Expended	Unit Cost	Total Cost
AGM-114 Hellfire (Semiactive laser-guided)	30	$35,127	$1,053,810
BGM-71 TOW (Anti-tank, optical wire-guided missile)	38	$15,000	$570,000
Total	68		$1,623,810
Grand Total			$603,266,739

Source: The Directorate of Supply HQ USAF/LGS, Combat Support Division (LGSP); OP-411D

Statistical Appendix

Table 31: Desert Shield/Storm: USMC Weapons Cost and Utilization (FY 91$)

Air-To-Air Missiles	Expended	Unit Cost	Total Cost
AIM-7M	7	$225,700	$1,579,900
AIM-9M	12	$70,600	$847,200
Total	19		$2,427,100
General Purpose Bombs	**Expended**	**Unit Cost**	**Total Cost**
MK-82 (500 lb General Purpose Bomb)	6,828	$498	$3,400,344
MK-83 (1000 lb General Purpose Bomb)	8,893	$1,000	$8,893,000
MK-84 (2000 lb General Purpose Bomb)	751	$1,871	$1,405,121
MK-20 (Rockeye II / Anti-Materiel/Anti-Tank Cluster)	15,828	$3,449	$54,590,772
CBU-72 FAE (High-speed Fuel Air Explosive)	254	$3,800	$965,200
CBU-78 Gator (Anti-Personnel/Anti-Tank)	61	$39,963	$2,437,743
Total	32,615		$71,692,180
Guided Bombs	**Expended**	**Unit Cost**	**Total Cost**
GBU-10 (Laser/Mk-84)	58	$22,000	$1,276,000
GBU-12 (Laser/Mk-82)	202	$9,000	$1,818,000
GBU-16 (Laser/Mk-83)	3	$150,000	$450,000
Total	263		$3,544,000
Anti-Radiation Missiles	**Expended**	**Unit Cost**	**Total Cost**
AGM-45 (Shrike)	7	$89,000	$623,000
AGM-88 (HARM/ High-speed, anti-radiation missile)	233	$257,000	$59,881,000
Total	240		$60,504,000
Air-To-Surface Missiles	**Expended**	**Unit Cost**	**Total Cost**
AGM-123A Skipper (II)	3	$31,240	$93,720
AGM-62B Walleye (II)	2	$70,000	$140,000
AGM-65C	5	$110,000	$550,000
AGM-65E (Maverick/Laser-guided missile, penetrator/blast frag)	36	$101,000	$3,636,000
Total	46		$4,419,720
Helicopter Munitions	**Expended**	**Unit Cost**	**Total Cost**
AGM-114 Hellfire (Semiactive laser-guided)	159	$35,546	$5,651,814
BGM-71 TOW (Anti-tank, optical wire-guided missile)	255	$15,000	$3,825,000
Total	414		$9,476,814
Grand Total			**$152,063,814**

Source: The Directorate of Supply HQ USAF/LGS, Combat Support Division (LGSP); OP-411D

Table 32: Desert Shield/Storm: Total USAF, USN, and USMC Weapons Cost and Utilization (FY 90/91$)

Air-To-Air Missiles	Expended	Unit Cost	Total Cost
AIM-7M	88	$225,700	$19,861,600
AIM-9M	86	$70,600	$6,071,600
Total	174		$25,933,200

General Purpose Bombs	Expended	Unit Cost	Total Cost
MK-82 LD (500 lb Low Drag General Purpose Bomb)	69,701	$498	$34,711,098
MK-82 HD (500 lb High Drag General Purpose Bomb)	7,952	$1,100	$8,747,200
MK-83 (1000 lb Low Drag General Purpose Bomb)	19,018	$1,000	$19,018,000
MK-84 (2000 lb General Purpose Bomb)	9,578	$1,871	$17,920,438
MK-84 HD (2000 lb High Drag General Purpose Bomb)	2,611	$2,874	$7,504,014
M-117 (750 lb Low Drag Demolition Bomb)	43,435	$253	$10,989,055
UK-1000 (1000 lb General Purpose Bomb)	288	$16,222	$4,671,936
CBU-52/58/71 (Fragmentation Bomb)	17,831	$2,159	$38,497,129
CBU-87 (Combined Effects Munitions, Anit-Armor, Anti-Personnel)	10,035	$13,941	$139,897,935
CBU-89 (Gator/ Anti-Personnel/Anti-Tank)	1,105	$39,963	$44,159,115
MK-20 (Rockeye II / Anti-Materiel/Anti-Tank Cluster)	27,987	$3,449	$96,527,163
CBU-72 FAE (High-speed Fuel Air Explosive)	254	$3,800	$965,200
CBU-78 Gator (Anti-Personnel/Anti-Tank)	209	$39,963	$8,352,267
Total	210,004		$431,960,550

Guided Bombs	Expended	Unit Cost	Total Cost
GBU-10 (Laser/Mk-84)	2,637	$22,000	$58,014,000
GBU-12 (Laser/Mk-82)	4,493	$9,000	$40,437,000
GBU-15 (Electro-optical and Infrared/Mk-84)	71	$227,600	$16,159,600
GBU-16 (Laser/Mk-83)	219	$150,000	$32,850,000
GBU-24 (Low-level Laser/Mk-84)	284	$65,000	$18,460,000
GBU-24 (Low-level laser/BLU-109 2000 lb penetrating warhead)	897	$85,000	$76,245,000
GBU-27 (Laser/BLU-109 2000 lb warhead)	739	$75,539	$55,823,321
GBU-28 (Laser/4000 lb penetrating warhead)	2	$100,000	$200,000
Total	9,342		$298,188,921

Anti-Radiation Missiles	Expended	Unit Cost	Total Cost
AGM-45 (Shrike)	78	$89,000	$6,942,000
AGM-88 (HARM/ High-speed, anti-radiation missile)	1,961	$257,000	$503,977,000
Total	2,039		$510,919,000

Statistical Appendix

Table 32 (continued)

Air-To-Surface Missiles	Expended	Unit Cost	Total Cost
AGM-132A Skipper (II)	12	$31,240	$374,880
AGM-62B Walleye (II)	133	$70,000	$9,310,000
AGM-65B (Maverick/EO guided missile, shaped charge)	1,673	$64,100	$107,239,300
AGM-65C	5	$110,000	$550,000
AGM-65D (Maverick/IR guided missile, shaped charge)	3,405	$111,000	$377,955,000
AGM-65E (Maverick/Laser-guided missile, penetrator/blast frag)	36	$101,000	$3,636,000
AGM-65G (Maverick/IR guided missile, penetrator/blast frag)	177	$269,000	$47,613,000
AGM-84B SLAM (Stand-Off Land Attack Missile)	7	$346,000	$2,422,000
Total	5,448		$549,100,180

TLAMS & CALCMS	Expended	Unit Cost	Total Cost
BGM-109 TLAM (Tomahawk Land Attack Missile)	298	$1,100,000	$327,800,000
CALCM (Conventional Air-Launched Cruise Missile)	35	$1,500,000	$52,500,000
Total	333		$380,300,000

Helicopter Munitions	Expended	Unit Cost	Total Cost
AGM-114 Hellfire (Semiactive laser-guided) - USN	30	$35,127	$1,053,810
AGM-114 Hellfire (Semiactive laser-guided) - USMC	159	$35,546	$5,651,814
BGM-71 TOW (Anti-tank, optical wire-guided missile)	293	$15,000	$4,395,000
Total	482		$11,100,624

Grand Total			$2,207,502,475

Sources: The Directorate of Supply HQ USAF/LGS, Combat Support Division (LGSP); 1990 Weapons File; OP-411D

Appendix Three

The First Twenty-four Hours of the Air War

The following maps depict air operations during the initial unfolding of the air campaign. These depictions are taken from Williamson Murray, *Operations,* Vol. II, Part 1, Gulf War Air Power Survey (Washington: GPO, 1993), 122–41. The emphasis in these maps, as it was in the initial attacks, is on operations to suppress the Iraqi air force and air defense system. The targets included airfields, aircraft, sector and intercept operations centers (SOCs and IOCs), air defense headquarters, and air defense radar sites. These operations in the suppression of enemy air defenses (SEAD) delivered a stunning blow to the Iraqi air force and air defense system from which the Iraqis never recovered. Not depicted but crucial to these operations were the hundreds of coalition combat air patrol sorties, principally F-15Cs and F-14s, flying in protection of the attack aircraft; these Coalition aircraft destroyed eight Iraqi interceptor aircraft during the first day of combat. Note too that only a sampling of the air attacks are depicted (nearly seven hundred Coalition combat aircraft were in Iraqi airspace during the first night); for instance, none of the Proven Force attacks from Turkey appear. All times are given in Iraqi local time. (See chapters 1 and 3 for further analyses of gaining control of the air.)

The First Twenty-four Hours of the Air War

Map 1—0239 to 0320, 17 January, local time. The initial attacks begin. Apache helicopters destroy radar sites in western Iraq, clearing the way for F-15Es to attack Scud sites. Meanwhile, F-117s, which had crossed the border twenty minutes earlier, attack the Nukhayb IOC to further degrade the air defense system, while others, along with the TLAMs (Tomahawk cruise missiles), proceed to targets in Baghdad. Attacks there on leadership, command and control, and air defense targets apply the first stunning blows of the war.

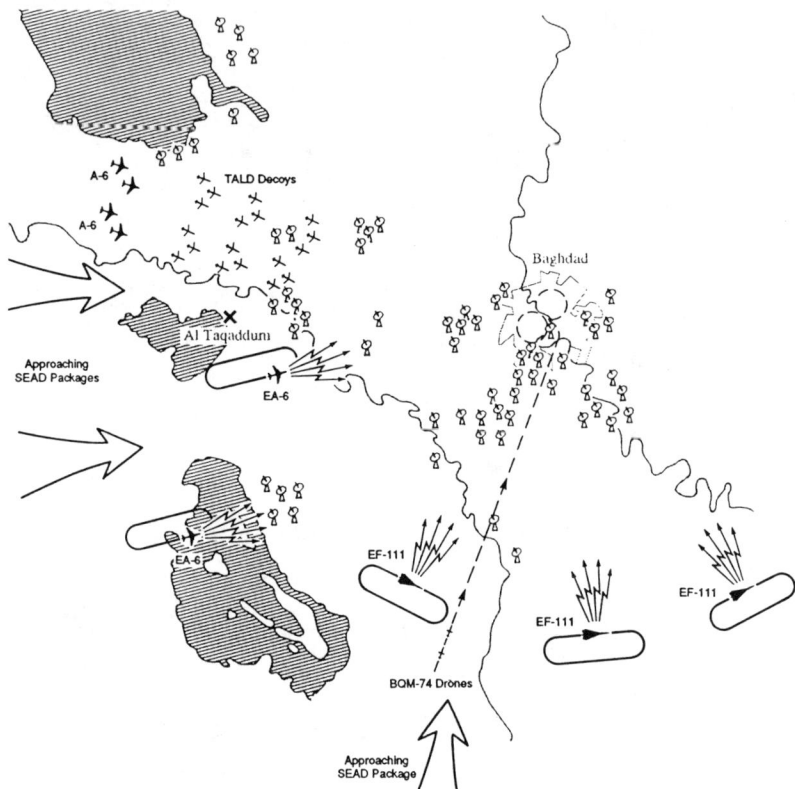

Map 2—0346. Decoys, drones, and aircraft providing electronic jamming approach central Iraq and the Iraqi radars that have been alerted and are awaiting the further arrival of Coalition attack aircraft.

The First Twenty-four Hours of the Air War

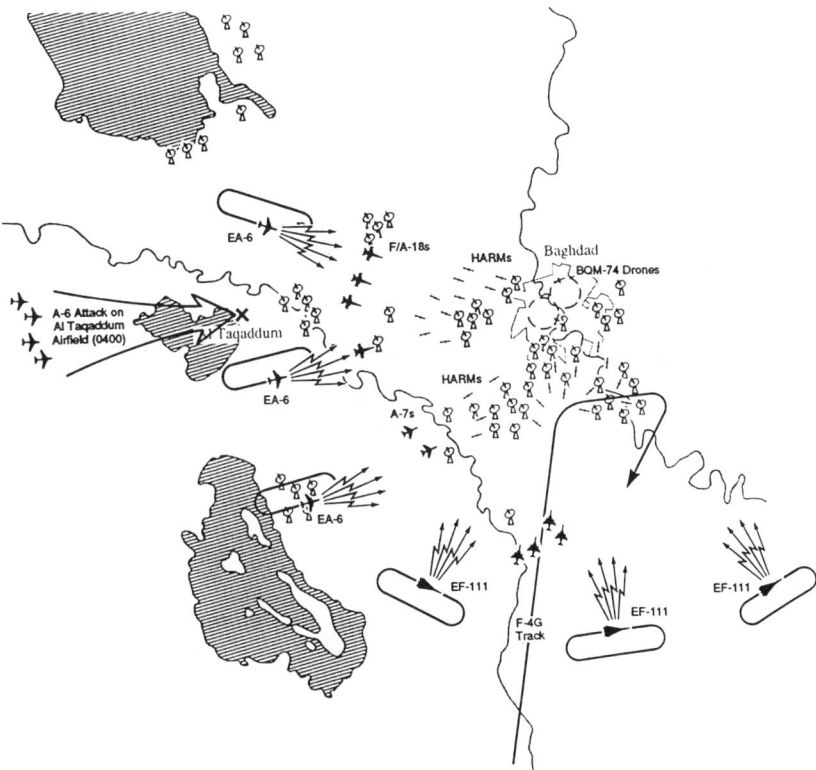

Map 3—0348 to 0355. The Iraqi radars are saturated by the detection of decoys and drones, mistaking these targets for the expected attack aircraft. Instead, Coalition aircraft launching HARM (antiradiation) missiles appear in the following wave.

Map 4—0320 to 0430. While the concentrated SEAD attacks described in maps 2 and 3 take place in the Baghdad area, airfield attacks by B-52s, GR-1s, and other aircraft are underway throughout Iraq.

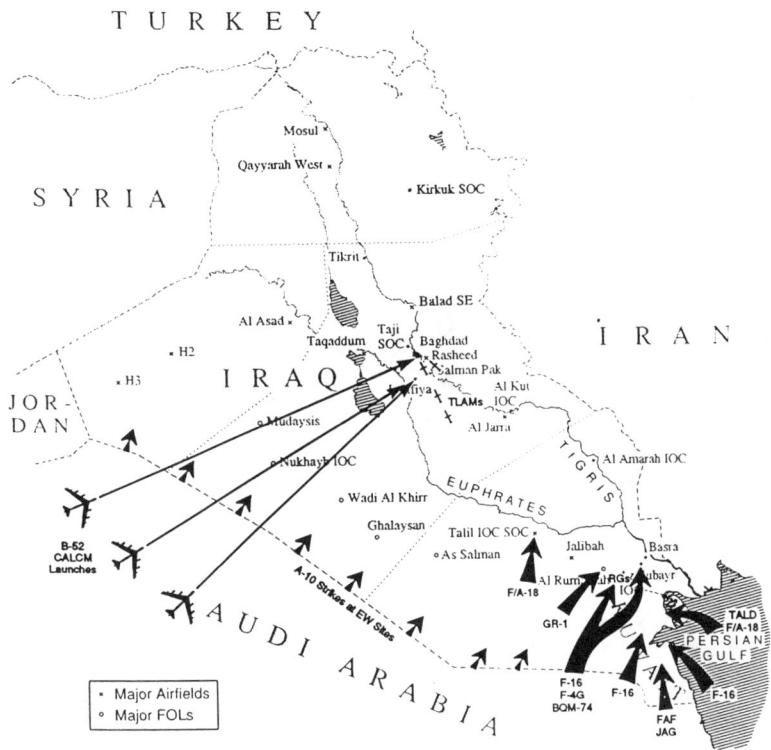

Map 5—0600 to 1300. Daylight attacks concentrate on radar and surface-to-air missile sites, airfields, and air defense facilities in southern Iraq and Kuwait, while cruise missiles (TLAMs and CALCMs) strike targets in the Baghdad area.

Map 6—1300 to 1830. Attacks against the Iraqi air defense system, airfields, and Scud sites continue amidst the more general attacks on the Iraqi army in the Kuwaiti theater. TLAMs keep the Baghdad area under attack.

The First Twenty-four Hours of the Air War

Map 7—1830, 17 January, to 0300, 18 January. Completing the first twenty-four hours of the war, F-117s and TLAMs again attack targets in Baghdad. Targets in Baghdad and other areas include the SOCs and IOCs, electric power, leadership, NBC, and communication sites. In the south and west, Saudi and British Tornados (GR-1s) attack airfields, while the Kuwaiti theater undergoes continued attacks on Republican Guard and other ground forces, attacks that will continue and increase in intensity throughout the war.

Appendix Four

Summary Data for F-117 and F-111 Strikes

The summary data of F-117 and F-111 (E and F) strikes, showing day-by-day targeting against places listed on the Master Target List, was prepared by Barry D. Watts using information from the GWAPS Missions Database and the 37th Wings (F-117s) History.

Summary Data for F-117 and F-111 Strikes

As of 22-Apr-93	STRIKES against Targets by Black Hole Categories													Total Strikes	ND (No Drop)	Total Bomb	Bombs Hit	Bombs Miss	Hit %	WxND /Cnx	WxND /Miss	%WxND or Miss
	SAD	SAM	CCC	L	C	A	MS	RR	SC	E	O	RG	N	BR	?									
Day 1 (17 Jan)	24	8		16	4		9									61	19	64	41	23	64%	7	21	25.3%
Day 2 (-4)	15	6		5	3		3	3	5							40	28	44	20	24	45%	27	49	68.1%
Day 3	6	5		7	4		1	2	1							26	21	29	21	8	72%	18	25	50.0%
Day 4	6	2	4	1	5		7		3							28	15	38	17	21	45%	6	13	24.5%
Day 5	9	4		9	11					1						34	4	62	47	5	90%	0	0	0.0%
Day 6					1	24		5	7		2					41	6	45	39	6	87%	1	1	2.0%
Day 7		10		4					6							17	38	22	14	8	64%	34	40	66.7%
Days 1-7	60	35	4	42	27	26	26	18	10	1	2					247	131	294	199	95	68%	93	149	35.1%
1st Week %s:	24%	14%		17%	11%	10%	10%																	
Day 8 (24 Jan)	1			1	18		14	8								42	26	46	34	12	74%	23	26	36.1%
Day 9	1	1			7		7	15								31	15	31	21	10	68%	12	18	36.1%
Day 10 (+6)	3			4	26	1	1		14							49	25	51	42	9	82%	17	17	22.4%
Day 11	2	2	3	10	28	9	5	4							1	63	6	65	54	11	83%	0	0	0.0%
Day 12		4	4	14	3		13	5	2			3				48	6	67	47	10	82%	0	1	1.6%
Day 13 (+8)		3	2	2			10	9	2		2	1				30	19	42	24	18	57%	18	20	32.8%
Day 14	4	4		6			9	22	1		2	1				49	15	65	37	18	67%	8	8	11.4%
Days 8-14	11	0	14	10	37	82	42	62	46	0	2	5	0	0	1	312	112	347	259	88	75%	79	90	19.6%
2nd Week:				12%	26%	13%	20%	15%																
Day 15 (31 Jan)	7			1	2	6	15	1		2						34	6	61	36	15	71%	0	0	0.0%
Day 16 (1 Feb)	7			3		5	15	11		4						45	9	50	44	6	88%	1	1	1.7%
Day 17						12	2									14	13	13	12	1	92%	11	11	42.3%
Day 18		3		1	25	3	2		1							35	31	38	25	13	66%	26	33	47.8%
Day 19		8	11	11	28		1	3		1						61	4	62	49	13	79%	0	0	0.0%
Day 20		2	2	2	21	10	10		3			1				55	10	58	51	7	88%	0	0	0.0%
Day 21	2	5	6	6	16	26	2		7				2			69	7	58	51	7	88%	7	7	10.8%
Days 15-21	2	32	20	32	94	63	25	33	23	0	0	7	2	0	0	293	80	330	268	62	81%	45	52	12.7%
3rd Week:		11%		11%	32%	18%	9%	11%	8%															
Day 22 (7 Feb)	8	10		3	31	6	6	1								63	10	60	55	5	92%	2	2	2.9%
Day 23					26				23							62	5	63	54	9	86%	1	1	1.5%
Day 24	4	6		3	2	6	13	5	9							46	4	51	41	10	80%	2	3	5.5%
Day 25 (+2)	10	14		3	3		12		2							58	6	65	56	9	86%	1	1	1.4%
Day 26	5	6		13	25		8		8							66	4	66	57	9	86%	0	0	0.0%
Day 27	6	1		32					3							66	8	59	53	6	90%	0	0	0.0%
Day 28	8	14		2		4			2				2			52	13	69	47	12	80%	1	1	1.4%
Days 22-28	41	33		56	87	10	39	9	45	1	0	0	2	0	0	392	50	423	363	60	86%	7	8	1.7%
4th Week:	10%	20%		14%	22%		10%		11%															

Appendix Four

As of	STRIKES against Targets by Black Hole Categories													Total	ND (no	Total	Bombs		Hit	WxND	WxND	%WxND
22-Apr-93	SAD	SAM	CCC	L	C	A	MS	RR	SC	E	O	RG	N	BR	?	Strikes	Drop)	Bomb	Hit	Miss	%	or Cnx	or Mis	or Miss
Day 29	1	3	19			16	8		4			2				63	8	60	52	8	87%	0	0	0.0%
Day 30 (15 Feb)	6				6		18	2	5					23		60	8	64	54	10	84%	3	3	4.2%
Day 31			8		13	4		6	10							41	5	52	46	6	88%	2	2	3.5%
Day 32	3				15	5	17		13							53	14	60	42	18	70%	8	11	14.9%
Day 33				6	4	37	4	2	3							56	7	66	48	18	73%	5	5	6.8%
Day 34						6	2	1	7							16	23	32	30	2	94%	19	19	34.5%
Day 35			2			8	19	2								31	1	45	41	4	91%	1	1	2.2%
Days 29-35	1	12	29	6	52	62	68	13	42	0	0	2	0	23	0	310	66	379	313	66	83%	38	41	9.2%
5th Week:			9%		17%	20%	22%		14%															
Day 36 (21 Feb)			11	4	27			5	7			1				55	3	64	52	12	81%	0	0	0.0%
Day 37				8	22		5									35	8	57	51	6	89%	0	0	0.0%
Day 38			4	9	18		12									43	14	57	44	13	77%	12	16	22.5%
Day 39				16	4		11	11								42	14	53	48	5	91%	5	5	7.5%
Day 40	All F117 sorties cancelled by CENTAF due to weather.															0	0	0	0	0		0	0	100.0%
Day 41				2			4									6	78	10	8	2	80%	78	78	88.6%
Day 42 (-1)				14	8	2	7	11								42	7	51	47	4	92%	3	3	5.2%
Day 43	No F117 sorties on ATO Day 43 due to the war ending at 0800L, 28 Feb 91.															0	0	0	0	0		0	0	
Days 36-43	0	0	15	63	79	2	39	27	7	0	0	1	0	0	0	223	124	292	250	42	86%	98	102	24.5%
6th Week:			7%	24%	35%		17%	12%																Excluding Day 40

SUMMARY DATA:																	Total	No	Bombs				WX No Drop/	% of
	SAD	SAM	CCC	L	C	A	MS	RR	SC	E	O	RG	N	BR	?		Strikes	Drops	Hit	Miss			Miss	Bombs
	115	40	205	187	376	234	238	162	173	2	2	16	4	23	1		1777	663	1652	413			442	18.9%
	6.5%	2%	12%	11%	21%	13%	13%	9%	10%	.1%	.1%	1%	.2%	1%	.1%		100%		Hit%	80%				

TARGET CATEGORIES: SAD = Strategic Air Defenses, SAM = Surface-to-Air Missiles, CCC = C3/Telecommunications, L = Leadership, C = Nuclear/Biological/Chemical, A = Airfield, MS = Military Support, RR = Railroads/Bridges, SC = SCUD, E = Electricity, O = Oil, RG = Republican Guard, N = Naval, BR = Breaching, and ? = Unknown.

NOTES: ** Discrepancies with GWAPS AIF counts. The "(-4)" annotation for Day 2 indicates that 4 strikes must be subtracted to get the AIF strike count for that ATO day. Such unresolved discrepancies exist on a total of five days as annotated. The final AIF strike total was 1788 (versus 1777 in this table).
** ATO Day 1 had two nights worth of F-117 strikes: the nights of 16/17 and 17/18 January 1991.
** Except for 4 Mk-84s on Day 37, all F-117 drops were precision-guided munitions (laser-guided, 2000-pound GBU-10s or GBU-27s).

COMMENT on the IMPACT of WEATHER: The high percentages of no drops or misses due to weather during the first ten days shows the dependence of laser-guided bombs on clear air. By the second week of the war, the Black Hole planners had begun working around this limitation. In the last few days, with a 72-hour target list to be hit and war termination looming, working around the weather ceased to be possible and it again became a major constraint (Days 40 and 41).

SOURCE: GWAPS Missions Database supplemented by the 37th Wing's unit history.

Summary Data for F-117 and F-111 Strikes

As of 30-Oct-93		Target Categories													Total Strikes	Aborts Air	Aborts Grnd	Notes
		SAD	SAM	CCC	L	C	A	MS	RR	SC	E	O	RG/GOB	?				
Day 1 (17 Jan)	PGM				2	4	24			8					38		3	Day 1: 48th TFW only, hit suspected Scud/BW bnkrs on 10 airfds
	NonPGM					8	9	8		4					29		3	
Day 2 (18 Jan)	PGM	12				4	14			1					19	35	5	Day 2: 12 Proven Force (20th TFW)
	NonPGM					3									15	5	1	Scud/BW bnkrs on 4 airfds
Day 3 (19 Jan)	PGM	3				1	5	1		2					12	15	3	Day 3: 8 no-tanker air aborts; bnkrs Tikrit, Balad, Qalat Salih alfds
	NonPGM	4					1	2		4	4	4			19	5	15	
Day 4 (20 Jan)	PGM						4								4	2	2	Day 4: Mostly CBU87 on Balad; PF Mk82 on Mosul
	NonPGM	4				6	15	6							31	5	5	
Day 5 (21 Jan)	PGM	1					3	8		4					16	18	1	Day 5: 16 no-tanker air aborts, H2 & H3, Scud bnkrs
	NonPGM	18		6			7								31	7		
Day 6 (22 Jan)	PGM	1		3			20								24	3	0	Day 6: Mostly 2 bunkers/111F at Al Asad, 14 HHQ Cnx
	NonPGM			2	1		5	8							16	8	2	
Day 7 (23 Jan)	PGM						19								19	43	5	Day 7: 30+ air aborts WX! Counted 2 DMPIs/111F in some cases on alfds
	NonPGM						12								12	1		
Days 1-7		43	0	11	3	26	138	33	0	23	4	4	0	0	285	158	22	132 Precision Strikes
		15%		4%		9%	48%	12%		8%								153 NonPrecision

		Target Categories													Total Strikes	Aborts Air	Aborts Grnd	Notes
		SAD	SAM	CCC	L	C	A	MS	RR	SC	E	O	RG/GOB	?				
Day 8 (24 Jan)	PGM			4			31								35	19	1	Day 8: Talill, Taqaddum, Al Jarrah
	NonPGM	13					5		4						22	1		Proven Force never reports aborts!
Day 9 (25 Jan)	PGM						14		8						14	37	2	Day 9: 30 Wx aborts! Excl 7 HHQ cnx
	NonPGM													4	12			for relgting. A few double DMPIs
Day 10 (26 Jan)	PGM						18			4		2	2		26	18		Day 10: oil manifolds (in MS)
	NonPGM						8								8	1		Excludes 3 Opns cnx
Day 11 (27 Jan)	PGM	4		6			44			3					47	11	3	Day 11: some double DMPIs; mostly busting shelters on airfds
	NonPGM						11								21	2		
Day 12 (28 Jan)	PGM			5			20	4	7	2				1	38	13	3	Day 12: Excludes 1 Opns cnx
	NonPGM						3	3	2						9	4		
Day 13 (29 Jan)	PGM					4	7	8	14	4					37	23	1	Day 13: Excludes 1 Opns cnx Al Jarrah alfd, Basrah SCUD
	NonPGM					2	12	4							18	2		
Day 14 (30 Jan)	PGM			1	7	5	56				1		2		72	6	1	Day 14: Excludes 1 Opns cnx. 20 double-DMPIs/111F on airfields
	NonPGM							4			8				12	0		
Days 8-14		17	0	16	7	11	229	23	35	13	9	2	5	4	371	137	12	269 Precision Strikes
		5%		4%			62%	6%	9%	4%								102 NonPrecision

		Target Categories													Total Strikes	Aborts Air	Grnd	Notes
		SAD	SAM	CCC	L	C	A	MS	RR	SC	E	O	RG/GOB	?				
Day15 (31 Jan)	PGM					2	54								56	10	1	Day 15: Some 2/4 DMPts/111F on airfields; excludes 2 Opns cnx
	NonPGM							7	8	4					19	3		
Day 16 (1 Feb)	PGM						19								19	33	1	Day 16: air aborts for no tnkrs & wx, excl 1 HHQ cnx
	NonPGM						12	8							20			
Day 17 (2 Feb)	PGM					3	18	8	10						39	33		Day 17: Latifyah SSM (in MS). Shelter busting at H3
	NonPGM	4				8		8	8	8					28	1		
Day 18 (3 Feb)	PGM			2		1	29		12						44	3		Day 18: Tallil, Taqadidum, Shayka Mazhar airfids
	NonPGM						7				8	8			23	1		
Day 19 (4 Feb)	PGM					8	31	3	3	8	4				53	10	3	Day 19: C11 (Tuwaitha); excludes 1 1 Opns cnx
	NonPGM						4	8							16			
Day 20 (5 Feb)	PGM						28	1	1		4		2		36	18	4	Day 20: 1st GBU-12 tank/arty hunt (1 sortie), logged as 2 RG strikes
	NonPGM			4			7					8			19	1		
Day 21 (6 Feb)	PGM		1	1			3	2	7				143		157	8	3	Day 21: No Proven Force; 1st day of tank plinking (all strikes "masked")
	NonPGM														0			
Days 15-21		4	1	7	0	22	219	46	37	16	16	16	145	0	529	121	13	404 Precision Strikes
						41%		9%	7%				27%					125 NonPrecision

		Target Categories													Total Strikes	Aborts Air	Grnd	Notes
		SAD	SAM	CCC	L	C	A	MS	RR	SC	E	O	RG/GOB	?				
Day 22 (7 Feb)	PGM	3	1				13	20		6					43	11	2	Day 22: SCUD related H2, H3; 2 Centcom Taskings
	NonPGM						8	1				25			34	1		
Day 23 (8 Feb)	PGM					5	23		2	2			94		124	5		Day 23: Tallil & H3—mostly double DMPts; tank plnkng (94 masked strks)
	NonPGM						4				4	8			16			
Day 24 (9 Feb)	PGM						10		4				149		163	3	6	Day 24: Al Shabah afld, tank plinking (149 strikes "masked")
	NonPGM											12			12			
Day 25 (10 Feb)	PGM					6	1		9	3			130		149	3	3	Day 25: excl 4 Opns cnx; PF on oil Tgts, plinking mostly masked
	NonPGM											12			12			
Day 26 (11 Feb)	PGM			1				14	1				38		54	21	4	Day 26: tank plinking mostly AF?; Latifyah SSM, Shayka Mazhar afld
	NonPGM					4		8							12			
Day 27 (12 Feb)	PGM						2	9	9	4			183		207	2	3	Day 27: plinking Medina, Hammurabi RG; Centcom taskings logged MS
	NonPGM	4				4						4			12			
Day 28 (13 Feb)	PGM					3	8		18				176		205	5	3	Day 28: Medina & Hammurabi Rep Gd divs
	NonPGM			4		4		4							12			
Days 22-28		7	1	5	0	26	69	56	41	15	4	61	770	0	1055	51	22	945 Precision Strikes
						7%		5%				6%	73%					110 NonPrecision

Summary Data for F-117 and F-111 Strikes

		Target Categories												Total Strikes	Aborts Air	Aborts Grnd	Notes
		SAD	SAM	CCC	L	C	A	MS	RR	SC	E	O	RG/GOB	?			
Day 29 (14 Feb)	PGM	3						2	13	4			178		196	5	3	Day 29: Medina & Hamurabi
	NonPGM														12			
Day 30 (15 Feb)	PGM					4	38	4	10	4			181		229	4	3	Day 30: Medina, 17 AD, kill box AE6, As Salman N, 4 GBU24s=4DMPIs
	NonPGM						8								12			
Day 31 (16 Feb)	PGM								12				91		103	13	6	Day 31: Medina & Hammurabi; kill boxes AF7, AG7, PF cnx.
	NonPGM														0			
Day 32 (17 Feb)	PGM					8	5	7		2			27		49	30	2	Day 32: Excl 3 HHQ CNX; Medina & Hammurabi; AF7
	NonPGM					4		8							12			
Day 33 (18 Feb)	PGM	3				11			13				103		130	7	2	Day 33: Medina, Hammurabi,AF7
	NonPGM							12							12			
Day 34 (19 Feb)	PGM							19	4				121		140	14	6	Day 34: Medina & Hammu; AF7SE, AF7SW, AG7SW, AF6NW; tank hunt
	NonPGM					8							4		12			
Day 35 (20 Feb)	PGM					2		14	4				13	5	25	16	3	Day 35: Many Mk84s rdr del thru wx (vice laser GBU12s); AF7
	NonPGM							8							5			
Days 29-35		3	0	0	0	37	51	74	56	10	0	0	718	5	957	94	25	872 Precision Strikes
							5%	8%	6%				75%					85 NonPrecision

		Target Categories												Total Strikes	Aborts Air	Aborts Grnd	Notes
		SAD	SAM	CCC	L	C	A	MS	RR	SC	E	O	RG/GOB	?			
Day 36 (21 Feb)	PGM			4				3	5				144		156	5	4	Day 36: Medina, Hammurabi, AG7, AF7; VIP bunkers & Winnebago
	NonPGM							12							12			
Day 37 (22 Feb)	PGM					12	3		9				228		240	4	3	Day 37: Tawakalna, IZ/KU border, & west of KU
	NonPGM														12			
Day 38 (23 Feb)	PGM			10				12	11				118		139	12	5	Day 38: PF Taji tnk repair
	NonPGM														12			
Day 39 (24 Feb)	PGM							14	8				163		171	1	2	Day 39: Tawakalna; excludes no drops
	NonPGM														14			
Day 40 (25 Feb)	PGM						32		4				74		110	13		Day 40: Bad wx led to GBU-12s dropped by rdr; GBU-12 on arflds
	NonPGM					4	8		3				16		28	2		
Day 41 (269 Feb)	PGM						1						5		9	2		Day 41: Some "plinking," but mostly CBU-87s on GOB
	NonPGM	5				4		8	43				2		62	18	4	
Day 42 (27 Feb)	PGM	2		4					7						13	18	3	Day 42: 18 air aborts WX, GBU28s on Taji; lots of CBU-87s on GOB
	NonPGM							16	7	2			11		36	4	1	
Day 43 (28 Feb)		The war ended at 0800L on 28 February. Hence no F-111 sorties on the night of ATO Day 43.													0			
Days 36-43		2	5	14	4	20	44	65	97	2	0	0	761	0	1014	61	22	728 Precision Strikes
						4%	6%	10%				75%						148 NonPrecision

F-111E/F Summary Data by Target Category:

Target Categories													Total Strikes	Aborts Air	Aborts Grnd
SAD	SAM	CCC	L	C	A	MS	RR	SC	E	O	RG/GOB	?			
76	7	56	14	142	750	297	266	79	33	83	2,400	9	4,212	622	106
1.8%	.2%	1.3%	.3%	3.4%	17.8%	7.1%	6.3%	1.9%	0.8%	2%	57.0%	2%	100%		

Appendix Five

Attrition of Armor and Artillery in Iraqi Heavy Divisions

	Totals	Armored							Mechanized			
		Hammurabi RG	Madinah RG	3rd	6th	10th / 12th	17th	52nd	Tawakalna RG	1st	5th	51st
Tanks												
Prewar holdings[a]	2,665	294	283	270	218	444	224	185	209	203	160	175
Remaining in prewar deployment areas on 1 March 1991[b]	1,135	39	64	82	130	312	134	144	63	99	51	17
Moved to fight or flee during ground war[c]	1,530	255	219	188	88	132	90	41	146	104	109	158
APCs												
Prewar holdings[a]	2,624	236	240	205	157	394	160	195	260	246	245	286
Remaining in prewar deployment areas on 1 March 1991[b]	827	63	39	102	41	164	58	122	101	78	50	9
Moved to fight or flee during ground war[c]	1,797	173	201	103	116	230	102	73	159	168	195	277
SP Artillery												
Prewar holdings[a]	305	25	65	18	18	72	36	0	36	35	0	0
Remaining in prewar deployment areas on 1 March 1991[b]	175	11	17	18	15	67	0	0	23	24	0	0
Moved to fight or flee during ground war[c]	130	14	48	0	3	5	36	0	13	11	0	0
Towed Artillery												
Prewar holdings[a]	584	36	33	52	17	6	6	86	115	168	65	0
Remaining in prewar deployment areas on 1 March 1991[b]	218	4	5	6	12	6	4	33	39	84	25	0
Moved to fight or flee during ground war[c]	366	32	28	46	5	0	2	53	76	84	40	0

Source: Directorate of Intelligence, Central Intelligence Agency, "Operation Desert Storm: A Snapshot of the Battlefield," Report IA 93-10022.

[a] These are counts of major equipment in the Iraqi heavy divisions before the ground war. Figures for most divisions are from early 1991. Figures for the 3rd Armored and 5th Mechanized Infantry Divisions were derived before the late January Iraqi attack on Ra's al Khafji, Saudi Arabia, in which these two divisions lost undetermined amounts of equipment. Figures for the 10th and 12th Armored Divisions are combined because they occupied adjacent areas before the ground war, and the precise demarcation between them was unclear.

[b] These are the counts from 1 March 1991 of equipment remaining in the prewar deployment areas. This equipment remained in these areas because it had been destroyed or damaged during the air campaign, was inoperable because of poor maintenance, or was abandoned when the unit's personnel withdrew after the ground war began. Figures listed for equipment remaining in the 5th and 51st Mechanized Infantry Divisions' areas are incomplete.

[c] These figures represent the difference between prewar division holdings and equipment remaining in pre-24 February deployment areas on 1 March. The category includes: equipment in units redeployed to new locations in the Iraqis' effort to defend against coalition attacks, equipment repositioned within prewar deployment areas to face an expected attack (particularly in the 3rd Armored Division area), and equipment abandoned outside pre-24 February deployment areas after the unit's personnel withdrew or fled from the battlefield.

Appendix Six

Gulf War Air Power Survey Principal Staff

Dr. Eliot A. Cohen	*Director*
Col. Emery M. Kiraly	*Executive Director*
Lt. Gen. Robert E. Kelley (Retired, USAF)	*Senior Military Advisor*
Dr. Wayne W. Thompson	*Senior Historical Advisor*
Mr. Ernest D. Cruea	*ANSER Program Manager*
Maj. Joseph W. Patterson	*Executive Officer*
Mr. Lawrence J. Paszek	*Publishing Manager*
Lt. Col. Daniel T. Kuehl	*Chief, Statistics*
Lt. Col. Robert C. Owen	*Chief, Chronology*
Dr. John F. Guilmartin	*Chief, Weapons, Tactics and Training*
Mr. Richard A. Gunkel	*Chief, Logistics, Space, and Support*
Dr. Thomas C. Hone	*Chief, Command, Control, and Organization*
Dr. Alexander S. Cochran	*Chief, Strategy and Plans*
Mr. Barry D. Watts	*Chief, Operations and Effects*
Dr. Thomas A. Keaney	*Chief, Summary Report*

Review Committee

Hon. Paul H. Nitze, *Chairman*
Diplomat in Residence
Paul H. Nitze School of Advanced International Studies

Gen. Michael J. Dugan (USAF, Retired)
Multiple Sclerosis Society

Adm. Huntington Hardisty (USN, Retired)
Center for Naval Analyses

Dr. Richard H. Kohn
The University of North Carolina at Chapel Hill

Dr. Bernard Lewis
Princeton University

Mr. Andrew W. Marshall
Office of the Secretary of Defense

Mr. Phillip Merrill
Former Assistant Secretary General for Defense Support, NATO

Dr. Henry Rowen
Stanford University

Hon. Ike Skelton
U.S. House of Representatives

Gen. Maxwell Thurman (USA, Retired)
Association of the U.S. Army

Maj. Gen. Jasper A. Welch, Jr. (USAF, Retired)
Former Assistant Chief of Staff (Studies and Analysis)

Dr. James Q. Wilson
University of California at Los Angeles

A Note on Sources

Most of the paper and electronic records used by the Gulf War Air Power Survey (GWAPS) are available to researchers with appropriate clearances at the United States Air Force Historical Research Agency (AFHRA), Maxwell Air Force Base, Alabama. The agency began to accumulate Gulf War records before the Survey was established in Washington during the summer of 1991. Early in Desert Shield, the Air Force deployed more than thirty enlisted historians under Chief Master Sergeant John R. Burton to the theater, where they collected documents, conducted interviews, and drafted unit historical reports. More than five hundred rolls of agency microfilm reached the Survey during its research phase, and a thousand rolls were available by the end of the writing phase. Agency microfilmers shot the first hundred rolls in Riyadh, the second hundred at Langley Air Force Base, Virginia (headquarters of Tactical Air Command and CENTAF Rear), and the rest at Maxwell.

During the Vietnam War, the Air Force had begun the practice of microfilming paper records in the field to ensure their preservation, but the Service did not meet with as much success in preserving the electronic records of that war. Since then electronic records have grown rapidly in quantity and importance. The Survey gathered a large collection of electronic records, many of which have been integrated in the three principal Survey databases; the missions database, the sortie database, and the target database. When the Survey was established, work on these databases was already underway at Langley Air Force Base. The chief of Langley's Gulf War database team, Maj. Lewis "Dough" Hill, moved the project to the Survey, where his team's work was the foundation of the statistics report, *Statistical Compendium*.

The target database permits researchers to determine quickly whether a potential target appeared on any of several intelligence or planning lists. The sortie database gives researchers information on Coalition sorties, both attack and support; this database was introduced in Riyadh by Maj. Roy Lee of the Tactical Air Control Center. Most of the Survey's database development effort has been expended on the missions database, which attempts to pull together all available information about strikes on targets. The Survey counts as a single "strike" one aircraft delivering any number of munitions against a single target on one sortie. If four aircraft bomb a target, that is counted as four strikes. If one aircraft bombs two targets on a single sortie, that is counted as two strikes. In addition to its utility in building cumulative statistics on Coalition air attacks, the missions database enables a researcher to learn when a particular target was struck by particular aircraft and munitions; damage assessments are included.

The missions database relies heavily on the mission report messages saved by a CENTAF intelligence computer, the Limited Enemy Situation/Correlation (LENSCE) message processor. The Survey was disappointed to learn that information storage devices associated with operations computers in the theater were reused after thirty days, wiping out much of the electronic record of the war. Fortunately, some of that electronic record was preserved by LENSCE. While most mission report messages were saved only electronically, the Survey obtained a large volume of other printed messages (many of which were not saved electronically). These comprise about a third of more than 500,000 pages of the Survey's paper records.

The Survey's archive of paper records is divided into four sets: (1) records of CENTAF's Black Hole planning group (2) records of the Air Staff's Checkmate planning group (3) records of the Air Staff's Operations Center, and (4) new acquisitions. The first three sets came to GWAPS at the outset and are maintained in the filing systems of the organizations that created them. New acquisitions include the reports of other agencies studying the Gulf War as well as wartime records subsequently acquired by Survey researchers. Many footnotes in the Survey's reports cite these records, using identifiers listed below:

GWAPS File Series Abbreviations

Black Hole Files . . . . BH

Checkmate Historian's Files

    Desert Shield . . . . CHSH
    Desert Storm . . . . CHST
    Planners . . . . CHP
    Chain of Command . . . . CHC
    Overviews . . . . CHO
    Video, Audio . . . . CHV
    Target Photos . . . . CHT
    Special Compartmented Information . . . . . . CHSCI

A Note on Sources

Checkmate Office Files

Central	CC
ATO	CATO
BDA	CBDA
Intelligence	CI
Gulf War Office	CG

Hq USAF Operations Center Files

Contingency Operations Branch	COB
Contingency Support Staff	CSS

New Acquisitions File............. NA

GWAPS CHSH 100-29 indicates the twenty-ninth document in the hundredth folder in the Checkmate Historian's File on Desert Shield. GWAPS NA 6 indicates the sixth folder in the New Acquisitions file. Air Force Historical Research Agency microfilm records are referenced by AFHRA followed either by a six-digit computer index (IRIS) number or a five-digit roll number.

The Air Force Historical Research Agency is cataloging GWAPS paper records to allow electronic retrieval through IRIS but the Agency will retain a cross-reference to the original GWAPS identifiers. Automated finding aids helped the Survey to begin studying the large body of records on the Gulf War, but much remains to be done. Survey reports should themselves be seen as finding aids for those who will continue the study of this war.

Much of the information used in writing the GWAPS reports and this book came from documents that at the time of the research carried a security classification. In preparation for publication of the unclassified reports, a special declassification team reviewed the drafts and secured declassification of the information. Footnotes in this book show no security classification for the documents cited, but an unknown number of these documents retain a security classification or other restriction.

Glossary

AAA	Antiaircraft Artillery
AAR	After Action Report
AB	Air Base
ABCCC	Airborne Battlefield Command and Control Center
Abn Corps	Airborne Corps (U.S.)
ADP	Air Division (Provisional)
AFB	Air Force Base
AFHRA	Air Force Historical Research Agency
AI	Air Interdiction
AIF	Automated Installation-Intelligence File
ALARM	Air-Launched Anti-Radiation Missile
ANG	Air National Guard
AOR	Area of Responsibility
APC	Armored Personnel Carrier
ARCENT	U.S. Army Forces, Central Command
ATACMS	Army Tactical Missile System
ATO	Air Tasking Order
AWACS	Airborne Warning and Control System
BDA	Bomb Damage Assessment
BE or BEN	Basic Encyclopedia Number
BVR	Beyond Visual Range
BW	Biological Warfare
C3	Command, Control, and Communications
CAFMS	Computer Assisted Force Management System
CALCM	Conventional Air-Launched Cruise Missile
CAP	Combat Air Patrol
CAS	Close Air Support
CBU	Cluster Bomb Unit
CEM	Combined Effects Munition
CENTAF	Air Force Component, Central Command
CENTCOM	U.S. Central Command
CES	Civil Engineering Squadron
CIA	Central Intelligence Agency

Glossary

CINC	Commander-in-Chief
CINCCENT	Commander-in-Chief, Central Command
CJCS	Chairman, Joint Chiefs of Staff
CNN	Cable News Network
COMUSCENTAF	Commander, U.S. Air Force Component, Central Command
CRAF	Civil Reserve Air Fleet
CSAR	Combat Search and Rescue
CVBG	Aircraft Carrier Battle Group (USN)
D-Day	Unnamed day on which an operation begins
DIA	Defense Intelligence Agency
Div	Division
DMAAC	Defense Mapping Agency Aerospace Center
DMPI	Desired Mean Point of Impact
DOD	Department of Defense
DSB	Defense Science Board
ECM	Electronic Countermeasures
EMIS	Electro-Magnetic Isotope Separation
EPW	Enemy Prisoner of War
FAC	Forward Air Control
FLIR	Forward-Looking Infrared
FLOGEN	Flow Generation computer model
FOL	Forward Operating Location
FSCL	Fire Support Coordination Line
GOB	Ground Order of Battle
GPS	Global Positioning System
GWAPS	Gulf War Air Power Survey
G-Day	Day the ground war began
HARM	High-Speed Antiradiation Missile
HAB	Hardened Aircraft Bunker
HAS	Hardened Aircraft Shelter
IFF	Identification Friend or Foe
IIR	Intelligence Information Report
IOC	Intercept Operations Center
IR	Infrared
IRIS	AFHRA Computer Indexing System
J-2	Intelligence Directorate (Joint)
Jaguar	Land-based ground attack aircraft
JCS	Joint Chiefs of Staff
JDOP	Joint U.S.–Saudi Directorate of Planning
JFACC	Joint Force Air Component Commander
JFC-E	Joint Forces Command East
JFC-N	Joint Forces Command North
JIC	Joint Intelligence Center
JMEM	Joint Munitions Effectiveness Manual

JOPES	Joint Operations Planning and Execution System
JSTARS	Joint Surveillance Target Attack Radar System (E-8)
JTF	Joint Task Force
JULL	Joint Uniform Lessons Learned
KKMC	King Khalid Military City
KIA	Killed In Action
KTO	Kuwait Theater of Operations
LAMPS	Light Airborne Multi-Purpose System (USN)
LANDSAT	Land Satellite, NASA/NOAA Satellite Program
LANTIRN	Low Altitude Navigation and Targeting Infrared System for Night
LGB	Laser-Guided Bomb
LOC	Lines of Communication
MAC	Military Airlift Command
MAGTF	Marine Air Ground Task Force
MAJCOM	Major Command
MAP	Master Attack Plan
MARCENT	U.S. Marine Corps, Central Command
MEB	Marine Expeditionary Brigade
Mech Div	Mechanized Infantry Division
MEF	Marine Expeditionary Force
MEL	Mobile Erector Launcher used for mobile missiles
MLRS	Multiple Launch Rocket System
MPS	Maritime Prepositioning Squadron
MTM	Million Ton-Miles
NATO	North Atlantic Treaty Organization
NAVCENT	Naval Component, Central Command
NBC	Nuclear, Biological, and Chemical
NCA	National Command Authorities
NF or NOFORN	Not Releasable to Foreign Nationals
NIE	National Intelligence Estimate
OASD	Office of the Assistant Secretary of Defense
OCA	Offensive Counter Air
OPLAN	Operation Plan
OPORD	Operation Order
OSD	Office of the Secretary of Defense
PACAF	Pacific Air Forces
PGM	Precision-Guided Munition
POL	Petroleum, Oil, and Lubricants
POW	Prisoner of War
PSYOPS	Psychological Operations
RAF	Royal Air Force (U.K.)

Glossary

RCAF	Royal Canadian Air Force
RGFC	Republican Guard Force Command (Iraq); also referred to as RG
ROE	Rules of Engagement
RPV	Remotely Piloted Vehicle
RSAF	Royal Saudi Air Force
RSLF	Royal Saudi Land Force
SAC	Strategic Air Command
SAD	Strategic Air Defense
SAM	Surface-to-Air Missile
SANG	Saudi Arabian National Guard
SCUD	Soviet-made surface-to-surface missile
SCI	Sensitive Compartmented Information
SEAD	Suppression of Enemy Air Defenses
SECDEF	Secretary of Defense
SITREP	Situation Report
SNIE	Special National Intelligence Estimate
SOC	Sector Operations Center
SOCCENT	Special Operations Command, Central Command
SOCOM	Special Operations Command
SOF	Special Operations Forces
SPEAR	Strike Projection Evaluation and Anti-Air Warfare Research (USN)
SPG	Special Planning Group
SPINS	Special Instructions
STU	Secure Telephone Unit
SWA	Southwest Asia
TAC	Tactical Air Command
TACAIR	Tactical Air
TACC	Tactical Air Control Center
TACS	Tactical Air Control System
TACSAT	Tactical Satellite
TALD	Tactical Air-Launched Decoy
TARPS	Tactical Air Reconnaissance Pod System
TEL	Transporter Erector Launcher
TEMPER	Tent Expendable Modular Personnel
TFS	Tactical Fighter Squadron
TFW	Tactical Fighter Wing
TIALD	Thermal Imaging and Laser Designating
TIS	Tactical Intelligence Squadron
TLAM	Tomahawk Land-Attack Missile
TOT	Time Over Target
TPFDD	Time-Phased Force Deployment Data
UAV	Unmanned Aerial Vehicle

UK	United Kingdom
UN	United Nations
USAF	United States Air Force
USAFE	U.S. Air Forces Europe
USCENTCOM	Central Command
USCINCCENT	Commander-in-Chief, U.S. Central Command
USMC	U.S. Marine Corps
USN	U.S. Navy
USNAVCENT	U.S. Naval Component, Central Command
USSOCOM	U.S. Special Operations Command
WRSK	War Readiness Spares Kits

Index

A

A-4, 1, 13, 154, 166–67, 168
A-6, 13, 18, 20, 70, 153, 159, 163, 167–68, 193
A-7, 153, 165, 167
A-10, 13, 18, 41, 56, 73, 89–90, 96, 145, 167–68, 170, 172, 183, 194, 214
ABCCC, 161–62
Abu Dhabi, 2
Abu Ghurayb, 67, 71
AC-130, 17, 167
ad hoc organization, 210
aerial tankers, 24, 138, 194
AFHRA, 24, 145
AGM-65, 90
AGM-88, 164
AGM-114, 90
AH-1W, 90, 167, 170
AH-64, 90, 98–99, 103, 167, 170
Aidid, Mohamed Farah, 225
AIF, 73n, 115
air base security, 148–50
air defense, 48
Air Force Combat Ammunition Center, 178
Air Force Components, 183
Air Force Reserve, 182–84
Air Force Special Operations Command, 152
air interdiction, 57, 81–87, 98–102, 144
Air National Guard, 183–84
air refueling, 127, 128, 136, 142, 153, 159, 194, 220
Air Staff, 5, 29–30, 111–12, 117–18
air superiority, 12, 22, 24, 27–28, 31–32, 40, 48, 53, 78, 102, 135, 202, 208, 222
air supremacy, 12, 23, 48, 211
air tasking order, 5, 27, 116, 121, 127–29, 131, 135, 143, 159, 181, 186, 197, 217. *See also* ATO

air-to-surface missiles, 12, 89–90, 169–71, 191
Airborne Warning and Control System, 2, 51, 140, 150, 160–62, 199, 208
airfields, 4, 10–15, 26, 30, 33–35, 46–55, 102, 139–43, 146–51, 155, 202
Al Asad, 54
Al Firdos, 19, 58, 59, 130, 185, 214, 222
Al Khafji, 19, 80, 85–86, 94–96, 199, 209
Al Taqaddum, 206
Al Tuwaitha, 72
ALARM, 195n
An Nasiriyah, 81, 82, 144
anthrax, 67
antiaircraft artillery (AAA), 13, 48, 51–53, 80, 195
antiradiation missiles (HARMs), 12, 34, 49, 51, 56, 165, 191, 196
Apache, 90, 97–98, 170
ARCENT, 7, 114, 121–22, 131, 132
Argentina, 152, 158
Army Tactical Missile System, 168
Arnold, R. P., 146
Arthur, Stanley, 131
artillery, 7, 8, 19, 41, 71, 89, 91–93, 97, 109–10, 130, 131, 151, 200, 209
Assistant Secretary of Defense (Public Affairs), 17
assumptions, 70, 78, 120, 194
ATACMS, 168
Atlantic bridge, 138
ATO, 5, 27–28, 30, 32, 121, 127–29, 131, 159, 197. *See also* air tasking order
AUTODIN, 127
AV-8B, 13, 41, 89, 96, 131, 145, 167–68, 194
AWACS, 218. *See also* Airborne Warning and Control System

307

AWS, 144
Az Zubayr, 87

B

B-52, 4, 10, 13, 18, 20, 24, 42, 70, 90, 96, 124, 126, 132, 135, 139, 142, 150, 153, 167, 168, 182, 190, 222
bad weather, 133
Bahrain, 142, 150, 152, 164, 166
Baker, James, 38
Baptiste, Sam, 112
Basra, 21, 26, 65, 82, 83, 86, 144
BDA. *See* bomb damage assessment
Behery, Ahmed Ibrahim, 134
Belgium, 152
Berlin airlift, 155
beyond visual range, 51, 208
BGM-71, 90
biological warfare, 55, 67, 118
biological weapons, 4, 34, 67, 72, 192
Black Hole, 5, 28, 32–33, 35–36, 40, 43, 45, 55–56, 58, 60, 70, 81, 112–16, 121, 126–29, 135, 137, 197, 210
BLU-82, 18
BLU-109, 54
Blue Ridge, 131
bomb damage assessment, 14, 25, 61, 62, 79–82, 86, 89, 102, 103, 114, 119–23, 129, 130, 218–19
Boomer, Walter, 131, 132, 148
Bosnia, 213
botulinum, 67
breaching, 13, 18–20, 119
bridges, 5, 12, 21, 33, 35, 36, 42, 55–57, 81–83, 85, 86, 99, 103, 115, 117, 144, 193, 205
briefing, 2, 23, 28, 30–32, 40–41, 59, 73, 117–18, 122, 146, 149, 168, 175, 180
Brown outs, 62
Bubiyan, 87
Buccaneers, 167–69
Bush, George, 1, 2, 22, 27, 32, 38, 40, 215, 220, 224–25
BVR. *See* beyond visual range

C

C-5, 4, 51, 155–56
C-130, 4, 152, 158–59, 205
C-141, 4, 155, 156
Cable News Network, 58, 78, 215
CAFMS, 127, 197
Cairo West, 138
CALCM, 168, 190
Canada, 152, 158, 166

carrier battle groups, 2, 3, 6, 24, 27
carriers, 2, 3, 6, 7, 18, 24, 27, 87, 89, 127, 131, 141, 143, 153, 159, 160, 194, 200
Caruana, Patrick P., 126
CAS. *See* close air support
casualties, 13, 16, 30, 36, 58, 65, 190, 203, 209–10, 214–16
CBU-52, 90
CBU-87, 90, 178
CBU-89, 89, 90, 221
CENTAF, 2, 5, 7, 25–27, 29, 31–32, 35, 37, 40, 41, 45, 89, 90, 101, 111–14, 116–17, 120–22, 124–28, 132, 135, 165, 175–81, 192, 196, 210
CENTAF intelligence, 111–12, 114, 120–21, 126–27
CENTCOM. *See* Central Command
CENTCOM plan, Desert Storm: Phase I, 6–7, 29–39, 40, 42–43, 80, 112; Phase II, 6–7, 32, 39, 40, 42; Phase III, 6–7, 32, 39, 40–43, 110; Phase IV, 6–7, 39, 42–43
center of gravity, 30–33, 39, 81
Center for Naval Analyses, 18, 80, 89, 124, 128, 165, 170, 178, 220
Central Command, 2, 5, 7, 10, 13, 16, 18, 24–26, 28–29, 31, 35, 37, 39, 40, 41, 60, 73, 79, 80, 91–93, 95, 106, 110–12, 114, 116–17, 119, 122–26, 129, 136–37, 143, 148, 150, 162, 174, 175, 180, 198, 216, 218
Central Intelligence Agency, 65, 71, 92, 101, 108
CF-18s, 166
Checkmate, 29–31, 34, 45, 58, 112–14, 118, 127, 184, 197, 210
chemical weapons, 4, 5, 11, 14, 21, 26, 28, 30, 33–35, 43–44, 55, 56, 67, 70–72, 117–18, 130, 150, 192
Cheney, Richard B., 2, 32, 38, 188
Chief of Staff, 29, 36, 87, 122
CIA. *See* Central Intelligence Agency
civil reserve air fleet, 4, 155, 158
Clinton, William, 220, 225
close air support, 16, 19–21, 24, 42, 97, 104, 125, 133, 166, 168
cluster bombs, 179, 221
CNN. *See* Cable News Network
Coalition, 47, 188, 215, 221, 223–24
Cold War, 1, 123, 173, 185, 188
combat air patrol, 166
Combined Bomber Offensive, 202
combined OPLAN, 39–40

Index

command and control, 5, 10, 22, 24–25, 32–33, 37, 45, 51, 57, 60, 115, 135, 137, 140, 152, 153, 160–62, 171, 172, 208, 210, 218
composite wing, 14, 143
computers, 216–19, 225
contingency plan, 2
Corder, John, 122, 126, 134
Corps: VII Corps, 7–9, 10, 85, 102, 133, 171, 211; XVIII Airborne Corps 7, 8, 133, 134, 159, 171, 211; XVIII Corps, 6, 7, 99
CRAF. *See* Civil Reserve Air Fleet

D

DCS, 196
D-Day, 28, 32
deception, 88, 107, 110, 118
Defense Department. *See* Department of Defense
Defense Intelligence Agency, 7, 8, 16, 54, 56, 58, 61, 67, 74, 78, 81, 85, 106, 107, 114, 116–17
Defense Mapping Agency, 117
Defense Science Board, 76, 181
Defense Support Program, 162
Department of Defense, 220
Deptula, David, 13, 34, 37, 56, 58
Desert Express, 176
desertion rate, 8
Dhahran, 28, 39, 148–50, 155, 158, 175
DIA. *See* Defense Intelligence Agency
Diego Garcia, 139, 142, 150, 167, 194
doctrine, 221
DOD. *See* Department of Defense
drones, 11, 49, 51, 152, 164
DSB. *See* Defense Science Board
Dugan, Michael, 224

E

82d Airborne Division, 3, 28
E-3, 3, 51, 160, 193
E-8, 16
EA-6s, 12
EC-130s, 161, 165
EF-111s, 12, 142, 153, 165, 207
Egypt, 139
Eisenhower, Dwight D., 189
electrical power, 11–12, 45, 63, 79, 201, 223
electricity, 33, 56, 61–65, 211
electronic warfare, 126, 153, 163, 164–65, 171, 172, 195, 220
enemy prisoner of war, 16, 85
enriched uranium, 72
European Command, 43, 136
European Express, 176
exercises, 7, 107, 135

F

F-1, 49, 166, 186
F-4, 205
F-4G, 12, 51, 142, 153, 164, 195, 196
F-5, 13, 167, 168
F-14, 12, 165
F-15C, 51, 165
F-15E, 11, 13, 18, 20, 41, 70, 73, 76, 78, 121, 160, 167, 168, 169, 182, 192–94
F-16, 13, 20, 41, 53, 70, 89, 98, 163, 164, 166–68, 169, 172, 183, 192, 214
F-105, 205
F-111, 13, 18, 20, 153, 167, 168
F-117, 10, 11, 14–16, 19, 25, 30, 34, 54, 57–58, 60, 70, 116, 117, 121, 145, 153, 164, 167, 168, 189–92, 204–8
facsimile (fax), 113, 196
Faylakah, 87
fire support coordination line, 98, 133–34
fleet defense, 125, 131
FLIR, 76, 207
forward air control, 126
France, 152, 158, 166–67, 186, 201
Franks, Frederick, 131–33
fratricide, 17, 19, 133, 208
French Air Force, 169
FSCL. *See* fire support coordination line

G

G-Day, 103
Gates, Robert, 38, 71
GBU-10, 50n, 206
GBU-12, 90, 205–6
GBU-15, 16
GBU-27, 54, 57–58, 192, 206–7, 211
GBU-28, 21, 221
generator halls, 36, 61
Germany, 79, 146, 152, 155, 182, 204
global war, 2
Glock, John, 112, 113, 116, 120
Glosson, Buster C., 5, 13, 29, 31–32, 35, 37, 39–41, 43, 53, 59, 61, 69, 89, 112–13, 117–18, 126–27, 129, 130, 197
GR-1, 54, 70
Great Britain, 32, 79, 139, 152, 157, 166–67, 195
Greece, 139

Griffith, Glenn, 205
ground forces, 5–9, 11–13, 15–16, 18–19, 21, 22–23, 26–28, 31, 34, 40–42, 46, 52–55, 66, 80, 95, 97–98, 101–3, 114, 119, 129, 131–34, 144, 153, 162, 171, 209, 211, 215, 223
ground order of battle, 116
Guam, 179

H

H-2, 73
Hammurabi, 9, 92
hardened aircraft shelter, 46–47, 54–55, 207, 219
HARM, 12, 56, 165, 191, 195–96, 203
Harvard Study Team, 64
Harvey, Bernard E., 118
HAS. *See* hardened aircraft shelter
Hawk, 166
Hawr al Hammar, 99–101, 144
helicopters, 1, 3, 5, 10, 11, 13, 32, 41–42, 50, 87, 90, 97, 98, 125, 127n, 134, 153, 158, 168, 170, 180, 223
Hellenikon Air Base, Greece, 139
Hellfire, 90, 171
highway of death, 21, 99, 133, 215
HMS *Gloucester*, 89
Horner, Charles A., 2, 5, 19, 27, 28, 31–32, 34, 43, 53, 59, 79, 83, 107, 111, 122, 124–26, 129–35, 149
hospital, 148
Hussein, Saddam, 4, 16, 30–31, 36–39, 44, 49, 57, 60, 61, 64–65, 118, 141, 185, 222–24

I

I-2000, 54, 207
IADS. *See* integrated air defense system
IL-76, 50
Incirlik, 14, 43, 143, 149, 150, 160, 163–64
India, 139
infantry, 9, 13, 93, 110
Information Age, 216–20
infrared, 18, 20, 48, 51, 73, 76, 80, 107, 191, 207
infrastructure, 5, 55, 60, 66, 73, 118, 148
Instant Thunder, 5, 30–31, 33–34, 36, 39, 111, 117, 118
integrated air defense system, 10, 48, 102, 109, 195
intelligence staff, 105, 111, 126
Intelligence and Threat Analysis Center, 66, 84

interdiction, 19, 25, 42, 57, 80, 86, 97, 98, 124, 133, 144, 158, 166, 168
Internal Look, 25–27, 106, 111, 120
International Atomic Energy Administration, 107
IR. *See* infrared
Iran, 8, 12, 15, 17, 23, 46, 49, 54–55, 67, 75, 95, 109, 141, 192, 208, 217
Iran-Iraq War, 8, 15, 49, 67, 75, 95, 109, 208
Iraqi air force, 12, 15, 17, 44, 46–49, 54, 108–9, 135, 152, 192, 208, 211, 221
Iraqi army, 7, 12, 16, 18, 21, 89–104, 108–10, 130, 144, 149, 192, 208–9
Iraqi navy, 17, 80, 87, 89
Iraqi target study, 26
Iraq's nuclear, biological, and chemical facilities, 30, 34, 70, 103
Israel, 4, 14, 36, 75, 77, 140, 141, 154, 210, 216, 224
Italy, 152, 167
Ivory Justice, 2
IZAF, 54

J

J-2, 85, 111, 113–14
J-5, 24, 28, 34, 40
Jaguar, 167
Jamerson, James L., 140, 161
Japan, 152
JCS. *See* Joint Chiefs of Staff
JDOP, 39
JFACC. *See* Joint Force Air Component Commander
JFC, 7, 9
JFC-E, 7, 9
JFC-N, 7, 9
Johnston, Robert, 34
Joint Chiefs of Staff, 22, 24, 30, 31, 32, 34, 36, 110, 113, 124
Joint Directorate of Planning, 39
Joint Force Air Component Commander, 4, 5, 125–37, 203
Joint Intelligence Center, 114
Joint no-fire target list, 38
Joint Staff, 30, 36, 110, 114, 125, 134, 162
Joint Surveillance Target Attack Radar System, 16, 95, 98, 150, 153, 161–63, 199, 204, 210, 218
Joint target list, 26
Joint Task Force, 2, 14, 43, 136, 140, 161
Joint Task Force Middle East, 2

Index

JOPES, 174, 198
Jordan, 65
JSTARS. *See* Joint Surveillance Target Attack Radar System
JTF. *See* Joint Task Force
Just Cause, 38, 155, 192, 204

K

KA-6s, 159
KARI, 51, 109
KC-10, 4, 155, 159
KC-135, 2, 142, 155, 157, 159
Kelly, Thomas W., 60
Khafji, 16, 17, 19, 80, 85–86, 90, 94–96, 199, 209
Khalid, Bin Sultan al-Saud, 4, 134, 148
Khamis Mushait, 147, 148
kill box, 43, 89, 91, 133
killer scouts, 18
Kimmitt, Robert, 38, 39
King Fahd, 22
Kirkuk, 205
KTO. *See* Kuwaiti theater of operations
Kuwait, 1, 2, 3–6, 9–11, 13, 14, 16, 18, 19, 21–23, 25, 27, 29–32, 36, 39–43, 45, 46, 48, 51, 54, 57, 60, 65, 66, 80, 82, 84–87, 89–91, 96–103, 106, 109, 110, 116, 119, 121, 123, 128, 130–32, 142–45, 151–53, 166, 170, 192, 194–96, 202, 209, 211, 215
Kuwaiti Air Force, 1
Kuwaiti theater of operations, 6, 11, 13, 51, 60, 66, 82–84, 90, 91, 101, 116, 128, 132, 215–16

L

Lajes, 138
LANDSAT, 163
Langley AFB, Virginia, 111, 175, 210
LANTIRN, 20
leadership, 5, 9, 10, 13, 22, 25, 30–35, 37, 45, 48, 55, 56–58, 63, 65, 106, 117, 148, 173, 187, 189, 192, 202, 210
leaflets, 16
Leavenworth, 40
LGB, 191–93
Libya, 138
Linebacker I, 205
Linebacker II, 53, 195, 202
lines of communication, 42
logistics, 55, 65–66, 80–87, 97–99, 154, 158, 174–79
Loh, John M., 29, 118

Luftwaffe, 203
Lynx, 170

M

M1A1, 97
MAC. *See* Military Airlift Command
Madinah, 9, 95, 102
mail, 158
maintenance personnel, 157, 179
maintenance squadron, 184
MARCENT, 7, 9, 114, 132
Marine Corps. *See* U.S. Marine Corps
Marine Expeditionary Brigade, 7, 28
Marine Expeditionary Force, 148
Marines, 7, 17, 53, 102, 124, 126, 131, 133, 136, 163, 166, 181, 223
Marshall, Andrew, 201
master attack plan, 56, 75, 128, 136, 209
Mauz, Henry, 131
Maverick, 56, 89, 90, 170–71, 191, 203
MC-130s, 18
McConnell, J. M., 110, 113–14, 127
McGuire AFB, New Jersey, 157
medical, 151
MH-53, 180
MiG-25, 50
Military Airlift Command, 155, 156, 174–76, 198
military production, 30
military support, 21, 34, 36, 55, 141
Ministry of Defense, 37, 39
Mirage 2000s, 166
Mirage F-1, 1
missile, 4, 7, 10, 12–14, 17, 33, 34, 35, 45–46, 48–51, 55, 56, 67–70, 73–78, 80, 88–90, 107–9, 115, 117, 127, 130, 141, 150, 151, 152, 153, 162, 164, 165, 168, 170, 171, 189–91, 195, 196, 200, 202, 203, 208, 210, 211, 219, 221, 223
Missouri, 117
MK-20, 90
MK-82, 90, 206
MK-84, 90
mobility, 98, 118
mobilization, 111, 155
Moore, Royal, 131, 163
munitions, 4, 11, 13, 14, 25, 41, 53, 57, 58, 65, 70, 71, 80, 89, 90, 93, 97, 148, 159, 169–71, 178, 188, 191, 192, 196, 203, 205, 220–21
munitions shipments, 178
munitions storage, 13, 14, 148

mustard, 67, 71
Mutla Ridge, 21, 99, 100

N
National Intelligence Estimate, 105
National Security Agency, 180
National Security Council, 2, 27, 32, 38
NATO, 53, 135, 138, 139, 140, 152, 160, 162, 173, 180, 210
naval, 7, 11, 17, 24, 26, 33, 35, 42, 80, 87–89, 114, 124, 153, 164, 167–71, 178
NAVCENT, 7, 114
navigation, 20, 144, 153, 162, 180, 207, 211
Nellis AFB, Nevada, 73, 135, 220
Netherlands, 152
New York Times, The, 7, 61, 71, 165
New Zealand, 152, 158
Ninth Air Force, 125
Noriega, Manuel, 38, 184
North Vietnam, 52, 124, 185, 191, 195, 203, 205
NSC. *See* National Security Council
nuclear, 5, 11, 14, 21, 26, 28, 30, 33–35, 55–56, 66–70, 72, 79, 103, 106, 118–19, 139, 192, 199–200, 211, 219
nuclear weapons, 35, 55, 56, 72, 119, 139, 199, 211, 200

O
OA-10s, 161
offensive, 1, 5, 16, 18–23, 27–30, 33, 36, 39, 42, 79, 94, 97–99, 112, 117, 122, 126, 129, 133–34, 140, 160, 170, 200, 202, 208
Office of the Assistant Secretary of Defense, 37
Office of the Secretary of Defense, 201
oil, 5, 11, 14, 26, 28, 30, 33, 35–36, 55, 61–63, 65–66, 102, 117, 133, 144, 201
oil production, 5, 11, 28, 30, 36, 61, 65, 102
Oman, 142, 176
Omnibus Agreement, 125
operational control, 125
operational level of war, 48, 118
operations order, 27, 32–33, 36–37, 39, 41
OPLAN 1002-90, 2, 24, 26, 125
OPLAN, 2, 24, 26–28, 40–42, 111, 125
OPLAN Desert Storm, 40–42
OPORD, 32, 33, 40

order of battle, 106, 116–19, 123
OV-10s, 161

P
Panama, 155, 192, 204
Patriot, 3, 78, 141, 150, 181
Perry, William, 188
Persian Gulf, 2, 7, 15–16, 22, 24, 29, 66, 72, 87, 133, 140–41, 143, 146, 160, 174, 185, 187, 193, 196, 203, 221, 223
PGMs, 191
planners, 1, 9, 13, 21–23, 28–31, 34–35, 51, 54–59, 61, 64–69, 78–79, 89, 108, 111, 113, 115, 116, 120, 122, 128, 138, 146, 164, 173, 184, 186, 196, 203, 205, 211
planning, 2, 4, 18, 23–25, 27, 31, 36–39, 43, 51, 79, 89, 112, 115, 117, 121, 125–29, 135, 164, 173–74, 197, 203, 210
POL, 26, 66, 87
population, 36, 38, 134, 148, 150
Powell, Colin, 22, 24, 31, 32, 37, 38, 110, 115, 216
presidential palace, 28
priority system, 175
prisoner of war, 16, 46, 85, 86, 94, 95
Proven Force, 5, 14, 21, 43, 63, 136, 140, 143, 149, 160, 169, 205, 208
psychological operations, 16, 18, 190
public affairs, 17, 37
Punishment ATO, 28, 30
Purvis, Joe, 40
push CAS, 42

Q
Qasr, 87
Qatar, 152
Quayle, Dan, 38

R
RAF. *See* Royal Air Force
RAND, 155, 174, 175, 215
RC-135, 3, 12, 163
reconnaissance, 3, 9, 14, 15, 16, 34, 15, 120–22, 125, 152, 153, 162–64, 166, 171, 172, 194, 197, 199, 210, 219
Red Flag, 135
Red Sea, 7, 142, 143, 160, 194
refueling, 11, 128, 136, 142, 153, 154, 155, 159, 160, 166, 171, 172, 176, 189, 193, 194
Republican Guard, 1, 5, 7, 9, 13, 18, 26, 33, 35, 39, 41, 42, 48, 80, 89, 92, 93,

Index

96, 103, 108, 133, 209, 214, 221, 224
research and development, 72, 115
reserves, 6, 10, 86, 130, 155, 158, 172, 182, 183
revolution in warfare, 188, 200–201, 226
RF-4Cs, 163
RF-5C, 163
Rhein-Main AFB, Germany, 155
River Joint, 3, 163
Rockeye, 90
ROE. *See* rules of engagement
Rolling Thunder, 184
Roosevelt, Theodore, 87
Royal Air Force, 3, 32, 53, 171, 192
Royal Saudi Air Force, 32, 112, 134, 135
rules of engagement, 19, 38, 131

S

S-3s, 159
SAC. *See* Strategic Air Command
Salman Pak, 67, 70
SAM. *See* surface-to-air missile
satellite communications, 57, 162, 180
Saudi Air Force. *See* Royal Saudi Air Force
Saudi Arabia, 1, 2, 4, 5, 16, 22, 27–28, 39–40, 72, 75–77, 108, 111, 134, 139, 141–43, 146–50, 152, 155, 157–58, 160, 165, 167, 174, 176, 180, 184, 210, 220
Schwarzkopf, H. Norman, 2–7, 13, 22, 24, 27, 29, 31–32, 37–41, 48, 59, 71n, 73n, 80, 92, 105, 110, 117, 119, 122, 124–26, 129–34, 149, 209, 216, 220
Scud, 10–11, 14, 26, 33–35, 56, 66–69, 72–78, 89, 103, 107–8, 115, 118–19, 140, 150, 162, 221, 223
Scud alert, 150
Scud hunt, 14, 78, 107–8
SEAD. *See* suppression of enemy air defenses
sealift, 4, 23, 151n, 177
SECDEF. *See* Secretary of Defense
Secretary of Defense. *See* Richard B. Cheney
Secretary of State. *See* James Baker
sector operations center, 203
secure telephone unit, 113, 128, 180, 189, 196–99
security police, 149, 184
Sherman, William Tecumseh, 224–25

Sierra Army Depot, 178
signals intelligence, 86, 106
Silkworm missile, 7, 18, 87–89, 102
SKYNET, 162
smoke, 133, 144, 193
SOCCENT, 7n
software, 198
Somalia, 225
Southeast Asia, 52, 124, 146, 185, 191
space war, 181
Spain, 139, 142, 155
spare parts, 85, 95, 158, 175–76, 179, 186, 196, 210
SPEAR, 108–9
special forces, 78
special instructions, 128
Special Operations command, 73, 152, 159
SPINS. *See* special instructions
SPOT, 163
State Department, 38
stealth, 10, 14, 25, 58, 153, 171–72, 189–91, 195, 204, 207, 220
strategic air campaign, 5, 12, 14, 19, 23, 31–39, 43, 65–66, 113–14, 118, 129–30, 190
Strategic Air Command, 124, 139n, 155, 163
strategic air defense, 33, 35, 49, 204
STU. *See* secure telephone unit
SU-7/17, 50
SU-25, 50
suppression of enemy air defenses, 186, 202–3
surface-to-air missile, 12, 48–53, 78, 80, 102, 108–9, 195–96
Syria, 142, 202

T

TAC. *See* Tactical Air Command
TACAIR, 42, 198
TACC. *See* Tactical Air Control Center
TACS. *See* Tactical Air Control System
Tactical Air Command, 151, 196, 198
Tactical Air Control Center, 59, 96, 101, 126, 128, 132, 134, 137
Tactical Air Control Party, 42
Tactical Air Control System, 125–29, 133
Tactical Air Reconnaissance Pod System (TARPS), 120
tactical control, 125
Tactical Fighter Wing, 3, 18, 182
Taji, 67, 68, 71
tank plinking, 18, 132, 207

tankers, 2, 24, 25, 127, 128, 159–60, 193–94
tanks, 7, 18, 41, 46–48, 92–93, 97, 103, 109–10, 116, 130, 132, 200, 207, 219
target list, 25–26, 34–36, 38, 70, 106 7, 113, 115–16, 136
Tawakalna Division, 9, 92, 102
Tenoso, Edwin E., 126
terrorism, 149
TFW. *See* Tactical Fighter Wing
TLAM. *See* Tomahawk
Tomahawk, 10, 12, 31, 63, 116, 153, 168, 190, 208, 221
Torrejon AFB, Spain, 139, 155
TR-1, 163
Tristar, 159
Turkey, 5, 14, 43, 136, 139, 140, 143, 149, 152, 160, 163, 183, 186
Tuwaitha, 68, 69, 72

U

U-2, 163
UK. *See* United Kingdom
UN. *See* United Nations
United Arab Emirates, 2, 142, 152, 157, 158, 176
United Kingdom, 87, 157, 158, 159, 163, 166, 167, 171
United Nations, 1, 4, 6, 22, 37, 46, 64, 65, 71, 72, 79, 107
United Nations Special Commission, 71, 107
United States, 216, 220–23
USAFE, 14, 128, 140, 198
USCENTAF. *See* CENTAF
USCENTCOM. *See* Central Command
USCINCCENT, 5, 22, 24, 32, 38, 41–42, 111, 125, 132, 136
USEUCOM. *See* U.S. European Command
U.S. Air Force, 3, 5, 14, 111, 135, 139, 143, 148, 158–72, 195, 202, 205, 221, 224
U.S. Army, 7, 40, 41, 90, 96, 130, 148, 163, 167, 168, 170, 171
U.S. European Command, 43, 136

U.S. Marine Corps, 3, 7, 31, 32, 41, 90, 96, 97, 102, 120, 124, 125, 128, 130, 133, 152, 156, 159, 163, 165, 166, 169, 172, 178, 195
U.S. Navy, 3, 7, 10, 24, 31, 32, 87, 90, 108, 109, 120, 124, 125, 127, 130, 131, 143–44, 152, 156, 159, 160, 163, 165–71, 177, 178, 181, 195, 205
U.S. Special Operations command, 73, 167
USS *America*, 87
USS *Independence*, 2, 3
USS *Midway*, 87
USS *Ranger*, 87, 215
USS *Saratoga*, 50, 87
USS *Theodore Roosevelt*, 87

V

VC-10, 159
Vietnam, 52, 53, 110, 124, 130, 132, 136, 139, 146, 169, 173, 179, 184–85, 191, 195, 198–99, 201–3, 205, 207, 208, 217, 222–23

W

Waller, Calvin, 132
Walleye, 171
war of the cities, 72
Warden, John A., 29–31, 34, 39, 118, 184
Washington, D.C., 18, 28, 54, 105, 113, 114, 121, 123, 126–27, 130, 142, 197
Washington Post, The, 99, 110
weaponeering, 12–13, 115–16
weapons of mass destruction, 35, 71
Weasel Police, 196
weather, 13, 19, 21, 58, 89, 101, 121, 129, 133, 144–46, 152, 170, 180
World War I, 222
World War II, 124, 148, 191, 193, 200, 201, 202, 204, 207, 210
Wurtsmith AFB, Michigan, 139

Y

Yeosock, John, 131, 132
Yugoslavia, 213

About the Authors

Thomas A Keaney is a professor of military strategy at the National War College, Washington, D.C., and director of its core course on U.S. military strategy and operations. A graduate of the National War College, he holds a B.S. from the U.S. Air Force Academy and both an M.A. and a Ph.D. in history from the University of Michigan. During a twenty-nine year career as an officer in the U.S. Air Force, his assignments included duties as a forward air controller in Vietnam, an associate professor of history at the U.S. Air Force Academy, and a B-52 squadron commander. In 1991 and 1992 he was a researcher/author with the Gulf War Air Power Survey. He coauthored two reports of that survey—*The Summary Report* and *The Effects and Effectiveness of Air Power*.

Eliot A. Cohen is professor of strategic studies at the Paul H. Nitze School of Advanced International Studies (SAIS) of the Johns Hopkins University. He graduated from Harvard in 1977 with a B.S. in political science and earned his Ph.D. there in the same subject in 1982. From 1982 to 1985 he was assistant professor of government at and assistant dean of Harvard College. In 1985 he joined the strategy department of the Naval War College and taught there for almost five years. He joined the policy planning staff of the office of the secretary of defense in February 1990. Dr. Cohen is a contributing editor at *National Review* and *The New Republic* and military book editor at *Foreign Affairs*. He directed and edited the eleven book-length reports (one of which he coauthored) of the Gulf War Air Power Survey.

The Naval Institute Press is the book-publishing arm of the U.S. Naval Institute, a private, nonprofit society for sea service professionals and others who share an interest in naval and maritime affairs. Established in 1873 at the U.S. Naval Academy in Annapolis, Maryland, where its offices remain today, the Naval Institute has more than 85,000 members worldwide.

Members of the Naval Institute receive the influential monthly magazine *Proceedings* and discounts on fine nautical prints and on ship and aircraft photos. They also have access to the transcripts of the Institute's Oral History Program and get discounted admission to any of the Institute-sponsored seminars offered around the country.

The Naval Institute also publishes *Naval History* magazine. This colorful bimonthly is filled with entertaining and thought-provoking articles, first-person reminiscences, and dramatic art and photography. Members receive a discount on *Naval History* subscriptions.

The Naval Institute's book-publishing program, begun in 1898 with basic guides to naval practices, has broadened its scope in recent years to include books of more general interest. Now the Naval Institute Press publishes about 100 titles each year, ranging from how-to books on boating and navigation to battle histories, biographies, ship and aircraft guides, and novels. Institute members receive discounts of 20 to 50 percent on the Press's nearly 600 books in print.

For a free catalog describing Naval Institute Press books currently available, and for further information about subscribing to *Naval History* magazine or about joining the U.S. Naval Institute, please write to:

Membership & Communications Department
U.S. Naval Institute
118 Maryland Avenue
Annapolis, Maryland 21402-5035

Telephone: (800) 233-8764
Fax: (410) 269-7940

THE NAVAL INSTITUTE PRESS

REVOLUTION IN WARFARE?
Air Power in the Persian Gulf

Set in Fenice and Franklin Gothic
by Blue Heron, Inc.
Lawrence, Kansas

Printed on 50-lb. Husky White
and bound in Holliston Roxite A
by Quinn-Woodbine, Inc.
Woodbine, New Jersey